THE MARK OF HONOUR

CANADIAN STUDIES IN HISTORY AND GOVERNMENT

A series of studies edited by Kenneth McNaught, sponsored by the Social Science Research Council of Canada, and published with financial assistance from the Canada Council.

1. *Church and State in Canada West, 1841–1867.* By John S. Moir
2. *The French Shore Problem in Newfoundland: An Imperial Study.* By Frederic F. Thompson
3. *The Alignment of Political Groups in Canada, 1841–1867.* By Paul G. Cornell
4. *The Private Member of Parliament and the Formation of Public Policy: A New Zealand Case Study.* By Robert N. Kelson
5. *The San Juan Water Boundary Question.* By James O. McCabe
6. *The Mark of Honour.* By Hazel C. Mathews

THE
MARK OF
HONOUR

BY

Hazel C. Mathews

UNIVERSITY OF TORONTO PRESS

© University of Toronto Press 1965
Printed in Great Britain by
Hazell Watson & Viney Ltd
Aylesbury, Bucks
Reprinted in 2018
ISBN 978-1-4875-8142-8 (paper)

PREFACE

IT IS DOUBTFUL if a finer tribute to the Loyalists of the American Revolution could be found than that written by their contemporary, John Ferdinand D. Smyth, as the concluding paragraphs to *A Tour of the United States of America* ... (London, 1784). An Englishman who wished to learn more about America than could be found in travel books of the period, he began his tour just before the Revolution broke, and being imprisoned twice on suspicion of being a British spy Smyth came to know many Loyalists well. He wrote of them:

> How sad has been the fate of all those truly meritorious but unhappy men, the *American Loyalists* of every denomination! True to their king, faithful to their country, attached to the laws and constitution, they have continued firm and inflexible in the midst of persecutions, torments, and death. Many of them have abandoned their homes, their friends, their nearest and most tender connections, and encountered all the toils of war, want, and misery, solely actuated by motives the most disinterested and virtuous.
> In short they have undergone trials and suffering, with a determined resolution and fortitude, unparalleled in history; and have submitted even to death sooner than stain their integrity, honour, and principled loyalty with the odious guilt of rebellion against their king....
> No compensation whatever can be adequate to the loss sustained by these deserving men, not only of their possessions, and the society of their friends and relations, but of that apparently established felicity and affluence, which they themselves, and their posterity after them, had the prospect of enjoying for ages to come.

My interest in the Loyalists grew out of my first book, *Oakville and the Sixteen*. In that book I had been concerned chiefly with second-generation Loyalists, so it was not unusual that I should later wish to learn something of their forebears, the original Loyalists. I soon found myself concentrating upon a particular group representative of the poorer Loyalist immigrants who had been somewhat neglected as a class and whose background and life prior to arrival in Canada had received very little attention. It became evident as I went on that my particular group was also representative of the Loyalists as a whole.

The place of beginning in the research was, of course, the claims, memorials, and supporting evidence submitted by Loyalists for the losses they had sustained during the Revolution. To find the modern equivalent of places they named therein seemed a hopeless task until I encountered the map of the Province of New York drawn by Claude Joseph Sauthier and published in London in 1779. The discovery that even the smallest details, whether of province or state, crossed the desk of a governor led to the use of the correspondence of Governor Frederick Haldimand of Quebec in conjunction with that of Governor George Clinton of New York. These documents produced a wealth of material relative to the war period. In fact, it seemed unbelievable that the whereabouts of so many individuals could be accounted for over the five-year period, 1777 to 1783. George Chisholm emerged as a principal in this story, not because of family records—his were virtually non-existent—but by reason of his given name. Being the only George in a welter of Williams and Johns made him relatively easy to trace with some degree of certainty.

In pursuing the facts about locations, I soon came across the problem of the terms "town" and "township." In New York State the former, borrowed from New England, is used instead of the latter, which is the British form. When New York was a British province the larger settlements were "townships" which took the name of the patent (Minisink Township) or of the patentee (Kortright Township), or that chosen by the owners (Cherry Valley, Harpersfield, etc.), but after the Revolution "town" replaced "township" and many names of British origin were discarded. Frequently the name of the largest village is the same as that of the township (Town of Schoharie in the Town of Schoharie in Schoharie County). In his *Travels through the Northern Parts of the United States in the Years 1807 and 1808* (3 vols., New York, 1809), Edward Augustus Kendall wrote in explanation:

> Among their founders the word *town* seems to have been synonymous with *settlement*. . . . Every new *settlement* was called a new *town*. In making a *settlement*, certain limits were assigned, or assumed; and the limits of the *settlement* were said to be the limits of the *town*. The town-proper was of course the collection of dwellings; but, in the vulgar acceptation, the same word embraced the entire district or township, and use has given a local sanction to its meaning.

In Upper Canada the British form of "township" was retained. For this book I have kept to the practice of contemporary usage wherever possible, so that "township" appears uniformly throughout this history and serves for the same political division in both the United States and Canada.

In a work of this kind it is a question as to which aspect is the more intriguing, the indoor search for fact in the archives and libraries of several countries or the outdoor explorations to locate areas and places and describe them. Both lead to memorable meetings and experiences: the one with a variety of people, the other with contrasting countrysides.

To all those to whom I am indebted for a great variety of assistance over the years I am sincerely grateful. My appreciation is not at all lessened by the impracticability of individual mention of so long a list. The greatest debt is owing to the Social Science Research Council of Canada whose grant from funds provided by the Canada Council made possible the publication of this work.

Erchless HAZEL C. MATHEWS
Oakville, Ontario

CONTENTS

	PREFACE	v
	INTRODUCTION	ix
1	To the Hills of the New World	3
2	The Forest: With Axe and Plough	17
3	The Rift: Rebel or Traitor?	30
4	The King's Men: With Hatchet, Knife, and Gun (Part I)	42
5	The King's Men: With Hatchet, Knife, and Gun (Part II)	60
6	The River and the Fort	76
7	The City: With Sword and Musket	93
8	Peace beside the Sea	107
9	The British Way of Life	127
10	A Journey to Kortright, 1804	145
11	A Cherished Legacy	161
	APPENDIXES	
A	Some Loyalists of Kortright, New Stamford, and the Head of the Delaware in the Province of New York	171
B	A List of Officers Employed in the Indian Department with Their Rank and Pay, June 15, 1777; A List of Persons Employed in the Indian Department, as of Use with Their Pay; A List of Persons Employed as Rangers in the Indian Department, June 15, 1777	175
C	From the "Boston Chronicle," March 12, 1782	177
D	Extract from Albany Newspaper, May 26, 1783	178
	NOTES	179
	GLOSSARY	202
	INDEX	207

ILLUSTRATIONS

PLATES *(between pages 132 and 133)*

Colonel John Butler's home on Switzer Hill, Fonda, N.Y.

John Chisholm's house on the Portage Road, Stamford Township, Welland County, Ontario

Allan Macdonell's plan of the "New Settlement—Niagara River Line," March–April 1783

Part of the town of Shelburne, Nova Scotia, 1789, with barracks opposite

Well in Mowat Street, Shelburne, from which George and Barbara Chisholm drew water

MAPS

Northern Frontier of the Province of New York at opening of Rebellion as taken from Claude Joseph Sauthier's map, *page 27*

British and Indian Territory lying between the Hudson River and Lakes Erie and Ontario, *facing page 52*

INTRODUCTION

SCOTLAND WAS LOSING her sons and daughters to the American colonies. The grinding poverty of over-population was forcing them to take leave of their homeland and try their fortunes in the new country beyond the seas. The intensive migration which drew cries against "depopulation" and would culminate in governmental prohibition of Scottish emigration had been gathering momentum since 1765. In Highlands and Lowlands hundreds prepared to follow those who had gone before. From the grey stone cottages of towns and little tenant-farms of hill and glen they walked down to the sea coast to embark for the long voyage to the New World. Singly or in pairs they came, in family groups and in organized associations of several hundred persons. By 1773 fewer tears were being shed because those left on shore believed that they would soon follow. This year and the next, the decision to migrate was reached by men scattered over the country whom fate would bring together in the Province of New York.

In the Roxburghshire town of Hawick, where tweeds were woven of Cheviot fleeces, were Archibald Thomson, younger son of a mercantile family, and his friend James Park. In the seaboard parish of Stranraer in county Galloway (now Wigtown and Kirkcudbright) were the brothers Thomas and John McMicking, stonemasons, who planned that their mother and sisters should soon join them. Alexander Leal, native of Forres, Morayshire, who as a lad had witnessed the Jacobite disaster on Culloden Moor, would depart with his wife Ann Cummings and their several children. Here in the Highlands where arable land was divided into minute holdings by an ever crowding population people in droves planned to leave their native Inverness-shire. In the parish of Croy were the minister's sons, James and William Calder, and around Kilravock Castle a number of Roses. James, Hugh and his family and sixteen-year-old brother Daniel, and William belonged to Clan Rose whose chieftains had occupied the castle in Strath Nairn since its building in 1460. Known to the Roses as members of the same parish were the Chisholms of Easter Leys whose sons George and John were also going off to the colonies. Westward William McKenzie, farmer, with his wife Mary, nine children, and two servants planned to leave kith and kin in the McKenzie country of Wester Ross.

To the south in Inverness-shire four Macdonells of Glen Garry, three brothers and their first cousin, were organizing a large company from their glen and nearby Glen Moriston, Glen Urquhart, and Strath Glass. The brothers of this branch of Clan Donald lived in the vicinity of their stronghold Invergarry Castle on Loch Oich, laid in ruins after Culloden by the Duke of Cumberland. According to Highland custom the Macdonells were known by the names of their properties: John of Leek, situated a few miles south of Fort Augustus; Alexander of Aberchalder (mouth of Calder burn) on Loch Oich; Allan of Collachie (Cullochy) on the opposite shore; and

John of Scottos* in the Isle of Skye. It was Scottos the cousin who was destined to become military leader in his community in the New World. The Macdonells were Roman Catholics and John like his father before him was sent to Italy to be educated for the priesthood at the Scots College founded 1600 in Rome. He ran away at the age of fifteen and joined an Irish regiment in the service of the King of Spain operating in Italy, thus gaining considerable experience in actual warfare, an officer's commission, and the name of Spanish John. In 1746 (when eighteen) he was charged with a secret mission to Prince Charles Edward and headed for Inverness. Upon landing in full regimentals, with a wig and black bag, "a la mode to Paris" he got the "dismal news" that on the day he had sailed from Dunkirk the battle of Culloden had been fought and lost in a sleet storm; "that the Highlanders were all dispersed, and nobody knew what was become of Prince Charles Edward."[1] That night his portmanteau was slashed and a canvas bag containing one thousand guineas for the Prince's use was stolen. His attempts to recover the gold and find the Prince make very interesting reading. Mistaken for his cousin he was taken by the English and detained "for imaginary crimes" for about a year. After being released he married his cousin Catherine Macdonell † in 1747 "and lived a most happy life for a number of years on my property. At last," he wrote in conclusion, "my disposition given rather to roving induced me to leave my native soil, and come to this great Continent of America, where I have resided ever since."[2]

Although those with whom we are concerned were mostly very poor, there were also some men of substance who were leaving their homeland. Hugh Fraser with two hundred guineas was accounted a wealthy man. And there were men with special training like James Stuart who in 1740 enrolled as surgeon's mate in the 42nd Regiment of Royal Highlanders (Black Watch) and later served for fourteen years as army surgeon. Stuart was a native of Inverness and according to family tradition a descendant of James Stuart, Earl of Moray, natural son of James V and half-brother of Mary, Queen of Scots.[3] His reason for migrating was his "numerous family of young boys."[4] In Britain surgeons, both army and civilian, were "mister" but upon reaching America James Stuart became "doctor."

John and George Chisholm were the sons of John Chisholm and his wife Janet MacGlashan. John Sr. was elder for Easter Leys in the Parish of Croy[5] when the parish church was built in 1767. It replaced (on the same site) an older church of pre-Reformation times and has been in continuous use for almost two hundred years. The bell which rings out each Sabbath would seem to be still older for a session minute of 1688 reads: "The Kirk bell is com [sic] home from London in a new cast."[6] John Chisholm was also a Freemason and the symbols on his masonic apron which went to America with George show John to have been a brother of St. John's Lodge, probably at Inverness.[7]

Dr. Samuel Johnson who passed this way with his friend James Boswell in the autumn of 1773 remarked upon setting out from Fort Augustus: "We were now ... to enter a country upon which perhaps no wheel has ever rolled."[8] In Glen Moriston

---

* This name also appears as Scotus and Scothouse, but John Macdonell wrote Scottos in his memoirs.

† Catherine's father Donald Macdonell fell at Culloden and is said to have been carried off the field by marauders from a vessel in Loch Ness. He was sold as a slave, later seized by Turkish pirates, and held in bondage for the rest of his life.

the Doctor found little English spoken and it was here that he "first heard of the general dissatisfaction which is now driving the Highlanders into the other hemisphere."[9] Seventy inhabitants of this glen and many more from those adjoining had only just gone off with the Macdonells. "According to a letter from Fort William of Aug. 20 three gentlemen of the name of Macdonell, with their families, and 400 Highlanders, from the countries of Glengary, Glenmoriston, Urquhart, and Strathglass, imbarked [sic] lately for America, having obtained a grant of lands in Albany."[10] The Macdonells had been in communication with their kinsman Sir William Johnson, a descendant of the MacIan branch of the Macdonells of Glencoe and an extensive landholder in Albany County, Province of New York. They and their company set sail from Fort William in the chartered ship *Pearl*. Being Roman Catholics the Macdonells had taken with them their own priest, Reverend John McKenna,[11] but the company also included a number of Presbyterians, for in the Highlands Catholic and Protestant wore their faith easily and were tolerant of each other.

Whether or not the Roses, George Chisholm, Archibald Thomson, and James Park had joined the Macdonells or like the Leals had crossed the Atlantic independently is uncertain, but somewhat more is known of those who departed the following year. Lists of emigrants which the government now required from customs officers show various reasons for persons' leaving their native land : "For Poverty and to get Bread," "High Rents and Deerness [sic] of Provisions," and such.[12] Thomas and John McMicking who shipped aboard the *Gale*, Henry Jefferson, master, at Stranraer on May 16, 1774, gave "want of employment" as their reason. (One of the 147 passengers gave "curiosity" as his reply to the question.[13]) On November 14 William McKenzie of "Auch hall," with his family and two servants embarked in the *Peace and Plenty*, Charles McKenzie, master, at Port Stornoway in the Isle of Lewis. All of the fifty-nine passengers were emigrating "on Account of their being greatly reduced in their Circumstances."[14] Another farmer who headed for New York was Robert Grant of Strathspey with his wife Mary and nine children.[15] On September 15, 1775, emigration from Scotland to America was prohibited altogether by the British government.

For some emigrants the voyage was short and uneventful like those in the *Pearl* who reached the port of New York in six weeks' time. Others such as Alexander Leal and his family were exposed to many dangers and suffered great hardship. Two of Leal's sons died at sea and the survivors "met with many remarkable deliverances," to use Leal's words.[16] In the opinion of James Boswell who inspected an emigrant ship the accommodation was very good. "A long ward I may call it, with a row of beds on each side, every one of which was the same size every way, and fit to contain four people."

The northwestern frontier of Albany County, the objective of these migrating Scots, was far removed from New England where the old struggle against taxation had been gathering momentum since 1765. Whereas the mounting dissatisfaction with the mother country was almost universal in these older colonies, in New York it was more or less confined to the mercantile classes of its seaport, York Town. In consequence the Province of New York was still the Loyalist stronghold of America, and the Scots who rallied round the Macdonells were to form the backbone of the Loyalist resistance during the Revolution.[17]

THE MARK OF HONOUR

At the Council Chamber at Quebec on Monday, November 9, 1789, "His Lordship intimated to the Council, that . . . it was his wish to put a mark of honour upon the families who had adhered to the Unity of the Empire, and joined the Royal Standard in America before the Treaty of Separation in the Year 1783."

CHAPTER ONE

TO THE HILLS OF THE NEW WORLD

York Town situated on the southern tip of York Island was a typical colonial seaport. Within an area of about one square mile bounded on the south by Bowling Green and Fort George, and on the north by the "Fields" (site of the present City Hall) lived 20,000 inhabitants of the city. The most populous section lay along the East River where places of business intermingled with private residences. Shops, market places, auction rooms, churches and burial grounds, taverns, dwelling houses with gardens, and warehouses were jumbled together along narrow and tortuous streets. The gracious homes of the wealthy gentry stood around Bowling Green, along Broad Street (originally a watercourse flanked by footpaths), and on Dock Street paralleling the East River. Wall Street followed the line of an ancient palisade running east and west, and the path used by Dutch maidens when carrying clothes to wash in a fine run of spring water retained the name of Maiden Lane. Queen Street (now Pearl Street) and Hanover Square were the business centres. Broad Way, the tree-bordered main street connecting with Bowery Lane, was fronted by elegant and stately buildings for the length of a mile. The older buildings, mainly of wood construction, were interspersed with brick edifices of Georgian architecture, some of them four-storeyed. Along Broad Way in front of Trinity Church, the Anglican place of worship, lay the parade ground named the Mall by the British army.[1] Here umbrellas carried by British officers were the first seen in the city. Broad Way was the only thoroughfare running through the farms, woodlands, and settlements such as Greenwich, Bloomingdale, and the Dutch farming community of Haarlem to the upper reaches of York Island. Along this road were the country seats of wealthier citizens to which they resorted in times of epidemic. Though much refuse was conveyed to the East River by means of sewers, or was carried away by slaves at night, the streets were cluttered with trash. Hogs grunted contentedly in garbage until kicked by cartmen or chased away by householders.

This was a city of castes headed by officers of the Crown and the landed gentry. Next came merchants and traders of the mercantile class who, though they earned good livings, were without prestige, either social or political. At the bottom of the scale but far in the majority were the poorer land owners, mechanics, journeymen apprentices, and labourers who constituted the "inhabitants" or, as they were more commonly characterized, the "mob." The largest non-English group in the cosmopolitan population was the Dutch. Scots were numerous, Ireland was well represented, there were some French and a few Portuguese Jews. Members of the Church of England were outnumbered by Presbyterians, the Scots having their own kirk in Cedar Street.

In the estimation of Judge William Smith, the city was "one of the most social places on the continent. Men collect themselves into weekly evening clubs. The ladies, in winter, are frequently entertained at concerts of musick or assemblies, and make a very good appearance. They are comely, and dress well; and scarce any of them have distorted shapes. . . . There is nothing they so generally neglect as reading, and, indeed, all the arts for the improvement of the mind. . . ."[2] (*Rivington's New-York Gazetteer* of October 14, 1773, carried the announcement of the opening of a French Night School for ladies and gentlemen.) The upper classes followed the fashions of London although by the time the latter reached the colonies they were out of date.

"Our merchants," wrote Judge Smith, "are compared to a hive of bees who industriously gather honey for others. . . ."[3] Their advertisements in the September and October issues of the newspapers[4] in 1773 show surprisingly wide ranges of merchandise. "At the Sign of the Looking-Glass and Druggist's Pot—a curious Assortment of valuable goods" included a great variety of engravings, painters' and limners' colours, articles of pewter and steel, carpeting and "paper hangings" as well as the expected mirrors and sconces. The Three Sugar Loaves had received from London a large quantity of excellent porter and Cheshire cheese of the first quality. Another merchant offered "Green Glass-goggles, most excellent preservatives of tender eyes in summer from dust and wind, in winter from snow, etc., . . . tooth pick cases mounted in gold, truly elegant presents for either sex." James Rivington, editor and publisher of the *Gazetteer*, was taking subscriptions for an engraving of "A view of the Cataract of Niagara . . . one of the most wonderful aspects of Nature." John Roosevelt in Maiden Lane offered "the most elegant and extensive variety of pictures ever imported into this place, one in particular with a very handsome frame and glass, of Regulus, opposing the entreaties of the Roman Senate, importuning him not to return to Carthage, price £14." The upholsterer, cabinet and chair maker from London at the Royal Bed and Star, Wall Street, made "all sorts of canopy, festoon, field and tent bedsteads and furniture; also every sort of drapery." The stock of another merchant included such widely assorted goods as Bath and Brussels lace and Axminster and Wilton carpets in variety. The leather-dresser at the Crown and Breeches in Queen Street undertook to make breeches of different quality ranging downwards from the finest buck and doe skin to the humble sheep skin. A hatter engaged to fashion hats "to exceed in fineness, colour and cock," a jeweller to make silver shoe-buckles "both manly and Macaroni." A stay-maker had "lately received an assortment of patterns of the newest fashion, from the Queen's stay-maker, in London. . . . Ladies at any distance accommodated upon sending measurements."

The Highlanders arrived at a time when the city was seething with excitement over what *Rivington's Gazetteer* dubbed "the Tea Occasion"; in fact the announcement of the safe landing of the *Pearl* appears just below the reports of this affair in both this newspaper and the *Gazette*. On October 15 a consignment of tea from the East India Company had arrived but it was refused entry because of the importation duties of three pence per pound as laid down by Parliament. Citizens in public meeting approved the action in the following address to merchants and others who had taken this stand: "Gentlemen—Your prudent Conduct in refusing the Freight of the India Company's Tea, justly merits the Approbation and Applause of every Well-Wisher to the Liberties of this or any other Country."[5] The Sons of Liberty, as the noisiest faction of the Whigs chose to call themselves, passed a resolution that all those who imported, stored, bought, or sold tea were to be considered enemies of American liberty.

Hugh Gaine, well-known printer, bookseller, and stationer at the Bible and Crown in Hanover Square (and publisher of the first American edition of *Robinson Crusoe*), informed the readers of his *Gazette* that "on Monday last arrived the Ship Pearl, Capt. Tucker, in 6 Weeks from Fort William, in the Highlands of Scotland, with a great Number of very respectable Passengers full of Health, and Ready Money to purchase each Man his Freehold. They are justly esteemed a great Acquisition to this Province, in some Part of which they propose to settle. There are in the whole about 280 Souls, all of them, about a single score excepted, of the Clan M'Donald, coming Chiefly from fam'd Lochabar, and Glenmuir."[6]

Inquiries were instituted by the Scots concerning land proprietors, and two who resided in the city, Goldsbrow Banyar and Lawrence Kortright, were recommended. The former, an Englishman who preferred to use a contraction of his Christian name, Goldsborough, had come to America about 1737 and had soon risen to prominence. He had been registrar of the Colonial Court of Chancery and officer of the Prerogative Court which handled the granting of marriage licences and the probating of wills, before he was appointed deputy secretary under Governor Cadwallader Colden of the Province of New York. Lawrence Kortright, who used the Anglicized form of the Dutch Louwrens Kortreght, was a son of Cornelius Jansen Kortright, a native of Beest, Gelderland, who in 1663 at the age of eighteen had migrated in the *Brindle Cow*.[7] Cornelius became a merchant and married Hester, beautiful daughter of another equally successful merchant, John Cannon. After her husband was accidentally killed at Kortright's Wharf Hester raised her six young children by going into business for herself.[8] Lawrence made a fortune privateering during the Seven Years' War,[9] and was one of the founders in 1770 of the New York Chamber of Commerce.[10] He married Hannah Aspinwall and with his family of one son and four daughters lived in his town house on Dock Street. His eighty-four-acre farm situated eight miles north of the city lay between the highway and the East River some four miles below Haarlem.[11] The Kortrights were closely allied to the Gouverneurs and other prominent colonial families.[12] Banyar and Kortright had secured patents to adjoining lands lying between the Head of the Delaware and the Charlotte River, a tributary of the Susquehanna. The representatives chosen by the Highlanders to discuss terms with these landholders would seem to have been Alexander of Aberchalder, Hugh Fraser, and John Cameron.

The ninth day following the arrival of the *Pearl* the Scots lost one of their number when a young man by the name of Gordon died of "a putrid inflammatory fever."[13] The next day, October 28, the company set out for the north. "Thursday last," runs a news item in the *Gazetteer*, "the Gentlemen and other passengers that arrived here last Monday se'nnight, in the ship Pearl, Captain Tucker, from that part of North Britain called Glengary, embarked on board a sloop for Albany : on going on board they drank his Majesty's health, and prosperity to the province; and expressed the highest sense of gratitude for the civilities shewn them by the inhabitants of this city."[14]

From one to two weeks were required to sail by sloop up the one hundred miles of the Hudson River lying between York and Albany. Richard Smith, who belonged to an old family in Burlington, New Jersey, had made the same journey four years earlier, when, upon becoming one of the patentees of a tract situated in the same area as the lands of Banyar and Kortright, he had set out to inspect and survey the Otego Patent. A man of knowledge and education, and a keen observer who was intensely interested in all that he saw, Smith recorded in his journal his impressions of the journey. Although sloops on the Hudson were engaged primarily in commerce, he was agreeably surprised at their appointments. "These Albany sloops contain very convenient Cabins. . . . We eat from a regular Table accommodated with Plates,

Knives, & Forks & enjoy our Tea in the Afternoon."[15] He noted that the masts of the sloops stood vertically and not with the usual slant so that sails might be more quickly lowered in the Highlands where the wind was gusty. Upon leaving York Smith "found it extremely agreeable Sailing with the country seats of the Citizens on the Right Hand, and the high Lands of Bergen [now known as the Palisades] on the Left and the Narrows abaft. . . . This morning the Sloop passed Col. Philips's Mansion House and Gardens situate[d] in a pleasant valley between Highlands." Built in 1682 and now nearly three hundred years old, Philipse Manor had then stood nearly a century. Where the river winds through the Highlands the immigrant Scots caught their first glimpse of the "mountains" which resembled so closely the "hills" of their homeland. Smith observed "a bold Shore encircled on either Hand by aspiring Mountains & thro them there is a View of a fine Country above."

Another traveller describes the beautiful Highlands of the Hudson. After stating that at the top of Tappan Sea "the banks approach each other so closely that the channel . . . is not perceived until you almost enter it," he continues:

> Here we suddenly found ourselves in a narrow pass between precipitous mountain tops, rising on both sides from the water's edge to an elevation of 1200 to 1500 feet . . . and the entry to them seemed to us the most remarkable point on the river. . . . The river course continues to run in this defile among romantic hills covered with wood, sweetly inlaid with plateaus of green pasture, and of table land, for about twenty miles. Farm-houses and villages look as if they hung on the cliffs, or rose by terraces from the water's edge . . . projecting rocks often force [the river] to change its direction, so much, indeed, that you frequently appear to be sailing in a lake, from which you cannot discover an outlet. . . . After leaving the Highlands the banks of the river are comparatively low. . . .[16]

Here the great manors and patroonships stretched away from the east shore of the Hudson River. "The Lords of Manors," wrote Richard Smith, "are called by the common People Patroons." At Beekman Manor he visited Dutch tenants living in stone houses; "one Woman had Twelve good Countenanced Boys and Girls all clad in Homespun both Linen and Woolen." The sloop's skipper acting as interpreter, Smith learned how according to the old Dutch system tenants leased their land for a term of three lives—those of a father, son and grand- or god-son for twenty skipples of wheat per annum, a skipple (Anglicized form of the Dutch scheepel and the German scheffel) being equal to three pecks. At Kaatskill he saw his first Indian, a Mohican named Hans clad in a "shattered Blanket . . . & had a Scunk Skin for his Tobacco Pouch." Near Albany Smith saw his first batteau, the French substitute for the bark canoe. Usually built of pine boards the batteau was flat-bottomed, of twenty to twenty-five feet in length with a depth of about two feet. This craft was capable of carrying heavy loads through shallow rivers and swift rapids, and being sharp pointed at both ends was rowed, poled, or sailed in either direction.[17]

To Richard Smith Albany was much like York. The town contained about five hundred dwelling houses exclusive of stores and outhouses. The streets were irregular and badly laid out,

> some paved others not. . . . Most of the Buildings are Pyramidically shaped like the old Dutch Houses in N York. We found [Richard] Cartwright's a good Tavern tho his charges were exorbitant. . . . The Court House is large and the Jail under it. One miserable Woman is now in it for cutting the Throat of her Child about 5 years old. There are 4 Houses of Worship for different Denominations and a Public Library. . . . Most of the Houses are built of Brick or faced with Brick. The Inhabitants generally speak both Dutch and English & some do not understand the latter. . . . Some Lime or Linden Trees as well as other Trees are planted before the Doors as at N York and indeed Albany has in other respects much the Aspect of that City. The Houses are

for the most part covered with Shingles made of White Pine, some few with red or black Tiles. . . . there is a Town Cloc which strikes regularly.[18]

These and similar scenes on the river and in the town were what met the eyes of the company of Highlanders. Almost immediately after their arrival Alexander Macdonell, John Cameron, and Hugh Fraser set out to view the lands of Banyar and Kortright at the Head of the Delaware while Allan Macdonell and other representatives went to Johnstown and opened negotiations with Sir William Johnson at his baronial home, Johnson Hall.

From York Island to Albany colonization was pushing westward by way of the four great rivers in the province : the Hudson on the east, the Mohawk on the north, and the Delaware and Susquehanna on the west. Settlements of Dutch and German Palatines had spread from the Hudson into the Mohawk Valley; British from Sir William Johnson's settlements on the Mohawk had gone south along the Delaware and Susquehanna to be followed by New Englanders mostly from Connecticut who clashed with German Palatines moving northward from Pennsylvania. Whereas York was the centre of the southern section of the Province of New York, the old Dutch town of Albany, situated near the confluence of the Mohawk River with the Hudson, was the northern centre of the province which extended along both sides of its busy waterway, the Hudson River. Since the earliest times, the Hudson-Champlain watershed lying between the Berkshire Hills and the Green Mountains on the east, and the Kaatskill and Adirondack mountains on the west, was the great north-south thoroughfare between the seaboard and the St. Lawrence River. The way westward to Lake Ontario lay up the Hudson's most important tributary, the Mohawk River which flows eastward through its valley lying between the Adirondacks and the Kaatskills. South of the Mohawk, where the mountains rise to two and three thousand feet, rivers and streams flow in all directions. Kaats Kill (Dutch for Wildcat Creek) and Esopus Kill flow into the Hudson; Schoharie Kill and the Canajoharie find their way to the Mohawk; many other streams flow south to join the Delaware or the Susquehanna.

This was the country of the Mohawks, Indians of the tribal family known to the French as Iroquois and to the English as the Six Nations (until the admission of the Tuscaroras about 1712 it had been the Five Nations). "The Iroquois," wrote Francis Parkman, "was the Indian of the Indians. A thorough savage, yet a finished and developed savage, he is perhaps an example of the highest elevation man can reach without emerging from his primitive condition of the hunter." [19] The six tribes, Mohawks, Onondagas, Oneidas, Cayugas, Tuscaroras, and Senecas, had occupied all the territory lying south of Lake Ontario between the Hudson and Lake Erie. Here they lived side by side, bound together by the Six Nations Confederacy, the fundamental principle of which was to establish permanent peace among its members and to ensure their unified action in time of war. Unlike the roving tribes in other parts of the continent these people lived in permanent castles,* some very ancient. "Along the banks of the Mohawk [again to quote Parkman], among the hills and hollows of Onondaga, in the forests of Oneida and Cayuga, on the romantic shores of Seneca Lake and the rich borders of the Genesee, surrounded by waving maize fields and

---

* "Fortified towns built on a high point of land in the fork of confluent rivers" (Francis Parkman, *The Jesuits in North America in the Seventeenth Century* (Boston, 1896), p. xxxix). "Ye Mohawkes were all gone to their Castles with resolution to fight it out against the french . . ." (E. B. O'Callaghan, ed., *The Documentary History of New York* (Albany, 1850), vol. I, p. 71, "A Relation of the Govern^r of Canada, his March with 600 Volunteers into ye Territoryes of His Royal Highness the Duke of York in America [1666]").

encircled from afar by the green margin of the forest, stood the ancient strongholds of the confederacy." [20]

Inevitably settlements crept westward from the Hudson into the Mohawk Valley and along lesser streams of the Mohawks' country, the names of the communities bespeaking the origin of their founders, whether Dutch, Palatine German, English, or ancient Mohawk. Under the patronage of Queen Anne the Palatines had come to the New World to escape religious persecution in their native section of Bavaria. Because of the common bond of the Protestant faith, England had lent a helping hand and large numbers had settled in Pennsylvania where they became known as "Pennsylvania Dutch" (Dutch being a corruption of Deutsch meaning German). Some groups had found refuge in New York,* and succeeded in living peaceably beside the Indians. The principal stronghold of the Mohawks was the Lower Castle strategically situated at the confluence of the Schoharie with the Mohawk River. The fort erected here in 1711 to mark the western frontier was named Fort Hunter in honour of the new governor from England. Upon his arrival in June 1711, the Scotsman Robert Hunter, in accordance with the Queen's instructions, saw to the erection adjacent to the fort of a mission school and a little limestone chapel twenty-four feet square where the Indians might receive instruction in the Christian faith. Queen Anne's Royal Chapel to the Mohawks, dedicated in 1712, was endowed by the Queen who sent communion silver, Bibles, an organ which for fifty years was the only one west of Albany, and other furnishings, some of which exist today. In time the Mohawks, of all the Six Nations, became the best acquainted with the manners of the English.

Few settlers had come to the Mohawk Valley until Sir Peter Warren was granted a tract of 15,000 acres extending along the river east from Fort Hunter and until he promoted emigration from Ireland and Scotland. Sir Peter, an officer of the Royal Navy (who later won renown as commodore of the fleet at the taking of Louisbourg in 1745) appointed his twenty-four-year-old nephew to dispose of his holdings. Young William Johnson came out from Ireland in 1738. He cleared land, built mills, and opened roads in the settlement which he named Warren's Bush and to which he brought sixty families, Scotch-Irish † like himself, in 1741. Here he carried on an active trade with the Indians and set up a trading post on the Susquehanna at the ancient village of Oquaga. His success in establishing amicable relations between the British government and the Six Nations gained him a position of great influence as the following "Extract from a journal written in America" shows:

* The story of how the Palatines or "High Dutch" came to settle in the Mohawk Valley, though long believed and often repeated, has been proved legendary by modern research. This story runs to the effect that in the spring of 1710 when the four Indian kings who had accompanied Peter Schuyler to England to implore Queen Anne's help against the French saw the wretched Palatines encamped in the environs of London, they became so touched at the distress of these poor folk that they offered the Schoharie tract as a new homeland for the refugees. In *Queen Anne's American Kings* (Oxford University Press, 1952) Richmond P. Bond states on page 11: "We know now that the Kings did not even see the 'High Dutch' on Black Heath. The Palatines had boarded transports for New York four months before the arrival of the sachems, and though long delayed in proceeding on their voyage, thus missed the visit of the sachems." (The visit of the four Indian kings was celebrated by the printing of a little book entitled *The Four Kings of Canada, being a succinct account of the Four Indian Princes lately arriv'd from North America* (London, 1710).)

† Scotch-Irish, an Americanism originating well before the Revolution and yet in current use, denotes Scots who had first migrated to the North of Ireland before coming to America. George S. Pryde, who did extensive research on Scottish influences in the colonizing of America, wrote: "The term seems to me to be open to two objections: (i) the word 'Scotch' is not, accord-

Major General Johnson (an Irish gentleman,) is universally esteemed in our parts, for the part he sustains. Besides skill and experience as an officer, he is particularly happy in making himself beloved by all sorts of people, and can conform to all companies and conversations. He is very much of the fine gentleman in genteel company. But as the inhabitants next to him are mostly Dutch, he sits down with them and smokes his tobacco, drinks flip, and talks of improvements, bear and beaver skins. Being surrounded with Indians, he speaks several of their languages well, and has always some of them with him. He takes care of their wives and children when they go out on parties, and even wears their dress. In short, by his honest dealing with them in trade, and his courage, which has often been successfully tried with them and his courteous behaviour, he has so endeared himself to them, that they chose him for one of their sachems or princes, and esteem him as their common father.[21]

Because of the confidence he inspired Johnson was appointed superintendent of the North American Indians. His sons-in-law acted as his deputies, Guy Johnson in the management of the affairs of the Six Nations and Western Indians and Daniel Claus in those pertaining to the Canadian tribes. In the Seven Years' War the elder Johnson won the loyalty of the Iroquois to the British, gained renown as a military leader, and was knighted after the victory over the French at Lake George.

As colonization spread westward, however, the discontent of the Indians mounted until it became imperative that an agreement be reached. In 1768 Sir William Johnson negotiated a treaty with the Six Nations at Fort Stanwix, one of a chain of British forts erected on the route to Lake Ontario during the Seven Years' War. This treaty fixed "The Line of Property" "between His Majesty's subjects and the Indian Country." The northern limits of this line were so drawn as to allow the greater number of Iroquois castles to remain within the territory of the Six Nations. Since it had been British policy to stay out of Iroquois country this vast wilderness was relatively unknown to white men. Hunters and trappers habitually skirted it by water— Lake Ontario, the Niagara River, and Lake Erie. Though forts along the waterways had changed hands many times no attempt had been made to penetrate the interior. When, in 1771, Guy Johnson was drawing his map of the country under his jurisdiction, he wrote that what lay beyond the boundary line "having never been surveyed or even thoroughly Explored is chiefly laid down from my Journals and the Sketches of intelligent Indians and other Persons."[22]

The Mohawk River throughout its length, the headwaters of the Delaware, the sources of the Susquehanna, and those of several of its tributaries lay within the region purchased by the Crown and added to Albany County. In the northern section the Delaware, called Kithane by the Indians, traverses this county in two branches which nearly parallel each other. The East Branch, the Popachton or Popatunk Branch of the Indians, rises on the northeastern slope of Mount Utsayantha which towers 3,214 feet above sea level. The river sweeps around the Moresville Range to flow towards the southeast. It is swift for a considerable distance, and except in the places where it receives tributaries its valley is rocky and precipitous and unfit for cultivation. The West or Mohawks Branch of the Delaware, rising at about 1,886 feet above the sea, is different. From little Lake Utsayantha,* named for a maiden

---

ing to the best modern usage, interchangeable with 'Scottish' or 'Scots' as a general adjective; it should qualify only a few special words, such as terriers, firs, whiskey, wool: (ii) 'Scotch-Irish' suggests a mixture of stocks . . . which is belied by the evidence. . . . In 1610 and the following years, the Ulster 'planters' came very largely from the Scottish Lowlands; in their new homes they became even more aggressively Scottish and Presbyterian, more bitterly anti-Irish-Papist, than they had formerly been. . . ." (George S. Pryde, "Scottish Colonization in the Province of New York," *New York History,* vol. XVI (1935), p. 140fn.)

* Long considered the source of the Delaware River. The true source, the spring which feeds the lake, rises in the hills to the north above which lies what is said to be the highest cultivated field in the state of New York.

famous in Indian legend, the river is little more than a shallow stream flowing through a valley well adapted to farming. In this portion of its course the varied scenery of its hills and wooded banks is exquisitely beautiful. Flowing tortuously through the plateau in a deep trough until it emerges from the Kaatskills the East Branch joins the West Branch to form the main course of the Delaware. The river then continues its southerly course to meet tidewater at Trenton, New Jersey. Paralleling the West Branch to the northwest is a tributary of the Susquehanna named the Charlotte River by Sir William Johnson in honour of the Queen. Between the three rivers the surface of the country is broken and diversified by high ranges of hills extending in a northeasterly and southwesterly direction. The arable land of the valleys and flats, composed of fine alluvion and rich mould, was superlatively productive, and was, as it is still, exceeded by none for grazing.

In anticipation of the treaty signed in November 1768 but not ratified until July 21, 1770, land speculators rushed in to deal directly with the Indians and secure large tracts cheaper than they could be got from the Crown. On June 14, 1768, John Harper Sr. and others purchased 250,000 acres from five Indians of Oquaga.[23] William, James, John Jr., Alexander, and Joseph were the sons of John Harper (Harpur), a native of County Derry in the north of Ireland. He had migrated to Maine in 1720 but after twenty years removed his family to Windsor, Connecticut, and thence (in 1754) to Cherry Valley, the community which would now serve as the model for a settlement on the new purchase.

These lands lay between the West Branch of the Delaware on the southeast and Sir William Johnson's tract of 100,000 acres, acquired in 1751, bordering the Charlotte on the northwest. On the northeast they adjoined the Strasburgh Patent granted to John Butler in 1769, while spreading over the Kaatskills to the southeast was the Great Hardenburgh Patent, an early grant of 2,000,000 acres. The Harper tract was divided into about a dozen smaller tracts. Because individuals were limited to 1,000 acres apiece syndicates were formed for the purpose of securing patents from the Crown. On December 8, 1769, a patent was issued to John Harper and twenty-one others for the 22,000 acres on the northeast, and on February 24, 1770, Lawrence Kortright and others were given title to the 22,000 adjoining acres on the southwest.[24] The next tract westward was divided under two patents issued to Goldsbrow Banyar and others in June 1777, and called the Goldsborough Patent. One of the conditions of these patents was that within three years a family should be settled on each 1,000 acres and that at least three out of every fifty acres of arable land of these grants should be brought under cultivation.[25] The Harpers called their settlement Harpersfield, a name that was soon applied to a large section of the upland lying between the Delaware and the Charlotte. The upper valley of the West Branch was known as the Head of the Delaware, and the Kortright and Banyar patents were given the name of Kortright Township.*

Since time immemorial this region, shown on early maps as the Endless Mountains,[26] had been the hunting grounds of the Mohawks and was reached by that well-beaten track, the Mohawk-Susquehanna trail. From the Mohawk River the path led up the Schoharie, struck over the hills to Lake Utsayantha and continued down the

* Throughout the eighteenth century no villages or towns existed on the frontier; therefore, the names encountered here refer not to villages and towns of the same names found there today but to settlements spreading over wide areas which in most cases became townships after the close of the revolutionary war.

east bank of the West Branch of the Delaware. At the great bend it crossed overland to the Susquehanna, down to Oquaga, and ultimately to Chesapeake Bay. Another branch followed the Cobuskill, a tributary of the Schoharie, to its head (Summit Lake at 2,068 feet above the sea), crossed to the Charlotte, and followed that river to its junction with the Susquehanna.

The opening of the territory acquired by the Fort Stanwix Treaty resulted in a fringe of new frontier settlements along the border of Albany County adjoining the Indian country. On March 12, 1772, a new county was set off from Albany County which was honoured with the name of the royal Governor, William Tryon. Sir William Johnson's settlement of Johnstown situated in the hills a short distance north of the Mohawk Valley was designated the county town, and Sir William promptly provided a brick court house whose cornerstone was laid June 26, and a stone gaol. The county was further divided into districts of which only two need be mentioned here. The Palatine District extended north and the Canajoharie District south of the Mohawk River. Because the West Branch of the Delaware River formed a part of the boundary between the old and the new counties, the Harper, Kortright, and Banyar patents together with Cherry Valley lay within the Canajoharie District of Tryon County. In the spring of 1774 alterations made in the county boundaries placed the east side of the West Branch of the Delaware within the jurisdiction of the new county of Ulster. By the following spring the country beyond the Susquehanna had become so well settled as to warrant its being erected into a district within Tryon County on April 5, 1775. Its name, the Old England District, shows the extent to which this section of the province was being populated by immigrants from the mother country.

The Head of the Delaware was the outpost of settlements which had pushed in from two directions, the Mohawk Valley on the north and the Hudson Valley on the east. It was almost equidistant from the old Dutch and Palatine settlement of Schoharie and the newer colony of Scotch-Irish and New Englanders at Cherry Valley situated on a tributary of the Susquehanna. The latter was the largest and most important settlement south of the Mohawk, and the road leading from it northward to the point where Canajoharie Creek enters the river was the first in this section of the frontier. When James Lindesay, a Scot of some fortune and distinction, had first come to live there he had called it Lindesay's Bush. Before securing (with others) in 1738 a grant of 8,000 acres of unbroken wilderness at what was then considered the head of the Susquehanna, Lindesay had been naval officer at the port of New York and sheriff of Albany County. That he sought patent to land so remote when unoccupied lands nearer to populated areas were available was doubtless due to the likeness of the rolling hills to his native Scotland. He sedulously cultivated the friendship of the Mohawks. During the Lindesays' first winter when deep snows made travel impossible and the family was on the verge of starvation, they were discovered by Indians who journeyed on snowshoes to the Mohawk and returned with provisions on their backs. Lindesay prevailed upon a young Presbyterian clergyman, born in Ireland and educated at Trinity College, Dublin, and in Edinburgh, to come to his settlement. In 1742 Reverend Samuel Dunlop arrived with about thirty Scotch-Irish families from Londonderry, New Hampshire, among them James Campbell and David Ramsey, to settle in Lindesay's Bush.[27] Others like the Harpers soon followed.

Being strict Presbyterians the Harpers planned to attract to their new settlement of Harpersfield the same type of Scotch-Irish families from New England. The principal industry was to be the manufacture of maple sugar, a product much in demand,* for which the only equipment needed was a sap kettle and a supply of wooden troughs. Harpersfield was heavily timbered with maple, beech, and other hardwoods, and therefore easier to clear than land upon which pines and other evergreens predominated. Among those who invested in lands both at Harpersfield and Cherry Valley was Richard Cartwright, the prominent innkeeper at Albany.[28]

In the spring of 1769 William Harper and Samuel Campbell, also of Cherry Valley, set forth with the King's surveyors to bound the Harper Patent and lay out the land in farm lots. On June 2 they encountered the surveying party of Richard Smith engaged in running the boundaries of the 100,000-acre Otego Patent lying south of Otsego Lake. The two expeditions met at the junction of Otego Creek with the Charlotte (below modern Oneonta), and all sat down to dine in an old orchard planted by Indians. Besides Smith, there was in this gathering another man of importance to this narrative. He was the young Mohawk chieftain, Thayendanegea, known to the British by his civilized or Christian name of Joseph Brant, whom Smith had engaged as one of the two Indian guides. "This Mohawk it seems is a considerable farmer," comments Smith, "possessing Horses and Cattle and 100 acres of rich Land at Canajoharie.† He says the Mohawks have lately followed Husbandry more than formerly, and that some Hemloc Swamps when cleared will produce good Timothy Grass."[29] Both guides had been schoolmates of William Harper's brother, John, at Dr. Eleazor Wheelock's Indian mission school at Lebanon, Connecticut. Joseph, at this time twenty-six years of age, had brought with him his wife Margaret, daughter of an Oneida chief,[30] and their small child. When remarking that some Indian women wore silver brooches which passed as money among the Indians, each to the value of a shilling, Smith states: "Brant's wife had several Tier of them in her Dress to the amount of perhaps 10 or £15."[31] And again, "Some of the Chiefs . . . imitate the English mode and Joseph Brant was dressed in a suit of blue Broad Cloth as his Wife was in a Callicoe or Chintze Gown."[32] He tells how Joseph and the other guide James built a bark canoe in a day; how Joseph kept the party supplied with deer and bear meat, safe from rattlesnakes, and warm in wet weather in bark shanties erected in half an hour's time.

About the regions being surveyed at the time of this festive meeting, Smith provides additional first-hand information. He describes the primordial forest, reporting the trees "very tall and lofty, sometimes 200 Feet high and strait, but not proportionally large in Circumference, except some white Pines and a few particular Trees of other Kinds which are both long and bulky."[33] The size was apparently relative because Smith mentions a birch measuring twenty-six feet in circumference. Small fruits grew in the wildest profusion and plum, apple, and cherry trees were found everywhere. The hosts of brightly coloured birds frequenting these mountains delighted him as they still delight the people of today. What he noted near the confluence of the Charlotte with the Susquehanna, "a few Flats but the Bone is more

---

* Some names of farms in Harpersfield a century later were Sugar Bush, Sugar Land, Maple Square, Maple Row, Maple Grove, Maple Shade, Maple Wood (*Atlas of Delaware County, New York* (New York, 1869)).

† The Canajoharie or Upper Castle of the Mohawks was situated in the township of Danube west of Fort Plain. This Indian village should not be confused with the white settlement of that name which grew up at the confluence of Canajoharie Creek with the Mohawk River.

plentiful than the Flesh," is not true of Harpersfield where the hills are for the most part tillable. Upon gazing over Otsego Lake while visiting Colonel Croghan * Smith remarked, "It rained again. The Elevated Hills . . . seem to intercept the flying vapors and draw down more moisture than more humble places. So Nature wisely feeds the two great Rivers whose sources are here...."[34]

Starting on the uplands above the Charlotte at the southeastern border of Sir William Johnson's lands William Harper and Samuel Campbell proceeded to lay out farm lots of 150 acres each, irrespective of hill or dale. Because an earlier grant of lands bordering the Delaware had been made in 1738 to Arent Bradt, little more than half of Harpersfield and none of Kortright extended to the river. Banyar fared best, having secured title to several miles of the river valley below Betty's Brook,† the northwestern limit of the Bradt Patent.

The Harper, Kortright, and Banyar patents were opened for settlement in the spring of 1771, at which time John Jr., who was to take charge of land transactions, moved his family to Harpersfield. After erecting a temporary shelter formed like a wigwam Harper went away on business, leaving the raising of the log house to men he had brought to assist the surveyor and under the direction of his wife Miriam. When he returned the walls had been raised, and upon being roofed the house was ready for occupancy. Like the Lindesays at Cherry Valley the Harpers faced starvation during their first winter in the wilderness. They had subsisted for some time on cornmeal until rescued by friends from Schoharie who brought them supplies. To keep his cow alive, John Harper travelled five miles over the hills on snowshoes to natural meadows in the Delaware Valley and carried back hay on his shoulders.[35]

Whereas Harper drew settlers of the second and third generations of Scotch-Irish Protestants from New England, Kortright and Banyar contacted new immigrants at the port of their arrival, most of whom were Gaelic-speaking protestants from Scotland and Ireland. They reached the area by travelling either over the mountains from Kaatskill on the Hudson or by the easier route from the Mohawk by way of the Schoharie. It was by the latter route that Hugh Fraser, Alexander Macdonell, and

---

* George Croghan, one of Sir William Johnson's deputy superintendents, lived at the foot of Otsego Lake. Next to Sir William he was the most prominent Indian agent of his time, and was one of the first Englishmen to foresee the future greatness of the wilderness beyond the Appalachians. He had engaged in organizing western land companies (*Dictionary of American Biography*), and, wishing to compensate him for land in Pennsylvania purchased from them and lost under the terms of the Fort Stanwix Treaty, the Indians had granted him 100,000 acres bordering on Otsego Lake. Intending to settle his tract Croghan raised money by mortgaging it to William Franklin, son of Benjamin Franklin, and lost the lands by foreclosure. The title eventually passed to William Cooper and Andrew Craig of Burlington, New Jersey, the home of Richard Smith. Upon viewing the tract in 1785 Cooper decided to settle it, laid out a village, and lived there alone for three years, naming his settlement Cooperstown. He brought his family to the lake in 1790 when his son James Fenimore was a year old. A series of letters written by William Cooper and published as *A Guide in the Wilderness*. . . . (Dublin, 1810) proved a valuable source for this history. His son, the author of the "Leatherstocking Tales" and other famous works, lived in the village, and today family relics are on view at Fenimore House. Across the way is the Farmers' Museum where various aspects and activities of a pioneer agricultural community are perpetuated in early buildings brought from far and near and set about along the little street.

† Although the origin of the name of this brook is elusive it was probably acquired in the usual manner, from a settler who once lived in its valley. It appears thus in a description of roads dated May 22, 1788, signed first by John Harper as one of the three road commissioners (Montgomery County Court House, Liber 3, pp. 45-57), but the spelling is probably his inimitable phonetic spelling. Once legalized by its recording, the spelling in this document endured although the chances are that it is a corruption of a proper name such as Beatty (James Beatty's?) or Bettys, a name then common in Schoharie.

John Cameron reached the Head of the Delaware to view the lands offered by Kortright and Banyar. They were so favourably impressed with this country that upon returning to Albany they reported "the most flattering encouragement" and immediately set out for York to negotiate with Kortright and Banyar.[36]

Meanwhile Sir William Johnson submitted proposals for settlement on his land. These were received on November 14, 1773, by Allan Macdonell who met with his "friends" the same evening and accordingly committed their observations to writing. Macdonell then dispatched these observations to Johnson, along with a covering letter which stated: "We have great desire of Settling under your wing and in which we may have a mutual Interest, you have Large estates to make & we some influence over people . . . that may be of consequence in Subsequent years." The meaning of some of the observations is clouded by the English of one whose native tongue was Gaelic, but those relative to the "Land in the neighbourhood of the Sisquehanna" are comparatively clear. Macdonell asked what the tract was in fee simple and "if any advantages of saw or Grist Mills fish or Fowl attend it," remarking that answers to the following questions were all the more necessary because of the proposals of other proprietors thereabouts. He continues:

> The people here are still in a fluctuating Situation but we believe they will adhere to us if Sir William gives the encouragement their Sobriety & Industry will Merit. The principle of which is a years Maintenance to each family that will Settle upon his estate: for which they would become bound to pay him. If their endeavours are found worthy of a Cow and a Horse or the Value its Hoped they will be indulged in it upon giving security for the Principal & Interest. We have a double motive for requesting the last the peoples Interest & Intention of frestering [frustrating?] the designs laid of inveigling them from us. It would be agreeable to us that there be room or Scouth in our Vicinity in order that such of our friends & Countrymen as will incline to follow our fate may sit down in our Neighbourhood we have reason to hope that severals of them will appear on the Continent if fortune does not frown upon us or force us to lay an Interdict on their intention.
>
> Should Any of us calling themselves Gentlemen incline to remove after a few years expence And toil in clearing land &c. it is hoped Sir William will agree to Accept of their Plantation at the Appreciation or estimation of honest men Mutually chose.[37]

The suggested assistance was in accordance with the prevailing custom whereby the patroon or lord of the manor furnished his settlers with seeds and stock, to be repaid in kind.[38] Although lands in Harpersfield and Kortright were given "on lease forever" the terms were somewhat different. Tenants were to be free to rent for the first eight years; thereafter they were to pay 6d. sterling per acre yearly forever. Thus settlers who took 150 acres might have ample time to become well established before the annual rental of £3.15.0 sterling came due.[39]

The Scots chose lands according to their liking. Some went among the Catholic Highlanders in Johnson's Bush near Johnstown.* The larger number, however, preferred the valleys of the Delaware and Charlotte rivers or the higher lands between the rivers where they searched for relatively level terrain. In this hilly upland broken by valleys and narrow ravines level land was not readily found so their holdings were scattered over the whole area. John, Alexander, and Roderick Macdonell "seated" themselves on the Charlotte, the water highway between the Schoharie and the Susquehanna (see Appendix A). A short distance upstream lived Christopher Servos

---

* At Johnson Hall is a huge ledger showing in large copperplate script the name of each of Sir William's tenants at the top of each page. Though never used before his death this ledger was kept when the great volumes of his papers were sold for scrap during the Civil War period.

who in January 1772 had acquired 1,500 acres of Johnson's land. There were also Servos' neighbours, the brothers Benjamin, Thomas, Joseph, James, and John Bartholomew, who between them occupied a 1,000-acre tract along the river adjoining the northeast corner of Harpersfield.[40] A daughter of John Bartholomew was the wife of Alexander Harper. George Chisholm and the Roses preferred the bottom lands along the Delaware where the deep valley lying east and west widens for a stretch of some eight miles. William Rose settled on the north side at the mouth of Betty's Brook and James located on the south side above the stream soon name Rose's Brook. The 100 acres that Chisholm purchased were also on the south side of the river[41] in the neighbourhood of Rose's Brook.

Other Scots like Archibald Thomson and James Park took Harper's land but the greater majority took those of Kortright through his resident agent, Alexander Mills. It was the area at the head of Betty's Brook where according to legend they clustered most thickly. Alexander Leal and Daniel McGillivrae took adjoining lots in a bowl-like depression rimmed by low uplands.

Whether in the outlying valleys of the Charlotte or the Delaware the Scots were all within a radius of six miles as the crow flies from the centre of the settlement.* Although it was far from the sea the northern section of Tryon County, spreading over the foothills of the Kaatskills, differed little from the newcomers' native land. That they came here for this reason is traditional among some of their descendants. The mountains proper,† rising suddenly from the surrounding country and too wild and forbidding even as a tribal home for the Indians, are lost after passing the Delaware River. The surface of Harpersfield and Kortright is rolling upland, broken by narrow valleys bordered by gradually sloping hills arable to their summits. Also it is a land of red rocks and bright red soil formed of soft sandstone alternated with shale and clay. Field stone, flat shale, and round hard conglomerates (called "pudding stones" since they look to be stuffed with plums) litter the ground in such abundance as to discourage the plough. In the latter quarter of the eighteenth century the whole Kaatskill region was covered by a continuous forest of hemlock which grew almost solid from the deepest gully to the loftiest summit. The colour of the mountains was that of the unbroken sea, a dark blue approaching black, and thus the reason for the name the Blue Mountains.[42] More than a century has passed since the woods were described by the master-craftsman, Francis Parkman: "One vast, continuous forest shadowed the fertile soil, covering the land as the grass covers a garden lawn, sweeping over hill and hollow in endless undulation, burying mountains in verdure, and mantling brooks and rivers from the light of day."[43] The foliage of standing hemlock was so dense that the sunlight could not penetrate it even at noonday. Trees of other species could not live in this dark, shadowy, and silent forest where only ferns and moss grew in the carpet of needles. Shandaken, the Indians called it, "the place of the hemlocks." Those whose trunks measured 4 feet in diameter were common, and many measuring up to 12 feet and standing as tall as 150 feet were found by men who came to strip them of their bark. It was the bark peelers who in the 1830's and

---

* In modern times this area is roughly bounded on the north by North Harpersfield, on the south by Bloomville, on the west by Davenport and Fergusonville, on the east by Stamford and Hobart in Delaware County, New York. What is known of individual locations is listed in Appendix A.

† Now set off as the Catskill Park under the jurisdiction of the State of New York.

thereafter swarmed over the mountains to fell these lofty trees of the virgin forest, strip them of their bark, and leave them to rot on the ground. Thus the Kaatskills were denuded of their hemlocks to supply the tremendous quantities of tan bark required by the tanning industry, and the blue aspect of the mountains gave way to the softer greens that we know today.[44]

CHAPTER TWO

THE FOREST: WITH AXE AND PLOUGH

THAT THE SETTLEMENT of the Gaels should succeed in the wilderness was only to be expected, for they were well prepared to endure the primitive life of the colonial frontier. In their homeland they had known hardship, privation, and isolation, and were inured to travelling long distances on foot over mountainous country. Like the Palatines, Scotsmen were noted for the nationalism of their settlements; wherever they might be transplanted they retained their language and ancient customs. "Ged chaidh an sgadpdh air gach taobh, cha chaochail iad an gnath" (although they scattered in every direction they did not change their ways) sang a Gaelic bard of his countrymen.[1] William Cooper, a contemporary well acquainted with their type, wrote:

> The Scotch succeed in the woods as elsewhere, being frugal, cautious in their bargains, living within their means, and punctual in their engagements; if a Scotchman kills a calf he will take the best part of it to market, and husband up the price of it; if he consumes any part at home, it will be the coarsest and the cheapest; the American will eat the best part himself, and if he sells any, will lay out the money upon some article of show; the odds are, that when the Scotchman buys a cow, he pays ready money, and has her for a lower price; the American pays with his note, gives more, and is often sued for the payment....[2]

There is no lack of evidence however, that, in settling their land, the Scots adopted most of the accepted procedures of the American frontier.[3] For matters beyond their ken like building log houses, using oxen as beasts of burden, and cultivating unfamiliar crops, they drew on the knowledge of experienced neighbours. Such a one was Jacob Stoneburner (Steenbrander), blacksmith, a native German reared in the colonies, who had purchased no less than 500 acres on the south side of the Delaware. He had been there a year when the Roses and George Chisholm became his neighbours. And up the adjacent valley at New Stamford were the New Englanders and a scattering of others whose names are long since forgotten, who were also old hands at settling wild land.

The ways of frontiersmen were time-worn, some having originated with the Indians long before either the colonists of Jamestown or the Pilgrim Fathers set foot on the continent. Temporary shelters such as the Scots would have learned to make according to Indian methods were adequate and tolerably comfortable. Four crotched stakes placed in the ground so that the two in front were tallest were crossed with poles and covered with wide hemlock bark. After spending several nights in such a shelter a traveller wrote that a large cheerful fire was raised in front of the "Kitchin and Bed Chamber wherein after broiling Salt Pork for Supper we rested . . . very comfortably."[4] Fires were kept burning throughout the night both for warmth and for protection against wild beasts of the forest. Another practice possibly unknown to the Gaels was the blazing of trees to mark a route. The white appearance of a large chip sliced through the bark on the side of a tree served to direct the way by night as well as by day. These marks were usually a mile apart so that the distance between points could be determined. The Scots also learned that a tree felled to bridge a stream was a "foot-log" to New Englanders and a "raccoon bridge" to Pennsylvanians.

Such co-operation among settlers, much vaunted as an outstanding feature of life on the American frontier, was not new to these people accustomed to "frolics" any more than it was to the Indians, particularly those of the Six Nations. Of a custom which prevailed among the latter even before the coming of the Jesuit missionaries Parkman wrote: "When one or more families were without shelter, the men of the village joined in building them a house. In return, the recipients of the favor gave a feast, if they could; if not their thanks were sufficient."[5] Whether or not it was borrowed from the Indians the feast was the crowning feature of the house raising of white settlers. The American counterpart of that old Scottish institution, the "frolic," which was a gathering of neighbours to unite their labours for the benefit of one of their number, was a "bee." Those giving assistance expected only a return in kind, one day a season being considered sufficient for any individual. "The New Englanders," wrote a Scottish traveller after asserting that they would work only for hire, "sometimes give their assistance for the sake of the Frolic—dinner & drink etc.—which takes place in the afternoon, but if they can persuade a man to give the dinner early they are off presently."[6] Although both bees and frolics transformed the performance of necessary tasks into occasions for community entertainment it was only at the Scottish gatherings that each activity was accompanied by its own song adapted to the rhythm of the work.

For their food frontier settlers depended upon the same products that for centuries had been the staples of the Indians whose methods of planting, cultivation, and manufacture had been little if any improved by the whites. Nor had the colonists evolved any clothing better adapted to frontier activities than the soft leather garments worn by the Indians. Conversely, Indians of the Six Nations, in particular many of the Mohawks, had adapted with reservations the white men's clothing and his habitations, both the framed and the humbler log house. The renowned King Hendrick, one of the Mohawk sachems presented to Queen Anne in 1710, had lived in a large framed house near the Upper or Canajoharie Castle. Mrs. Grant relates how the King's house, like the traditional Iroquois long house, was without partitions, giving it "the appearance of a good barn." From cross beams hung a laced hat, a fine saddle, and pistols, and on the floor beside a large pile of wheat and surrounded by baskets containing various kinds of dried berries sat King Hendrick. "He was splendidly arrayed in a coat of pale blue, trimmed with silver; all the rest of his dress was the fashion of his own nation. . . . All this suited my taste exceedingly," adds Mrs. Grant who at the time was about five years old.[7] (In 1758 the old chief fell on the shore of Lake George in the battle which had won fame and a baronetcy for William Johnson.)

Building with logs was a new technique to the Scottish settlers who in their homeland had built with stone. The log house, a traditional symbol of the frontier, had come into use as a dwelling house only about fifty years before the Scots arrived in America. Modern research has proved that the English colonists at Jamestown used wattle and daub and that the Pilgrims who landed at Plymouth relied on another construction which goes back to the Middle Ages, the oak frame sheathed with weatherboard (soon called clapboard in New England) and roofed with thatch. It is now recognized that the Swedes and Germans of the fur-trading colony of New Sweden founded at the mouth of the Delaware in 1636 introduced the log dwelling house to the American colonies. This type of construction had no appeal for English colonists, so it would seem that the Scotch-Irish who came in large numbers after 1718 were the first English-speaking race to adopt it. "From and through the Germans and Scotch-Irish," wrote an authority on the subject, "it spread rapidly through the English colonies and by the American Revolution had become the typical American frontier dwelling from Maine to Tenessee." [8]

Using axes, a logging chain, and a yoke of oxen, a few brawny workers could lay open a clearing (about one-eighth of an acre), keeping its centre beyond the reach of falling trees, and roll up a log shanty in a remarkably short time. This temporary dwelling, which might later serve as a barn, was small with low walls of round logs and a slanting roof to shed the rain. Trees were felled, their branches lopped off for burning, and the timber cut to the desired length and roughly notched so that each log might fit into the next. Upon base-logs set on flat rocks the walls were raised to the required height, poles set into position for rafters, and the building roofed in with strips of black ash or elm bark set two feet wide in four-foot lengths. "When spread out and . . . pressed down with poles or small timbers, the rough side exposed to the weather [the bark] makes a good roof that will last several years and shed the rain quite well," wrote Levi Beardsley.* A hole cut in the roof allowed the smoke to escape from a fire built beneath it on the earth floor.† Cracks between the logs were chinked with wood wedges, clay, or moss, and the entrance way hung with a heavy quilt in lieu of a door.

Throughout the first winter men battled with the forest to clear a patch of ground for tillage in the spring. It was a hard life but to that the majority of the Scots were accustomed. All in all they were well pleased with this new country, and on the strength of such reports as reached their homeland numbers of kinfolk and friends set out to join them early in the spring. With these new arrivals during the summer of 1774 settlement spread farther up the Delaware and down the valley of Banyar's Brook which rises in the uplands of Kortright and flows southwest into the Delaware. Hugh Alexander and Dougal McAslin (McCausland?) took tenant farms from Goldsbrow Banyar in the valley of this brook. Daniel Rose, Thomas Shearer, and Thomas McMicking also became Banyar's tenants, McMicking locating on the Delaware within a short distance of the mouth of Banyar's Brook. Of those who took lands on the south side of the river Hugh Rose settled at the mouth of Rose's Brook. The brothers Alexander and John More, William Fraser, and his son Simon settled below New Stamford in the valley of the stream which was later named Town Brook where they were soon joined by the brothers Dingwall, James and John. Dr. James Stuart bought 400 acres at the mouth of Town Brook near Jacob Stoneburner. Also among

---

* Judge Levi Beardsley's *Reminiscences* (New York, 1827) have been heavily drawn upon for information on settlement practices in this section of New York. His family, originally from Connecticut, settled in Richfield not far from the Tunnicliffs at the foot of Canadarago Lake on land bought of Goldsbrow Banyar in 1789. Levi's grandfather was a brother of John Beardsley (b. 1732), who was chaplain in the Loyal American Regiment commanded by Colonel Beverley Robinson and who accompanied his regiment to Nova Scotia at the close of the Revolution. Thus John Beardsley's son, Bartholomew Crannell Beardsley of Oakville, Ontario (see the author's *Oakville and the Sixteen* (Toronto, 1953)), was Levi's cousin, and both became judges in their respective countries. William Chisholm, founder of the town of Oakville, was a son of George Chisholm who appears in this narrative.

† More than half a century later another newcomer to the forest found that "four thick slabs of limestone, placed upright in one corner of the shanty with clay well packed behind them to keep the fire off the logs, answered very well for a chimney, with a hole cut through the roof directly above to vent the smoke." (Samuel Strickland, *Twenty-seven Years in Canada West* (London, 1853), vol. I, p. 92.)

the newcomers was George Chisholm's elder brother John who seemingly spent his first year labouring for hire before taking his leasehold of 150 acres from Lawrence Kortright.[9] Hugh Clarke, John Livingston, and his son Neil became tenants of Kortright—all under terms as outlined above.[10]

The first crops planted for subsistence were those grown since ancient times by the Indians, corn, beans, and squash. Corn was the best cereal crop for the rude clearings because it could be planted with little soil preparation, its yield was more certain than that of any other food-giving crop, and it could be utilized with less trouble than any other grain. Beans were planted in the same hill with the corn so that the cornstalks might support their clambering vines. The hills laid out at random were interspersed with pumpkins, squash, and sunflowers. And like the Indians white men had learned to hoe and hill their corn fields: "to cull out the finest seede, to observe the fittest season, to keep distance for holes and fit measures for hills, to worme it and weed it; to prune it and dress it as occasion shall require."[11] Even though the same hills were used year after year, the yield was great. Statistics are lacking respecting the yield of newly cleared land at the Head of the Delaware, but in all probability it was even greater than that of older, established farms in the Mohawk Valley where harvests so impressed travellers. Figures vary from the 40 to 60 bushels of marketable shelled corn per acre reported in 1768[12] to the 75 to 90 bushels exclusive of hog corn quoted thirty-two years later.[13]

The husking peg, the slatted crib set upon posts in which corn is dried by air circulation, and the scarecrow to keep away birds were all devised by the Indians. Dried corn was soaked in lye to remove the hulls and to obtain hominy, and then pounded until fine in wood or stone mortars. When charred (parched) and mixed with maple sugar, corn was so diminished in bulk and weight as to be easily portable on journeys and to allow storage for several years. About a quarter of a pint of meal boiled in a pint of water provided "a hearty travelling dinner when 100 miles from any habitation," according to John Bartram * who had travelled the Indian country in 1743.[14] Green corn, beans, squash, and the fat meat of dog cooked together constituted the Indians' festive and sustaining food, succotash. White men omitted the squash and showed preference for pork rather than dog meat. The stalks and blades of corn were stacked for the cattle's fodder, so all in all corn was the "crop of crops for the pioneer."[15]

Clearing the arable land of the dense growth of trees was the most arduous task facing the settlers. Underbrush and small trees which New Englanders called "staddles" were cut out and piled for burning. The quickest but the most laborious method of clearing land was to cut down living trees with an axe, and the Scots learned how to fell them parallel to facilitate logging. Logs were cut in lengths of about fifteen feet, dragged with logging-chains by oxen, and rolled into piles and burned. Another method was the Indian practice of girdling; when dead and dry the trees were more easily felled and the stumps burned out. Although some risked the dangerous Indian procedure of burning the standing timber, most settlers cut and piled it in heaps which the Scots called black forest (*coille dhubs*) or burnt forest (*coille*

---

* Quaker naturalist whose botanical garden surrounding his homestead was the first established in the American colonies. The large stone house that he built with his own hands beside the Schuylkill is now within the city of Philadelphia, and both it and Bartram's Garden are open to the public. Some thirty years before the Revolution, at first alone then accompanied by his son William, he explored the interior of the colonies from the Six Nation country bordering Lake Ontario to the upper reaches of the St. John's River in sub-tropical Florida.

loisgte). A contemporary writer tells of a Scottish settler who having been "employed with his man, clearing and burning wood off his land, came home in the evening as black as a collier." [16] A bard sang of this work:

> Gur h-iomadh ceum anns am bi mi 'n deis laimh
> Mu'n dean mi saibhir mo theachd-an-tir;
> Bidh m' oabir eigneach mu'n tior mi feum aisd'
> 'S mu'n dean mi reiteach air muin a cheile
> Gu'n d' lasaich feithean a bha 'nam dhruim,
> 'S a h-uile ball diom cho dubh a sealltainn,
> Bidh mi 'gam shamhlachadh ris an t-suip.

("Many a labour I'll be involved in before I can make my living secure; my work will be exhausting before I get any returns from it and before I make a clearing for the plough. Piling tree-trunks on top of each other in bonfires has strained every muscle in my back, and every part of me is so black I'm just like soot." [17])

A good chopper could clear an acre of trees and pile the brush in seven to eight days, and three men with a yoke of oxen could log an acre a day and sometimes more. According to John Cameron "it cost £3 per acre to make it fit for Corn," and William Rose estimated that clearing and fencing cost him £4 per acre.[18] John McKay's "clearing with House, Barn & Stable" had run to £5 per acre,[19] and George Chisholm's improvements totalled £30.[20] But a barn as well as a house of such size to accommodate a family of five grown sons and several daughters cost Dr. Stuart £12 in cash, and his clearing ran to £6 sterling per acre.[21].

Incidental to land clearance was the making of potash for which there was a constant demand in England. This white solid substance, known to chemists as potassium carbonate, had been made in America for use in the manufacture of soap and glass since the beginning of the seventeenth century. In fact, the making of potash was among the primary reasons for sending the first English colonists to Virginia in 1607, and in November of the following year the first shipment of "Sope-ashes" was sent to England from the new settlement of Jamestown.[22] Since then American potash had become a commodity of increasing importance on the English market. As to its value to new settlers Tenche Coxe, a leading economist of the time, had this to say:

> The settler in making his clearing must take care to burn the brush and wood, in such manner as to preserve the ashes. Out of the wood ashes, thus saved, he should make as much pot ash, or pearl ash, as he can; and he should dispose of this for ready money, strong clothing, axes, spades, ploughs or such other things for his farm, or family, as it would otherwise be necessary for him to procure by selling or bartering grain or cattle, if he had them to spare. It is believed that the pot ash or pearl ash will procure him as much value as all the expense and labour of clearing, during the season, would be worth in cash. He will therefore obtain as much money or goods as will enable him to hire assistance, in the next season, either to farm, or to clear land, or to make his improvements, so as to save his own time, or labour, intirely [sic] for clearing more land, or to help him in doing it. He must again make pot ash or pearl ash, and he must again supply the money or goods it sells for, to the clearing of the next season.—In this way it is plain, that he will derive money enough from the clearing and pot ashes of every year, to do much of the same in the year following.[23]

Ashes scraped together from burned log piles and taken to an ashery brought about 7d. or 8d. per bushel payable in goods at Cherry Valley,[24] and approximately 450 bushels made a ton of potash.[27] The process was simple and required little equipment other than deep iron kettles, some holding forty gallons or more. First, the strong alkali solution, lye, was obtained by pouring boiling water through wood ashes. The lye was then strained through coarse linen cloth, poured into an iron pot and evaporated over a quick fire. The crude product was "black"; when purified by calcination and recrystallization it was "pearl-ash." Thus the giants of the forest, some centuries old, were reduced to a powerful caustic of various industrial uses.

Two men could make above a ton a month of pearl-ash (worth £40 per ton in 1769), payable in goods upon delivery at the Mohawk River.[26] Christopher Servos had a potash works on the Charlotte equipped with three large kettles, a fair enterprise at this period.[27] At about the time the price rose to £50 per ton George Chisholm and Daniel Rose formed a partnership with two other unidentified men, undoubtedly Scots, for making potash on the Delaware. They invested in two iron kettles and established their works on the 100-acre holding Rose had leased from Banyar. Rose also allowed the use of his oxen [28] and Chisholm valued his share in "the utensils for a Potash Manufactury" at £8.[29]

Another source of revenue to new settlers was maple sugar, and nowhere on the continent were (and still are) there better sugar maples than those crowning the hills of Harpersfield. Maples marked for clearing were usually tapped before being felled. Most settlers made several hundredweight of maple sugar very spring, but Hugh Fraser who acquired six sugar kettles evidently undertook to produce it on a large scale. One traveller tells of encountering a woman near Canajoharie who made up to 400 pounds per year and sold it for 9d. per pound. "And she has exchanged 2 pounds of this for 3 pounds of West India Sugar, the People esteeming the former best." [30] When well made, loaf sugar manufactured from maple sap was white, harder and finer grained than cane sugar. Though it was not as sweet and would therefore not go as far some people found that maple sugar had no particular flavour to distinguish it from the West India cane sugar of the period.[31]

The making of maple sugar was yet another Indian skill upon which white men had failed to improve. In early spring when the sap began to flow a notch was cut in the tree with an axe, and below it a hole was made by driving a tapping gouge into the wood with the axe, into which a spile (or spigot) was inserted. The sap was collected in a wooden trough, generally scooped out of butternut and holding the equivalent of a pailful of liquid, set beneath the spile at the foot of the tree. It was turned into an iron kettle set up on crotched sticks over a fire in the bush and evaporated by boiling for several hours. The quantity sufficient to make a pound of sugar would ooze from a tree in a day's time.[32] If removed when only partially evaporated the product was molasses.

The crops that settlers counted on for an immediate cash return were Indian corn and wheat. Corn was grown in the bottom lands of valleys and dales. Here the black vegetable mould was too rich for wheat which thrives on knolls and hillsides. The markets for wheat, long the chief agricultural product of the Province of New York, were New England, the West Indies, and Europe. Both summer and winter wheat were grown,[33] the seed being sown broadcast. Contemporary writers almost unanimously assert that new settlers rarely tilled their land for the first crop, but only raked the ground clean, sowed the wheat, and covered it either by harrowing or by drawing a bush over it. For harvesting grain the Dutch and Palatines had long employed the hand tools familiar to the Scots. The *corran* or reaping-hook, a six-inch iron finger set at right angles to the handle, was used in the left hand to gather grain which was then sheared with the *speal* (scythe) [34] or a sickle mounted on a wooden handle with handgrip. The swaths were raked and the grain bound into sheaves by hand to be threshed in early winter with the flail (*suist*). Upon being riddled through a seive (*criather*), it was ready for grinding. Gaelic housewives were well used to doing their own milling and many had brought with them so cherished a possession as the *bradh* (quern or stone hand-mill). Those without were obliged to carry their grain by pack horse to grist mills on the Schoharie some twenty miles away over the hills. One situated on a small tributary of the Schoharie was that of Adam Chrysler. About 1750 his family of Palatine origin (Chrysler, Krysler, Kreisler, etc.) had acquired a large tract of Vroomansland, and Adam retained the old homestead.[35] Before long, however, the community at the head of the Delaware had its own grist and sawmills, one erected by Hugh Alexander near the mouth of Banyar's Brook,[36] and another by Hugh Rose near the mouth of Rose's Brook.[37] James Calder located his mills on the western limits of the Kortright Patent where the Delaware sweeps to the southeast about a mile below Banyar's Brook. John Harper built a grist mill not far from his home on Center Brook (so named because in its upper reaches its valley divides Harpersfield into two parts) which flows westward into the Charlotte. On the Charlotte in the northeast corner of Harpersfield and only a short distance above the Macdonells were the grist and sawmills of Christopher Servos.* Here the Indian trail leading from the outlet of Otsego Lake met the trail which followed the Charlotte down to its confluence with the Susquehanna.

Year after year the same land was ploughed and sown to wheat. Wooden two-wheeled ploughs drawn by three horses abreast were common in long-settled communities, and sometimes the horses were driven at full trot by a boy astride one of them.[38] But on newly cleared land covered with stumps and the large boulders found at Harpersfield and the Head of the Delaware only ploughs drawn by one or at most two draught animals could be used. Both the gunsmith and blacksmith at Cherry Valley made iron plough shares and coulters which required frequent sharpening for 1s. per pound weight[39] and for which the settlers themselves fashioned the wooden parts. Dr. Stuart paid £4.6.0 "cash for plough, coulter and share."[40] John Chisholm, who had brought his blacksmith's tools with him from Scotland, would have done much of his own iron work and probably that of others as well. Wherever possible wood was made to serve instead of iron, and was used for an infinite variety of purposes, many of them learned from the Indians : withes of elm bark were woven into ropes,[41] and crotches of trees were shaped into log-boats, stone-boats, and the log sleds which conveyed grist to the mill, produce to the barn, or the family on long-distance visits over horse tracks yet impassable for wheeled vehicles.

Horses were commonly relied upon for farm work in New York whereas in New England oxen took preference. One man with a pair of horses hitched to a plough could turn twice as much acreage between sun-up and sun-down as could two men with a yoke of oxen, one to drive them and the other to guide the plough. Horses descended from those brought by early settlers from Holland and known as Dutch horses were used for farm work, and English horses, which in this district had been improved by the breeding of Sir William Johnson, were used for riding. Horses cost from £7 to £15 and oxen from £10 to £25 depending upon age and weight. Out of fifteen Scots on record six owned one horse (Hugh Fraser, John Livingston, John McKay, William Rose, Alexander and Roderick Macdonell), four owned a pair of horses (George and John Chisholm, Archibald Thomson, John Cameron, James Dingwall), and only two owned any more (John Macdonell, six; Thomas McMicking, four). Dr. Stuart, Daniel Rose, and Duncan McKenzie each owned a yoke of oxen but no horses; McMicking had both.[42]

* At or close to modern South Worcester in Otsego County, New York.

Cattle were of mixed breeds from Holland, England, and Scotland, and averaged, "small & great," about £5 per head. In winter they fed on "blades" (dried stalks and blades of Indian corn) and the tops of maple and bass-wood trees felled daily for their use. "On hearing a Tree fall the Cattle set off full scamper towards it," wrote an observer.[43] Modern writers tell of the scrawny sickly cattle of the early settlers but the findings of contemporary chroniclers would seem to belie this belief. We are told that George Croghan's cows looked well after being out in the woods without any hay, and that cattle wintered well in the forest "and soon became thrifty and sleek."[44] The custom of allowing cattle to range prevailed until after the turn of the century.[45]

Hogs also roamed at large. Much emphasis has been placed on the ferocity of the American wood-hog and its ability to endure hardship. It has been described as long in leg, narrow in back, and short in body with flat sides and a long snout, "in make ... like a fish called a perch." It would seem to have been more agile than our modern domesticated hog: "you may as well think of stopping a crow as one of these hogs. They will go a distance from a fence, take a run, and leap through the rails,* three or four feet from the ground, turning themselves sideways."[46] They were very fond of hunting rattlesnakes which they would eat with avidity.[47]

Unlike the other farm animals, sheep were yarded at night in pens which resembled the bodies of log houses and which guarded against the depredations of wolves, wildcats, and "painters" as frontiersmen called the tawny panthers or mountain lions so prevalent in these hills. In winter sheep like other livestock lived on blades and Indian corn. Although most settlers kept a few sheep for their wool Dr. Stuart's twenty-four ewes and thirty-six lambs would seem to be an exceptionally large flock.[48] The various kinds of black-faced sheep were found to have the greatest endurance while the wool of the rat-tailed sheep from Holland, generally from four to six inches in length, was especially soft and fine. Because only the cleanest wool was used it was not uncommon to see sheep on the hills clipped of all wool except that on their bellies and tails.

An important event in the spring routine was the harvesting of wool. After the sheep were shorn late in May each fleece was rolled up and firmly tied. The handling thereafter was women's work. Girls learned at an early age to separate good wool from poor (the average yield of a fleece was three pounds when washed), and to card it into rolls for spinning. The mistress set aside the best wool for stockings, the next best for clothing for the men folk, and the rougher wool for blankets.[49] Although some housewives through necessity or preference continued to spin their wool into yarn with distaff and spindle, a majority would have used a spinning wheel. The motions of the person using the great wheel—setting it slowly in motion with the right hand and backing away while pulling out the fibres with the left and twisting them with the right until a long strand of twisted yarn extended from the spindle, then while the machine was still coasting walking quickly towards the spindle so that the finished yarn was automatically wound around it—led to the name of "walking wheel." When wound off the spindle onto a swift, a kind of hand reel that their American neighbours called a "niddy noddy" evidently because of the oscillating motion of its use, the yarn was in skeins and ready to be balled for knitting or warping a loom.

* For their first enclosures the Scots split rails and laid them end to end to form the "snake" fences ("horse high and hog tight") so common in the colonies. Gradually as more land was cleared the boulders strewing the ground of Harpersfield were used in laying the stone dykes the Scots knew so well how to build. Surely some of the drystone walling now climbing the valleys and uplands at the Head of the Delaware must rest on footings set by the Scots.

The women wove stout worsted cloth about twenty-seven inches in width, a fine cloth for petticoats and gowns, and a strong durable checkered cloth for aprons.[50] They made the same *drogaid*, called linsey-woolsey in America, a homespun with wool weft and linen warp of home-grown flax, that they had made in their homeland. The method of cleansing and thickening both this cloth and the hand-woven blanket fabric was called fulling, that is working the cloth when wet to raise the nap. This occasioned a milling frolic in which numbers of people could participate, and as they sat around a long trestle table the workers rhythmically pounded and flicked the cloth to the beat of a milling song (*oran luaidh*).[51] Thus the performance of so necessary a task was converted into entertainment for the community.

The settlers soon adopted the clothes of the frontier which for the women generally consisted of black skirt, white or callico "short gown," and occasionally a full calico or chintz dress. Indoors the head was usually uncovered, but some older women wore caps. Except in winter they went barefoot, although when making a visit they carried buckled shoes and stockings to put on before entering a house. On week days the men discarded the kilt for the "leather britches" mentioned by Thomas McMicking, James Rose, and others,[52] the homespun jacket, and the flannel shirt which had long been the garb of the frontier. For the breeches the skins of elk, deer, and sheep were smoked and dressed in the Iroquois manner which differed little from that of Scotland. According to Levi Beardsley the sheepskin breeches which he wore in his youth rattled like parchment "or an old snuff bladder." When wet they stretched and became flabby, and after drying were shrunken and hard.[53] ("A parcel of Indian dressed Deer-skins fit to make Breeches . . . sheep skins fit to make negro breeches," advertised a merchant of the period.[54] Sang an immigrant bard, "However good your trousers are they'll do no good without two pairs of stockings and hair-lined moccasins that are tightly laced with thongs. It is the latest fashion to wear the hide, hair and all, just as it comes from the beast the day before."[55])

The Scots soon learned to adapt their eating habits to the products that their new home had to offer. They found that one indispensable food was the versatile Indian corn : the young "roasting ears" could be boiled and eaten with drawn butter; the cornmeal could be cooked plainly as mush, combined with meat, or mixed with water, laid on a board or shingle before the fire to bake, and eaten hot; or eggs and milk could be added to produce the "nice cake" found in the homes of the "better sort of people," although the food of the poor people in back settlements was the simpler form made by the Indians, the white man's "Johnny cake." The settlers also found that the most popular breakfast bread in the country was buckwheat cakes topped with butter and maple molasses. They became acquainted with substitutes for high-priced commodities; for example, the inner part of white pine bark, sassafras, and various roots served as tea. Salt brought in barrels from great distances was precious indeed, but the needs of the frontiersmen were simple and nature was bountiful. Deer roamed the hills, the forest teemed with smaller game, both feathered and furred, and the valley abounded in fish. Venison could be traded for salt pork, and the softness of the water gushing from the hills was no small blessing.

Before winter set in more adequate log houses replaced the shanties which thereafter were used as barns. Though identical in construction to its predecessor this log house was better finished and possessed the added refinements of floor, fireplace, and chimney. The floor was made of split basswood logs partially hewn on one side. A small cellar for the storage of roots and fruits was excavated underneath and was entered by removing one of the logs of the floor.⁵⁶ The fireplace and chimney were built either of stone or of mud and sticks to be later replaced by stone. There was also a low garret which was reached by a ladder and some houses were probably lined later with boards obtained at a sawmill. For door catches and hinges wood was substituted for iron. The latch was raised from outside by a leather string prassed through a hole in the door. When the string was drawn inside the door could not be opened; thus the phrase "the latch string is always out" indicated hospitality. Furniture consisted of axe-hewn benches, a plank table, and bunks frequently filled with cedar boughs. Travellers lay on straw pallets in front of the fire. The assertion by Neil McKay that he "had made most of his buildings with his own hands assisted by his neighbours" was applicable to these and other settlers on the frontier. In the colonial idiom his buildings and clearing were his "improvements," his farm his "plantation," his implements his "farming utensils," and, if his land was freehold, he was a "yeoman." ⁵⁷

This predominantly Protestant settlement lost no time in forming itself into congregations, one in Kortright and the other in Harpersfield where the Harpers being Presbyterians had set aside a plot of ground for a future church. In Kortright they met at a private house and the services were opened by an elderly Scot, John Blair.⁵⁸ Upon application to the Associate Presbytery of New York and Pennsylvania Reverend R. Annan was sent from New Jersey to minister to both these congregations. He officiated at Harpersfield on the Sabbath and at Kortright on a weekday.⁵⁹ Families came eight or ten miles over the hills, many on foot, to attend services beginning at 9.30 A.M. and continuing with an hour's intermission until 3.00 P.M.⁶⁰ When the congregations united for communion, members who came from a distance were welcomed by those living nearby because services starting on Friday lasted until Monday afternoon.⁶¹

"The Scotch colonists," wrote Timothy Dwight, a contemporary who was destined to become president of Yale College, "preserve, unaltered, the character which they brought with them. They are industrious, frugal, orderly, patient of every hardship, persevering, attached to government, reverential as to religion, generally moral, often pious. . . . As a body they are better citizens than any other class of immigrants." ⁶²

The area our group first inhabited is within a region now famous for its pasturage and dairy cattle. The farms along roads that follow valleys or climb over hills to drop down into adjoining valleys grow no wheat, only oats and corn for ensilage. On the slight chance that some evidence might yet be found of the occupation of the earliest settlers I circled the area, following the paths shown by William Gray on his map of 1778.⁶³ Starting where the valley of the Delaware widens at Town Brook I drove down the west side of the river to Banyar's (now called Wright's) Brook, followed it northward for about 4½ miles, then went eastward over the watershed and down into the village of Harpersfield. Turning south I recrossed the divide within a mile of the lake on Gray's map and descended into the Delaware valley near the place where I had started.

It was spring when the redness of the cultivated soil is heightened by the brilliant greens of fields of young oats and hillside pastures lying between crowding masses of trees; when enclosures within drystone walling greyed by lichens are dotted with the white bloom of low spreading hawthorns; and when yellow mustard streaks distant hillsides crowned with dark pines. In its upper reaches the West Branch of the Dela-

Northern Frontier of the Province of New York at opening of Rebellion as taken from Claude Joseph Sauthier's map
Fort Stanwix
Oriskany
FORT STANWIX TREATY LINE 1768
German Flatts
Mohawk River
Upper Castle of the Mohawks
Johnstown
Butlersbury
Stone Arabia
Tribes Hill
Fort Johnson
Fort Hunter
Warren's Bush
Corry's Bush
Richfield
Little Lakes
Springfield
Youngsfield
Canadarago Lake
Canajoharie Creek
Cherry Valley
Otsego Lake
Turlach
Tianderha (Unadilla) River
Butternut Creek
Schenevus Creek
Charlotte R.
Sir Wm. Johnson
Strasburgh (J. Butler)
John Harper
Lawrence Kortright
Goldsbrow Banyar
Banyar's Brook
Lake Utsayantha
Town Brook
Arent Bradt
Rose's Brook
Breakabean Creek
Schoharie Creek
Foxes Creek
Susquehanna River
Outeout Creek
Unadilla
Scotch Settlement
Various other patents extending to the treaty line
Mohawks or West Branch Delaware River
Delaware River
Papacunck
Popachton or East Branch
Delaware River
Tryon County
Albany County
Ulster County

ware is a narrow stream threading its course like a silver ribbon through lush fields, the earliest ever to be tilled. The hills standing away to north and south, once made blue by their heavy covering of hemlock, are now the feathery green of deciduous trees which rise in thickly clustered regiments on either side. Where the hills fall abruptly roads round their shoulders to enter the cool shade of woods, and some of these places are deer crossings. When at this season the wild creatures come down into the valleys for food it often becomes necessary to stop and wave them off the road. The more gentle slopes are cleared for orchards and pastures through which stone walls run up to meet the trees that crown the hills. Cattle are fond of the young shoots of the prolific red thorn, and constant trimming forces these trees to grow outward first in round mounds, then in the shape of cones until the centre shoots are beyond the cattle's reach. Finally the trees grow upward into the strange hour-glass shape so characteristic of the foothills of the Kaatskills.

While passing along this nine-mile stretch where the first Scots had settled I noted two of the farm sites which it has been possible to identify: William Rose's at Betty's Brook and Hugh Rose's across the valley at Rose's Brook, the two separated only by the windings of the Delaware. Because these lots include more level land on the river bottom than is usual in this hilly country, they are undoubtedly among the choicest in this section of the valley. Upon turning north (at what is now Bloomville) at Banyar's Brook I found, in the spot shown by Gray, the old mill pond now almost solid with white water lilies. Continuing up the valley known so well to the Gaels I saw that its floor sloping up from the Delaware to an altitude of some fifteen hundred feet above sea level is almost flat and wide enough for extensive farms. Meadows sloping up on either side become gradually steeper until at $1\frac{1}{2}$ miles farther up, where Hugh Alexander once lived, the valley begins to narrow. From the road I looked down into the valley at the knoll where Alexander's log house must surely have stood. Now the site is occupied by a frame house built by a New Englander in a simple adaptation of the Greek-revival style of architecture introduced by Thomas Jefferson * as befitting the new democracy of the United States of America. While I was noting the height and almost incredible steepness of some upland slopes now under cultivation on this farm a young doe which had come down to the brook to drink leaped through a meadow, over a stone wall, and disappeared into the bordering woodland on the hill. As my car climbed steadily upward I saw that only the land beside the brook in the valley below was arable, and that the line of the watercourse through sloping fields and grassland is marked by tall pines, great oaks, white willows, beeches, and large stands of hemlock. To the east stone walls climb the upland to elms and hard maples standing high above against the sky.

Upon reaching the point where Gray shows three paths converging on "McCash-

---

* It is of interest to note that in 1786 Lawrence Kortright's daughter, Elizabeth ("Eliza"), married the Virginia lawyer, James Monroe. In announcing his engagement to his close friend, Thomas Jefferson, Monroe wrote that Eliza was "the daughter of a gentleman of reputable character and connections in this [New York] State, though injured in his fortunes in the late war" (George Morgan, *The Life of James Monroe* (Boston, 1921), p. 210). In 1798 Monroe built the charming house called Ash Lawn for which Jefferson had drawn the plans. It is situated within sight of Jefferson's own Monticello sitting high on its hilltop near Charlottesville, Virginia. The garden of Ash Lawn is protected by a 300-year-old white oak and its paths bordered by venerable boxwood. James Monroe, author of the Monroe Doctrine, was minister to England, France, and Spain. In Paris Eliza Monroe was called "la belle Americaine" (*ibid.*). She was hostess in the White House during her husband's term (1817-25) as fifth president of the United States.

lands" (Dougal McAslin's), a mile above Alexander's and 3½ from the mill pond, the valley again broadens and levels to admit of a farm. Where the road forks I took the middle one, Braehead Hill Road, which according to Gray's plan would lead over the hills to the house of John Harper. While climbing ever more steeply I was overtaken by a shower of hail and rain. Before reaching the top of the divide (700 feet above the Delaware and 2,200 above the tide) I paused to watch the storm sweep down the valley of Banyar's Brook toward the Kaatskills looming darkly in the far distance to the south. Billowy white clouds floated high above in the clear blue sky, and below them the racing black thunder-heads threw patches of shadow on the green hills, the greener fields, and the red soil lying brilliant in the sunshine. As I continued upward to the top of the pass between the highest hills in Kortright where the road is almost level for a mile (at approximately five miles above the mill pond), trees growing along the narrow dirt road reached out to form an archway overhead. Throughout the last mile the descent is sudden and steep. I dropped rapidly into Kortright Center which, as the name attests, is the centre of Kortright Patent and the starting point of its earliest settlement. Turning due west onto the old Catskill Turnpike by which the Hudson and the Susquehanna were joined in 1803, in less than a mile I reached the corners where it crosses the road leading down the valley of Banyar's Brook to the Delaware. Here high on the hill near the northwest corner is the old burial ground still known as Covenanters' Cemetery. Turning northeast then (at eight-tenths of a mile) northwest I struck up over the hills on an old road which leads directly down into Fergusonville. Once well travelled as the shortest route from Kortright to holdings of the Macdonells and Christopher Servos in the valley of the Charlotte, the northern section of this road, because of its steep gradient, is now closed to modern mechanized vehicles. Returning to Kortright Center I turned east and passed the farms once owned by Leal and McGillivrae and the site of Harper's grist mill on Center Brook at West Harpersfield. Another two miles brought me to Harpersfield Center where a boulder near the cemetery marks the site of John Harper's house overlooking the valley of Center Brook. Again I climbed over the watershed between the Charlotte and the Delaware and drove down to the Head of the Delaware, well content with the proof that the paths of the Scots are the roads of today.

CHAPTER THREE

THE RIFT: REBEL OR TRAITOR?

HARDLY HAD THE immigrants from Scotland become established than they became embroiled in political difficulties with their neighbours. Like the mass of the frontier population they took little interest in the taxation quarrel between the New England provinces and the British ministry. Content with the established order, they wished only to get on with their work of carving farms from the wilderness. The Colonists who did sympathize with the New Englanders and who accordingly voiced their sentiments were almost invariably native born of Dutch, Palatine German, or Scotch-Irish extraction. Unhappily for the Scots these were the people who were foremost in the nearest settlements of Schoharie and Cherry Valley. The Scotch-Irish in the latter community and also at Harpersfield were held by strong family ties with New England. The Scots were at a further disadvantage in that they were continually under the vigilance of such ardent Patriots as the Harpers.

Throughout the province the Scotch-Irish Presbyterians who were so hostile to the British government ranged themselves on the side of the Patriots, as the Whigs had chosen to call themselves. In consequence of the oppression experienced in earlier times at the hands of the English they were intensely liberal and democratic, those at Cherry Valley almost aggressively so. This settlement had made great progress but not until after its founder had been forced to abandon the enterprise. James Lindesay had sunk all his fortune in providing a grist and sawmill, a log church, a schoolhouse, and other conveniences for his settlers. In 1743 Reverend Samuel Dunlop had opened a classical school for boys, the first in the province west of Albany. He combined teaching with farm work, his pupils repeating their lessons while following him around the fields and during the performance of his daily chores. Some of the young men educated by Mr. Dunlop were among the most influential Patriots in the Mohawk Valley. By 1765 there were forty families living in Cherry Valley. The log church had been supplanted by a Presbyterian meeting house which was new when Richard Smith attended service there in 1769. He described it as "large and quite finished," and found that the congregation "tho not large made a respectable Appearance, several of them being genteely dressed."[1] By 1774 with sixty families numbering nearly three hundred persons[2] Cherry Valley was the most important settlement south of the Mohawk. It was the centre where the Scots from the Delaware could trade their produce for gun powder, shot, rum, and other necessaries. Most of the tradesmen like the general merchant Wells had come originally from the northern seaboard provinces where "to buy, to sell, to exchange, or, as they term it to *swap*, are pursuits in which [the people] wish constantly to be engaged."[3] The principal product of this prosperous community was cheese.

Over the hills to the north in the Mohawk Valley were a number of other thriving communities where large areas of rich land were in the height of cultivation. Side by side with the Indians lived a white population of various racial origins each clinging to its own language and customs. The Scotch-Irish and New Englanders of Warren's Bush lived across the Schoharie from the Indians at the Lower Mohawk Castle, Fort Hunter. On the opposite side of the Mohawk were the estates of Sir William Johnson's family by a German wife: Guy Park, built 1766 by Sir William for his youngest daughter Mary (Polly) and her husband, Guy Johnson, who was Sir William's nephew; Mount Johnson, the residence of his son Sir John, the first American-born baronet, and his wife Mary (also Polly) Watts, a beautiful and wealthy girl who was related to the prominent De Lancey and Van Cortlandt families; and midway between, Claus Manor, the home of Sir William's eldest daughter Ann (Nancy) who had married Daniel Claus. These houses, built of the grey stone so plentiful in the valley, were situated close to the river about a mile apart. Northward lay the Highland Scottish settlement of Johnson's Bush near Johnstown. In the hills east of the road leading from Johnstown to the Mohawk River was Butlersbury, which since his father's death in 1760 was the settlement of Colonel John Butler and which was attracting New Englanders. Adjacent to Johnson's Bush on the west were the Palatine Germans of Stone Arabia, now after fifty years of settlement one of the most prosperous sections of Tryon County. Thus up the valley to the Upper Mohawk Castle and the outlying white settlement of German Flatts, the Holland Dutch, Palatine Germans, Scotch-Irish, English, Scots, and Mohawks lived together.

Although the quality of the Scots' relationship with the Indians may not be truly assessed, documents of a later date imply that from the outset a particular friendliness existed between the two races. The Gaels possessed the advantage of being unencumbered with the prejudices, antagonisms, and above all the fear that characterized the attitude of native-born Americans, particularly New Englanders, towards the Indians. Living as the immigrants did on the main route to the Indians' hunting and fishing grounds it is evident that their contact, especially with the Mohawks, was both continual and close. Several of the Indian chiefs, having been reared among the English, spoke the language and had to some extent adopted English ways. There is every reason to believe that at least four became well known to the settlers around the Delaware. There was David Hill "whom every one that knew him allowed to be the handsomest and most agreeable Indian they have ever seen." [4] Sometimes David was called the Little Mohawk Chief [5] and at others Little David. And there was his eldest son Aaron, a "young Indian gentleman, of very agreeable looks and mild manners." [6] Another was William Johnson, natural son of Sir William by Caroline Peters, a niece of the famous Mohawk sachem King Hendrick. To his own people he was known as Tageheunto and to historians as "William of Canajoharie," but to Thomas McMicking and other Scots he was "Sr. Wm. Johnson Jnr." [7] Finally there was Joseph Brant in whom so many of the Scots and hosts of other frontier settlers would place their confidence as time wore on. Brant was a chief of the noblest descent among his nation: a son of the Canajoharie Mohawk chief and grandson of one of the four sachems who had voyaged to England with Peter Schuyler in 1710 to implore Queen Anne's help against the French. Joseph was born at the Canajoharie or Upper Castle of the Mohawks in 1742 and at the age of fifteen had joined the warriors of his tribe who had fought under Sir William Johnson in the Seven Years' War.[8] He was among the Mohawk guides who led the Bradstreet expedition to Fort Frontenac and was with Sir William when Niagara fell to the British in 1759. He had an even more personal connection with Sir William in the latter's alliance with "Miss Molly," also known as "Brown Lady Johnson," who was Mary Brant, sister of Joseph. Sir William's close contacts with the Brants further strengthened the Indians' trust in him and their loyalty to the British government.

Among the numerous undertakings of Sir William for improving the lot of the Mohawks was that of educating promising young Indian boys. About 1760 Joseph and William "junior" were sent to the school at Lebanon (modern Columbia), Connecticut, conducted by Dr. Eleazor Wheelock.* In later times Joseph was fond of relating the following anecdote of William. When ordered one day by Dr. Wheelock's son to saddle his horse, William refused on the grounds that he was a gentleman's son. Young Wheelock inquired if he knew what a gentleman was. "I do," replied William, "a gentleman is a person who keeps race horses, and drinks Madeira wine, and that is what neither you nor your father do,—therefore saddle the horse yourself." [9] The boys left school to take part in the Pontiac war, and in the spring of 1764 Joseph returned to Canajoharie. After his marriage he became a Christian, and following upon their meeting in the winter of 1771 he became closely associated with Reverend John Stuart, missionary to the Mohawks, who officiated at Queen Anne's Chapel at Fort Hunter. The two men collaborated in translating into the Mohawk language the Gospel according to St. Mark, part of the Acts of the Apostles, a short history of the Bible, a concise explanation of the Church Catechism, and additions to the Indian Prayer Book. The translations were carried to London by Daniel Claus where they were published at the order of King George III.[10] Before long Joseph had become a substantial farmer on his hundred acres of rich land at Canajoharie. He owned horses and cattle and lived in a frame house of which the cellar wall was still standing in 1878.[11]

During the last years of Sir William Johnson's life when he passed many responsibilities to George Croghan he frequently employed Joseph on public business. When Sir William died in May 1774, Guy Johnson succeeded him as superintendent of the Indian Department, Daniel Claus was appointed his deputy and Joseph Brant his secretary. Sir John Johnson succeeded to the post of major-general of Tryon County militia.

The war of pen and petition which preceded the actual battle of arms in Tryon County began in the Palatine District where a public meeting was held to protest the closing of the port of Boston (result of the "Boston tea party"). The minutes of the proceedings noted that:

Whereas the Brittish [sic] Parliament has lately passed an Act for raising Revenue in America without the Consent of our Representatives to abridging the Liberties and privileges of the American Colonies and therefore blocking up the Port of Boston; the Freeholders and Inhabitants of Palatine Dist. in the County of Tryon . . . , looking with Concern and heartfelt Sorrow on these Alarming and Calamitous Conditions, Do meet this 27th Day of August 1774, on that purpose at the house of Adam Loucks Esq at Stonearabia.

The meeting resolved that "the King George the Third is Lawful and Rightful Lord and Sovereign"; that they would bear allegiance to him and "Will with our Lives and Fortunes support and maintain him upon the Throne of His Ancestors"; that taxes laid and exacted without the consent of the colonies were unjust and unconstitutional,

---

* This was the Indian Charity School founded 1748 by Joshua Moor of Mansfield, Connecticut. The school later removed to Hanover, New Hampshire, and in 1796, when enlarged under the patronage of the Earl of Dartmouth, it was incorporated as Dartmouth College, and Dr. Eleazor Wheelock, a graduate of Yale, became its first president.

and that the last acts of Parliament encroached on their rights as British subjects; that the blocking of the Port of Boston was "oppressive and arbitrary", therefore they considered the Bostonians "as Brethren in the Common Cause . . . that we will join to support and defend our Rights and Liberties. That we think the sending of Delegates from the Different Colonies to a general Continental Congress is a Salutary Measure, and absolutely necessary at the alarming Crisis"; and that they would abide by and adhere to the regulations made and agreed upon by said Congress. A committee was appointed "to convey the sentiments of the County in a Sett of Resolves to New York," and recommendations were made to the inhabitants of other districts in Tryon County to appoint their own committees of correspondence for the same purpose.[12]

The formation of a committee of correspondence was in accord with the instructions of the "helmsman of the Revolution," Samuel Adams, who in 1772 had written, "Let Associations and Combinations be everywhere set up to consult and recover our just Rights."[13] Those appointed to the Palatine committee were John Frey, prime mover in its organization, Christopher P. Yates, and Isaac Paris. The Freys, originally from Zurich, Switzerland, had lived on their tract bordering the Mohawk south of Stone Arabia since its purchase from the Indians in the 1730's. Hendrick Frey, namesake of the original settler, was a Tory but his brother John was an ardent Whig. John's brother-in-law, Christopher Yates, was a lawyer and all three of these men had attended the school of Mr. Dunlop at Cherry Valley. Isaac Paris was an Alsatian, a merchant and trader living at Stone Arabia, who had come to America in 1737.[14] Other districts in Tryon County formed committees of correspondence. On the Canajoharie District committee were John Moore and Samuel Campbell, both prominent citizens of Cherry Valley, and Nicholas Herkimer[15] whose father was one of the patentees of German Flatts. Next to the Johnsons the Herkimers were perhaps the most influential family in the Mohawk Valley.

In the spring of 1775 events followed one upon another in close succession. Upon learning that on April 19 at Lexington Common New Englanders had carried the Patriot cause from the arena of politics onto the battlefield, sympathizers in the vicinity of Butlersbury made ready to erect the first liberty pole in Tryon County. The attempt was frustrated by the arrival of the Johnsons, John Butler, Daniel Claus, and a number of Highlanders who caused the crowd to disperse. When in May Fort Ticonderoga fell to Ethan Allen, Benedict Arnold, and their "Green Mountain Boys," John Butler and other residents of the county rushed to defend Fort St. John's against this army of "rebels." In July 1775, when Guy Johnson, Daniel Claus, Gilbert Tice, John Butler, and his son Walter were attending an Indian council at Oswego, Nicholas Herkimer advised the Canajoharie committee "that Col. Johnson was ready with 800 or 900 Indians to make an Invasion of this County, that the same Indians to be under the Command of Joseph Brand [sic] and Walter Butler, and that they were to fall on the Inhabitants below the Little Falls, in order to divide the people in two parts. . . ."[16] But Johnson, accompanied by almost the entire body of the Mohawks and many leading Tories of Tryon County crossed into Canada and descended the St. Lawrence to Montreal where the Indians allied themselves with the British. Brant told of this decision in the following words:

> We were living at the former residence of Guy Johnson, when the news arrived that war had commenced between the King's people and the Americans. We took but little notice of this first report; but in a few days we heard that five hundred Americans were coming to seize our superintendent. Such news as this alarmed us, and we immediately consulted together as to what

measures were necessary to be taken. We at once reflected upon the covenant of our forefathers as allies to the King, and said, "It will not do for us to break it, let what will become of us." ... On this occasion General Haldimand told us what had befallen the King's subjects, and said, now is the time for you to help the King. The war has commenced. Assist the King now, and you will find it to your advantage. Go now and fight for your possessions, and whatever you lose of your property during the war, the King will make up to you when peace returns.[17]

According to tradition it was just prior to this time that Dr. Wheelock tried to influence his former pupil to keep the Mohawks neutral by writing him a learned dissertation on the aspect of the times. In his courteous reply Brant recalled the many happy hours he had spent with the family, making special reference to the doctor's prayers at the daily devotions. One passage in particular, he stated, had been so often repeated that it could never be effaced from his mind. This was his good preceptor's petition "that they might be able to live as good *subjects*—to fear God, and *honour the King*."[18] Another anecdote was handed down by Sir John Johnson's brother-in-law, John Watts. It seems that during the operations on Long Island when Brant was with Governor Tryon at Flatbush they and others were strolling through an orchard in the village. Brant picked a crabapple from a tree, but upon tasting it threw it away remarking that it was as bitter as a Presbyterian.[19]

The lines between Whig Patriots and Tory Loyalists were becoming sharply drawn. To Tories the Whigs were "rebels"; to Whigs the Tories were "traitors." In the Continental Congress meeting at Philadelphia a Tory was defined as "a thing whose head is in England and its body in America, and its neck ought to be stretched." This the Yankees of Cherry Valley, all ardent and outspoken Patriots, set about to do with a will. Following upon a large and spirited meeting held in the Presbyterian Meeting House, when numbers pledged themselves to support the Continental Congress by signing a general association, increasing pressure was exerted on outlying neighbours to follow their example. When one William Wood of Marbletown in Ulster County refused to sign a general association his name was written on the reverse side of a document dated June 6, 1775. Here was drawn the picture of a gibbet and in the space below the arm where a body would hang suspended "William Wood" was perpendicularly inscribed.[20] Two days later settlers of New Turlach drew up the following singular declaration :

8 June 1775

We the inhabitands of new turlach * do hereby certify that whereas william Spornhaier sets himself op for a commity at the first he invidet the boys to his hous to give them a frollick and when they were in their frollick he cat them to sign then he went aboud and toche who he could git and derecdit them with lyes till he gad them to Sign for him one of the inhabitants asked him what he meand by such action he answered he dit it out of Sport and he Shuld hender it if he could therefore if we have neet of a committi we will meat boblick to gether and chose 1 who we tinck for it. we have been to gether and have chosen officiars who we thought fid for it.[21]

By late summer there was no longer any thought of fealty to King George. The committees of correspondence became committees of safety which assumed all authority in civil and military affairs. Officers were appointed to organize a Patriot militia, and Nicholas Herkimer was placed in command of the men in the Canajoharie District. At a meeting held in August at the house of John Harper, a vigilance committee was appointed to watch the movements of suspected persons and the Indians

---

* "This early settlement formed by immigrants from Dorlach in Germany spread over the rolling country of the present townships of Seward, Sharon and the 'Rock District' of Carlisle in Schoharie County. The variety of spellings of New Dorlach ... was due to the Germans pronouncing it 'Turlagh' as their descendants still do at the present time." (William E. Roscoe, *History of Schoharie County, New York* (Syracuse, 1882), pp. 226-27.)

under Brant.[22] Loyalists who refused to sign articles of association were "found under Obligation of £100 to appear before the Albany Committee . . . for their Tryal." [23] A case in point is that of Lewis Clement, a substantial farmer and owner of several Negro slaves, whose lands at Tribes Hill* adjoined Colonel Butler's settlement of Butlersbury. Since his father Joseph had settled there in 1749 Lewis Clement had extended the holding to over 300 acres. With 75 cleared, 60 of which were rich lowlands, three houses, and a large orchard he had become well established in the Mohawk Valley.[24] Clement had already been informed against when he made a journey "towards Canada" for which he was unable to give an explanation satisfactory to the committee. "I am heartily sorry," he wrote to the chairman, "that my behaviour has given you so much offence, and I hope you will be kind Enough to Excuse that which is past Attributing it to my ignorance, or any other Cause, but a malicious Design of Enslaving My Country." [25] Clement was promptly arrested, found guilty of "Misconduct against our American Cause," and sentenced to pay £25 or spend three months in gaol (at his own expense). "The prisoner Lewis Clement," reads the minute of the proceedings, "doth choose the confinement and refused to pay a single copper. Resolved unanimously, and it is hereby Ordered, that the proceedings of the Tryal and Determination of said Lewis Clement shall be kept Secret, and not revealed to any Body." [26]

Other arrests were planned but most of the suspects succeeded in escaping to Canada. When rumour reached the committee that Guy Johnson, John Butler, and others who had gone to St. John's were about to return to their homes, preparations were made to take them prisoners. "Upon this dangerous Return of our proved Enemies [reads the minute], who left the County to serve against us in a hostile Manner, as much as it did lie in their power, and did actually fight themselves agst. our Forces near St. John's, but also tried their best to set up the Savages against us"—resolved that they be taken "by Force of Arms if Need Requireth" and that "a Spy-guard" of two or three men be set up to spot them.[27] But these "enemies" did not at this time return to the Mohawk Valley.

Meanwhile the Scots at Harpersfield and the Head of the Delaware seem to have avoided any serious trouble although some were forced to sign associations and to serve with the militia. Terence McAlister signed an association "for the defence of liberty and property . . . but his conduct was so adverse to the rebellion that in 1776 he was forced to live much in the woods." [28] Harpersfield, Kortright, and New Stamford were under the jurisdiction of the militia stationed at Schoharie and commanded by Colonel Peter (Pieter) Vrooman who had served as captain during the French or Seven Years' War. Loyalists were avoiding difficulties just so long as they took no part in demonstrations against the rebels. The Committee of Safety was so engrossed with such matters as procuring arms and ammunition, reducing the "Days Wages" paid John Moore of Cherry Valley as district representative to the first provincial congress (from 12s. to "Eight Shillings N. York Currency pr. Day and no more" [29]), and setting a date of muster for the militia that it was some time before "disaffected persons" in remoter districts caught its attention. Measures that the committee saw fit to adopt were driving many persons sympathetic to the American cause into the ranks of the Loyalists who stood for law and order and the unity of the Empire. They rested secure

* So called for the three clans, Onondagas, Cayugas, and Senecas who in earlier times had lived here in the village of Ogsadaga. During the Colonial period this name frequently appears as Tripes Hill.

in the belief that before long the rebel upstarts would be put down and dealt with severely.

It was unfortunate that the family of Thomas and John McMicking should arrive from Scotland just at this time. Their mother Janet Mulwain McMicking and sisters Sarah and Janet, the latter widow of James Cooper with two young sons Thomas and James, had set out from New Luce in Galloway. At Port Stranraer they shipped on board the *Jackie*, Captain James Morrison, master, on May 13, 1775.[30] The voyage across the Atlantic was a difficult one. Twenty-one-year-old Sarah died and was committed to the sea, and Captain Morrison lost his reckonings and had to sail aimlessly about in the open sea until he fell in with another vessel which helped him find his course. Upon learning of the rumoured closing of ports he obtained his passengers' consent to land at the first harbour he could find. He thus disembarked the two women and their charges at Philadelphia and arranged their passage to New York where they were met by Thomas and John McMicking and taken to their new home beside the Delaware.[31]

In the autumn of 1775 Guy Johnson, Daniel Claus, Joseph Brant, and Gilbert Tice went to England. At the same time, John Butler was appointed Johnson's deputy in the Indian Department and ordered to Niagara, a posting for which Butler's family background and experience had well fitted him. His father, an Irish army officer who had come to America with his regiment about 1709, had gained influence with the Indians during his services on the frontier. In 1733 the elder Butler received a Crown grant in Schoharie, land which was later bought by Sir Peter Warren as part of the Warren's Bush tract, and two years later he acquired from the Mohawks some 5,000 acres known as Butler's Purchase south of Johnson's Bush on the north side of the Mohawk River. Here he established his settlement of Butlersbury. Included in the purchase was a part of Old Caughnawaga and its early church founded by Jesuits as an Indian mission. To the east on the crest of a hill (Switzer Hill near Fonda) was the Butler homestead built in 1742, a clapboard house with centre door flanked by windows. This typical New England "salt box," from which one sees the Mohawk winding out of the hills on the western horizon, is one of the few wooden homesteads in the region to have survived the ravages of both time and the Revolution.

John Butler was born at New London, Connecticut, and educated in that province, before his father moved the family to the Mohawk Valley. John's son, Walter, eldest of five children, was born at Butlersbury when his wife was only seventeen years old. At an early age, John took up a military career, and in 1753, when a lieutenant, he was stationed at Fort Hunter where his father was commandant. At the beginning of the Seven Years' War he joined Sir William Johnson and was appointed to the Indian Department. He led the Indians in most of the important battles fought throughout the war. "In 1760," he wrote, "when the Officers of the Indian Department were principally dismissed, Sir William Johnson thought proper to continue me, on Account of my Knowledge of the Indian Languages & after Sir William's Death I acted under his Successor Colo. Guy Johnson the Acting Superintendent."[32] He narrates how, upon his arrival at Niagara November 17, 1775, he found that many "Rebel Emissaries . . . were using every Artifice to seduce [the Indians] from their Attachment to the King." He succeeded in pointing out to them "the insidious Designs of the Rebels & the pernicious consequence of their joining the King's Enemies . . . & the Rebel Emissaries were obliged to quit the Indian Country." [33]

Meanwhile Joseph Brant, the "tower of strength among the warriors of the wilderness" [34] and the war chief of the Six Nations, had crossed the Atlantic in company with Captain Gilbert Tice, an American of English extraction and veteran of the French War in which he had served under Colonel Claus.[35] Tice had married Christian Van Slyke of the old Dutch family in New York, and had been a considerable landholder in the Mohawk Valley until he got into financial difficulties, was imprisoned for debt, and had his land sold under execution. Upon building a tavern at Johnstown Sir William placed Tice in charge, and it became a rendezvous for Johnson and his cronies. Tice's account books which are now at Johnson Hall contain many entries for refreshment furnished at meetings of the Freemasons' Lodge. His long experience and skill in dealing with the Indians made him a suitable guide for Joseph Brant.

Various reasons have been ascribed for the Mohawk Chief's visit to England, but none may be given with any degree of certainty. Not only was he well received but his society was courted by gentlemen of rank and station. He became intimate with James Boswell and at his request sat for a portrait. The most famous portrait, commissioned by the Earl of Warwick and painted by Romney, shows Brant in his native dress which he wore at Court and upon other state and ceremonial occasions. Ordinarily he wore European dress in London. During this visit, Brant gained the friendship, destined to endure throughout his life, of Lord Percy, later the Duke of Northumberland. Also, he was commissioned captain, the highest rank for Indians in the British army.

During Brant's absence his neighbour Hendrick Frey was arrested and thrown in Albany Gaol whereupon his son Philip Rockell Frey, a lad of about fourteen, returned home to Canajoharie from school in Schenectady. Upon refusing to join the rebels Philip was put in Johnstown Gaol. When given permission to visit his mother he and another prisoner escaped to Molly Brant who hid them in the woods for a week and supplied them with provisions and an Indian guide. They travelled to the Oneida country by way of Canaseraga and Onondaga and were well cared for in other Indian villages along the way. Upon arriving at Niagara Philip Frey enrolled in the 8th or King's Regiment as gentleman volunteer (or "cadet").[36]

Early in the spring of 1776 Brant and Tice made a secret landing near York Island, and wearing disguises they stole their way through a hostile population to Canada. They arrived in time for Brant to lead his Mohawks to victory against invading rebels at the Cedars near Montreal where they found Sir John Johnson in command of a corps of Loyalists from New York. Sir John had been in the Montreal area since early in the new year. Some six months before that, when he had fortified his house and the Scots and Mohawks had stood about him for protection, the Americans had claimed that he was preparing for an attack on the Mohawk Valley. Accordingly he was arrested, his Highlanders disarmed, and he was released on parole. Six Scots, of whom at least five were Macdonells, one of them Allan of Collachie, were held for the good behaviour of Sir John, and because they chose to be prisoners of war rather than hostages they were sent to gaol at Lancaster, Pennsylvania.[37] Persistent rumours that the Indians were being secretly incited by Sir John resulted in the dispatching of militia to take him into custody. Forewarned, Sir John hastily assembled a party of friends, Highlanders, and other tenants, and guided by three trusty Mohawks struck out for Canada, travelling due north through the heart of the Adirondack Mountains.

Unprepared for this nine-day winter journey, the travellers suffered great hardship and reached Canada in a pitiable condition. Sometime later, Sir John wrote to Daniel Claus:

> Exiled from all that was dearest to me in life and what rendered my situation still more unhappy was that, before I got to my Journey's end, I received letters from my Dear Polly, informing me that she was ordered to go to Albany with such part of her family as she thought necessary to take with her there to remain as Hostages for my behaviour—the keys of every place were demanded and all papers which were not concealed were taken, my Books distributed about the Country, and my house made a Barrack of. The most of my Tenants went to different parts of the Country, there to linger out their time in utmost distress, in want of every necessary while their families are equal Sufferers at home for want of their assistance. I had removed many things both of yours and Guy's to the Hall, all which together with everything I had in the world except my Plate and our title, Deeds, Books of account, &c., which I had Buried, were made plunder of by those ungrateful Rebellious Miscreants. After Lady Johnson had been at Albany a considerable time I advised her, as I constantly corresponded with her by Indians and white men that I sent through the Woods, to try to prevail upon Mr. Schuyler or the Committee to let her return home, or come down to this place with her friends—they refused saying "that while they had her and the Children in their possession I would not dare to head the Indians or act agst. the Country; if I did, she would have reason to dread the consequence, for that she would not be saved from the Violence of the people." . . . Upon my arrival at St. Regis with my party consisting of one hundred and seventy men who were almost starved and wore out for want of provisions, being nine days without anything to subsist upon but wild Onions, Roots and the leaves of the Beech trees, I was received in the most friendly manner by the Indians. . . .*[38]

The Americans claimed that Sir John had "shamefully broken his parole" whereas he considered the intent to arrest him as an automatic release from any agreement. Nevertheless, Lady Johnson, Mrs. John Butler, and their families were retained as hostages, and Johnson Hall continued to be used as a barracks. Sir John was commissioned by the British to recruit among Loyalists and to raise two battalions for the King's Royal Regiment of New York. One by one the Macdonells who were prisoners contrived to escape, and all joined Sir John Johnson's new corps, popularly called the Royal Yorkers by the British and Johnson's Greens by the Americans.

When the inhabitants of Cherry Valley heard rumours that they were in "Eminent danger of being cut off by the Savages, our Enemies, whom we understand are Bribed by Sir John Johnson and Colonel Butler," they petitioned for help in their defences. They stated that people from the Old England District and other exposed locations to the west "are daily flying into our settlement."[39] Before long Fort Stanwix was strengthened and other fortifications were erected along the Mohawk River.

The mission of enlisting the settlers of Kortright, Harpersfield, and the Head of the Delaware on the side of the Patriots was entrusted to John Harper, but a majority eluded his grasp. He wrote to the Committee of Safety:

HARPERSFIELD June the 19th 1776

GENTLEMEN
upon my arrival at home I call'd the people of Kortrights pattan together & laid the New Association before them 10 of which I voluntary swore myself & asked if they would swear to the same, they make some scruples on which account they have sent some of their own people to receive their Instructions from your selves. This is all from
                                      Gentlemen
                                      Your Verry Humble Servt
                                      JOHN HARPER
                                      Chairman [40]

---

* About 1900 two old brass cannon of the type that had been mounted in front of Johnson Hall but had disappeared at the time of Sir John's flight were discovered south of Big Tupper Lake. The gun carriages of these English fourteen pounders had rotted away and inside a metal tire of one of the wheels had grown a beech tree two feet in diameter which tree experts judged to be more than a century old. (T. Clarke Wood, *The Bloody Mohawk* (New York, 1940), p. 196.)

When failing to secure a signature to an association, Patriots applied pressure to obtain an oath of neutrality, similar to the following :

County Tryon
I John Thomspon do solemnly swear on the Holy Evangelists of Almighty god, that I will not during the present troubles between America & Great Britain, be aiding or assisting Coll. Guy Johnson or any other person in his department with provisions or any other Necessarys or Intelligence whatsoever, Neither will I be aiding or assisting in causing the same to be done by any person whatsoever, Whom I may Suspect or cause to Suspect to be Aiding or acting for that purpose without the Consent or direction of the Committee from this County, or any Sub: Committee of this County knowing it be by such.[41]

The adoption on July 4, 1776, of the Declaration of Independence by members of the Continental Congress meeting at Philadelphia cut off all hope of terminating the war by other means than a triumph of arms. Every colonist had now to choose between remaining a subject of Great Britain in which most had taken great pride, and becoming a citizen of the new republic and thus a traitor to the Crown. There was no longer any middle ground, no hope of compromise. Five days later, on July 9, a Commission of Sequestration was given power to seize the property, real and personal, of "persons gone to the Enemy." They were empowered to sell the personal effects for the benefit of the state and to rent the real estate. Among the six commissioners appointed in Tryon County were John and William Harper.[42]

Although the battles that took place before the onset of winter were fought on fields far removed from the frontier of Tryon County the settlers continued to prepare for the worst. The Scots in the area around the Head of the Delaware were ready to follow the lead of their social superiors, the Macdonells, who were loyal to the House of Hanover. The Kortright and Banyar patents soon became recognized as a nest of Scottish Toryism and Captain John Macdonell, "Spanish John," of the Charlotte River, the leader. Nor did their landlords champion the rebellious movement, because they were among the large proportion of Loyalists who although unsympathetic towards the measures of the British Parliament believed in resolving the differences by constitutional methods rather than war. Lawrence Kortright remained quietly at York and Goldsbrow Banyar retired into obscurity at Rhinebeck, New York. Captain Macdonell had organized a company of Loyalists "probably in concert with Sir John Johnson, and also as a measure of protection against raiding militia from Schoharie," according to the county historian, John D. Monroe.[43] "The troops of either side," he wrote, "did not take much pains to distinguish those who adhered to the British from those who favoured the Americans."[44] Macdonell induced men who would not enlist to take an oath of neutrality which was probably similar to that adopted by Patriots and quoted above.

That the Scots were being closely watched is indicated by resolutions passed December 18, 1776, by the Committee of Safety of which John Harper was now a member. The committee ruled : (1) that settlers along the road running between the Charlotte River and the West Branch of the Delaware should improve said road; (2) that the inhabitants along the Charlotte be formed into a militia company and Christopher Servos' son Daniel be commissioned ensign; (3) "that the McDonalds, Scotch Inhabitans ... of the said Charlotte River and like shall join the said company and train under the said command."[45] At the same time George Ramsey and Hendrick Huff of the Harpersfield–Cherry Valley area were brought before the committee for examination. Upon the assertion of John Harper that they "were desperate fellows and, that ... they ought in his Opinion be prevented from going at large" Ramsey and Huff were sentenced to confinement at Poughkeepsie.[46] While on the way to this prison two nights later they and fourteen others escaped from the Fish Kill guard house.[47] John Harper promptly sequestered their property. Huff went to Canada to join Sir John Johnson, but upon returning at a later date for his family he was again seized by Harper together with a number of Loyalists who "had deserted from Confinement at Albany." Huff succeeded in making a second escape and joined Joseph Brant.

Early in the new year, 1777, the Indians were gathering in such large numbers as to cause great uneasiness to settlers along the frontier, and John Harper was dispatched by the provincial congress to Oquaga. According to W. L. Stone (and other historians) Harper was instructed merely "to ascertain their intentions," and "was well received by the Indians."[48] But the report of a committee on dispatches from General Schuyler throws a different light on the matter. The committee resolved that "it will be of great service to the American Cause to apprehend Joseph Brant, wherefore no Cost should be spared for the purpose and that it will be of use to recommend to Gen¹ Schuyler that Mr John Harper of the County of Tryon is a proper Person to be employed in that Service. . . ."[49] Harper set out February 19 and upon reaching Oquaga eight days later "found Brant away."[50]

With the arrival of spring in 1777 came the news that the British were preparing a large-scale offensive on the Province of New York. Brant appeared at Oquaga, the ancient Indian village so beautifully situated where the valley of the Susquehanna broadens out into a wide space between the hills. Here he was joined by Indians in large numbers, and that the Loyalists to the east might also reach him he marked a path through the forests and valleys of the Kaatskills between Oquaga and the Hudson River.[51] As his forces increased so did the uneasiness of the Patriots in outlying settlements. On April 25 the Palatine District Committee of Safety was warned by its Schoharie counterpart that according to information received from responsible persons at Harpersfield it seemed advisable "to send for Mr. William Wills . . . and examine him about the behaving of Captain John MacDonald in his presence."[52] John Harper informed the Committee of Safety at Albany that "the peopell of Harpersfield onfortunately fell into the hands of McDonald, who amediately Swor them not to take arms against the King of Britain."[53] It has been stated that the Scots in this area together with those in the vicinity of Johnstown who continued their allegiance to the Macdonells were "to form the backbone of Loyalist resistance in New York."[54]

As a result of these and similar rumours a party of militia from Schoharie went hunting for Tories. One of their number, Peter Swart, tells how they "turned out to Harpersfield, from thence to the Delaware to take up the Disaffected . . . after we had about twenty-five of them went to Albany and delivered them to jail. A few days afterwards went to Harpersfield; then thence to the Charlotte river to take McDonald, and send him to jail."[55] But they did not take John Macdonell, and of those who were seized only the record of Hugh Fraser has been found. Fraser, who laid claim to being the "first man that opposed the oath to Congress" was taken to Albany Gaol.[56] On May 1, 1777, the properties of John, Allan, and Roderick (Rory) MacDonell along the Charlotte and of John Cameron, Hugh Clarke, George Chisholm, John Livingston, Donald McLeod, and Hugh McMullan in Kortright were seized by the Commission of Sequestration. As commissioners, John and William Harper sold the personal property and attempted to rent the real estate of those listed above. The properties of

Hugh Clarke remained untenanted,[57] but the farm of Lewis Clement* at Tribes Hill on the Mohawk, seized four months later, rented for twenty skipples of wheat, and that of Hendrick Huff brought the new State of New York £14 per annum.

An expedition made in July under General Herkimer, an old acquaintance of Brant's, had descended the Susquehanna to Unadilla ostensibly on a friendly mission but more probably to seize Brant. Thereafter rumours of retaliation flew through the settlements, and numbers of avowed Patriots in Harpersfield and elsewhere, including the Harpers, sought the protection of the militia stationed at Schoharie. "I was informed," stated John Harper, "that a party of indens was sent by Brant to take me & those other persons that ware most active in the american caus on which my Self my brother Alexander and Some other famelys maid our ascaip to Scohary and I went to kingstown to inform the convention who ware then Seting their."[58] About the middle of July the raising of two companies of rangers and minute men for the defence of the frontier was authorized and John Harper was commissioned captain and his brother Alexander first lieutenant.[59] Although busily engaged in recruiting Captain Harper was, however, unable to enlist more than one company of rangers.

By this time when war finally reached the Province of New York the Scots were experiencing considerable persecution at the hands of Patriots. A number, including Hugh Fraser, who escaped from Albany Gaol,[60] were forced to follow the example of Terence McAlister and live much in the woods, and two of Dr. Stuart's sons, one of them the eldest, had flown to York Town where they were to serve in the Waggon Master General Service throughout the war.[61] The sequestration of the many properties listed above at so early a date would indicate that at this point in the story much of importance is unfortunately elusive, and that events took place which, however dramatic, must remain untold.

* Gone to Niagara to enlist in the Indian Department.

CHAPTER FOUR

THE KING'S MEN: WITH HATCHET, KNIFE, AND GUN
(PART I)

WHEN IN THE SUMMER of 1777 Major-General John Burgoyne brought war into the Province of New York large numbers of Loyalists on the frontier prepared to take up arms in allegiance to their King. They no longer feared to declare themselves for Parliament, so certain were they of the rapid subjugation of the rebels and the end to the hostilities. They only awaited the opportunity presented by the arrival of British forces. The military strategy was designed to cut off New England, the hot-bed of the rebellion, from New York down the Hudson Valley line by armies converging from three directions upon Albany. While General Burgoyne, lately arrived in Canada with 8,000 regulars, forced his way up the Richelieu River into Lake Champlain, a detachment under Colonel Barry St. Leger would make a diversion to liberate Loyalists in the Mohawk Valley. St. Leger's forces would consist of about 2,000 men: a few regulars, Sir John Johnson and his Loyalist regiment of Royal Yorkers, Colonel John Butler heading a small party of rangers enlisted among refugees who had reached Niagara (see Appendix B), and Joseph Brant and his Indian warriors. Concurrently, another expedition under General Howe would move up the Hudson, destroying all opposition to the Crown. Thus New England would be isolated, the water route from north to south opened throughout its length, the Loyalist province of New York freed from the grasp of the rebels, and the erring colonists brought back to their former allegiance.

General Burgoyne took the field in June. St. Leger ascended the St. Lawrence and Lake Ontario to Oswego and prepared to proceed inland to capture Fort Stanwix on the upper Mohawk, the rebel garrison of which was expected to offer little resistance, and sweep down the Mohawk Valley. Sir John summoned to Oswego the leading Loyalists of Tryon County, among them Captain John Macdonell.[1] "I met Sir John at said place [Oswego], under the command of Brigd^r St. Leger, going to the siege of Fort Stanwix, he ordered me, to go into the Country to raise my comp^y," wrote Macdonell. "I went accordingly, raised and armed fifty four men . . ."[2] and called them together at the houses of Dr. James Stuart and Neil McKay.[3] Among the fifty-four men who in the first week in August shouldered their guns were James and John Park, John and George Chisholm, Archibald Thomson, Thomas McMicking, and Daniel Rose (who by now had a wife Jane). Other Scots who rallied to the call were Hugh Alexander who had escaped from Albany Gaol, Hugh Clarke, Hugh Fraser, John McKay, William Rose, John Cameron, John Livingston, Terence McAlister, Jacob Stoneburner's two eldest sons, and of course Dr. Stuart and Neil McKay. Marching to the skirl of bagpipes,[4] Macdonell led his recruits over the Delaware hills to the Breakabean, a tributary of the Schoharie, and thence to the house of Adam Chrysler, mill owner in the Schoharie Valley (at modern Fultonham). A commissioned officer of the provincial militia since 1768 Chrysler had also been gathering recruits. For five months he had maintained in provisions and at his own expense "all the Indians that were at Schoharie which was twenty-five,"[5] and, acting upon instructions from Joseph Brant, he had in readiness seventy white settlers whose meeting place was the inn of Captain George Mann near the Stone Fort in the Schoharie settlement. After allowing the Highlanders a day and night of rest Macdonell combined forces with Chrysler to take possession of the house of Peter Swart about four miles down the river at the lower end of Vroomansland (now the township of Fulton) where the 160-odd men remained another thirty-six hours.[6]

The alarm soon spread that Macdonell and a band of Highlanders were prowling through the hills, probably heading for Schoharie. The first preparation for Continental defence was the fortifying of the stone house of Johannes Becker in the Schoharie Valley. It was surrounded with ramparts, called Fort Defiance, and placed in the charge of Colonel Peter Vrooman, commander of the Schoharie militia. Vrooman was a neighbour of Adam Chrysler in the valley.[7] He and about twenty-five of the militia barricaded themselves within the fort, and the first entry on an itemized account of supplies would indicate that to put heart into the defenders was of primary importance: "to Peter Becker one-fourth of a Barrel of Cyder—15s."[8] John Harper, recently promoted to colonel, rushed off on horseback to Albany for assistance. During the thirty-six hours that the Loyalists rested he returned with "a small party of Light Horse ... procured at the risk of his life, and six Frenchmen raised at his own expense," according to Vrooman.[9] Upon learning of the rebel reinforcements Macdonell and Chrysler "thought it proper to retreat until we saw a convenient place to make a stand, which was at my house," stated Chrysler. Thirty-five men were detached to the Breakabean, should the rebels come that way, but "in the meanwhilst" the enemy approached from another direction. The Loyalists waited in ambush at a place called The Flockey (probably meaning swampy ground).[10] When the rebels came within gunshot the Loyalists gave them a volley, killing one and wounding three militiamen and "nine of their Light Horse." Lieutenant David Wirt died of wounds, and the above-mentioned account of expenses shows the entry, "Aug. 15, 3 boards for a coffin for one of the Light Horse."

"It being such a great shower of rain that we could not pursue them," continued Chrysler's narrative of the engagement, "we retreated back into the woods ... where we held a consultation and concluded that with the small number of men we had it would be madness to attack their increasing numbers which was already 4 to our 1, but collect all together and proceed from Oswego to the Army."[11] David Brass, millwright from Somerset County, New Jersey, and likely in Chrysler's employ, was dispatched to bring back the detachment from the Breakabean, but he reported that they had dispersed to join Sir John Johnson at Oswego. Thereupon Macdonell and Chrysler also set out over the hills for the Indian country, and thus ended the action of August 13 known as the battle of The Flockey. One of the earliest and perhaps the first of the frontier skirmishes, it was claimed as a victory by both sides. Macdonell and Chrysler had proceeded on their march when on the fourth day the latter fell ill and was obliged to remain behind at the Butternuts, sending his men ahead with Macdonell.[12] His parting with the company breaks the thread of this narrative, but it is certain that news of other recent British action caused Macdonell to hurry forward.

Meanwhile, on August 3 the British had appeared before Fort Stanwix, renamed by the rebels Fort Schuyler, over which waved the first national emblem of the United States of America (according to tradition) to be flown in the face of the enemy. It had been made out of an old white shirt, the red petticoat of a soldier's wife, and a blue coat captured from a British soldier.[13] This flag showed the red and white stripes of the one adopted eighteen months before by the Continental Army, but instead of the crosses of St. George and St. Andrew of the earlier flag it figured a constellation of thirteen five-pointed stars on a blue ground.* Under a flag of truce Captain Gilbert Tice carried St. Leger's summons to the rebels to surrender but it was met with shouts of defiance from the 600 Continental militiamen who defended the fort. The course of events was related to General Burgoyne by St. Leger in a letter "brought through the woods by an Indian, dated before Fort Stanwix, August 11, 1777."

> After combating the natural difficulties of the river St. Lawrence, and the artificial ones the enemy threw in my way at Wood Creek, I invested Fort Stanwix the 3^d instant. On the 5th I learnt from discovering parties on the Mohawk River,† that a body of one thousand militia were on the march to raise the siege. On the confirmation of the news, I moved a large body of Indians, with some troops the same night, to lay an ambuscade for them on their march. They fell into it. The compleat victory was obtained: above 400 lay dead upon the field, amongst the number of whom were almost all the principal movers of rebellion in that country.[14]

This was the battle of Oriskany, fought August 6 between brothers, fathers, sons and neighbours, and perhaps the bloodiest of the Revolution. The carnage was particularly frightful among the Indians, and for a long time Chief Brant was wont to speak of the sufferings of his "poor Mohawks" in their first engagement of this war.

Early in the battle a bullet killed the horse and shattered the leg of General Nicholas Herkimer in command of the Continental militia. Ordering his saddle placed at the foot of a beech tree he sat down upon it, lit his pipe, and shouted orders to his men. When advised to seek a more protected spot the general replied that he would face the enemy. After the conflict was over General Herkimer was carried on a litter to his home 2½ miles below the Little Falls in the Mohawk River, but unskilled amputation of his leg soon caused his death. This stalwart veteran of sixty years died propped up in bed while smoking his pipe and reading his huge family Bible. His house, built in 1764 of lovely rose-white brick, a product of the countryside, still stands on the south bank of the river.

In spite of the victory of Oriskany St. Leger's expedition was doomed to failure. The garrison of Fort Stanwix refused to surrender; the Indians decamped and fled at the approach of General Benedict Arnold at the head of a large Continental force; the panic of the Indians soon spread among the soldiers; and on August 22 St. Leger abandoned his siege. Assembling his scattered forces he started back to Oswego, and thence to Montreal. There have been various explanations of this retreat, one being that it was due to a ruse of Arnold who succeeded in circulating a report that General Burgoyne was totally defeated and that a great American army was on its way to rescue Fort Stanwix. However, the reasons given by Daniel Claus who was on the spot seem more credible than most:

---

* Though singular it is nevertheless true that in January 1776 the Continental Army had adopted unchanged the ensign of the British East India Company, but by order of Congress in June 1777 the crosses were replaced by the stars (William H. W. Sabine, ed., *Wm. Smith's Historical Memoirs 1763–76* (New York, 1956), vol. II, p. 433fn.).

† Notably Indians sent by Joseph Brant's sister at the Canajoharie or Upper Castle of the Mohawks (John Romeyn Brodhead, ed., *Documents relating to the Colonial History of the State of New York* (15 vols., Albany 1853–87), VIII (1857), pp. 718–23, Claus to Knox, Oct. 16, 1777).

The Chiefs advised the Brig^r to retreat to Oswego and get better artillery at Niagara, and more men, and so return and renew the siege [to which St. Leger agreed]. . . . On our arrival at Oswego the 26th and examining into the state of the troops' necessaries, the men were without shoes and other things which could only be got at Montreal, the Brig^r at the same time having rec^d a letter from General Burgoyne to join him either by a march thro' the woods back of Tryon County (which was impracticable) or the way he came. He adopted the latter, on account of procuring necessaries for the men. . . . Thus had an expedition miscarried, merely for want of timely and good intelligence. . . . All the good done by the exped^n was that the Ringleaders and principal men of the rebels of Tryon County were put out of the way.[15]

The precipitate departure of the British forces left many Loyalists, numbers of whom had come from as far as Wyoming on the Susquehanna, the alternative of joining Burgoyne who was encamped above Albany, of going to Canada, or of returning to their homes. Although Captain John Macdonell's company dispersed a majority of them followed him to Canada [16] to enlist in Johnson's Royal Yorkers (see Appendix A). George Chisholm, answering the call of General Burgoyne for all Loyalists to join him, made his way eastward to enroll with the artificers as carpenter. After remaining some time with the Indians, Hugh Fraser, Daniel Rose, Thomas McMicking, Thomson, James Park, the McKays, Alexander, John Chisholm, and others returned to Harpersfield and Kortright. Fraser stated that he "was with the Indians 13 weeks . . . some of the Party went to Canada, some returned home, and then tried to go to Niagara." [17] Adam Chrysler remained in the Indian country until the end of November when, accompanied by about one hundred Indians, he journeyed to Niagara.[18] There he encountered his brother Philip who had abandoned his extensive holdings at New Turlach, which included a blacksmith's shop and large potash works, to join St. Leger at Fort Stanwix.[19]

Upon reaching Canada Colonel Butler went to Quebec where he was empowered "by beat of Drum, or otherwise forthwith to raise" a corps of eight companies of rangers "to serve with the Indians, as occasion shall require," each company to be composed of a captain and fifty-seven rank and file.[20] The same day he was ordered to march with such rangers as were already serving and as large a body of Indians "as you can collect" and to join General Burgoyne as soon as possible.

Burgoyne in the meantime had opened his campaign on July 1. He ascended Lake Champlain and surrounded Fort Ticonderoga, the formidable stone fortress standing on a rocky promontory jutting into the lake and thus known as "the Key to a Continent." He found that the Continentals had failed to fortify Sugar loaf Hill which rises at the confluence of Lake Champlain with the outlet of Lake George and is the highest elevation in the vicinity. Lieutenant Twiss of the Engineers and his men performed the astonishing feat of building a road up this hill, dragging cannon up the steep incline, and beginning the construction of a large block house on the summit—all in somewhat over twenty-four hours.* When the Continentals holding Fort Ticonderoga "awoke to see English cannon and scarlet uniforms frowning down upon them" [21] they evacuated the fort July 6.

Continuing southward the British army was slowed down by the rough terrain and delaying tactics of the Continentals. Felled trees obstructed the road; the rebels' destruction of their crops and dispersal of horses and cattle caused a shortage of provisions; and the fleet had not started up the Hudson River from the south. Bur-

* "Plan of Ticonderoga . . . showing . . . the Extensive Communication which was made in one day . . . Including Sugar Hill . . ." drawn at the command of Lieutenant Twiss shows "New Road made by the Artificers on the 5th July in the afternoon and the following night; Block houses begun for the defence of this important post." The name of Sugar loaf Hill was later changed to Mount Defiance.

goyne crossed the west branch of the Hudson on a bridge of boats and prepared for battle with the Continental army under command of General Horatio Gates. To secure a retreat, should such become necessary, seventy-two artificers were put to work raising a fortification on the summit of Sugar loaf Hill. All went well until the small band of artificers was attacked on the night of July 18. The details of this action were fully related by Ira Allen whose brother Ebenezer led the Continental attack, and by John Clunes who in the spring of 1776 had crossed the Atlantic in the same ship with fur-trader's clerk, Francis Goring (who will be encountered in other chapters of this history), and now in the summer of 1777 was master carpenter in charge of the work on Sugar loaf Hill.

The Continentals' over-all plan was to cut Burgoyne's communications by first taking Fort Ticonderoga,[22] so under cover of darkness three contingents consisting of rangers, militia, and volunteers attacked simultaneously, one against Mount Independence on the east side of Lake Champlain, another under Colonel John Brown * against the landing of Lake George, while a third, Captain Ebenezer Allen and his rangers, climbed Sugar loaf Hill. Allen and his Green Mountain Boys "scaled the craggy rocks with much danger. . . . He commenced the assault with a hideous yell, and to use his own expression, *his Men came after him like a stream of hornets to the charge*. . . . Allen and his men were soon in possession of the parade and garrison. Such men as were not killed, or wounded, ran down the cut towards Ticonderoga, and were taken . . . by a party . . . stationed at the bridge for the purpose."[23] According to Clunes, "after a retreat almost incredible to believe, without seeing the precipises," he and a few of his men reached the water. "Our difficulty was to get over to Tyconderogo," he continues, "but fortunately I saw an old batteau which . . . was so leaky that it was likely to sink with us. But we kept bailing her out with hats and caps the best way we could," and reached Fort Ticonderoga. Besides all his clothes Clunes lost a purse containing forty guineas "by a stump that tore my breeches. . . . As soon as General [Brigadier Henry W.] Powell saw my condition . . . he clothed all my few people with me. Some were half naked, as we were asleep when the cowardly villains surprised us."[24]

The greater part of four companies was taken prisoner "at the Portage, Sugar loaf Hill, Blockhouse and Davis's farm a little beyond the lines."[25] Among the twenty-five artificers[26] seized was George Chisholm who, according to his own statement, lost £20 when "taken upon Lake Champlain."[27] The rebel forces laid siege to Fort Ticonderoga for about a week, but thereafter they gave it up. "A few days after," continues Clunes, "we had news of Gen. Burgoyne's army being prisoners." When the plan of the campaign had miscarried and reinforcements failed to arrive the general was completely encircled by Continental forces, and the attempt to break through, known as the battle of Saratoga, had brought total defeat. "About three weeks after," wrote Clunes, "Gen. Carlton sent orders up to Gen. Powell to burn Tyconderogo to the ground and return to Canada with his men which he did."[28]

The battle of Oriskany, particularly the employment of Indians in the warfare, struck such fear into the hearts of the rebels along the frontier that they huddled near their strongholds leaving their work undone. In asking protection from the Council

* John Brown, native of Massachusetts and graduate of Yale, who had practised law at Johnstown 1772–73, commanded the detachment of men which had initiated the invasion of Canada in September 1775. He combined forces with Ethan Allen to capture Montreal, but the attack failed and Allen was taken and held prisoner in Canada until some eight months after his brother Ebenezer's seizure of Sugar loaf Hill.

of Safety "on behalf of themselves and the Inhabitants of Tryon County" William Harper and Frederick Fisher stated :

> That the late Incursions of the Enemy & their Savages . . . have reduced the Inhabitants to the utmost distress. The Harvests not yet gathered in are rotting on the Ground. The Grass uncut. The fallow Grounds not yet ploughed. The Cattle in a great measure destroyed.
> That altho' by the Blessing of God the Siege of Fort Schuyler hath been raised, yet the Inhabitants labour under the greatest Apprehensions, and in the opinion of your memorialists those apprehensions are not ill founded. The known method of warfare among the Savages, and the Infamy annexed to those who suffer their Friends to fall unrevenged, give but too much reason to believe that the Fears of those unhappy People will be realized. . . .[29]

Fears resulted also in the people's reluctance to enlist in the Patriot cause, and Colonel John Harper had to advise "the Honbell, the Presead't of the Council of Safety at Kingstown" as follows :

SCHOHARY FORT DEFEYANCE August the 20 1777

SIR :
> On my Return to this place I found the wholl Country in alarm; and the popell So intimidated that it was out of my powir to inlist aney Considerabell number of men; and thos that Did ingage were So Scatred that it had ben out of my powir to Colect them as they had to go hom for their Necasarys. . . .

JOHN HARPER [30]

Loyalists who had borne arms against the Patriots were now being hunted down as traitors to the cause of freedom. In calling General Clinton's attention to Tryon County's "dismal situation" and requesting directions, a committee informed him that "the late Trial of the County, drove Numbers of Disaffected Inhabitants into the Woods, many of whom actually joined the Enemy at Fort Schuyler; several returned since the Flight of the Enemy to their respective homes, some delivered themselves up to this Board others is brought Prisoners before us." [31] Jacob Stoneburner "was imprisoned on acct. of having sent his Sons into the Army" and confined for a year before being realeased on parole in Connecticut; Hugh Clarke "was very soon obliged to quit his home and shelter in the Woods. Kept skulking in the Woods, sometimes got upon his own lands." [32] Neil McKay was advertized in the newspapers and ordered to leave the country "or he would suffer for it." [33] Even unprotected families suffered dispossession. To cite two instances among many, the wife of Terence McAlister "was turned out of doors" and Mrs. John Macdonell "off the land" by rebels.[34] In the north, at Turlach, one George Walker, "Chief of the Tories," was accused of tying "a Handkerchief to a Stik" and crying out "Huza for King George," found guilty, and confined to gaol. Adam Young, founder of Youngsfield on the Little Lakes which empty into Otsego Lake, had only recently returned from eleven months of confinement for refusing to sign an association. Being an Indian trader he was suspected of supplying provisions to parties of Loyalists fleeing to Canada. A witness declared that upon the approach of a group of persons whom he mistook for Patriot militia Young "immediately hided himself and would not come to the Hauss." However, upon discovering his error he had ordered "victuals to be given to them and supplied them with flour," and had unwisely used the term "damned Rebels." [35] Thereafter, Adam was visited by rebels who carried away all such "moveables" as farm stock, household furniture, and articles of Indian trade and then set fire to his house, sawmill, potash works, trade store, and other valuable buildings. "With scarce sufficient clothes to cover him" Young and two of his sons went away to join Colonel Butler at Oswego and enlist in Butler's Rangers.[36] A third son John was already serving in the Indian Department.[37]

Colonel John Harper was no longer in Harpersfield. "About the last of December [1777]," he wrote, "I removed to torlough [Turlach] the better to Secure the frunteers and allso the property that was Sequestrated." [38] So that Harper and the other commissioners would be protected while they were seizing and disposing of Loyalists' effects a number of settlers at the Head of the Delaware were impressed into the Patriot service. Archibald Thomson, Thomas McMicking, and Angus McMullin are listed on "A Payroll of a Company of Rangers Commanded by Captn Alexander Harper, in Guarding the Commission of Sequestration Whilst they were Collecting and Selling the Personal Property of Persons Absconded to the Enemy in the Service of the State of New York, Being for the Month of January 1778—By order of Col^o Jno Harper one of ye commiss^{rs}." [39] This document shows that as privates each Scot received £2.13.4 plus £1.5.10 for rations, a total of £3.19.2 for the month of January 1778, which Alexander Harper declared upon oath had been paid.

The greatest danger to the inhabitants during 1778 was the raids carried out by Butler's Rangers stationed at Fort Niagara. The British commanders in Canada found themselves in a precarious position after the surrender of Burgoyne's army, because the remaining troops were required to defend the scattered garrisons and were thus unable to undertake any major offensive. Until such time as reinforcements could be sent from England the British officers were forced to concentrate on delaying actions. Both the Loyalist corps and Butler's Rangers which were organized to serve with the Indians were used for this purpose. To employ rangers to act in conjunction with the regulars was far from an innovation. Rogers' Rangers had fought through the Seven Years' War, and at this period the Queen's Rangers, commanded by Major John Graves Simcoe, were on active service in the southern theatre of the Revolution.* Whereas Simcoe's rangers acted as a flying column in support of the regulars the functions of Butler's men were to range far and wide on scouting expeditions, to harass the enemy, to destroy as much as possible of their food supply, to collect Loyalists who had been unable to escape, and to drive cattle and horses to Niagara. Butler's men, particularly those attached to the Indian Department, were "to mix ... with the Indians when on service, and be commanded by Indian Officers." [40] Two of his companies were to be comprised of "People speaking the Indian Language and acquainted with their customs and manner of making War" at 4s. New York currency per day. The other six companies composed of "People well acquainted with the Woods, in consideration of the fateague they are liable to undergo" were paid 2s. per day. Owing to this high rate of pay recruits were expected "to cloathe and arm themselves at their own expense." [41] Each company was under the command of a captain assisted by a lieutenant, both of whom Butler chose from among men holding commissions in the provincial militia. Joseph Brant was placed in command of a company in the Six Nations Department of Butler's Rangers, and other Mohawks such as David Hill, his son Aaron, Jacob Lewis, and William Johnson "jr" also received commissions.

---

* The *Royal Gazette* carried the following notice on March 31, 1779:

All aspiring Heroes
Have now an opportunity of distinguishing themselves
by joining the Queen's Ranger
HUSSARS
commanded by
Lieut. Col. Simcoe
Any spirited Young Man will receive every encouragement, be immediately mounted on an elegant Horse, and furnished with cloathing &c. to the amount of
FORTY GUINEAS
... Whoever brings a recruit shall instantly receive Two Guineas.

Brant continued to exert his influence to keep his people faithful to their pledge to the British cause, now more important than ever because their country lay between Canada and the enemy.

As fugitives filtered into Niagara the ranks of Butler's Rangers began to fill up. Many of the best recruits had come from settlements along the Susquehanna where all suspected persons were keenly persecuted and many like John Glassford had come "almost naked into Niagara." [42] Although they had little knowledge of military drill or discipline they possessed the practical knowledge and endurance so essential to survival in the forest. Soon recruits were issued uniforms of the dark green worn during the Seven Years' War by Rogers' Rangers and at the present time by the Queen's Rangers. The equipment consisted of jackets, buckskin breeches, and low flat caps bearing plates monogrammed "G.R." encircled by "Butler's Rangers." From Niagara parties went out to perform various duties according to their instructions. The silence and lightning rapidity with which they struck and vanished, to reappear where and when least expected, caused great fear to sweep through the settlements. Inhabitants on the frontier from Johnstown on the north, German Flatts on the west, and Unadilla on the south soon became an armed yeomanry. Men watched at home and took turns standing sentinel when labouring in the fields. They were continually harried by conflicting rumours, and often the first intimation that the foe was in their midst was the glare of a neighbouring house in flames. This fear, though it proved an asset to the Rangers, gave rise to tales of such extensive ferocity and atrocity as are impossible of belief. Probably the rebels' bitterest complaint, that white men disguised themselves as Indians, was unwarranted because this ruse had been used by both sides throughout the French wars.

Early in 1778 a party of Rangers was taken prisoner. They had joined St. Leger at Fort Stanwix, but when the seige was abandoned had obtained leave to go home "in order to fetch their families into Niagara, as they had been drove by the enemy from their habitations." [43] They had also had orders to drive cattle from the settlements to Niagara. In this party conducted by Lieutenant James Secord were Jacob Bowman, his sixteen-year-old son Adam, Philip Buck, Adam and John Young of Youngsfield, and Michael Showers. Excepting the Youngs all were settlers from Forty Fort and its vicinity in the Wyoming Valley of the Susquehanna. They had reached their homes when on January 3, 1778,[44] twenty-seven of them were "taken up and secured." *The Remembrancer* reported that "the white inhabitants" had discovered that "many of the villainous Tories, who had stirred up the Indians, and been with them in the fighting against us, were within the Settlements. . . . Of these 18 were sent to Connecticut, the rest, after being detained some time, and examined, were for want of sufficient evidence set at liberty; they immediately joined the enemy. . . ." [45] Secord and Showers were among those released but Buck, the Youngs, and the Bowmans were sent to gaol.

Jacob Bowman and his wife Elizabeth were natives of the Mohawk Valley. Upon securing a grant of land in Wyoming for his services in the Seven Years' War they had left his father's settlement situated north of Cherry Valley spreading along the stream which would continue for another century to be known as "Bowman's or Canajoharie Creek." [46] At the time of Jacob's arrest his house was pillaged, his grain destroyed, his cattle driven away, and his wife and children left without provisions and with only one blanket between them. Soon after her husband and eldest son were marched away Elizabeth gave birth to her seventh child, and to keep the family from freezing Peter, age eleven, cut and drew wood on a hand sleigh barefoot. They might have perished had not friendly Indians brought them provisions, and shoes and a blanket coat for Peter. In the spring Elizabeth Bowman took her children to the Mohawk Valley where they planted corn and potatoes.[47] Although not so stated by her descendant, the narrator of a later period, Elizabeth undoubtedly returned to Bowman's Creek where she had lived when first married. She later reached Canada in safety. The families of the Youngs, Secord, Showers, Buck, and Hendrick Nelles were also in dire straits. It was said that among the five women and thirty-one children of these families there was only one pair of shoes. Learning from Indians of their plight, Colonel Mason Bolton, commandant at Niagara, sent a party of rescue, and the distressed families were thus led to Quebec where they remained under government care until the end of the war.

Meanwhile Buck and the Bowmans were exchanged to New York, and not knowing that their families were in Canada they set out for the Susquehanna. On the third day they attracted the attention of enemy scouts by shooting ducks. Buck escaped but the Bowmans, being sorely wounded, were again taken. "Loaded with irons," they were removed from gaol to gaol (once Jacob "lay in Chains" for twenty weeks) and were kept in confinement throughout the war.[48]

The news of the fate of Secord's party was brought to Niagara by one of the first men to join Colonel Butler at Niagara, John Depue, who had been sent to seek recruits among his former neighbours in Wyoming. He reported that many Loyalists awaited the chance to join Butler should he raid the area. Such an opportunity was soon forthcoming because by spring the alarm of the Indians caused by rumours of Continental attacks on their villages led Colonel Butler to lay plans to march to their support. For his headquarters he fixed on Unadilla as being within striking distance of the frontiers of New York, Pennsylvania, and New Jersey. From Niagara the expedition moved across the Seneca country and down the Chemung to Unadilla on the Susquehanna, where they remained for some time while gathering recruits and provisions for the coming offensive.

It was at this time that a party of Scots left Harpersfield and Kortright to avoid further service in the Patriot militia, among them Daniel Rose, James Park, Archibald Thomson, and John Chisholm.[49] Their effects were promptly seized by the Harpers as commissioners of sequestration and a detachment of militia from Schoharie descended upon Harpersfield and seized a number of settlers. That these four Highlanders chose to fight with the Indians rather than with the Rangers and that they journeyed as far as Tioga Point to join Joseph Brant could only have been owing to their friendship with Brant or his recruiting ability—probably a combination of both. Early in May he had appeared in the Old England District accompanied by six Indians and several Rangers described as "green Coat soldiers."[50] He warned Loyalists of their danger and tried to persuade families he knew to go with him, pointing to his inability to protect them. Unless they sought a place of safety they must "take their own risk."[51] Continuing northward Brant and his men laid waste Springfield and other settlements, and drove off a large number of cattle. Several families from the Old England District went with him to Unadilla and others soon followed.[52] "I am so happy to find," wrote Sir John Johnson from Quebec, "the Mohawks have accomplished their errand to the Mohawks Country . . . [and] that Joseph has at length had another Opportunity of drubbing those wretches who have so unjustly injured us all. . . ."[53]

Brant's search for provisions and recruits had taken him among the Scots at the Head of the Delaware. One of those who were unable to leave their families was Thomas McMicking whose mother, young brother, sister, and two small nephews needed his protection. Thomas therefore "was desired by Joseph Brant to remain in the Country for the purpose of getting Intelligence and supplying British Scouts with Provisions."[54] To gather cattle and horses from his neighbours and turn them over to officers commanding scouting parties without being detected was risky business. A subterfuge commonly employed was that of leaving the animals in exposed situations near trails where scouts could easily find them; thus the landholder was able to claim that he had been plundered by the enemy.

From Unadilla Brant went to Oquaga, but upon orders from Colonel Butler proceeded to Tioga Point where a council of war was called in May. Tioga (Teaoga) was the Iroquois name for the wedge of land situated where the Chemung enters the Susquehanna. Here was the apex of a triangle of pathways leading through the territory of the Six Nations, Albany forming the eastern angle, the Great Falls of Niagara the western, and the trail from the Hudson to Lake Erie the base of the triangle. In Indian times as in our own the Old Iroquois Trail through the Mohawk Valley was the greatest of all New York highways. A well-worn Indian trail was described as being from twelve to eighteen inches wide and often beaten to the depth of a foot below the level of the surrounding earth. On the flatlands to the north of Tioga was the ancient Seneca stronghold, a town of seventy log houses where Queen Esther held sway. Esther Montour was a granddaughter of Madame Montour who had ruled the Seneca castle, known to white men as French Catherine's Town, at the head of Seneca Lake. In like manner the castle of the Tioga where Esther held court was called Queen Esther's town. Here the forces assembled for the incursion on the frontier, and Brant came to the council of war.

The Indians in council refused to form an expedition to go north unless they were first assisted in cutting off the inhabitants of the Wyoming valley on the Susquehanna. A treaty was signed in which it was agreed that Butler should attack Wyoming while Brant again went north on a forgaging raid until the colonel's return. The council lasted about nine days (during which time Thomson, Park, Rose, and Chisholm arrived to enlist [55]) after which Brant moved his men to Oquaga to prepare for the expedition to the north. Butler sent other Indian officers to assist him and also to engage recruits from the people who were flocking in from different parts of the frontier to avoid serving in the rebel militia.[56]

Moving his expedition down the Susquehanna on rafts Colonel Butler invaded the Wyoming valley on July 2. The "Massacre of Wyoming" became what is probably the war's most celebrated tale of horror and elaboration. One popular and much repeated fantasy is that found in *The Remembrancer*'s account of the raid as told by refugees:

<blockquote>
Partial Terry,* the son of a man who bore a very respectable character, had several times sent his father word, that he hoped to wash his hands in his heart's blood. Agreeable to such a horrid
</blockquote>

---

* Partial Terry, born in Connecticut, migrated to Wyoming with his family of which he was the only Loyalist member. He was commissioned lieutenant in Butler's Rangers, and later became a magistrate. In 1792–96 he represented the fourth Riding of Lincoln and Norfolk in the first Parliament of Upper Canada. He lived on Lake Erie near the mouth of Black Creek some seven miles west of Fort Erie until about 1793 when he removed to York to build the first sawmill on the Don River. He accidentally drowned in 1809 while fording the Don on horseback at night. (John Ross Robertson, *Landmarks of Toronto* (Toronto, 1898), vol. III, pp. 297–98; R. Janet Powell, *Annals of the Forty*, no. 5 (Grimsby Historical Society, 1954), p. 25.)

declaration, the monster, with his own hand murdered his father, mother, brother, and sisters, stripped off their scalps, and cut off his father's head. . . . (Among the strange articles of expense for the employment of the Indians, as laid before the House of Commons, is a charge of one hundred and fifty thousand pounds, for tomahawks, scalping-knives, *razors* and *spurs*, for the Indians. It is extraordinary: razors, and spurs, for Indians! who have neither beards nor horses! it was, no doubt, a *job*.) [57]

The most savage barbarity was attributed to "the Monster Brant" whereas the agreement reached at Tioga, the testimony of Philip Rockell Frey, a ranger who was present,[58] and above all Colonel Guy Johnson's report to his superior, Lord Germain, prove that Brant was certainly not there. Johnson wrote: "One division . . . proceeded with great success down the Susquehanna, destroying the Post & settlements at Wioming, augmenting their number with many Loyalists, and alarming all the Country, whilst another Division under Mr. Brandt, the Indian Chief, cut off 294 Men near Schoharie and destroyed the adjacent settlements. . . ."[59] Moreover, the *New-York Gazette and the weekly mercury* for August 24, 1778, stated that "Joseph, the Indian Chief, sent by Col. Johnson through the back Country . . . in May advanced against the Troops &c placed at the rich settlement of Schoary and Cobus Kill. . . ."

Brant and his men, among whom numbered at least four of our Scots, had ascended the Susquehanna and reached the Charlotte River early in June. From there parties went out to destroy the smaller settlements, and panic stricken inhabitants on Bowman's Creek and also at Springfield and around Otsego Lake fled to Cherry Valley. In his appeal for help Colonel Samuel Campbell stated that within a circumference of three-quarters of a mile there were between six and seven hundred cattle feeding which must inevitably fall into the hands of the enemy. On June 18 "Houses, Barns, even Waggons, ploughs and the Hay Cocks in the Meadows were laid in Ashes," Colonel Klock reported to Governor Clinton. "All the provision taken and Horses and carried off. Two hundred Creatures (Horses and Chiefly Cattle) were drove down the Susquehanna, last Sunday morning the Enemy set off with this Booty from the House of Tunnicliff. All this had been done [while] the garrison at Cherry Valley did not know the whereabouts of the Enemy, tho' Springfield is not above four miles Distant from said place. Several People, who have been prisoners and did Escape, affirm, that Brandt was the Commander . . . and his number increaseth daily."[60]

Information given by these and other escaped prisoners resulted in the arrest of the Tunnicliffs and the loss to Brant of what the enemy claimed was his headquarters on the northern frontier. Upon learning that Brant had visited the Tunnicliffs both before and after the raid on Springfield General Stark* ordered Captain W. H. Ballard of the garrison at Cherry Valley to investigate, and if Tunnicliff and others in the district "will not come within the Lines and Swallow oaths of Allegiance with a good Stomach, you must take the Trouble to Bring them in. . . ."[61] To these instructions Colonel Ichabod Alden added, "You will Indeavour to make Decoveries and Git all the Intelligence Possable of Brant & his Party."[62] Accordingly Captain Ballard marched his militiamen to Tunnicliff's home situated deep in the hills near the foot of Canadarago Lake on the trail leading from the Mohawk to the Susquehanna. They arrested John Tunnicliff and his son William, then proceeded to gather damning evidence against them. Sheep, cattle, and horses had been collected and left near the trail to be driven off at any time by the enemy; John had been overheard bargaining with Brant for oxen, five hundred weight of cheese, and so forth; he had

---

* John Stark, son of a Scot who had migrated in 1720 from Glasgow to New Hampshire and lieutenant in Rogers' Rangers during the Seven Years' War.

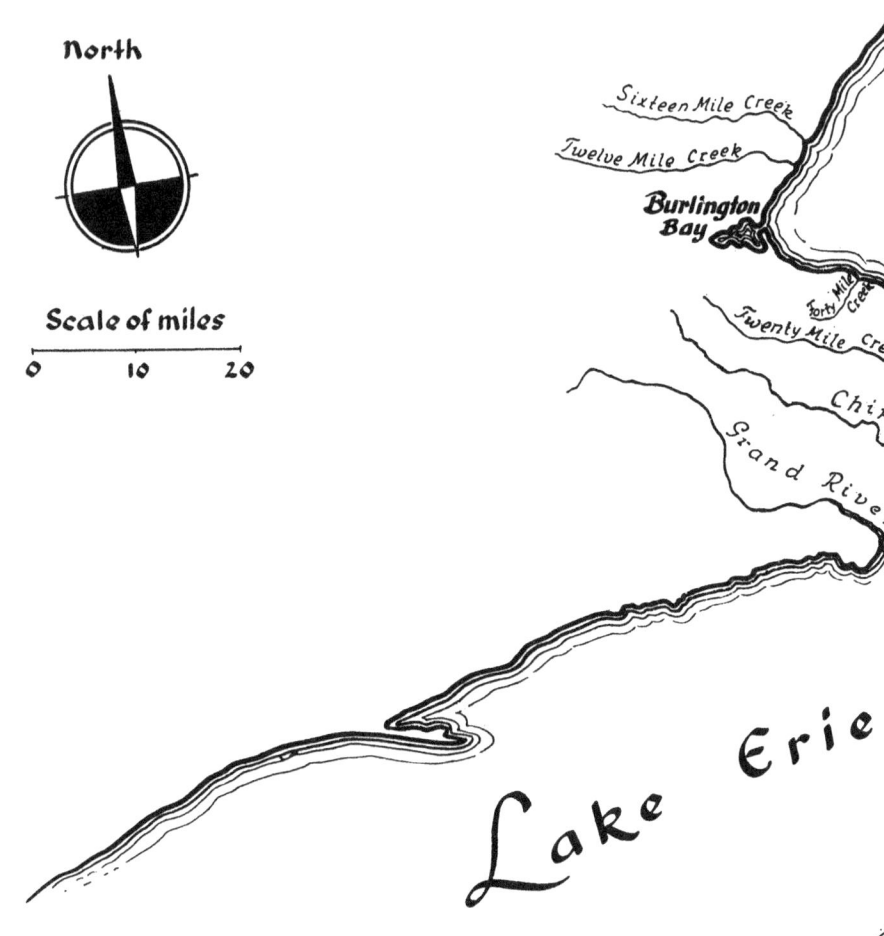

Lake Ontar

Fort Niagara
Lower Landing
Twelve Mile Creek
Niagara River
Great Falls
Fort Schlosser
Tonewanta Creek
Upper Landing
Canawaugus
Territ
Fort Erie
Buffaloe Creek
Chenussio
Conesus Lake
Canandaigua
of
Genesee River
Canaseraga
Six
Na
Canisteo
Ind
Allegheny River

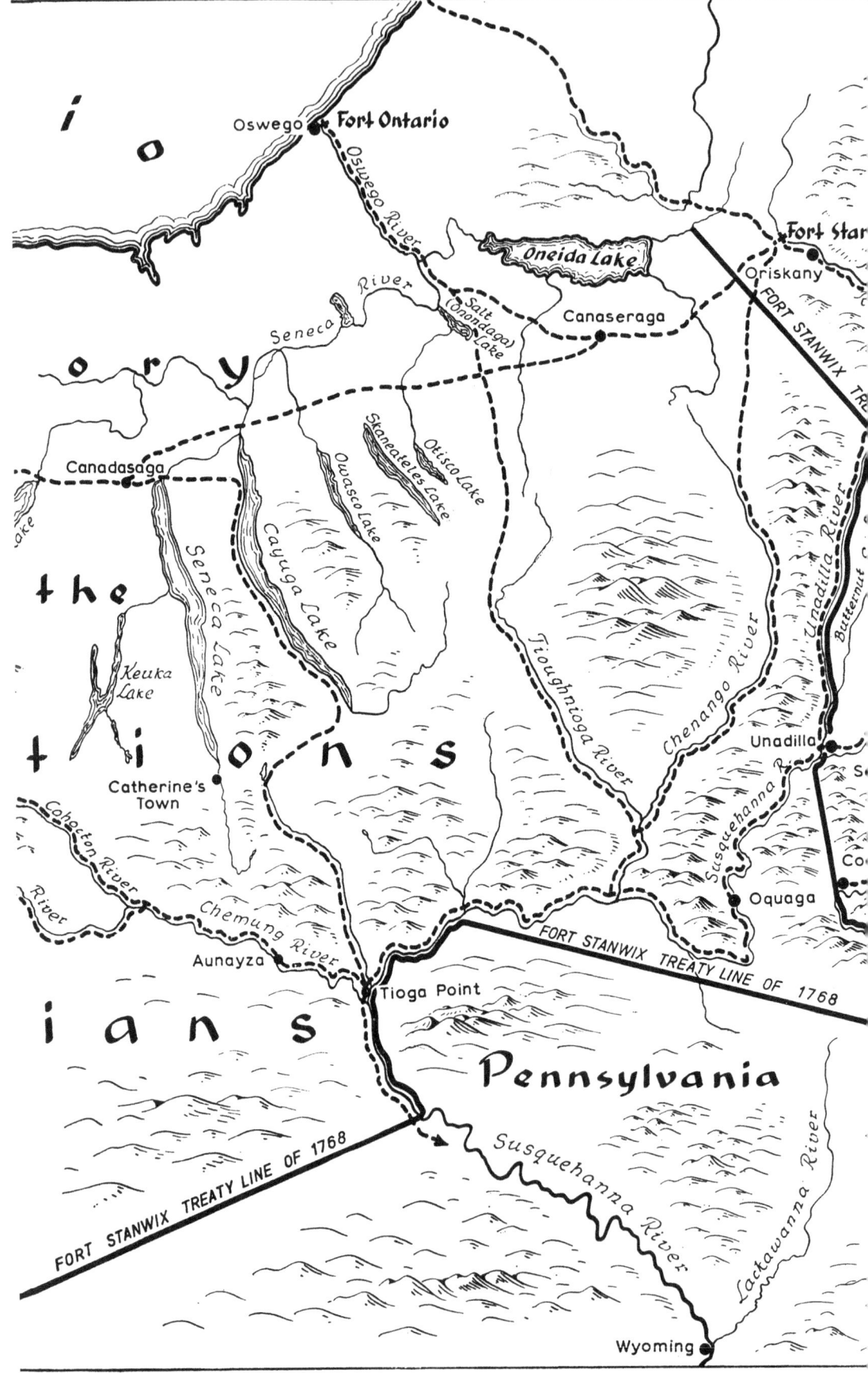

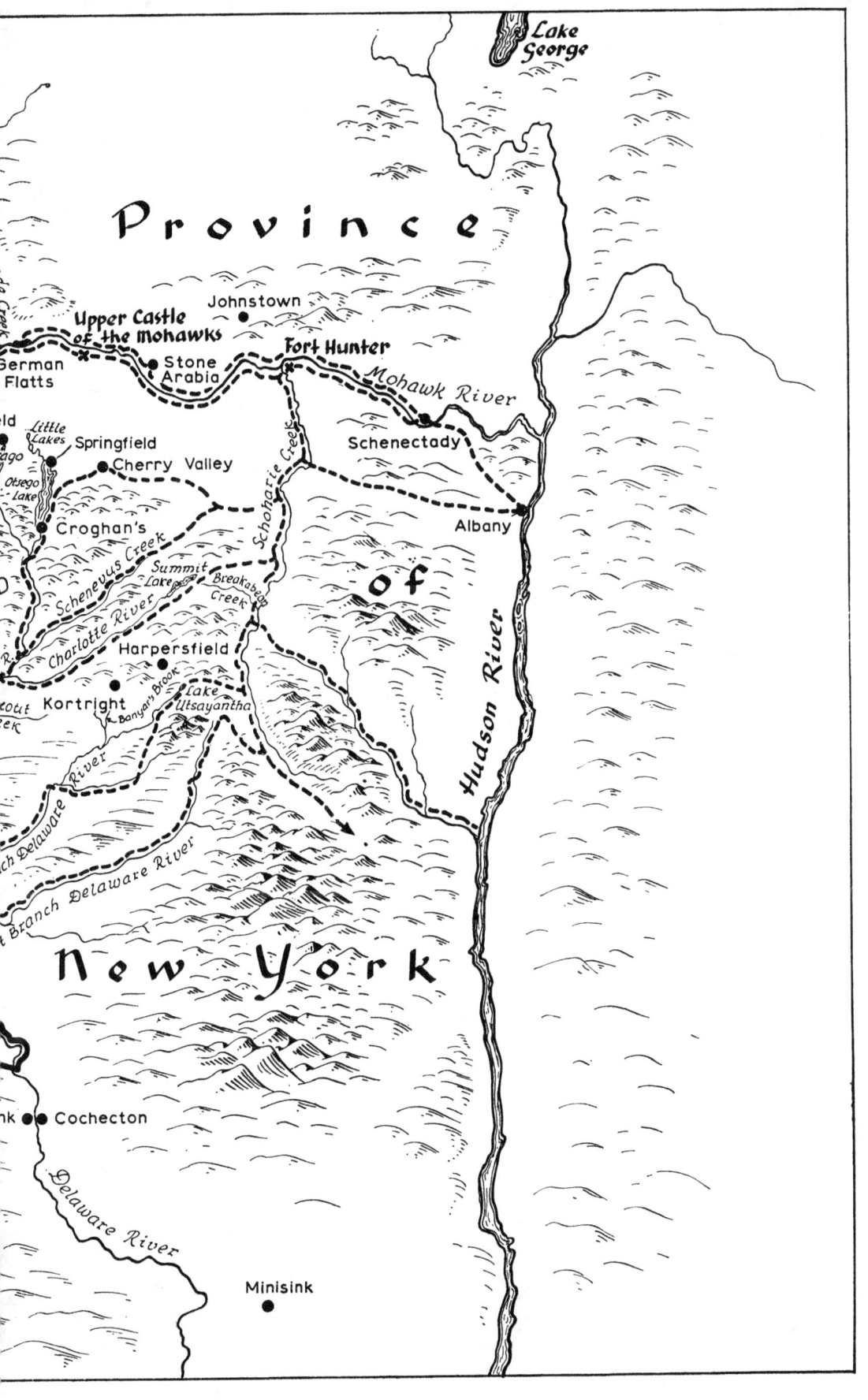

"supplied all Brant's Party with Provision Freely"; William had worn "the Same Token on his Hat that Brant's men wore, which was a Peaice of yellow Lace." [63] Ballard then proceeded some fifteen miles westward to the settlement named the Butternuts on a tributary of the Unadilla River. Here he and his men came upon fifteen more Tories, two of them Brant's men ("Clothed and painted like Indians"), engaged in collecting farm stock to be driven to Unadilla, but they had missed Brant who had left only a few days before. With seventeen prisoners, about one hundred head of cattle, forty sheep, and numerous horses Captain Ballard returned to Cherry Valley. On the instructions of General Stark to "Divide the Plunder as ... will do most Justice to the Party" the animals were taken away by his men instead of being turned over to the Commission of Forfeiture and Sequestration. After inquiring into the affair the Commissioners for Conspiracies deplored "the Spirit of plundering" so manifest among the Continental troops, particularly the regiment from Massachusetts stationed at Cherry Valley. "We cannot learn," they wrote to Governor Clinton, "that the People from whom the Cattle were taken have acted such a Part as to forfeit their Property. ... We have had Persons sent down by them under pretence of being guilty of Treason, but suspect in fact that the motive proceeded only from having a better Opportunity to appropriate their Effects...." [64] But the rumour that the Tunnicliffs and others taken at the same time were about to be released "and sent back to their Plantations again" reached Colonel Alden at Cherry Valley. "If you Please," wrote this intrepid New Englander to General Stark, "you may inform the Commite that if they send them Back, I will again take them Prisoners." [65] Whereupon the commissioners at Albany ordered the Tunnicliffs and others to be kept in close confinement.[66]

No sooner had Captain Ballard returned to Cherry Valley than Brant and Captain Gilbert Tice with some 300 Rangers and about 150 Indians attacked German Flatts in the Mohawk Valley. It was rumoured that Brant's party was expected at Tunnicliff's home, so again the Continental militia set out for it, arriving at noonday on August 21. They found that Indians had been there in the morning and that the women of the family had a "sumptuous meal prepared for the enemy." After making "good use of the victuals" the militiamen scouted the area, but found no signs of the enemy.[67] Similarly in September, Adam Chrysler's party of rangers and Indians on a flying visit from Oquaga eluded the Continental forces at the Tunnicliffs'.[68] However, the Tunnicliff family were soon obliged to abandon their home, although because it escaped confiscation they were able to return to it after the war.[69] The corner of a wall still standing (close to highway no. 51 a short distance west of Schuyler Lake) shows it was constructed of limestone and fieldstone with a frame of heavy squared oak timbers. An arched vault of superb stonework is still intact and has all the appearance of being quite as sound as when built in 1765.

Another supplier of provisions was John Burch, who, though his farm was located deep in the wilds of the Kaatskills, had little chance of escaping the notice of eagle-eyed Patriots. Burch was an Englishman who had migrated in 1772, and setting up at York as tinsmith and japaner had become a substantial tradesman. When pressed to sign an association in 1775 he had "retired to Albany to avoid it." [70] By then he had acquired from Colonel Johannes Hardenburgh, for more than £2,500, 6,710 acres of Great Lot 37 of the Hardenburgh Patent situated at Papacunck, an old Indian settlement on the East Branch of the Delaware. At Albany he added dry goods to his business of tinsmith and was preparing to build a grist and sawmill at Woodstock for which the iron work had been forged. Burch kept considerable livestock and a number of fine thoroughbred English horses on his estate at Papacunck which he placed in the hands of Thomas Cummings as overseer. To the house, barn, and other outbuildings that he had bought with the land, Burch, who was unmarried, added a dwelling house for himself. In the spring of 1778 he sent a message to Colonel Butler that he would supply him with cattle and men, though he himself was disqualified for active service by some physical disability. Butler sent a lieutenant of the Rangers and two Indian chiefs to accompany Burch, Cummings, and forty neighbours that Burch had induced to join Butler at Unadilla. They drove with them 136 head of cattle for the use of Butler's Rangers.[71]

Upon returning to Albany from Unadilla Burch learned that during his absence twelve prominent Loyalists of Albany who had refused to take the oath of allegiance had been ordered to remove within the British lines or, to use the Continental phrase, had been "sentenced to be banished." Among them was Burch's friend Richard Cartwright Sr. His inn had been plundered on two occasions, and on the last, the King's birthday, he had been beaten. The Commissioners for Conspiracies had ordered him and the other eleven Loyalists to appear before the city hall with fourteen days' provisions for themselves and such of their families as they wished to take with them, persons capable of bearing arms excepted. They were permitted to take "all their Cloathing and Household Furniture. The Charges of Transportation to the Enemies is to be defrayed by themselves." [72] The Cartwrights, except for Richard Jr. who had already slipped away to Canada,[73] were conveyed under guard to Crown Point on Lake Champlain. Rather than suffer the same fate at the hands of Patriots of Albany, John Burch quietly retired to the mountain fastness of Papacunck. He commissioned his servant, Janet Clement, a niece of Thomas Cummings, to "fetch off his most valuable property" from Albany. Aided by Hugh Alexander of Kortright Janet loaded the goods on three pack horses and started out for Papacunck. At Schoharie she and Hugh Alexander were seized and taken to gaol, and the horses, goods, and money were confiscated by the rebels.[74]

When John Burch's services to Butler became known he was visited at Papacunck by a large party of rebels who surrounded and plundered his house, burnt his buildings, destroyed the harvest from fifty acres of land, and drove off his thoroughbreds, eight working mares, forty hogs, and a flock of forty sheep. They carried away ploughs, harrows, waggons, a curricle, a pleasure sleigh, and all his farming utensils. Burch was attacked three times in like manner. Upon the last occasion he got through a window and with Thomas Cummings Jr. escaped into the woods. Thomas Sr. was caught, taken to gaol, and though "tried for his Life and Condemned for having assisted in supplying Butler with Cattle" was later released. What stock in trade remained in Burch's store was seized and sold at vendue; Thomas McMicking was present on that occasion probably as a guard of the Commission of Forfeiture.[75] Burch also lost considerable goods stored in towns along the Hudson, but the irons prepared for his grist mill were so well concealed as never to have been found.[76] Burch and young Cummings got into the Indian country and eventually to Niagara, where Burch, unfit for active service, was placed in charge of the Indian stores and was later appointed sutler of the Rangers.[77]

Christopher Servos, the Macdonells' neighbour on the Charlotte River, paid with his life for aiding Brant and his scouts. In June 1778 at the time of the raids in the area of Otsego Lake, he was denounced by a Continental scout who claimed that Brant had visited Servos "and sworn him & John Doxtader, to be true to George the

Third."[78] Because Servos was regarded as "a Noted Villain who has constantly supplied the enemy with necessaries" a Continental army rifle corps under Captain Long set out from Schoharie to place him under arrest. When the cavalry surrounded his house Servos was alone with his wife Clara, his three-year-old granddaughter Magdalene, and his servants. Daniel, the eldest son and father of Magdalene, lay imprisoned in Johnstown Gaol,[79] John was being held in Albany Gaol, and two other sons were absent. When informed that he must accompany the militia to Schoharie Christopher flourished an axe and was immediately shot down. Family and friends claimed that he had caught up the axe in self-defence but the rebels called it resisting arrest.*[80] "Because of the helpless situation of his widowed mother" John Servos secured his release some weeks later,[81] and when Daniel also regained his freedom the brothers went to Niagara to enlist in the Indian Department of the Rangers.[82]

When the bits of evidence which make up the story of Christopher Servos are pieced together it becomes apparent that he was more deeply involved than even the rebels suspected. He had assembled a party of Loyalists [83] and at the time he was killed was awaiting the arrival of Captain Charles Smith. The latter had been recruiting along the Delaware, the success of which endeavours are evidenced by the numerous denunciations that had been pouring into the Continental authorities since early spring. Francis Ellsworth of Shehawken was accused of selling provisions to the Indians, of taking "Orders on the King's quarter-master for pay," of having joined a group from Papacunck who had been so frequently among the Indians that "they seem to be of one mind and agree very well," and finally of having "gone with the Indians."[84] Robert Land, justice of the peace at Cochecton, had been absent since the middle of February "taking an express to York"; he and other King's men at Cochecton had asserted that in the event of a raid they, as known Loyalists, "would not be hurt."[85]

Smith was also attempting to persuade settlers to remain neutral. Some of the enthusiasm of his approach is apparent in the declaration submitted as proof of his activities in the area east of the Delaware:

Coshakton May 27th 1778

Gentlemen offesers and Cummanders at the Meaneasinks:
These Cumes to Inform you That the Volanteers and Indens Doth Not Intend to hurt aney of the frunteers if tha keep thare Selves Still, and Mynds thare Buysness, and Don't Hurt the frinds of government; for we are Informed that the Inhabatance is Moving a way for feer of Us, and I am Cum Down My Self to this place to Dezier the Inhabatance that tha Need Not be a frade of aney Hurt, if thay Stay at Home, But By thare Moving and Caring of fauls News, In Rages the pashon of the Indens, But thare is one thing that I Dezier of you as a frind, that is to Move your gards Back, for that In Rages the Indens, and Will Be the ocasion of the Indens fauling on that place and Distring all Before them; and if you Do that, the Inhabatence May Live in Safety; and if Not they Must Take What follows. I am one of the British offesers that am Sent to Look into these Maters, and a frend to all Human Nater, But your proceedince is Working your own Ruen, Which you Will find Before Long if you Dont Take My Councel; and for Robing and plundering of the Whigs it is Beneeth the Sparit of a British Offeser or Solder, altho you Have Made it your Busyness to Rob and plunder frinds of Government yet the Davel has Not so Much Power Over us as yet, and I hope Neaver Shall; But We Mean that Law Shall Take place in a Short Time and Make the gilty Siffer a Cording to thare Desarts; and I beag that you Wold

---

* Christopher Servos was shot down by Tim Murphy, "and the circumstances, as related by Simms," wrote Monroe, "strongly suggest murder on the part of Murphy, who took time to repulse the pleadings of Mrs. Servos with a ribald jest" (John D. Monroe, *Chapters in the History of Delaware County, New York* (Delaware County Historical Association, 1949), p. 70). It is indeed singular to find Timothy Murphy living after the war at South Worcester on land that formerly belonged to Christopher Servos.

Not Troubel the frinds of Government as Long as tha Lay Still; this is the advice of a frind; for feer of Wors following So No More from yours; But I am your Humble Sarvent

CHARLES SMITH, Capt.[86]

From the beginning until the end of the war messages of the same purport continued to be sent through the settlements by the British.

Having worked through the settlements to the Hudson, Smith was returning to the Rangers' headquarters at Unadilla with a company of recruits when he fell in with Archibald Thomson who was also on his way back after having fulfilled some mission. To him Smith entrusted the reports that he had made to Captain Walter N. Butler, Colonel Butler's son, and to Captain Brant, the whereabouts of the latter not having been determined. He had written to Walter Butler from Harpersfield on July 27 that the "Harvest being at Hand" settlers refused to leave until their grain was taken care of, but thereafter he expected many to join him; that he had urged Loyalists to show themselves so that they might not suffer with the rebels. He continues:

> I was Cuming to see you but met Archibald Thompson and Returned Back to bring out my men & Join as Soon as Possible . . . they Expect you at Schoharie, and make all the Preparations thay Can, but the Cuntry is in Great Confusion, and but Few Men to be had for tha are Struck with Tarror. . . . I shall see you Soon & hope I Shall march in Frunt of my men Panted and Some of My men Panted to give notice to my Brethren. Sir, I am Y'r H Ser't,
>
> CHARLES SMITH [87]

To Brant Smith wrote that he was coming for orders when he met Thomson and "have sent you a Little Tobacco by the Bearer." He then asked Brant that a letter be "left at Mr. Survises with Orders what to do."[88] Thomson travelled for a time with Smith's party which, unaware of the fate of Christopher Servos, was heading for his home to spend the night. Captain Long meanwhile had no sooner returned to Schoharie than he and his rifle company were ordered out to apprehend Smith who was reported as having "raised a Number of Tories and was Marching to Join the Enemy." The two companies met near Schoharie Creek "when Capt Long of the Riffle [sic] men [runs the report] fired at and shot Smith through the head. General Stark received his scalp last night. One prisoner was taken; the rest of the party of twenty four in number, escaped, owing to Schoharie Creek being between them and our men." The prisoner, who carried damaging letters, was identified as Archibald Thomson, and the death of "a Certain Service, a noted and Zealous defender of his King's bad Cause" was reported.[89]

Confined in Albany Gaol, Thomson was soon overtaken by illness. On August 22, the same day that John Tunnicliff and his son William were brought up for examination, the Commissioners for Conspiracies ordered that "Archibald Thompson . . . Janet Clement [and others] be removed to the Hospital on account of their being sick and that General Stark be requested to order a Centry to be placed at the Door of the Room in which they are to be put."[90] Despite these precautions Thomson presumably succeeded in escaping; neither was he brought to trial nor does his name again appear on the record.

Throughout the summer raiding parties under Brant and Colonel Butler had continued to lay waste the settlements. In September Brant with "a number of Indians and Friends of Government" penetrated the Kaatskills to within a few miles of the Hudson River. They burnt the wealthy settlement of Marbletown remarked for its "forardness in Rebellion," carrying off large numbers of men and cattle to Oquaga.[91] Thereupon the Continentals determined to raid Oquaga and Colonel John Butler's headquarters at nearby Unadilla. A force under the command of the Continental officer, Colonel William Butler, set forth from Schoharie, for two days descended the Delaware, then crossed over the hills to the Susquehanna where on October 7 he made "prisoner one Glasford" to guide him to Oquaga. They arrived to find the old Indian town deserted. "It was the finest Indian Town I ever saw [William Butler wrote in his journal], on both sides of the River; there was about 40 good houses, Square logs, Shingles & Stone Chimneys, good floors, glass windows, & &. On taking Possession of the Town I order'd a large number of fires to be made, in order to make my little Party loom as large as Possible; lay on our Arms and at daybreak, had my Bugle Horn blown when all got under Arms." They destroyed the town, farm produce, cattle, dogs, and poultry of the Indians. Upon returning they razed Unadilla, also a settlement on both banks of the river, including the only grist and sawmills on the Susquehanna. During these operations William Butler and his men had fared sumptuously but they were evidently short-sighted in preparing for the return march up the Delaware. Butler wrote that all he could furnish to each man was an ear of corn per day "which they parched." [92]

The Continentals' destruction of Oquaga sealed the fate of the settlers at Cherry Valley who for some time had been collecting grain and cattle under the protection of the Massachusetts regiment which manned the picketed fort. Captain Walter Butler, gathered at Canadasaga in the Seneca country his forces of rangers and Indians including Brant and his men. "Captain Butler's little army of Rangers & Indians amount to 800," reported Colonel Bolton from Niagara to General Haldimand, "& from his last letter intends to attack Cherry Valley where the enemy have a number of cattle & a large quantity of corn. Joseph I have not heard from for a considerable time. . . ." [93] They arrived at Cherry Valley in a heavy snowstorm which turned into a steady downpour of rain, and spent the night in hiding among the pine trees without tents, blankets or fires. The Continentals, having disregarded repeated warnings of an impending attack, were taken by surprise on November 11 and their commander, Colonel Ichabod Alden, was killed. While Butler and the main body of rangers engaged the fort, still in the chilling rain, the Indians defied their officers and dispersed through the settlement, killing, plundering, and burning. "I have much to lament," wrote Walter Butler to the commandant of Fort Niagara, "that notwithstanding my utmost precautions and endeavours to save the Women & Children, I could not prevent some of them falling unhappy Victims to the Fury of the Savages." [94] Brant and at least three of his Mohawk officers, Captains William Johnson, Jacob (Lewis), and Aaron (Hill), acted with humanity. "Little Aaron" protected the elderly Reverend Samuel Dunlop from injury though he was powerless to prevent the massacre of his wife and daughter. John Moore and Samuel Campbell were absent on militia duty, and their families were taken captives by the Indians along with James Ramsey and his two sons and daughters, William McClellan and his two children, and "Rev. Mr. Dunlop's negro wench." [95] Butler did what he could to rescue prisoners from the Indians, and those already in his hands he protected by placing them next to camp fires and surrounding them with the whole body of rangers.

The next morning destruction of the settlement was complete; "the Garrison all the while cooped within their Breastworks remained Spectators of our depredations which they made no attempt to interrupt," Butler affirmed.[96] He sent most of the Indians and some rangers off with a huge drove of cattle and horses, most of which never reached Niagara because the Indians used them for food on the way.[97] "I could not prevail upon the Indians to leave the Women and Children behind," continues Butler, "tho' the second morning of our March, Captain Johnson (to whose knowledge and address in managing them I am much indebted), and I got them to permit twelve who were Loyalists and whom I had concealed the first day with the humane assistance of Mr. Joseph Brant and Captain Jacob of Ochquaga, to return." [98] Altogether thirty-one persons were killed, thirty-eight prisoners were permitted to return, and thirty-three were carried away, among them the Campbells, Moores, Ramseys, and McClellans, and the Negro wench.[99] Travelling westward by the Susquehanna-Chemung route the prisoners were taken to Canadasaga, the Old Castle of the Senecas near the outlet of Seneca Lake. Mrs. Samuel Campbell and her four small children became separated, as did Mrs. John Moore and her grown-up daughters, because they were adopted into different families scattered throughout the Indian country. The system of adoption by which the losses of incessant wars were offset had been long practised by the Iroquois. When, by burning or butchering, the Indians had killed enough captives to sate their wrath the remainder of the captives were adopted into various families, and thus became incorporated into the nation. For nearly a century a goodly number of the population of the Six Nations had consisted of adopted prisoners of war.[100]

Among Patriot settlers and state officials there was considerable commiseration for the prisoners of war. On December 2 William Harper wrote as follows to General James Clinton:

> Sir, Mrs. Moore is my sister and Duty and nattier finds me to binds me to intret hur exchange and hur three daghters, whoo are all women grone, for whom my hart trembles. . . .
> Likewise Coln. Campble's wife and hur for small childring.
> I was informed . . . that Butler sade he would keep Mrs. Campble & Mrs. Moore & thare Childring till Mrs. Butler . . . and his other frinds are exchanged for them.[101]

Negotiations were initiated to effect the repatriation of these prisoners of war but it took reams of paper and several years before success was achieved. In the case of the Ramseys and McClellans Patriot sympathy was somewhat misplaced. James Ramsey, a native American, and William McClellan, an Irishman, had so successfully hidden their Loyalist sympathies as to be listed for some time as eligible for exchange. In point of fact they had "continued quiet" and awaited the coming of rangers and Indians as a means of escape. Seemingly Ramsey had been warned as "he had removed most of his things before ye House was burnt," [102] and Indians had destroyed McClellan's home "because the Americans should not find out who were Loyalists." [103]

More has been written about Wyoming and Cherry Valley than about any frontier raids which occurred during the war, and in both instances charges of wanton cruelty were laid and continue to be laid against Walter Butler and Joseph Brant. Wyoming need not concern us here because Brant and the four Scots who were serving with him, Archibald Thomson, James Park, Daniel Rose, and John Chisholm, were not involved, but they did take part in the raid on Cherry Valley. Various and singular explanations have been advanced in accounting for the fury of the Indians on that November day, but so far as this writer is aware the most obvious seems to have been passed over, though in that well-used source, the *Public Papers of George Clinton*, it is there for all to see. In a statement under date of December 13, 1778, four Iroquois chiefs among whom was Captain William Johnson, dispose of the matter in the simplest of terms: "Your Rabble came to Oughquago when we Indians were gone from our place, and you burned our Houses, which makes us and our Brothers the

Seneca Indians angrey, so that we Destroyed men, women and Children at Chervalle." [104]

The destruction of Cherry Valley, the seventh valuable settlement to be laid waste during the season, brought the campaign of 1778 to a close. The Indians of the Six Nations dispersed to their villages and Butler's Rangers went into winter quarters at Niagara, but from their own statements it is certain that our four Scots were not among them. It may be that they returned to the hills of Kortright, and, finding themselves "under sentence of Death for joining the Indians." [105] they eluded capture during the winter.

By now most settlers at the Head of the Delaware sympathetic to the rebel cause, such as Alexander Leal and Daniel McGillivrae, had taken refuge near the forts at Schoharie. When obliged to leave his cattle Leal had cut a large opening in the end of his log barn where the hay was stored, and having access to the fodder the beasts wintered safely.[106] And there were others along this frontier who made similar preparations for withstanding further attacks by the British.

CHAPTER FIVE

THE KING'S MEN: WITH HATCHET, KNIFE, AND GUN
(PART II)

THE LOYALIST CORPS, wrote Patrick Campbell, were the
smartest, liveliest, and most useful troops in the British service. Their sufferings were very great: they were often obliged to eat Horses, Dogs, and Cats, and yet were never heard to complain, if they could distress their enemies. They and the Indians went hand in hand; the former led on by a son of Colonel Butler, a gallant young officer . . . and the latter by the intrepid Captain Brant.
This chosen corps,—this band of brothers, was rarely known to be worsted in any skirmish or action, though often obliged to retire, and betake themselves to the wilderness, when superior force came against them . . . their advances and retreats were equally sudden and astonishing; and to this day the Americans say, they might as easily have found out a parcel of Wolves in the woods, as them if they once entered it. That the first notice of their approach, was them in sight; and of their retreat, their being out of reach. These two bodies were chiefly made up of Indians and Scotch Highlanders, who adhered closely to their country's cause. . . . I have known many of them, both officers and soldiers; and the account they gave of the fatigue and sufferings they underwent, is hardly credible, were it not confirmed by one and all of them.[1]

Campbell heard Loyalists relate their experiences during his travels in North America after the war, but it was not until after he had listened to those who had served with the Continentals in the Mohawk Valley that the above paragraphs were written. Because he was a Highlander from Fort William, Inverness-shire, and spent considerable time in the community where our Scots who fought under Brant were then living it is almost a foregone conclusion that Campbell had known them.

As their stories unfolded it would have become apparent that like earlier white men who had fought side by side with the Indians these men were trained in their own discipline. Armed with hatchet, knife, and gun they were partly hunters and partly woodsmen. Only by adapting themselves to the way of life and to the woodland warfare of the Indians, what Parkman called "their mysterious warfare of ambush and surprise."[2] could they survive long periods in the wilderness. "The Indian differs widely from the European in his notion of military virtue," wrote Francis Parkman who had lived among them and knew whereof he spoke. "In his [the Indian's] view, artifice is wisdom; and he honors the skill that can circumvent, no less than the valor that can subdue, an adversary. The object of war, he argues, is to destroy the enemy. To accomplish this end, all means are honorable; and it is folly, not bravery, to incur a needless risk."[3] The Scots were fortunate in having as their commanding officer an Indian of remarkable intelligence whose primitive inheritance was tempered by schooling in the English tradition. As war leader elected by his people Brant exerted his influence to control them and thus minimize atrocities.

Rangers attached to the Indian Department learned to travel light and to cover great distances. They threaded the pathways of the woods in single file, journeying through snow-encumbered forests on snow-shoes the Indians had taught them to fashion. In summer they took to the waterways, sometimes going downstream with raft and setting-pole. At day's end they bivouacked in the manner described a hundred years before by the Jesuit Father Galinee:

> Your lodging is as extraordinary as your vessels; for, after paddling or carrying the canoes all day, you find mother earth ready to receive your weary body. If the weather is fair, you make a fire and lie down to sleep without farther trouble; but, if it rains, you must peel bark from the trees, and make a shed by laying it on a frame of sticks. As for your food, it is enough to make you burn all the cookery books ever written; for in the woods of Canada one finds means to live well without bread, wine, salt, pepper, or spices. The ordinary food is Indian corn . . . which is crushed between two stones and boiled, seasoning it with meat or fish, when you can get them.[4]

In winter in time of war warmer shelters were constructed. Using their snow-shoes men scooped the ground bare, banking the snow as a protection against the wind. Small branches of spruce, fir, and hemlock served as beds and as the covering of the shelter constructed under the lee of the pile of snow. The beds being below the level of the snow and the slanting roof retaining the heat of the fire, only a single blanket sufficed for comfort. "I have been assur'd by gentlemen who have gone on winter scouts that these sheds or huts are warm even in the coldest time," wrote a British army officer. "The Indians are so expert at this kind of camping that in half an hour after they have stopt for the day everything is finished, and perhaps the pot—if they have any—is over the fire."[5]

In addition to hunger, fatigue, and the exigencies of weather the Rangers were beset by the pests and diseases so prevalent in the swamps and bogs of uncleared country. "Muscetoes" of incredible size and voracity rose in clouds, and malaria, called swamp fever and ague, was endemic. Colonel Butler relates how one of his officers "was so ill with Ague that he was under the necessity of having himself tied to his Horse."[6] When ill Brant is said to have made rattlesnake soup "which operated as a cure to the attack of the ague."[7] These venomous snakes, regularly used for food by the Indians, infested the Indian country in great numbers, and Brant killed them by running a sharp stick through the head.[8] Wild Solomon's seal and broad leaf plantain were considered effective antidotes to their bite.

Brant led his followers along the main routes through the mountains and hills of the Indian country. From Tioga Point they could travel by water throughout the length of the northern frontier with only the fifteen-mile portage between Oquaga on the Susquehanna and Cookoze on the Delaware. When pressed for time they frequently built rafts of old logs held together by poles laid crosswise and tied with withes. After floating downstream upon them, they abandoned the rafts at the portages. From Tioga Point the main route to the northwest lay up the valley of the Chemung and its tributary the Cohocton. Then began a long march over the mountains to the Genesee. Again taking to the water the men descended to the Seneca castle of Chenussio situated on the Genesee plains. At Chenussio (a phonetic rendition of the Indians' pronunciation of Genesee) there were at this time 128 framed houses which General Sullivan of the Continental army found "mostly very large and elegant." "The town was beautifully situated," continues Sullivan, "almost encircled with a clear flatt which extends for a number of miles, where the most extensive fields of corn were, and every kind of vegetable that can be conceived."[9] Upon leaving Chenussio travellers followed the windings of the Genesee down to Canawaugus where they left their craft to begin the long trek overland to Niagara in the west. The way eastward traversed the Cayuga country, skirting the northern tips of Seneca and Cayuga lakes to pass through the lands of the Onondagas, Tuscaroras, and Oneidas to reach the head of the Mohawk Valley. That the Indians chose well when laying their trails is evidenced by their adoption by white men and continuance as the main highways of today.

There were times when Captain Brant disappeared into the wilderness for long periods of time. As the chosen leader of a free and independent people who fought on their own terms as allies of the British he was allowed greater freedom of action than other officers of the same rank. His long absences tended to shake the confidence of some British officers who were inclined in general to distrust the Indians. Certainly, the loyalty of the Indians to the Crown was almost entirely dependent upon the leadership of their war chief, Thayendanagea. He was described as follows by a Continental officer from the Mohawk Valley who met him while in the guard house at Niagara :

> He was a likely fellow, of fierce aspect—tall and rather spare—well spoken, and apparently about thirty years of age. [Brant was thirty-eight.] He wore moccasins, elegantly trimmed with beads—leggings and breech-clout of superfine blue—short green coat, with two silver epaulets—and a small, laced, round hat. By his side hung an elegant silver-mounted cutlass, and his blanket of blue cloth, purposely dropped in the chair on which he sat to display his epaulets, was gorgeously decorated with a border of red.[10]

The last sentence in this quotation tends to confirm the report that Brant was even prouder of his commission in the British army than of the rank conferred upon him by his own people.

Unlike officers of the Rangers who kept journals of their expeditions Brant reported only the results of his engagements. Except when rebel informers or escaped prisoners identified acquaintances, the individual experiences and exploits of Brant's followers mostly remain unrecorded. In consequence the accounts of those of our Scots (Daniel Rose, Archibald Thomson, James Park, and John Chisholm) together with those of many hundreds of others have unfortunately passed into oblivion, but we know from their own statements that all four "volunteered the most dangerous Enterprises" and were "almost unremittingly on actual Service" throughout the war.[11] Although it is impossible to know who took part in the actions that follow it is certain that some if not all were with Brant in these major operations as well as in many minor actions of which no mention is made. In this record of fact there is no place for romancing and we must perforce be content with what data is extant.

Early in the spring of 1779 Captain Brant and his men appeared at Wyoming and "drove off all the Cattle and every Thing else without the Fort that was moveable."[12] By flag of truce he informed the inhabitants of Sussex County, New Jersey, that, "having been apprized that many of them who had last Year pretended Friendship and Attachment" to the cause for which he was fighting had since taken up arms, "he now gave them Notice, that no longer any regard to Professions of that kind would be attended to, for that every Man who did not join him upon his approach to their Country, should be deemed and treated by him as an Enemy...."[13]

In May 1779, enemy militia descended upon Kortright, apprehended Thomas McMicking, Hugh Rose, Alexander Carson, and Angus McIntosh, and imprisoned them in Albany Gaol. Upon appearing for examination before the Commissioners for Conspiracies on June 11 the prisoners were ordered committed to gaol.[14] On June 24 the commissioners, deciding that McMicking, Rose, and Carson had "always demeaned themselves in a peacable manner," ordered the three discharged from confinement and put under bond to appear on demand. Bail was set at £100.[15] A few days later McIntosh was also released under the same conditions.[16]

Although the enemy could secure no proof, McMicking was continuing to supply Brant with scouting parties. While he was awaiting trial at Albany a party led by the Mohawk chiefs, Captain Aaron ("Little Aaron") and Captain David, visited McMicking's "plantation" on the Delaware in search of provisions. They drove away six oxen, a bull and seven cows, four horses, and took from the house sixty-one pounds of butter, six quilts, six pairs of blankets to the value of £160 and £3.9.0 in cash, all York currency.[17]

Rumours were now circulating that the Continentals were planning a large-scale invasion of the Six Nations' country in retribution for the raid on Cherry Valley. To support the Indians and keep a sharp lookout towards the Susquehanna where enemy forces were assembling, Colonel John Butler with four hundred rangers marched to the Seneca castle of Canadasaga. He found the Indians starving, and by June when his own provisions became exhausted he was hard pressed for subsistence for his men.

A few items of news at this date are yielded by Richard Cartwright Jr. who since his flight from Albany had been acting as Colonel Butler's secretary. In this capacity he corresponded with Francis Goring, a clerk employed at Fort Niagara by Montreal merchants engaged in the fur trade. Goring salted his business correspondence with bits of news and gossip concerning happenings at the fort. In a letter dated July 1, after reporting that he had sent to Colonel Butler 110 pounds of tobacco at 8 shillings per pound he remarks that there is nothing of further interest to add "except the arrival of Aaron from Scoary with 18 prisoners, mostly Scotchmen, and thought to be friends of Government."[18] On the same day Cartwright wrote to Goring from Canadasaga: "The bearer of this, Samuel Lutes has several orders for cattle from him which Col. Butler desires you will pay in hard cash. . . . Give my compliments to Mr. Cunningham and Mr. Burch. I suppose Burch is quite disconsolate at the thought of parting with his widow.* Tell him, I say he will be well off if he keeps his intellect safe between her and the Lodge."[19] And some weeks later, "I am happy to hear Mr. Burch is so well employed, the Progress indeed from Brotherly Love to Sisterly Affection and from that to Matrimony is quite Natural and regular. I would however not have him delay the latter till my coming [to Niagara] as that is rather precarious and will not I fear be very soon."[20]

The reports of the proposed Continental invasion proved to be true. While the commander-in-chief, General John Sullivan, gathered his forces at Wyoming in the south, General James Clinton, brother of the Governor of New York, assembled a division in the north. The plan was that the two divisions would form a junction at Tioga Point and sweep northward to Niagara, destroying the villages of the Six Nations as they progressed. For transporting Clinton's army to Tioga batteaux were brought up the Mohawk to Canajoharie and thence portaged to Otsego Lake. Four horses were required to draw each batteau overland through the twenty miles of hilly country lying between the Mohawk and Springfield at the head of Otsego Lake. On July 6 General Clinton advised the Governor that he had transported "208 boats, with all the stores, provisions, and baggage of the army," and was in readiness to join General Sullivan. "I have thrown a dam across the outlet, which has raised the lake at least two feet."[21] The dam was situated close by the site of George Croghan's house which in all likelihood was still standing. Some two thousand men embarked in two hundred batteaux,[22] the dam was breached, and the "flotilla was . . . borne triumphantly along upon the pile of impatient waters accumulated for the

* John Burch married Martha Ramsey, widow of one of the Cherry Valley Ramseys.

occasion."²³ On this "majestic flood"²⁴ Clinton's division descended the Susquehanna, but it was not until August 22 that they joined Sullivan for their march up the valley of the Chemung.

During Clinton's operations two Ranger spies were captured and executed, although it was some time before even a rumour of the incident reached Niagara. Goring mentioned it in a business report to Robert Hamilton:

> Yesterday Capt. Peter Hare & Lt. Frey arrived here from Col. Butler but no news particularly, there is about 1000 men they report at Wyomen in order to protect the frontiers. Lt. Henry Hare, Sert. Newberry & some Rangers who went on a Scouting party to the Mohawk River. Of this the rebels got intelligence, surrounded his house, took him & tis said he was hanged at his own door, as it is only Indian news I hope it may prove false. Further news of this tragedy are not available, but it is certain that they were put to death in great haste.²⁵

Indeed, Hare and Newberry had been caught at Canajoharie where Clinton's men were portaging batteaux and stores from the Mohawk River to Otsego Lake. General Clinton wrote to his wife that he "had them both tried by general court-martial for spies, who sentenced them to be hanged, which was done accordingly at Canajoharie, to the satisfaction of all the inhabitants of that place that were friends to their country. . . . Each had a wife and several children * who came to see them and beg for their lives."²⁶

While Clinton and Sullivan gathered their forces during July and August Colonel Butler continued to use the small force of Rangers and Indians at his disposal in frontier raids calculated to weaken the enemy and at the same time to secure provisions for his men. Continental preparations at Wyoming were being pursued at so leisurely a pace that Captain Brant, weary of waiting for so tardy a foe, determined to raid the old settlement of Minisink on the border between New York and Pennsylvania. Among his company of sixty "Enjions" and twenty-eight white volunteers was John Chisholm,† according to the report of a deserter. The latter, in his deposition to a Continental officer, "Saith he left Shemong on ye 8th of July [with Brant's men] and he Heard Said Brand give Orders that they Should not Kill any women or Children, and if they Knew any persons to be a Torey not to Kill them, and any that would Deliver them Selves up to Take them prisoners, but any person Running from them to Kill them."²⁷ The raiding party descended the Chemung to Tioga Point, ascended the Susquehanna to Oquaga, crossed overland to the Delaware, and went downriver to Minisink where they arrived on July 19. In his report to Colonel Bolton, commandant of Fort Niagara, Brant stated that he had been disappointed not to have arrived until noon when all the cattle were in the woods; consequently they had got few of them. "We have burnt all the Settlement called Minisink," he continues, "one Fort excepted, round which we lay before about an Hour, & had one man killed and one wounded. We destroyed several small stockaded forts, and took four Scalps & three prisoners but did not in the least injure Women and Children. The Reason that we could not take more of them, is owing to the many Forts about the Place, into which they were always ready to run like Ground-Hogs. I left this Place about 8

---

* Henry Hare's widow was left with five children. She later married Adam Empey (Empie, Impie) of the King's Royal Regiment of New York, a native of Stone Arabia in the Mohawk Valley, and had four more children by 1788. (*18th Report Ontario Archives* (1928), p. 36.)

† Others mentioned are Hendrick (Hank) and John Huff, Lodovic Seeley from Papacunck on the West Branch of the Delaware, Rudolph Johnston, William Crum, Anthony Westbrook, Daniel Cole, Ebenezer Allan, John Barnhart, Nicholas Miller, Benoni Crum, and Joseph Cole. (P.A.C., Haldimand Transcripts, B. 105, p. 395A; Hugh Hastings, ed., *Public Papers of George Clinton, First Governor of New York 1777-1795* (8 vols., Albany, 1899-1904), V, p. 162.)

o'clock the next day, & marched 15 miles." Here rebels lying in ambush gave battle, but the Indians and volunteers succeeded in driving them out, a defeat readily admitted by the enemy. Brant reported: "We have taken 40 Scalps and one Prisoner, a Captain. I suppose the Enemy have lost near half their Men & most of their Officers —they all belonged to the Militia, and were about 150 in number. . . ."[28] The enemy claimed that out of 180 men only 30 had escaped the tomahawks of the Indians.[29] Thus ended the battle of Minisink.

Brant led his men back to the Susquehanna trail and struck north to the Mohawk, arriving on August 2 after a journey of twelve days. The following week, in a raid on a settlement at the Little Falls, Brant was wounded in the foot by swan shot, and his coat and breech clout showed holes where bullets and shot had passed through. So closely was the party pursued by rebel militia that they narrowly escaped capture, and lost their blankets and plunder in their flight.[30] The report flew through the country that Brant was "either killed or dangerously wounded."[31]

By August 15 Butler was preparing to move against the invading forces of General Sullivan, for Richard Cartwright wrote from Canadasaga to advise Goring at Niagara that "You need not send any of the Shirts at Present for as we are just going off to meet the Enemy the less we are encumbered with Baggage the better."[32] On September 1 Goring wrote to Robert Cruikshank, silversmith at Montreal, that "Col. Butler has gone down the Skemong to meet the rebels who are 12 miles from that at a place called Tioga, and certainly before this they must have come to action. The rebels have two strong forts on the point and are said to be in numbers between 6 & 7000."[33] And two weeks later, after reporting that about ninety men of the 32nd and Royal Emigrants had arrived from Carleton Island and left that morning to join Butler at Canawagorass, Goring continues: "just now arrived one of the Ramsays who left Col Butler Sunday last, who says the night before the rebels were at Aunayza, which is only a day's march from Conawagorass, where the Col. is, and that he was just setting out on his march (when he left) to meet the rebels."[34]

The King's men, both white men and Indians, took their stand at New Town, an Indian village of twenty houses situated on the Chemung below the confluence of the Canisteo and Cohocton with this river. Here was the southern gateway to the country of the Six Nations. The river sweeps round in a graceful curve, making a full semicircle, and enclosing several hundred acres of rich bottom lands upon which the Indians had their corn fields. Butler had marshalled all his forces but still they were outnumbered four to one, and illness was taking its toll. For some time they had "fed upon Herbs & roots which they found in the woods," and during the eight days they had awaited the enemy they ate "nothing but Corn . . . except a small proportion of five small Cattle."[35] In the face of such opposition Butler and Brant obstinately resolved to entrench themselves high above the river on a hill top commanding the bend in the river. Below, the wide valley and the Chemung winding around the hill could be seen for miles in both directions. Notwithstanding their weakened condition the men contrived to throw up more than half a mile of log breastworks and to hide them by sticking freshly cut trees into the ground. On the afternoon of August 29 the Continentals appeared, and in the battle that raged until dark, Brant and a Seneca chief flew from point to point to sustain their warriors by encouraging words and daring deeds. Rangers and Indians were driven from tree to tree until forced by overwhelming numbers to retreat, leaving behind their packs, blankets, and cooking pots.[36] "Finding that our numbers did not exceed 600 men we could not engage the enemy with a probability of success," Colonel Butler wrote from Shechquagao to Colonel Bolton. "Officers and men were without even a Blanket to cover them. . . . The consequences of this affair will, I fear, be of the most serious nature . . . at any rate those Families whose Villages & Corn have been destroyed will be flocking into Niagara to be supported, and you know the quantity of Provisions that they will consume."[37]

The victory of New Town Heights opened the way for Sullivan to sweep through the Indian country leaving desolation in his wake from the Susquehanna to the Genesee. Colonel Butler was heard to compare the advance to the driving of a wedge into a stick of wood; nothing stopped or disturbed its motion.[38] British reinforcements arrived too late to prevent complete devastation,[39] and Sullivan burnt 40 Indian towns and 160,000 bushels of corn (ears measuring 22 inches in length were noted), and cut down all the orchards, one of 1,500 trees. The general's amazement at the state of civilization attained by the Indians of the Six Nations is manifest in his report of the campaign to Congress.[40] Colonel Butler, who had retired to the Genesee River, hurried to the defence of Fort Niagara, but Sullivan, though within easy reach, turned back at Chenussio. Having delayed too long at the work of destruction he fell short of the major objective, Niagara, before the onset of winter.

The Indians of the Six Nations were now homeless in their own land. Deprived of food and shelter when winter was upon them they fled to Niagara where the British built huts for them around the fortress. Now more than ever this stronghold was a rallying place of Loyalists, both white and red. Throughout the summer settlers from the frontier had arrived in increasing numbers to seek safety for their families. Fort Niagara was quickly becoming an "island of congested humanity in an otherwise almost unpeopled wilderness."[41] It stood isolated except by water from the forts at Oswego 150 miles to the east and at Kingston even farther away at the foot of the lake. Its entrance gate with moat, ramp, and drawbridge was named the "Gate of the Five Nations" in honour of the Iroquois Confederacy, and the stone citadel, called the "Castle," within its ramparts was built in 1726 by the French. The first British commandant was Sir William Johnson, and according to one authority "it was from Niagara that he ruled half of America."[42] When Colonel Guy Johnson assumed charge of the Indian Department his headquarters were likewise at Niagara, and the Castle was described as "a structure of considerable magnitude and great strength, a handsome dwelling-house for the Superintendent of Indians."[43]

Daniel Rose, Archibald Thomson, James Park, and John Chisholm followed Brant to Niagara in October 1779,[44] at which time "Colonel Guy Johnson informed them that they could only draw pay from the day of their arrival at Niagara—and nothing from their preceding severe and dangerous Service of Eighteen Months—on which [they] replied that as they served the Crown from principle and not for the sake of Emolument, they would continue to serve without pay during the remainder of the war—Which they did—and they are happy to add, satisfactorily, being almost irremittingly on actual service."[45] These four Highlanders had been dispossessed of their holdings in Harpersfield and Kortright when on October 22, 1779, the estates of those adhering to the Crown were declared forfeited to the State of New York and were to be sold by the Commissioners of Forfeiture at auction or by private contract. Although the Scots possessed nothing but their arms and the clothes they stood up in, they were willing to serve as volunteers who were "unpaid, uncloathed, and unprovisioned."[46]

The authenticity of this assertion is attested by the total absence of their names from paylists throughout the period.

At Niagara the Scots went into winter quarters in the new range of barracks on the west side of the river opposite the fort. These barracks were built during the autumn of 1778 by Colonel Butler at a cost of £2,527.19.2.[47] and accommodated both his Rangers and the "distressed families" who were taking refuge at Niagara. The site was a clearing which had once been an Indian cornfield. The building yet standing would seem to be the oldest in Ontario today. It is of the squared timber construction usual in block houses, and is of two storeys. It measures eighty-three feet in length by twenty-six feet in width with a massive brick chimney at each end. Two entrances centred in the long sides lead into an entry where a stairway rises to the upper storey. A partition running through the building on the west side of the stairwell divides each floor into two rooms. This wall is of brick-nogging (that is, brick work in a timber frame), the same type of construction as was used in the colonel's old home, Butlersbury. The rooms on the ground floor have arched brick fireplaces five feet in width but in those upstairs stove-pipe holes are let into each chimney. The long narrow windows set high in the timber walls, eight along each side and two flanking each chimney, are said to have been enlarged from rifle slits.

Because most of their friends and neighbours at the Head of the Delaware had enlisted in one or the other of Sir John Johnson's corps the Scots found but few men at Niagara with whom they were acquainted. In the Indian Department there were Adam Chrysler from Schoharie and the Servos brothers, Daniel and Jacob, from the Charlotte River, all of whom held commissions as lieutenants. Also there was John Burch from Papacunck who was keeper of Indian stores. In Butler's Rangers were several Macdonells and a few other Scotsmen, but the great majority were of Palatine German or Dutch descent from the Mohawk or Susquehanna valleys and elsewhere along the Pennsylvania–New York frontier. Some of the latter group were among the first to join Colonel Butler in the spring of 1777; from Wyoming came Philip Bender, John Depue, and the Secords. Philip Bender had come as a child in the 1740's from Germany. He had been a neighbour of the Depues for only a short time when forced to leave Wyoming and flee to Niagara.[48] John Depue, already a lieutenant in the provincial militia, was entrusted by Colonel Butler with important missions such as carrying dispatches from Niagara to the British headquarters at York.[49] The Secords were descendants of Ambroise Sicard who had left France at the time of the Revocation of the Edict of Nantes and had settled in Westchester County in the Province of New York at a place named New Rochelle for his former home, La Rochelle, in France. About 1774 Peter, John, and James Secord went westward to find land on the Susquehanna on the border of the Indian country above the Wyoming Valley. Because these men were among Butler's earliest recruits their families had fled to escape the fury of the Sons of Liberty. James Secord Sr.'s wife, Magdalena (Badeau), was among those rescued by Colonel Bolton early in 1778 while her husband and three oldest sons were serving with the Rangers. Lieutenant James was sent on many arduous missions before transferring to the Indian Department where he now had easier work as "tavern keeper at this Post."[50] He continued in this capacity until May 1782,[51] and perhaps longer.

Also an early comer to Niagara was Captain Nelles from the Mohawk who was often sent on missions with Captain Brant. Hendrick William Nelles was a grandson of William Nelles who with his two brothers had joined the Palatine migration of

1710. In 1720 he became one of the twenty-seven patentees to Stone Arabia. Hendrick William, a substantial landholder on the north shore of the Mohawk, lived not far from Colonel Butler and had served as lieutenant in the Seven Years' War.[52] Early in the Revolution, according to his own statement, he had "abandoned a wife and eight sons to join the King and from his knowledge of the Indians, attached himself to Colonel [Guy] Johnson." His wife Priscilla and children had also been rescued by a party sent out by Colonel Bolton. Hendrick "recovered" his eldest son Robert who enlisted as a volunteer in the Indian Department and was commissioned lieutenant, and at times father and son were employed together as scouts.[53]

The Dolsons and Fields, neighbours in Wyoming, had come later to Niagara. They had remained on their lands until about the time of Butler's raid in the spring of 1778 when they fled in a great hurry. Isaac Dolson had left a 150-acre farm bought in 1774 for £1 York per acre, the prevailing price for wild land in Wyoming, paying "ye money down." He had cleared 60 acres and built a two-storey house. Upon refusing a captain's commission in the Continental militia he was thrown into gaol, and when released came away bringing his father, his wife, and small children. Although "persued so fast they could not carry all their effects with them," they contrived to drive away some cattle, but had left behind many sheep, calves, and fields turning green with young corn.[54] George Field and his three sons had brought most of their stock with them, and having learned the trade of blacksmith he and Daniel were useful as rangers.[55]

The tedium of life during the long winter of 1779–80 was relieved by news which concerned the prisoners of war from Cherry Valley, Mrs. Samuel Campbell and the Moores. The circumstances surrounding their release by the Indians is told elsewhere because their stories are closely related to those of the Scottish families of Allan Macdonell and Hugh Fraser (see pp. 96–98). The first event of interest was Mrs. Campbell's recovery of her four children from Indian families driven to Niagara by starvation, and the second was the courtship of a daughter of Mrs. Moore by a British officer of the garrison, Captain John Powell. "We have no News here at present worth communicating," wrote Francis Goring to an absent trader, "except Capt[n] Powell being married to Miss Jane Moore."[56] There was another marriage of note that winter. Some time previously Joseph Brant had by Indian rite taken a Mohawk princess as his third wife. After his first wife Margaret had succumbed to tuberculosis he had in 1773 married her half-sister Susannah who lived only a short time. Some say that his third wife Catherine was a daughter of George Croghan by an Indian wife; others that her father was head chief of the Turtle tribe, the first in rank of the Mohawk nation. Brant now availed himself of the opportunity of having the English ceremony performed by Colonel Butler as one of the King's Commissioners of the Peace of Tryon County.[57]

Despite the severity of this winter the British did not await the opening of spring before starting their retaliation for Sullivan's campaign. Some of the preparations are reflected in the accounts of the Indian Department which show the issue of such items as twenty-six oxhides at 16s. apiece for making snow-shoes, "Coating Trousers for Volunteers" costing 20s. a pair, and five gross of scalping knives.[58] Several kinds of scalping knives were furnished by one firm of traders at Niagara—"Redwood handled," "Buck handled," and "Camwood handled."[59] Early in February war parties began to march from Niagara.[60] Small forces of Rangers and Indians, all in war paint, raided German Flatts and other settlements north of the Mohawk. The dangers and hardships of parties on service were greatly multiplied by the destruction of the Indian villages, their supply bases, and they were reduced to living off the country. Their numbers became smaller and their marches longer and whenever possible they drove with them a few cattle each with a bag of salt and one of flour tied to its back. The necessity of continually searching for provisions seriously hampered their movements. The Indians, now more aggressive than ever, made little distinction between friend or foe, and carried the tomahawk and torch into districts hitherto spared.

It so happened that Archibald Thomson was of the war party which took Captain Alexander Harper and a group of enemy militiamen prisoners at Harpersfield. The first week in April Captains Brant and Nelles with eighteen Rangers, six Mohawks, and four Onondagas [61] appeared at the Head of the Delaware en route to the Upper Fort in Schohaire. From Thomas McMicking they secured provisions * and intelligence of enemy activities. When travelling eastward through Harpersfield the party came across a group of the enemy who under the command of Captain Harper were making maple sugar for the garrison at the Upper Fort and at the same time keeping watch on fellow-workers suspected of "disaffection." Rangers and Indians approached so stealthily that the sugar-makers, dispersed through the bush, were surprised at their work. As Harper bent to adjust his snow-shoes Brant was upon him, holding his tomahawk over Harper's head when he discovered his identity. At the same time Indians appeared beside other workers in different parts of the bush, and three who resisted were struck down.†

The party of Brant and Nelles with their prisoners of war lingered for several days in the vicinity of a grist mill on the Delaware, the location of which is disputed by historians. Simms placed it as the mill of Hugh Alexander on Banyar's Brook,[62] but Jay Gould identified it as the mill of William Calder a mile below on the Delaware, although he stated that some contemporaries with whom he had conversed after the war gave the owner's name as Rose.[63] In any case it was at the mill of one of these Scots that two letters were written, one by Harper and the other by Brant. Captain Harper wrote to his wife Mary:

* "Furnished Capt Brant and Nelles and a party of Mohawks
        12 Bushels Indian corn 6/   3.12.–
        81 lbs sugar 1/   4. 0.–
        1 full grown Hog 1.10   1.10.–
        10 lbs butter 1/   –.10.–"
(P.R.O., Great Britain, AO 13/91, Claim of Thomas McMicking, Sept. 18, 1784.)

† The brothers James and Thomas Hendry and James Stevens were buried in the fields. Their graves were marked by tombstones, later removed to a Harpersfield cemetery, which bear the following inscriptions:

        In memory of Mr. James Hendry who was killed by
   Indians & Tories April 7th 1780 in the 35th year of his age.
      While British tiranny oerspread this land was slain
                     by cruel hands

       Erected to the memory of Thomas & John Hendry who were
sacrificed by the Tory party April 7, 1780 for the Crime called Democracy
      When the British and tories oer this land bore sway
        A [eroded] cruel Indian my body did slay
                Thos Hendry
    When my Brother was murdered I was standing by
      But in a rebel prison I was doomed to die
               John Hendry

James Stevens Killed by Indians & Tories April 7, 1780

DELAWARE, 8th April 1780

My dear, by this you may know that I am a Prisoner: and I am very glad that I am fallen into the hands that has me, seeing that it is my Lott to be taken Prisoner, (to Witt, Captain Brant and Lieut. [William] Johnson ["Jr."]) who used me and all them that is taken along with me exceeding well, and as for them that was kill'd there is no accounting for it; ... I hope that you will spare not pains nor Cost, but apply immedate to the Governor, for an immediate Exchange, for I have been talking to Capt. Brant about an Exchange who says it can easily be obtained, and that it is the falt of the Country and none of theirs if it is not ... and as for my advice to you, I cannot give any; you must try to do the best you can. I will ad [sic] no more; only remain your loving Husband; likewise give my love to all my Friends & to Father & Mother. You must shew this immediately to the Commanding Officer.

ALEX. HARPER.[64]

Two days later Chief Brant wrote his "Indian letter":

That your Bostonians* ((alias Americans) may be certified of my Conduct towards all those whom I have captured in these Parts, know that I have taken off with me but a small Number—Many I have released—Neither were the weak and helpless subjected to Death, for it is a Shame to destroy those who are defenseless—This has been uniformly my conduct during the War—I have always been for saving and releasing—These being my Sentiments you have exceedingly angered me by threatening and distressing those who may be considered Prisoners—Ye are (or once were) brave Men—I shall certainly destroy without distinction does the like Conduct take Place in future—

Translated by Samuel Strickland Missionary

JOSEPH BRANT
on the Delaware April 10th 1780 [65]

These letters were entrusted to Walter Elliot of Harpersfield, one of the militiamen released by Brant, who reached Schoharie on April 12. Elliot reported to Colonel Peter Vrooman that on Friday April 7 "a party of Indians commanded by Joseph Brandt, 19 white Men and Indians, came to Harpers Field ... and killed three, and took Captain Harper and Eleven More Prisoners. ... The party that took them was designed for Schohary but happening to fall upon that place, these poor People became a Victim [sic] for them ... five white men were with the Party Vizt. Hendrick Nellis, Archibald Thompson, Benjamin Begraft, William Smith and Henry Huffson." †[66]

This capture, according to the modern historian John D. Monroe, "has been made the basis of much fabulous literature," including the story told by Josiah Priest as the narrative of Freegift Patchin, a young fifer who was among the captured.[67] Priest, a coach painter at Albany, became "an itinerant spectacle and nostrum peddler during which time he wrote, published and sold many highly coloured narratives of Indian captivities, all notoriously garbled and inaccurate."[68] However, Priest's version as related to him by General Patchin shortly before his death in 1830 (but not printed until 1833) is the only known source of the sequel to the capture at Harpersfield. The pamphlet is rare; only three complete copies are known to exist.

After the arrival of Captain Harper at Niagara Colonel Butler advised General Haldimand of his capture and inquired about his exchange. Haldimand replied, "Mr. Harper shall be kept in close confinement. No prisoners, a few very old and insignificant excepted, are exchanged from this army, but if it should happen, Harper shall not be of the number."[69]

The British continued relentlessly to raid the border. In May 1780, while Captains Brant and Nelles blockaded Fort Stanwix on the west, Sir John Johnson with a large force swept through the Mohawk Valley from the east, devastating a long stretch of

---

* The term "Bostonnais" as indicative of the people of New England had originated a century before with the French (Parkman, *Frontenac and New France under Louis XIV* (Boston, 1896), p. 335). It was still current in Quebec in 1816 as applying to Americans in general (Francis Hall, *Travels in Canada and the United States in 1816 and 1817* (London, 1818), p. 152).

† Listed as "Brant's Volunteers" are Henry Huff 48, and Benjamin Beacraft 22, forester and interpreter (P.A.C., Haldimand Transcripts, B. 105, p. 395A; B. 110, p. 103).

country. So secret was their advance from Lake Champlain that they were close to Johnstown before being discovered. The baronet even retrieved two barrels of valuables which he had buried in the cellar of Johnson Hall at the time of his flight and which were now carried back to Montreal in the knapsacks of some forty soldiers.[70] In the first days of August Brant too arrived to raid the settlements in the Mohawk Valley. At Canajoharie the alarm was given by a woman's firing a canon and at Johnstown where people were harvesting in the fields, by ascending columns of smoke from burning buildings.

In all actions on the frontier the decline in rebel opposition was becoming very marked. "Every party gives us accounts of the Distress of the Enemy," wrote Colonel Butler. "The Return of [59] Indian War Parties . . . that marched out from Niagara Between the third of February and that of September . . . 1780, with the success they had, against the rebels" shows that 43 totalling 1,403 men had returned and that 16 (892 men) were still out. Rebel losses were recorded as 142 killed, 161 taken, 81 women and children released; 247 horses and 922 cattle taken away; and 2 churches, 157 houses, and 150 granaries destroyed.[71]

In September Joseph Brant had returned, probably by rafting down the Susquehanna, to Tioga Point to prepare for an extensive operation under Sir John Johnson. He and the famous Seneca warrior, Corn Planter, assembled Indians of many tribes and early in October started north along the Susquehanna trail. At the Unadilla River they joined Sir John and Colonel Butler who had marched from Oswego. Johnson led his large force by the old route—up the Charlotte, over the divide, and on October 16 down into the Schoharie Valley which he laid in ruins as he swept towards the Mohawk River. Inhabitants in Johnson's Bush, having been informed in advance of Sir John's coming, provided quantities of bread they had baked for the use of his men.[72] The march westward on the return to Oswego was marked by a path of almost complete devastation on both sides of the Mohawk River.

Tales of excessive cruelty and atrocities committed by the Indian allies of the British were circulated by the Continental press. Such recitals were without doubt based on authentic incidents, and certainly the British attempted to discourage scalping by offering good prices for prisoners taken alive. Nevertheless one can imagine that the harrowing tales were sharpened by imaginative embellishments. Highly coloured versions of Johnson's raid on the Mohawk Valley caused General Haldimand to write that the reports "assiduously published upon all occasions by the enemy, of cruelties committed by the Indians, are notoriously false, and propagated merely to exasperate the ignorant and delude the people. In this late instance Major Carleton informs me, they behaved with the greatest moderation, and did not strip, or in any respect use ill, their prisoners."[73] The following paragraph purporting to be an "Extract from a letter from Quebec" had appeared the previous year:

> Everything is quiet in this country. The Indians have been ravaging the back settlements of Connecticut and New York provinces. We hear they have destroyed above 1000 families, and scalped the whole of them: they have brought fifteen prisoners into this province: they had at first 25, but had *roasted* and *eaten* ten of them in the woods at their war-feast. I heartily wish they had your Commissioners in the *bellies*, could that be a means of bringing about a reconciliation.[74]

The American historian William L. Stone writing at Albany in the 1830's stated that he was satisfied that "much of exaggeration and falsehood has obtained a permanent footing in American history"; that the "crude verbal reports of the day—tales of hear-say, coloured by fancy and aggravated by fear,—not only found their way into the newspapers but into the journals of military officers." [75] Probably the most flagrant example of anti-British propaganda was what William L. Stone called "the well known scalp story of Dr. Franklin—long believed, and recently [1830's] revived and included in several works of authentic history." [76] (See Appendix C.) Monroe who covered much of the same ground a century later observed that a comparison of the behaviour of white men and Indians "affords no basis for the assumption, common to fanciful writers, that the whites were less savage than the Indians." [77]

In general native Americans particularly New Englanders treated the Indians with contempt and a spirit of double-dealing. A case in point is that of Seth's Henry (sometimes called Seth Hendrick), a Mohawk well known to settlers at the Head of the Delaware. In 1738 his father Seth had assisted surveyors in laying out the Arent Bradt Patent along the Delaware adjoining Harpersfield and Kortright. At the time of the Revolution, Seth's Henry and three other Mohawks captured two Continental sympathizers who lived on the west side of the Delaware, Isaac Sawyer near Betty's Brook and St. Ledger Cowley below Banyar's Brook in the southwest corner of Kortright.[78] Sawyer and Cowley were taken to Tioga Point, assuring the Indians that they were Loyalists interested only in getting to Niagara. For eleven days they acted their parts so well that at night the Indians left them unbound and unguarded, whereupon Sawyer and Cowley set upon their captors and killed two in their sleep. Seth's Henry and another Mohawk escaped badly wounded. A few months later the state legislature awarded "to Isaac Sawyer and St. Ledger Cowley, each the sum of one hundred pounds as a gratuity for their valor and resolute conduct in effecting their escape when captivated by the Indians."

Sawyer and Cowley were well away from the Head of the Delaware by the time a party of Indians came looking for them. In frustration at losing their quarry the Indians wreaked their vengeance on the McKees living close to Odell's Lake high on a hill in Harpersfield. McKee, a known Patriot, was in Schoharie, where he had gone for news and flour, on the dark night when the Indians sounded the war whoop and shot his wife and a child in arms. His sixteen-year-old daughter, Ann, was taken a prisoner to Niagara where she was nearly killed in running the gauntlet. However, she was befriended by a Scottish family, obviously one of those from Kortright, until the end of the war when she returned to her father at Harpersfield. The site of the McKees' log house at the end of the road above Whiskey Hollow commands one of the most spectacular scenes in Harpersfield. From the rocky hillside where it stood beside the stream issuing from Odell's Lake a few hundred yards to the east, there is an uninterrupted view of the Kaatskills rising above Town Brook on the south. On the north the path, once a main trail of the Indians, disappears over the hilltop to lead down into Harpersfield Center. Lilacs, wild pink roses, ferns, and Indian paint brush now run rampant over this windswept height where, we are told by the historical marker standing at the roadside, the McKees were massacred by the Indians.

The McMickings also became the victims of an Indian attack, the perpetrators being a marauding band of Senecas who had evidently deserted Sir John Johnson during the time that he together with Colonel Butler, Captain Brant, and a large army was marching down the Schoharie Valley towards the Mohawk in the autumn of 1780. Johnson reported that Indians had been leaving "as they did not like going so low down in the country where it was whispered we would meet with Two Thousand men to oppose us." [79] On October 18 these Senecas suddenly appeared and surrounded the McMicking house. Thomas' mother Janet, having fractured her leg in a fall from her horse, was confined to the house. With her were her sons Thomas and John, her daughter Janet Cooper, and the latter's sons Thomas and ten-year-old James, all of whom were promptly taken prisoners. Because Mrs. McMicking was unable to walk the Indians determined upon killing her. That her family might not witness the deed they were led away from the house, one Indian remaining behind on guard. While he stood with his back towards her watching the others walk away Mrs. McMicking saw her chance. She crawled out of the house and around to the rear where she found a hiding place behind a log. Upon returning the Senecas decided that Janet McMicking must be hidden within the house, and though they discovered that there was a cellar by sounding the floor they were unable to find how it was reached which was probably by the usual method of raising one of the logs in the floor. Giving up, they pillaged the house, carrying away linen, blankets, "a fine Beaver Hatt," and more than £16 in cash,[80] then tossed in a firebrand. After the house had burned to the ground the Indians informed the captives that their mother had perished in the fire. However, Janet McMicking managed to crawl through the woods to the nearest house situated about a mile away, and when this family removed to Albany she was taken with them.[81]

Those who at this time removed to the relative safety of Albany were Neil McKay and Hugh Fraser. McKay stated that Indians "came down and destroyed two families and he was obliged to fly and went to Albany in 1780." Fraser established his family in the same district but before long both families were forced by persecution to abandon their properties.[82] John McKay, having recently supplied Sir John Johnson's expedition with provisions, was obliged to leave his large family and flee to Canada,"[83] and Hugh Fraser escaped to the British stronghold, York Island. Other settlers such as John Park and John Murray of Harpersfield who might be under suspicion, yet refused to leave their homes, were "laid under Restriction." In December 1780, Park and Murray were summoned to appear before the Commission of Safety at Albany for a renewal of their bail.[84]

The McMickings were meanwhile living as prisoners of the Senecas. A journey of several days had brought them to "the Indian Town on the Susquehanna River in the State of Pennsylvania,"[85] evidently the Castle of the Tioga. Some days after their arrival news was brought of the killing of three Indians by escaped Negro prisoners. The Indians in council resolved that in retaliation for the loss of the three warriors their white prisoners should run the gauntlet until three of their number were killed. Thus a scene both of amusement and punishment should be offered.

Forcing prisoners to run the gauntlet was an ancient practice somewhat like the trial by ordeal of mediaeval times. It was common to many tribes of North American Indians. Much depended upon the courage and presence of mind of the prisoner. If he started upon the race with force and agility he usually escaped serious injury, but he was accorded no mercy at the slightest manifestation of fear. At Tioga the white men, followed by the greater part of the town's inhabitants who had come to enjoy the sport, were taken to a gateway made of brush about a half mile away. The distance to be run lay between the gate and the chief's house within the town. If the prisoner, pursued by an Indian warrior, could reach the house without being killed, however badly wounded, he was pardoned. One of the last prisoners brought in was Thomas McMicking. He outran the Indian on the level, but his pursuer gained on him on a rise of ground, and only a few rods from the chief's house the Indian threw his tomahawk striking McMicking a glancing blow on the top of his head. McMicking won his pardon but was long recovering from his injury, "the scar of which he carried to his grave." [86]

After four months of suffering from cold and hunger a party of Senecas started for Niagara taking Thomas and other captives they had been holding for ransom. Janet Cooper and her sons remained behind and of John there is no mention. Each member of the party was given a sock full of parched corn on which he subsisted for ten days with the addition of a raccoon which was equally shared. Plodding by day and sleeping at night in the snow they reached Niagara in March 1781 [87] where Thomas was redeemed from the Senecas (average price paid for redemption of prisoner, £4 [88]) and provided with new clothing by Butler's Rangers. He enlisted in the corps as forester, and bought freedom for his sister and nephews who joined him the following spring. John McMicking also reached Niagara and enlisted in the Rangers.

By the summer of 1781 the New York frontier was feeling the full effects of the war. The situation of the Continental army was deplorable and underfed soldiers in large numbers were going over to the enemy. A good many were taken in by Loyalists and hidden until such time as they were able to join the British. Recruiting officers for the Crown were meeting with such successs that enlisting was openly carried on in the streets of Albany. The militia in the Canajoharie District had been reduced from 2,500 to a mere 800, and the commanding officer estimated that one-third of the population of the district had been killed or taken, another third had gone over to the enemy, and the remainder had fled to the interior. The few that were left could expect little if any protection, and those who could do so built block houses on their own farms.[89] British scouts were constantly in the region, entering even the thickly populated areas to snatch men from their beds, and leading citizens were disappearing with alarming frequency. A plan to abduct General Gansevoort miscarried, and a more daring attempt to seize General Schuyler very nearly succeeded notwithstanding that he was warned in advance. Scouts surrounded and had entered his mansion called The Pastures in the suburbs of Albany when the general shouted from an upstairs window as though to encourage approaching rescuers. The ruse succeeded and the invaders beat a retreat.

As the summer wore on rumours of a large-scale invasion caused the Continentals to look with growing concern towards the north although Butler's Rangers and Brant's Indians continued to ravage the settlements on the west. Nevertheless the rebels were taken completely by surprise when the British attacked late in October. Some five hundred men led from Canada by Major Ross had traversed the forest so secretly that they appeared near the Schoharie "as suddenly as though they had sprung from the earth." [90] Captain Gilbert Tice, who had been assigned command of one hundred hastily-assembled Indians, "the dregs of the tribes," tells in his journal of this expedition: how he left Niagara on October 5 and met Major Ross and Captain Walter Butler with regulars and Rangers at Oswego; how he learned that many Indians upon whom he had counted were unable to join him "because they had no Mockasons, or anything to go to War with"; how they reached Fort Brewerton and on October 15 set out for Otsego Lake by way of Canasarago Creek, Old Oneida, "passed Tunnacliff's Place & struck for Croghan's Lake . . ., encamped at a Creek running out of Young's Lake. . . . Marched & passed the upper end of Cherry Valley, & encamped within four miles of Durlach." The expedition continued eastward to the Schoharie, marched down the river and "halted within a mile of Warren's Bush till day break."

Tice was ordered to destroy this settlement which "we finished about 10 o'clock in the morning" of October 24 and re-joined Ross near Schenectady. They then "wheeled about, marched up the Mohock River, crossed at Fort Johnson and took the main road to Johnstown, went through the Town, passed the Hall & halted in the Fields above it, and began to collect Prisoners, all this time without interruption, from the Enemy." It was after 3 P.M. on the same day when Colonel Marinus Willett arrived with enemy militia from Canajoharie, and Tice describes the action which followed as "very obstinate on both sides, which lasted till dark when we left the Field. . . . The Enemy did not pursue us." [91] Major Ross then led his half-starved and exhausted men westward through the wilderness. Gilbert Tice states that during the period of time between October 25 and November 4 they had nothing to eat but horse meat, "& but little of that." [92] The endurance of these men amazed the enemy commander Colonel Willett who later commented that, notwithstanding they had been four days in the wilderness with only half a pound of horse-flesh per man per day, "yet in this famished situation they trotted thirty miles before they stopped." [93]

Because the warriors of the Six Nations wanted to return through their own country Major Ross met them at Captain Tice's "fireplace to thank them for their good Behaviour & shake hands with them." [94] The day following, October 30, Ross at the head of all the troops took the trail for Carleton Island at the foot of Lake Ontario while Tice with the Six Nations Department set out for Niagara. From straggling parties of Rangers met along the way Tice learned that on the day they had parted Major Ross had been overtaken by Continentals in Jerseyfield and that Captain Walter Butler had been killed. The spot on West Canada Creek, now called Ohio, where Colonel Butler's son was shot through the head is not many miles from the Butler homestead still standing high above the Mohawk Valley. This action fought nearly two weeks after Lord Cornwallis surrendered to the Continentals at Yorktown, Virginia, is generally considered the last skirmish of the Revolution to take place on the soil of New York. However, on November 2, in a deep gully a short distance north of Lake Utsayantha, Brant and Adam Chrysler with sixty or seventy Indians and volunteers fought a battle with militia from the Upper Fort on the Schoharie under the command of Captain Jacob Hagar.[95] And according to the journal of Captain Chrysler he and twenty-eight Indians made a foray for cattle on Schoharie as late as November 13 to 14. They were pursued by 150 rebels of whom five were killed and some wounded, and were forced by overwhelming numbers to relinquish fifty head of cattle. Chrysler's party did not reach Niagara until December 11.[96] By then both sides knew that the end of the war was near, and there followed a period of armed neutrality during which the exhausted combatants sought for peace. But the negotiations of the commissioners at Paris proved lengthy, dragging on through 1781 and 1782.

In the foregoing pages Fort Niagara has been seen only from afar and it has appeared solely as the military headquarters on the western edge of the Indian country. But this is merely one aspect of this ancient fortress, so while we await the outcome of the peace deliberations a closer view will be taken of Niagara and other reasons for its importance will be considered.

CHAPTER SIX

THE RIVER AND THE FORT

THE NIAGARA RIVER was the gateway to the West—to the four great lakes, the Ohio, and the Mississippi. On the east bank of the river stood Fort Niagara, the guardian of this vital passage and thus of Forts Detroit and Michilimackinac on the upper lakes. Serving as outlets for and affording protection to the rich trade in furs, these three outposts were strategically located on the lake and river system which divides the Appalachian from the Laurentian highlands and which throughout its length of more than 2,000 miles was then considered as the St. Lawrence River: "The River St. Lawrence and the Lakes thro' which it flows." * This mighty river may be said to rise at the source of the St. Louis River which empties into the head of Lake Superior, and then to flow from one great basin into the next through rivers and straits. From Lake Erie, the shallowest of the lakes, there is a sudden drop of 325 feet to Lake Ontario from the top of the escarpment which parallels its shore. The connecting river, or "this part of the St. Lawrence which is called the Niagara River," [1] pours over the shelf of the escarpment in the roaring mass of the Great Falls of Niagara to dash through the great spillway of the narrow gorge produced by the retreat of the waterfall.

In provisioning the upper posts the British government therefore experienced many difficulties in transportation. Nor were the Falls the only obstacle. Between Lake Ontario and Montreal the St. Lawrence is faulty and broken, dropping 225 feet in a series of boiling rapids spread over 120 miles. At times, the batteaux which were the freight carriers of the river were towed by batteaumen from the shore; other times, men toiled through water up to their arm pits; but where the current was strongest manpower was supplemented by horses, oxen, and windlasses. The Long Sault which drops the raging river 45 feet in 9 miles took a whole day to surmount. Batteaux travelled in brigades of ten or twelve so that their crews might aid each other; "coming up with the brigade" is a term frequently encountered at this period. Between May, when the "large fleet of victuallers" arrived from Britain, and late

---

* E. A. Cruikshank and A. F. Hunter, *The Correspondence of the Honourable Peter Russell with allied documents relating to his administration of the government of Upper Canada during the official term of Lieut. Governor J. G. Simcoe while on leave of absence* (3 vols., Toronto, 1936), II, p. 238. In 1798 a Moravian missionary wrote that Lake Erie "is connected with Lake Ontario, and the other great Lakes of N. America, by means of the river St. Lawrence, which runs through them all into the Atlantic Ocean" (Leslie R. Gray, ed., "From Bethlehem to Fairfield— 1798," pt. 1, May 13, 1798, *Ontario Historical Society, Papers and Records*, vol. XLVI (1954), no. 1, pp. 37–61). In 1804 Dr. Timothy Dwight, president of Yale College, spoke of the "River Niagara, properly called the St. Lawrence" (*Travels in New-England and New-York* (London, 1823), vol. IV, p. 69). This view was still held forty years later by the engineer Francis Hall (*Travels in Canada and the United States in 1816 and 1817* (London, 1818)), and by the botanist, John Goldie (*Diary of a Journey through Upper Canada and some of the New England States in 1819* (Toronto, 1897)).

autumn, stores sufficient to last during the six months that the St. Lawrence was ice bound were transported up the river. Thus the batteaux deeply laden with barrels of pork from Ireland and flour from London, stores, merchandise, arms, and men were rowed, poled, hauled, and dragged up the long miles of river to the foot of Lake Ontario where they met the lake vessels at Carleton Island. An "Estimate of One Batteau Load Rum from Montreal to Niagara" was given as £458.6.6 New York currency.[2]

Sometimes batteaux coasted the south shore of Lake Ontario to Fort Niagara where stores for that garrison were put down. They sailed upriver to the Lower Landing where they unloaded their goods for overland portage around the Great Falls and took on new cargoes for the return trip, peltries of fur traders brought down from the upper posts.[3] At this landing, situated on the east bank of the river at the foot of the escarpment, "the banks are extremely high," remarks Thomas Hughes, so "they have a contrivance to drag goods up with a windlass and large machine on skids."[4] This device has also been described as a cradle on tracks drawn up the fifty-foot bank by a capstan fixed at the top, and again as a sliding car with broad runners which ran over wooden rails. Thirty years later Christian Schultz was shown the remains of machinery reputedly used by the French. "This is a contrivance made prior to any roads or teams being used in the wilderness," wrote Schultz, "and so constructed that, with a kind of windlass and cable, one end would draw up a large frame made to contain three or four thousand weight of goods, while the other end, with an apparatus of the same kind, would descend with the same or a greater quantity of peltry."[5] After being loaded on carts or waggons the cargoes were transported along the portage road constructed in 1763 to the Upper Landing above the Falls. This point was called Fort Schlosser by the British, but correspondence of the fur-trader's clerk, Francis Goring, shows that the old French name of "Little Niagara" was still in use. The cargoes were again loaded into batteaux, carried upstream another eighteen miles to Fort Erie, and transhipped into lake schooners which plied between there and Forts Detroit and Michilimackinac. Forts Schlosser and Erie were fortified warehouses intended merely for the protection of stores and merchandise in transit.

Unlike the traders in the northwest who travelled great distances to reach the fur-bearing regions the traders at Niagara and Detroit conducted their business at the posts. For controlling the trade the British depended upon the discretion of their officers rather than upon the number of troops stationed at the garrisons. The officers learned the language of the Indians, compelled traders to deal equably with them, and by their conduct gained the respect of the natives, "thus managing them by address where force could not avail," as Sir Guy Carleton remarked.

The cost of provisioning the garrisons on the lakes was so vast as to cause Lieutenant-Colonel Mason Bolton, who was the officer commanding the upper posts and also the commandant of Fort Niagara, to exclaim that it seemed a pity they had not been abandoned to the Indians since they "were costing Old England far more than they were worth." Bolton's despair was not the result of inexperience because he had served more than twenty-five years as quartermaster of the 9th Regiment of Foot before taking command in 1776 of the 8th Regiment which was then garrisoning the outposts on the lakes.[6] His quarters on the officer's deck of the "Castle," having required little if any restoration, are substantially the same today as when he occupied them. The picture of the colonel sitting by the warmth of the fire while the light from burning logs in the fireplace played on the grey stone walls and the golden brown of the heavy beams of the ceiling, or standing at the casement window overlooking the water of Lake Ontario is a poignant one. However, he was now aging and his health was poor so that the manifold problems by which he was beset weighed heavily upon his shoulders. He was constantly harassed by the delays and uncertainties of the transportation system, and he was concerned about the welfare of the men at the garrisons, the strength of which had been considerably increased by the war, and of the mounting numbers of Butler's Rangers and other refugee Loyalists. And his trials were not lessened by the exacting demands of the Indians. In November 1778 he had written: "I have already bought up above fifty head of cattle from the People who lately came in here ... but all this is a trifling supply to the two or three thousands of Indians who will certainly assemble here in order to receive cloathing, &c."[7] The obvious solution to these problems of provisioning was an extension of the plan of cultivation in the vicinity of the posts.

For some years officers and men of the garrisons had been raising garden stuff on a small scale, owing chiefly to the efforts of Major Duncan, who during the Seven Years' War was commander of a Scottish regiment which was officered by young men just out of school. This regiment had suffered great hardships during its first action, the disastrous defeat at Ticonderoga in the summer of 1758. The depleted corps had then marched up the St. Lawrence to its station at Fort Ontario, the post recently built across the river from and as a reinforcement to Fort Oswego. Major Duncan was a learned and experienced officer who, although not old, was war-worn and gouty. That he might avoid the winds of Lake Ontario he lived in a house fixed on wooden wheels so that it could be moved around the parade ground. The board walls of the two rooms were hung with deer skins, and bear skins covered the floor. In the "breakfasting parlour" were his globes, mathematical instruments, flutes, dumb-bells, chess-boards, and extensive library while in his bedroom many stores were stowed. When the post was completely isolated in winter the major "did not allow this interval to waste in sloth or vacancy." He set his young officers to reading on subjects of their own choosing, inviting them regularly to breakfast in rotation and examining them on their studies. Thus they passed through the period of confinement without the usual quarrels and came to regard their commanding officer as their "guide, philosopher, and friend."

With the arrival of spring and the hunting by which fresh could be substituted for salt meat, Major Duncan made known the plan that he had hatched during the winter. It included the making of a large garden, a bowling-green, and a field enclosed with pallisadoes from the great stock left over from building the garrison. "This was a bold attempt when one considers that you might as well look for a horse in Venice as Oswego," commented the narrator Mrs Grant.[8] Except for dogs and cats the only tame creature at the post was the sutler's cow. The project was received with "curses not loud but deep." Each officer was to oversee the work of soldiers allotted to him. The major decreed that "as the summer was merely to be occupied in gardening and the chace [sic], the parade of military dress was both expensive and unnecessary." He ordered that soldiers' coats from a large surplus on hand be cut down by the regimental tailor to "a sort of undress frock," with little round hats to complete the outfit. "Thus equipped," continues the narrator, "these young Cincinnati set out ... on the horticultural enterprize."

From the stores concealed in the fastness of his bedroom Major Duncan produced "the food for future pigs and poultry; pease, beans and Indian corn," and the garden was prepared under the eye of an old serjeant who knew something of husbandry. The spot chosen by the major for his "ample garden" was partly cleared of trees which had been used for the winter firing of the garrison, but many mulberry, wild plum, cherry, and some lofty plane and chestnut trees were marked for preservation. By the end of May a summer-house in a tree, a fish pond, and a gravel walk had been completed, and every vegetable "known in our best gardens" had been planted. "These vegetables throve beyond belief or example. The size of the cabbages, the cucumbers, and melons, produced here, was incredible. They used, in the following years, to send them down to astonish us at Albany. On the continent they were not equalled, except in another military garden, which emulation had produced at Niagara. The major's œconomical [sic] views were fully answered. Pigs and poultry in abundance were procured, and supported by their Indian corn crop; they even procured cows, and made hay in the islands to feed them. . . . In short they all lived in a kind of rough luxury, and were enabled to save much of their pay. The example spread to all the line of forts. . . ." [9]

All this had been possible in times of peace but during the war there was little opportunity for such activities. None the less General Haldimand was of the opinion "that effectual measures could be fallen upon at All [the posts] for raising a supply within themselves." [10] He also stated that for many years he had "regretted that measures were not adopted to prevent the safety of the Upper Posts from depending upon Supplies from Home, so very distant, the Transport so extremely precarious and attended by such a heavy Expense to Government . . . and there is nothing wanted but a Beginning. . . ." [11] He suggested to Colonel Bolton to urge the contractor at the Carrying Place and any other capable person who could be found to cultivate as much land as possible about the fort "to lay a foundation by degrees" of supplying the garrison with bread, and in time to bring about the rearing of cattle.[12] He also advised that the Indians be induced to till the soil. "Nothing will so much contribute to the certainty of supplying this Post with Provisions necessary for the Garrison as the persuading the savages to cultivate near their habitations as much as possible. However difficult it may be to persuade them to it it is a thing to be endeavoured at, and to make them sensible they will in time from their labour reap great advantages as their produce would be purchased by Govenment at the Current price." [13]

After consulting with others "on the plan of agriculture" suggested by General Haldimand Colonel Bolton reported them to be of the opinion that "such a scheme might prove displeasing to our allies the six nations." According to the treaty that Sir William Johnson had effected in 1764 the Indians of the Six Nations had ceded land along the river to the Crown, but with the stipulation that, on the east side, only enough land was to be brought under cultivation as was necessary to support the oxen employed on the portage. At the same time, the Indians had granted land to John Stedman who had been appointed master of the portage in 1760. In 1763 Stedman had made a contract with Sir William Johnson to construct a road along the portage to facilitate the transportation of military supplies which were being moved from Oswego to Detroit at the time of Pontiac's uprising. The road passed near to Devil's Hole, a deep chasm which is situated about half a mile below the Whirlpool and the rim of which is above the tops of forest trees growing in its bottom. On a day in September twenty-five loaded waggons with twenty soldiers and their officers as guard started over the road under the charge of Stedman as contractor for the transportation of army stores. On the return trip Senecas lying in ambush at Devil's Hole killed all but Stedman who was on horseback, a wounded soldier, and a drummer boy who when falling into the chasm was caught on the limb of a tree by his drum-strap. An Indian seized the bridle reins of Stedman's horse and was leading it into the woods when his attention was diverted long enough for the contractor to cut the reins with his knife, and laying spurs to his horse to escape the "massacre of Bloody Run." At the peace which followed in a few months time the Indians made Stedman a grant of nearly 5,000 acres, all the land that he had galloped over in his flight. According to John Maude who got the story first hand, the Senecas "considered Stedman's escape so miraculous, and that this gift was atonement to him and the Great Spirit who protected him, for their guilt in trying to kill him."[14] Stedman cleared the land adjacent to the barracks and built a house which he surrounded with a large apple orchard, using seed brought from Fort Detroit. The apple trees at Detroit were descendants of those grown by the French from seed brought in earlier times from Normandie.[15]

By 1779, Stedman's farm at the Upper Landing had spread over such an area as to cause the Indians some dissatisfaction: yet without their friendship the posts could not exist. Bolton thus reported to Haldimand that not only was it impossible for the contractor to cultivate more land than would supply his cattle, but that it seemed unwise to encroach upon the lands of the Six Nations. "I beg leave to observe also that the Indians not only make free with the Corn Gardens but often with the Cattle belonging to Mr. Stedman & sometimes even with those under the Cannon of this Fort."[16] He had been advised that the soil on the west side of the river was preferable to that on the east side; that with the few livestock they had brought with them some of the distressed Loyalists might succeed in supporting themselves by the end of the second year and thereafter "might be useful to this Post."[17]

General Haldimand replied that if Bolton could find among the distressed families three or four "who were good Husbandmen" and who had dependants he wished them to be established on the west side of the river, and afforded every assistance "whether by a little provision or a few Labourers." But it was to be clearly understood that their labour was "to tend as much to supplying the garrison as to their private advantage." He also stressed the necessity of sending "every useless mouth," all prisoners, and "idle people from the frontiers" down to Canada.[18]

Among those who possessed the qualifications and applied for leave to settle on land were three Loyalists from the Susquehanna, the brothers James and Peter Secord and Isaac Dolson. James Secord, aged forty-seven,[19] had four children younger than Solomon, Stephen, and David who had come with him to Niagara to join Butler's Rangers in March 1777.[20] Peter Secord had recently been discharged from the Rangers on account of his age of fifty-three. He and his wife Abigail had five children ranging from six to fourteen years.[21] Isaac Dolson, aged thirty-seven, had besides his wife Elizabeth and five small children his seventy-year-old father John. Evidently Isaac had not enlisted as a Ranger but was employed in some capacity by the fur trader Captain Robinson. Early in August 1779, Francis Goring informed his employer that "Dolson is very anxious to leave the House [firm] as he and the Secords are going to farm it [sic] on the other side of the River facing the Landing."[22] But unexpected difficulties had arisen over ownership of the land when the Missisaugas claimed they had not been parties to the treaty of 1764. Until an agreement was reached no settlement could be undertaken on the west side of the river. Peter Secord stated that when he applied to Colonel Bolton for leave to settle on the land "no particular quantity could then be granted ... the land not then being purchased from the Indians." [23]

By November 1779 conditions had worsened at Fort Niagara. Before navigation had closed General Haldimand dispatched several pressing letters to the Secretary of War for the Colonies, emphasizing that if the upper country was to be preserved for the fur trade a solution must be found for provisioning the outposts. He asked the approval of his plan of agriculture and the authority necessary for the purchase of the land. However, a reply could not reach him until the following spring.

Glimpses of life in the outposts at this period are caught in the correspondence of Francis Goring. In September 1779 he wrote:

> I have lived at this place three years last August, and have had two masters in that time and am now getting a third, still in the same house [firm]. The first was Mr. Pollard,* he made a great fortune and left off. The second, Mr. Robison,† who was formerly a captain on these lakes, is now tired of business and assigns in favour of George Forsyth who has treated me with the greatest kindness and is ready to serve me in anything I should ask. I have had several offers by my employers to leave Niagara and live with them in Canada, but I believe I shall continue here which I prefer to Canada the popular place where everything is carried on with the greatest gaiety, and this place you may say is almost out of the world, in the woods, and frequented by nothing but Indians except the people of the garrison. . . . [Here] is carried on a business which consumes every year £30,000 sterling worth of merchandise of all sorts which is mostly retailed to the Indians. We employ four clerks of which I am the senior. For the first two years my salary was but small, but I have now (and I flatter myself that there is not in these parts a clerk that has as much) about fifty guineas per annum, being found in food and washing. By carrying on correspondence with my good friend Mr. Cruikshank ‡ who supplied me with silver work, such as the Indians wear, which I dispose of to the merchants in the country, and the profit arising therefrom is sufficient to find me in clothes. I have had several severe illnesses which has been occasioned by the ague and fever (which is subject to every person at this place annually) except last Christmas, which had it not been for the great care I was taken of by Mr. and Mrs. Robison I should certainly have died.[24]

From other clerks at Carleton Island Goring learned that men were snatched by enemy scouts in broad daylight within a hundred yards of the fort.[25] Another tells of batteaumen who, surly because of night loading by candle light, flung crates so as to ruin their contents; of the flock of sheep received, several with legs broken on the journey upriver; of the day spent in cutting grass on another island and ferrying it back that they might have fodder. After acknowledging a shipment of "hides" this clerk remarks that if the peltry of Goring's employer, Captain Robinson, "continues to be so good he will undoubtedly make a handsome fortune," as indeed he did. When ordering an assortment of Indian goods including "30 pair of mogozeens, 8 carrots of tobacco," the clerk adds, "P. S., There are upwards of 40 Canoes of Indians on the ground at present, having come in the other day, two small partys [sic] are now singing their war songs to go on a scouting party to Fort Stanwix. . . ." [26] Again after concluding his business he tells Goring that he had plenty of good milk "by means of L. Parlour who was sent with a party by our Commandant to bring off his family from Oswego." Parlour had found his home burnt and his son taken prisoner by rebels, yet had the good fortune to find that they had missed [in order of their importance] his

---

* Evidently Edward Pollard, an early British trader who established himself at Niagara and by 1779 had become prosperous enough to retire and return to England. He also acted as deputy commissary. (Milo M. Quaife, ed., *The John Askin Papers* (Detroit, 1928), p. 107; P.A.C., Haldimand B. 100, p. 62, Bolton to Pollard, Oct. 20, 1778.)

† Captain Samuel Robinson, a Scot and sailor from youth who was sent to Detroit in 1774 to take command of a vessel for merchants in the fur trade. In 1778 he married fifteen-year-old Catherine Askin, eldest daughter of John Askin, merchant at Detroit. (Quaife, ed., *Askin Papers*, p. 54.)

‡ Robert Cruikshank, " ye silversmith" at Montreal. (Quaife, ed., *Askin Papers*, p. 583.)

bag of piasters,* two milch cows, his wife and two daughters with all of which he succeeded in making good his retreat to this place." This correspondent continues that he hears that Captain Robinson has provided the merchants at Carleton Island with another companion "imported smoking hot from the great city [Edinburgh?] of the name of Hamilton who comes out for and by Commission of Mr. Pollard." [27] (Robert Hamilton was a Scot from Dumfries who would soon take his place in the upper country as "a gentleman of the first rank.")

Another of Goring's correspondents was John Clunes, the master carpenter whose party of artificers had been attacked on Lake Champlain in September 1777. Clunes wrote that he had accompanied Lieutenant Twiss † "who is my friend" to Carleton Island to fortify the garrison there. "I hope it will be an honour to our Engineers and a credit to the other master carpenters and me and every artificer concerned in the building of it. . . . I return you my very hearty thanks for your useful and generous present of potatoes, and depend if it ever lays in my power to serve you I will." [28]

It will be recalled that the winter of 1779–80 was exceptionally severe. In December the trader John Warren wrote to Goring from Detroit : "For god sake keep three or four pair of Womens small shoes till I come down, for our Folks are barefoot." [29] At the end of January he stated that at Detroit the snow drifts were over ten feet high; "the Sun is become a Stranger here, hardly ever shewing his Face, and when he does, it is thro' mist, as if he intended not to be too familiar. . . . My Ammunition will soon be expended, when I shan't have sufficient for a single charge and this cold weather it will be bad living by the scent of the Cask." [30] Although white refugees endured the hardships of intense cold and short rations the suffering and misery were much greater among the Indians, hundreds of whom died of scurvy and starvation.[31]

About this time Goring formed a partnership with Samuel Street, son of John Street, trader of Fort Niagara. Goring, Street and Company embarked on "the Trade of Furs &c at Niagara" which they were keeping a closely guarded secret despite the building of a storehouse at the landing. Street was at Montreal, and when sending him a list of goods to bring up in the spring Goring added :

. . . be sure not to forget to bring something for the Belley as provision is very scarce here Flour in Particular, if you could procure two or three cags [kegs] of Corn'd Beef I believe it will answer.
We have Experienced the Longest and Coldest Winter ever known here, the River was froze over from the 7th of Jan^{uy} to the 1st March and Passable for horses and Sleds almost the whole time, which has put us back in our building oweing [sic] to the Snow being two & three foot deep in the Woods—however the Weather has for this past week been milder in which time we have got all the Timber Cut & only wait for favorable Weather to Raft it home. . . . The spot is not yet fixt on as Col Bolton has not dared to show his nose out this winter. . . . Not a word has transpired or the least conjecture about our Copartnership, tis whispered about there is a House

---
* Spanish pieces of eight or dollars.

† William Twiss put Clunes and his men to work on the first canal to be built in Canada. It was a batteau canal at the sluicing cataract of the Long Sault and was six feet wide having forty-foot locks with iron flood gates. This improvement was planned by Twiss and built by the Royal Engineers during 1779–80. In the years that followed, navigation in the river was further improved by the construction of a series of batteau canals at other perilous places. (Arthur Weir, *The Beginnings of the St. Lawrence Route* (pamphlet, Toronto, 1899), p. 7.) Twiss had entered the Military Department of Ordinance in 1760 and three years later was commissioned ensign in the Engineers. He did duty in Gibraltar until 1771, was promoted to lieutenantcy and employed 1772–75 in fortifying Portsmouth, England. He embarked for Canada with General Burgoyne who appointed him commanding engineer of his army. At the close of 1778 he was commissioned captain and sent to fortify Deer Island, thereafter known as Carleton Island, at the foot of Lake Ontario. (E. B. O'Callaghan, ed., *Orderly Book of Lieut. Gen. John Burgoyne* (Albany, 1860), p. 14fn.)

going to be Built but no one can tell for who it is . . . Mr Stedman has lost his Cannon about a week agoe [sic] which in these times is very considerable being the only one to his Garrison and of no small Size—However I should not joke with Death for he will one time or other be revenged, on

Dear Street
Yours &c
F. Goring [32]

Robert Hamilton, with whom Goring had evidently had occasional private dealings,[33] wrote from Carleton Island: "After a long dreary winter the communication with our friends is now again to be opened and the summer campaign to begin, when by our activity we must try and make amends for six months idleness." [34] During 1780 Hamilton formed a partnership with Richard Cartwright Jr. in a mercantile business of which Cartwright handled the Carleton Island end and Hamilton removed to Niagara.

In the spring the encouragement of the Indians to plant corn for their own use began to meet with success. A "Return of Indians of Colonel Johnson's Department gone to plant at Different places, their villages having been destroyed," shows that by the end of May 1780 a total of 147 men, women, and children of "Captain Brant's Mohawks and other tribes" were busy at Buffaloe Creek. "About 200 more [are] preparing to go out to plant very soon, and more will soon follow." [35] Along Buffaloe Creek, which empties into the Niagara River opposite Fort Erie, was a stretch of "excellent flat land." [36] From the 200 bushels of seed corn procured for them they raised a crop of 20,000 bushels of which 2,000 was bought by the garrison.[37] Thus Captain Brant's own people produced the first crop under the agricultural plan of General Haldimand.

When Colonel Butler visited Quebec in the spring of 1780 the General seized this opportunity to discuss his plans with one who was familiar with frontier conditions and who had long farming experience. The mode of forming a settlement was arranged and Butler was given the necessary instructions, a copy of which was delivered to Colonel Bolton upon Butler's return to Niagara. The Commandant was advised by the General:

> By your letter . . . which will be delivered to you by Lieut Col Butler, you will be made acquainted with my intentions of settling Families at Niagara, for the purpose of reclaiming, and cultivating Lands to be annexed to the Fort. The Expediency of this measure is sufficiently evinced, not only by the injury the service has, and must always suffer from a want of sufficient supply of Provisions as well as for the present unavoidable consumption of the Indians, as for the support of the Troops. . . . I am therefore come to a resolution to extend this scheme to the several Posts in the Upper Country . . .
> My letter to Colonel Johnson . . . will inform you of the situation I have chosen at Niagara, which he is directed to purchase from the Mesessague Indians. Lieut. Colonel Butler with whom I have conversed fully upon this subject has promised to give you every assistance in his Power and from his knowledge of farming, his being upon the spot with his Rangers, and his acquaintance and influence with those who may be found to settle I am persuaded you will find him very useful. I have . . . desired him to engage any Loyalists He may find proper persons about Montreal and take them up with him. He informs me there are some good Farmers in his Corp who either advancing in years, or having a large family, he could dispense with. . . .[38]

Negotiations were then instituted for the purchase from the Missisauga Indians of the strip of land extending "from the River to four Mile Creek and from thence in a straight line to strike 4 miles west of Fort Erie." [39] This land was part of the tract already ceded to the Crown by the Senecas in restitution for the Devil's Hole massacre, but the consent of the Missisaugas had never been gained. That the latter might be treated fairly and to expedite the "Niagara Plan of Edible annex to fortresses" Colonel

Guy Johnson was authorized to treat separately with the Missisaugas. Although he was unable to arrange a council in the summer of 1780 because the Missisaugas had widely dispersed to their hunting grounds, the outcome would seem to have been certain since several families were established on the west side of the Niagara River at this time.

The area marked for settlement lies between Lake Ontario and the Great Falls and is almost equally divided into plateau and plain by the escarpment standing midway between. The latter landmark rises near the Genesee River, skirts the south shore of Lake Ontario to its head, and then passes north to Lake Huron. At Niagara the escarpment, rising abruptly with great outcroppings of rock to a height of 350 feet, commands the lowland plain spreading away in the distance. From the north and particularly from the lake it is visible for a great distance. To the white men, and possibly the Indians before them, the predominating feature of the landscape was "the Mountain." There were natural clearings on the lowland plain, Five Mile Meadow beside the river and Great Meadow in the upper reaches of Four Mile Creek, but much of the area was covered with swamps which extended as far westward as the Head of the Lake. The land was also scored by numerous streams, the larger of which rise above the escarpment. They had acquired their names by a system long established in the American colonies whereby smaller waterways were named according to their distance from some important landmark. Thus travellers were enabled to find sheltered anchorage. On the south shore of Lake Ontario the landmark was the Niagara River; therefore, between these two points are the One, Two, Three, Four, Six, Eight, Twelve, Fourteen, Fifteen, Sixteen, Twenty, and Forty Mile creeks. Walter Butler mentioned several of these streams in his "Journal of an expedition from Niagara along the north shore of Lake Ontario March 1779."[40] The ponds at the mouths of the creeks had been formed by bars of gravel and stone thrown up by the action of the lake across their entrances; the water was thus dammed back on the low lying land. Some were quite extensive such as those at the Four, Twelve, and Twenty Mile creeks, but from the lake they were almost invisible against the dark mass of the shore. At Twenty Mile Pond was "an Indian Cabbin on the banck inhabited by Messessaugoes."

As laid down in General Haldimand's instructions to Colonel Bolton, the conditions of settlement on this tract of land show that the exile of the Loyalists was considered as merely temporary. Allotments were to be "distributed to such Loyalists who are capable of improving them and desirous of procuring . . . a comfortable maintenance for their families until such time as by peace they shall be restored to their respective homes should they be inclined to quit their situation at Niagara." The land was at all time to remain the sole property of the Crown, the produce alone being the property of the settlers. They were to understand, however, that anything produced over and above their own consumption was to be disposed of to the commandant of the post for the use of the troops "and not to traders or accidental Travelers." The settlers would hold their allotments from year to year "according to their merits," paying no rent. For one year after they took possession a reasonable amount of provisions would be allowed: "Ploughs and other implements of Husbandry will be furnished them gratis" and Bolton was to "afford them every assistance Whether of horses or otherwise."[41]

On August 4, one year to the day since he had first mentioned the subject, Goring noted in his journal that "Secord commenced farming over the river." *⁴² James Secord, Peter Secord, Isaac Dolson, Michael Showers, Samson Lutes, and possibly one or two others went onto the land. (In time to come the distinction of being the first settler would be claimed both by Peter Secord⁴³ and for her husband by Hannah Showers.⁴⁴) As Goring had predicted the previous year Dolson and the Secords chose tracts opposite the Lower Landing. They were situated side by side at the foot of the escarpment: Dolson at the lower end of the portage on the west bank beside the river, James Secord adjoining on the west,† and Peter Secord where the waters of Four Mile Creek tumbling down the escarpment gave him potential water power. This stream rises in the mouth of a pre-glacial gorge and runs over a bed of boulders and fill laid down by glaciers. Adjoining Peter on the south in the upper reaches of the Great Meadow was Samson Lutes. Michael Showers chose a tract beside the river below the landing at Five Mile Meadow and set about raising a log cabin for his family who were still in Canada.

Obviously these men would have chosen open tracts requiring a minimum of clearing, and by autumn they had ground ready for sowing fall wheat. Unfortunately the seed arrived too late for planting and it went in the commissary's store as provisions. Also, "the harness sent up is not the Kind wanted, if dressed leather could be sent up I would get some of the Rangers to make the Kind Requisite," wrote Colonel Butler.⁴⁵ "Captain Twiss promised me a Forge for the Families who are to settle here but it never came up," he complained, "please put him in mind of it." ⁴⁶ Being entirely dependent upon Montreal for supplies Butler prepared well ahead for more extensive settlement in the coming spring. He ordered ten bushels of spring wheat and four bushels each of buckwheat, oats, pease, and small seeds; Indian corn harvested by the Indians was already on hand. "The Families will want four Grindstones and a dozen hoes for planting in the Spring—I have four or five Families who have begun and built themselves houses. . . ." ⁴⁷ This was no small accomplishment in view of the handicaps. Only a few months earlier, when telling how inadequate the twenty rooms in the two ranges of barracks were for officers and men of his eight companies, Butler observed that new construction was slow "as we can't get a Board, nail or even Tools to assist. . . ." ⁴⁸ He requested the services of a blacksmith for making and mending the first plough shares, hoes, and axes, suggesting that one of the Rangers or a soldier of the garrison might be employed "to work at a fixed Rate." ⁴⁹ General Haldimand expressed his regret for the delays which were hampering the farmers and assured Butler that the items requested would be forwarded by the first bateaux to go up in the spring.⁵⁰

In the autumn Colonel Bolton was drowned in Lake Ontario. He had been granted leave of absence and upon the arrival of Brigadier H. Watson Powell, who was to relieve him as commander of the upper posts, the Colonel made preparations to return to England. He embarked in the *Ontario*, a fine new vessel with eighteen guns, the largest on the lake. She set sail for Carleton Island on the last day of October

---

* Which Secord is referred to has not been determined. This fragmentary journal seems to have vanished since Dr. W. H. Canniff saw it about 1882, so we are dependent upon his brief notes. The above is all that appears. "Over the river" or "over the water" were common usage in that day. (Ontario Archives, Canniff Papers, Fragment of a diary.)

† In a memorial David Secord testified that "My father James Secord with the sanction of Colⁿ Mason Bolton (then Commandant) in the year 1780 Settled on Lots No. 42, 43, 44 & 50 . . ." and that the first land he had improved "was on lot 44" (Ontario Archives, Niagara Township Papers, Memorial of David Secord, June 21, 1794).

and two days later was seen off the mouth of the Genesee River, but thereafter was lost with all aboard.

Meanwhile, negotiations for the purchase of land still faltered. General Haldimand emphasized to Colonel Guy Johnson as superintendent of the Indian Department the urgency of assembling the Indians in council. "Every Ration of Provisions you issue," he wrote, "will remind you of the necessity of the measure...."[51] Finally in May of the following year (1781) Johnson reported that the matter had been brought to conclusion, and that "the Indians are well satisfied, having received about the value of Three Hundred Suits of Cloathing."[52] By May 20 the boundaries of these lands were being marked by a party of Royal Engineers[53] and the allotment of land under military direction went forward. No mention appears of the number or identity of the settlers, although there are occasional allusions to sows, grain, tools, rations, and the family of Michael Showers. "Lieut. Col. Butler desires me to present his respectful compliments," wrote Captain Walter Butler to Haldimand's secretary, "and would be glad if a dozen Breeding sows were sent up for the use of the Farmers. There is an old man in the Rangers named Michael Showers, tho' he is fit for service Lieut. Col. Butler has permitted him to Build a House, and he is clearing Planting & Commencing Farmer, he wants permission to bring up his Family...."[54]

Throughout this period the difficulties in supplying the upper posts persisted. In writing to Sir Henry Clinton late in September 1781, Haldimand stated that several times since the commencement of the war the Rangers had been "within a few days of evacuating Niagara for lack of provisions."

> When it is considered that provisions with every store necessary for 12 months for 2,000 men, and a supply of the former with presents for at least that number of Indians, (of which 3/4 are women & children) in addition to the present consumption in the upper country, (amounting at Niagara alone, one season with another to 4,000 rations per day,) must be conveyed in batteaux 200 miles up rapids, intersected by carrying places to the first lake, from thence to Niagara in vessels, then over a carrying place of 7 miles and up a rapid of 18 to Fort Erie, from thence they proceed to Presqu'Isle, it will appear to those who have a knowledge of the route a work of time.[55]

However, some of the problems were alleviated with the inauguration of the agricultural plan at Niagara and the consequent realization of the aim of reducing the number of rations issued to Loyalists. From the beginning the farmers had been allowed only half rations, one ration being the daily issue of one pound of flour and twelve ounces of beef or pork. After the harvest in 1781 they were able to maintain themselves without rations, and during the mild winter weather in December they were able to clear and prepare more ground for early planting in the spring.[56] "If they only begin to cultivate the Land in Summer," wrote Colonel Butler, "the Season is over before they can expect to draw any subsistence from their labour. I flatter myself," he predicts proudly, "that in a short time the Farmers will be found of essential use to this Post."[57] Listed under Niagara in the Accounts of Works and Fortifications for 1781 is the item, "For Seed, Grain and sundry Tools &c^a for Husbandry ... £212.11.8$\frac{1}{4}$."[58]

The agricultural settlement grew quickly. Several families, mostly refugees from Wyoming, settled along the river below the Mountain : elderly George and Rebecca Field, John and Mary Depue with their six youngest children, and Elijah Phelps. Elijah who lived to the age of 103 years was born at Nine Partners (modern Milbrook, Dutchess County), New York, shortly before his father Elijah Sr. and mother Jemima Wilcox removed to the Wyoming Valley. His was one of the unfortunate families divided by the war, bitterness resulting between him and two younger brothers who had sided with the Americans.[59]

Other settlers, the first of whom were Daniel Rose, Thomas McMicking, Philip Bender, and Francis Ellsworth located right on the Mountain. Rose's family had been at Niagara since late 1780 when he had returned to the frontier and brought off his wife Jane and two-year-old son Hugh. Evidently it was no longer safe for them to remain at the Head of the Delaware although they were the only members of the family who found it necessary to leave their homes. By the time he removed to the new settlement, Rose had two more sons, William born in the spring of 1781 and the new born infant John.[60] With McMicking came his sister Janet Cooper and her sons Thomas and James.[61]

The disadvantage of the Mountain site, that it had no access by water, would seem to have been mitigated by its height about the swamps which were responsible for so much fever and ague. Also fewer trees had to be cleared away because here the forest thinned out to an oak grove. In 1765 Robert Rogers described this area as being "thinly timbered with lofty oaks, which at first view, one would be apt to think were artificially transposed."[62] In the estimation of Patrick Campbell "the land on the Mountain appears to me to be the fittest I have yet seen for a poor man to begin upon, as it requires scarce any clearing, there being no more wood upon it than a sufficiency for rails, inclosures, and the necessary purposes of farming; so that if he chooses he may plough down the land the moment he acquires possession of it. Clearing land of heavy timber is both expensive and tedious...." *[63]

The area was made accessible by the ancient portage path leading around the Falls on the west bank of the river. It connected the natural goals of the landing below the escarpment, now on the farm of Isaac Dolson, and the mouth of Chippawa Creek where the Niagara River again becomes navigable. This path made by the Indians and used by the French and British was destined to become the first highway in the upper country, and it was beside it that the first three settlers on the Mountain chose their allotments. Daniel Rose's tract was situated about a mile from the face of the Mountain, and that of Thomas McMicking adjoined it on the south. Evidently Archibald Thomson was promised land below the Whirlpool[64] but it seems unlikely that he occupied it at this time. Philip Bender and Francis Ellsworth went five miles farther up the river at the head of the gorge close to the Great Falls of Niagara. Where Rose and McMicking were situated the gorge narrows and from its rim to the rapids below is a sheer drop of some 250 feet, but they built their log houses near the portage path where it swung away from the river towards the west. Rose's was twenty feet square and McMicking's two feet smaller.

Once more, as upon arriving in America eight years before, these two Scots began to convert wild land into farms. Requiring assistance in the work of clearing and planting, McMicking employed "a Young or Hired man" and owned the only slave, a male Negro, in the community.[65] A "Return of Negroes and Negroe Wenches brought into the Province" lists a number who had accompanied their masters and "others carried to Niagara by Indians and white men." They were known by such names as Nero, Boatswain, Jude, Diana, Cato, Jacoba Boy, and sold for prices ranging from £12.10 to £70.[66] Thomas owned his slave during this year only, as he disappears

---

* In 1804 Robert Hamilton told Lord Selkirk that when first settled the oak land and plains on the Mountain between the Lower Landing and the Chippawa were considered worthless; that the land chiefly settled by Scots was then, twenty-two years later, worth some two or three hundred thousand dollars (P.A.C., Lord Selkirk's Diary, May 21, 1804).

from the record thereafter.* By the end of the year McMicking had cleared eight acres and harvested ten bushels each of potatoes, oats, and Indian corn. He owned two horses, a cow, and twenty hogs. Daniel Rose had a clearance of six acres and his produce for that season was forty bushels of potatoes and thirty bushels of oats. His livestock consisted of two cows, one "steer or heifer," two horses and three hogs. The animals foraged the bush throughout the year because neither man built a barn for some time to come.

There were now sixteen farmers in the new agricultural settlement. The first census taken after the harvest of 1782 [67] shows that although more than half of the farmers were in possession of from three to six horses, none having less than two, there was not an ox in the settlement; that the most useful crops were potatoes and Indian corn. Except for two families without children, all the farmers had cows, twelve keeping from two to seven, and only Bender and James Secord had flocks of sheep. Any surplus over and above the needs of the sixty-eight persons comprising the sixteen families was sold, according to Haldimand's instructions.

The previous spring General Powell had been relieved as officer commanding the upper posts by Brigadier Allan Maclean, and it is of interest to note in passing that before his departure Powell had officiated at the christening of the encampment of the Six Nations Indians. This temporary village was situated about two miles east of the Lower Landing on the east side of the river. Joseph Brant and his family lived here in a log house standing near a spring which seventy-five years later was still being called "Brant's Spring." [68] There was a log church in which the services of the Church of England were read by someone attached to the garrison, or occasionally by an army chaplain or a missionary. The Mohawk version of parts of the Bible and Indian Prayer Book which Brant in collaboration with the Reverend John Stuart had translated before the war would have come into use. The bell that the Mohawks had brought away from their Upper Castle hung upon a cross-bar resting in the crotch of a tree.[69] General Powell found the Indians "comfortable settled and their fields well planted with Indian corn," and being "desirous of having a name expressive at the same time of their loyalty and unanimity, their village was christened Loyal Confederate Valley." [70]

General Haldimand continued to take a keen interest in the progress of the farmers at Niagara, and requested a plan of the settlement together with an estimate of the amount of land that had been brought under cultivation. Allan Macdonell, formerly sergeant of the Rangers, was employed to survey and mark the boundaries of allotments already made. Under the supervision of Lieutenant William Tinling of the Royal Engineers Macdonell began work early in March 1783. According to the account he submitted, two chain bearers and one marker were employed at 4s. per day for twenty-four days,[71] and the plan of the "New Settlement at Niagara from the Falls to Four Mile pond"† (reproduced between pp. 132 and 133) accompanied the account.[72]

---

* Slavery was abolished in Upper Canada in 1793, one of the first British colonies to take this step.

† Allan Macdonell's plan, long sought by historians, appeared quite unexpectedly during a search for maps of another area. Although undated and unsigned its relationship to Macdonell's account is verified by its reference which also shows its inclusion in a volume of "Additional MSS." Its importance lies in the fact that it is the first plan of any settlement in the region which eight years later was to become the Province of Upper Canada and eventually Ontario. The only colour, a blue wash to indicate water, is of so pale a shade that the Keeper of Manuscripts at the British Museum saw no advantage in reproducing it in colour.

It was when Macdonell was laying out the hundred acres allotted to Isaac Dolson that he (Dolson) expressed to his neighbour Elijah Phelps a view probably shared by the Secords whose allotments also lay at the foot of the escarpment. Dolson stated that he "did not wish to take the side of the Mountain" since "he expected when the Lands came to be granted that it would be thrown in to him."[73] Macdonell's plan shows that at this time no account was taken of the Mountain. It also shows John Chisholm as Elijah Phelps' neighbour on the south. Nothing more is known of John for the present, for no details of the agricultural progress were given on the census of 1783.

However, this census does tell us that Janet McMicking had been reunited with her family. There are two versions of how Mrs. McMicking reached Niagara. The first is the bare statement of fact that Thomas brought her from Albany.[74] The other is a fuller account of how she travelled alone from Albany for several days through the forest to the shore of Lake George. Upon finding three men with a boat she offered them a guinea to take her within sight of British shipping. After rowing only a short distance and upon rounding a point of land the boat came under the guns of the *Royal George*, a British man-of-war.[75] Mrs. McMicking was taken aboard, and when interviewed by the captain she related the capture of her sons, daughter, and grandsons, her fortuitous escape, and her journey from Albany. "The sailors hearing the tale of the guinea, offered to take it from the rascals and return it to her. She replied, 'Na, Na, they hae fulfilled their bargain, t'is nane o' mine.'"[76] Of the remainder of her journey by water through Lake George and Lake Champlain, down the Richelieu River to the St. Lawrence and up to Niagara there are no details, but to survive these experiences at the age of sixty-six required a rugged constitution.

Until such time as the grist mill could be got into operation the farmers were allowed to exchange their wheat for flour from the King's stores.[77] Delay in building the mill had arisen from a misunderstanding. In June 1782 Colonel Butler had informed General Haldimand that Peter and James Secord were about to build a saw and grist mill. Because they intended to purchase the mill stones and iron work in Canada they begged permission for these articles to be sent up in the King's batteaux.[78] The General promptly replied that he would not permit "anything of the kind as Private Property" and that the mill "must be undertaken entirely upon the same Footing as the Farms."[79] Butler explained that the Secords had never intended the mills for a private enterprise but for the benefit of the garrison and the whole settlement.[80] Nearly five months had elapsed when advice reached Niagara that, instead, the proposals of Lieutenant Brass of the Rangers, a skilled millwright, had been accepted. This was David Brass who had engaged in the battle of The Flockey and come to Niagara with Captain Adam Chrysler. He undertook the project for £500, the same amount as Colonel Butler had estimated for the building of a saw and grist mill at Peter Secord's farm. Common carpenters, all of them Rangers, who cut and squared the timbers were asking the exorbitant wage of 6s. per day, causing General Maclean to remark: "Its a maxim I find that has long been adopted in this Part of the world, that whatever can be got from Government, is well got, where no censure can ensue."[81] But Brass held down the costs and by early summer had completed the sawmill and a grist mill with two run of stones including the dam for £465 York.[82]

The site chosen for the government mills was on the west side at the upper end of the Four Mile Pond. Here the intervale is wide but the banks are low. To obtain an adequate drop for the water wheel the building was placed well below the level of the bank and the mill race cut on a higher level from the dam situated some distance above on the creek. Thus the water pouring down from the higher level turned the water wheel which set in operation the machinery of the mills. When the iron work failed to arrive from Quebec the farmers were "all in despair," but it was finally received just in time to get it installed and the mills going before winter set in. Daniel Servos of the Indian Department, who had settled nearby, became the first operator of these government mills. As the eldest son of Christopher Servos, Daniel had gained valuable experience in his father's mills before the war. In 1779, he had received his commission as "Lieutenant of Confederated Indians" [83] and had served in the Indian Department throughout the war.

In the meantime the outcome of the negotiations for peace, so eagerly awaited though not without misgivings, arrived at (New) York in March 1783. Article IV stipulated that Loyalist creditors should "meet with no lawful impediment" in the collection of debts. Article V for the restitution of all estates, rights, and properties which had been confiscated, provided that Congress would "earnestly recommend" to the different states that these be restored to Loyalists who had not borne arms; that all others might within twelve months recover confiscated property by paying the sale price. Article VI contained the clause that Congress would "earnestly recommend" that no future persecution be permitted. No mention whatsoever was made of the allies of Great Britain whose country east of the Niagara River lay within the territory ceded to the United States—the Indians of the Six Nations. Such treatment confounded the Indians because, as they explained to General Maclean, their "Ancestors granted permission to the French King to build trading houses or small forts on the water communication between Canada & the Western Indians . . . for the convenience of trade only without granting one inch of land but what the forts stood upon, and that at the end of the last war they granted leave to Sir Wm Johnson to hold these forts for their ally the King of England." They considered themselves faithful allies, not subjects; a free people, "subject to no power on earth." How then could the King cede away their land? "I should wish that Captain Brant might be detained in Canada for some time," Maclean wrote to General Haldimand, "he is much better informed and instructed than any other Indian, he is strongly attached to the Interest of his Countrymen, for which I do honor him, but he would be much more sensible of the miserable situation in which we have left this unfortunate People, that I do believe he would do a great deal of mischief here at this time; I do from my soul pity these People, and should they commit outrages . . . it would by no means surprise me." [84]

To the Loyalist exiles at Niagara, the accounts of the peace terms brought the realization that there was little hope of returning to their former homes. Colonel Butler stated that "none of his People will ever think of going to attend Courts of Law . . . where they could not Expect the Shadow of Justice and that to repurchase their Estates is what they are not able to do . . . and they would rather go to Japan than go among the Americans where they could never live in peace" [85] Therefore, with the idea of settling in the vicinity of Niagara a number of Rangers began looking for good farm land. Butler reported that if military claimants were compensated with grants in this district the land westward to Twelve Mile Creek and south of Lake Erie might be bought from the Indians for five or six hundred pounds sterling.[86] Those already settled, the farmers, were apprehensive about uncertain tenure and asked more security for the land which they had worked so hard to improve. This dissatisfaction is expressed in a politely phrased memorial to Colonel Butler entitled "The Humble Address of Farmers Residing on Lands On the West side of the River, Niagara," signed by Isaac Dolson, Elijah Phelps, Thomas McMicking and "Donal Bee" "on behalf of ourselves and the Rest of the Farmers." They related how the proposals of a year's provisions and the services of a blacksmith had not been met. They asked that they might be given leases or some other security for their farms and offered to pay rent after the term of eight years "as the footing we are on at present, We are Liable to be turned off our places when Ever the Commanding Officer pleases. We are happy for the present, being not under the least apprehention, But the Commandant[s] often change, which makes our Stay Uncertain." [87] The farmers, in reply to this address, were advised that in the final arrangements for settlement they would be shown every indulgence, but that at present General Haldimand awaited instructions from England.[88]

Some efforts were made to induce former tenants of Kortright Township to return to the Head of the Delaware. A newspaper advertisement entitled "Encouragement" which appeared over the name of Lawrence Kortright advised the "considerable number of families" who had left the township during the war that "as we now have peace, and once more expect to be happy in this country" he was prepared to make concessions to those who would return. He would "forgive" the payment of rent and interest money for five years.* [89] Only the families of Alexander Leal, Daniel McGillivrae, and Kortright's agent, Alexander Mills, are known to have returned to Kortright Township at this time.[90]

Whatever hopes this "encouragement" might have raised in the hearts of the Scots and other refugees from New York were dashed by reports of the animosity of victorious Americans. The copy of an Albany newspaper brought to Niagara revealed the bitterness and the contentious attitude of the inhabitants of the District of Saratoga who had called a public meeting to discuss the repatriation of Loyalists (see Appendix D). Tales of the sufferings of those who had had the temerity to return were equally discouraging. Benjamin Beacraft, who had been with Joseph Brant when Alexander Harper was taken prisoner, returned to his home in the Schoharie Valley. One day upon hearing a knock at his door he bade the caller to enter whereupon three men with whom he was acquainted filed into the room. Beacraft "arose, respectfully inquiring after their health, and offering his hand; the compliment was returned by a hearty and determined clench of his shoulders." He was taken outside to a hickory grove before a self-appointed "jury" of ten men. He was stripped, tied to a staddle (sappling), "to save him the trouble of running away," and after cutting hickory switches each man joined a circle and gave Beacraft fifty lashes on his back. They then warned him "to flee the country, and never more return to blast, with his presence, so pure an atmosphere as that where liberty and independence breath and triumph." [91] Compared with the experiences of others Beacraft would seem to have got off lightly. He returned to Niagara and with his wife Elizabeth Westbrook eventually settled on lot 11, concession 2, Ancaster Township.[92]

Meanwhile the settlement at Niagara grew apace. By early spring, 1783, 46 allotments had been made. Log houses stood on all but 2 and 20 farms had barns. Of

---

* Because Lawrence Kortright was evacuated with other Loyalists from New York to the St. John River in Nova Scotia where he remained for a time, this advertisement was manifestly placed by his son who seems to have taken over the handling of his father's estates.

the 713 acres that had been cleared 123 were under fall wheat and 342 stood ready for sowing in oats and Indian corn.

Rations were no longer needed by the earlier established families, even the largest. During 1783 no rations were issued to the Secords, Depues, Lutes, or Dolsons, although the Scottish families still received supplementary provisions. The allowance for Loyalists was two-thirds of a ration for adults and one-third for children. The Roses were issued one and the McMickings three rations per day during their second year on the land. These figures as gathered from a "Return of the Rise & Progress of a Settlement of Loyalists on the West side of the River, Niagara 18th April 1784"[93] show how well it had become established before the disbanding of the Rangers.

The Loyalists who participated in this agricultural experiment could not know or even suspect that they were the thin edge of a wedge of migration which was to populate the upper country of the Province of Quebec with an English-speaking people or that their settlement was the first link in a chain which would follow the north shores of Lake Ontario and Lake Erie from the gateway of Niagara. The Niagara River was now part of the new boundary line established by the treaty of peace, so that settlers once living on the frontier of the Indian country found themselves on a new frontier between Quebec and the United States of America. The same stroke of the pen which had given to the new democracy the country of the Six Nations and a great section of the fur country in the southwest gave also those old guardians of the fur trade, Forts Michilimackinac, Detroit, and Niagara.

During the time that the Scots along the river were once more beginning to convert wild land into farms, others from the Head of the Delaware were engaged in carving a town from a wilderness beside the sea. Leaving Brant's volunteers to their laborious task we will now step back in time to pick up the thread of events which had caused their compatriots to be caught up and set down on a shore of the Atlantic coast hundreds of miles away.

CHAPTER SEVEN

THE CITY: WITH SWORD AND MUSKET

OF THOSE SETTLERS who left Harpersfield, Kortright, and the Head of the Delaware, some had removed their families to places that were theoretically safe. Although out of danger from border raids most of these people were not permitted to remain; Hugh Fraser and Neil McKay, for example, had installed their families on leaseholds near Albany only to find them driven away by persecution. Others, like Jacob Stoneburner, who when released from gaol found themselves free in a hostile land without means of support, had no choice but to seek safety away from the frontier. And there were those such as George Chisholm who escaped while prisoners of war. Many of these displaced settlers eventually reached York Island, the last foothold of British occupation in the colonies.

Since the British seizure and occupation in 1776 (of the city on September 15 and of the whole island by November), York Island had become the haven of Loyalists from all the thirteen colonies from New Hampshire to Georgia. Upon the approach of the British army more than half of the population had fled; only some 5,000 people remained. This rapid change in population had resulted in great confusion particularly in the matter of housing. Though rebels' houses had been declared forfeit the military had first choice. This problem was further aggravated by the great fire which had destroyed one-quarter of the town. The young British officer Thomas Hughes estimated the number of buildings lost at about 4,000, mostly stone or brick. He was impressed by the "vast number of churches—the principal of which, St. Paul's, has escaped the fire though the houses round it were burnt to their foundations."[1] Trinity Church was a sombre ruin.

The refugees were also hard put to find employment in this garrison town. There being no regular poor tax, those who were unable to support themselves were dependent upon voluntary contributions. These unfortunates received assistance from army officers and wealthy Loyalists who took a deep interest in their plight. The first public charity, held on Christmas Eve in 1777, provided a dole of beef and bread to forty needy widows and householders.[2] Thereafter the rent of houses that were not occupied by the military and the money collected from licences and fines were appropriated to the relief of the poor. Soon funds were being raised by means such as the Associated Loyalists Lotteries, permits to cut wood on rebel estates, and contributions of money and clothing from England. Though markets were plentifully supplied with meat and vegetables from Long Island, to Hughes these products were "immoderately dear. Good fish is scarce but they have oysters by shiploads."[3] But supplies soon became inadequate to the demand because the enemy now controlled the shore of the mainland and American whale boats began to interfere with the transfer of supplies from Long Island. Some produce was brought from farms in the upper reaches of

York Island but the greater portion of provisions was sent from Britain in great fleets of victuallers under convoy which were often delayed in transit and always in danger of capture. The Commandant, General Pattison, determined the amount of food each family might buy; as is usual in times of war the civilian population was the first to suffer from shortages. Wood for fuel, being in short supply on the island, was brought across the water from Staten and Long islands. Fresh water was also scarce and high priced, the laying of wooden pipe lines in the city having been interrupted by the war. The sources of supply had remained unchanged in the last few years: Fresh Water Pond, Tea Water Pump at Roosevelt and Chatham Streets (now Park Row), and private wells. The pump which tapped one of the principal springs of the nearby pond had long supplied some 10,000 persons with water for their favourite beverage and carmen delivered it throughout the city.

Such was York Town when George Chisholm returned to it as a refugee in the winter of 1777. Where he had been imprisoned or how he reached the city have not been discovered, but it may be that like many others he contrived to escape. Hughes, who was then in the city, wrote on December 6, that "50 of Burgoyne's men who had made their escape arriv'd today. The guide who conducted them was allo'd [by military authorities] 1 guinea pr man. . . . I cannot help lamenting the deplorable situation of the Loyalists, who because they will not violate their oath of allegiance . . . are turn'd out of their houses, their estates sold, and themselves and families reduced . . . to beggary and want. Such is the Land of Liberty!"[4]

Sometime within the next three or four years George Chisholm set up as merchant although how or when has not been established, nor has the type of business in which he engaged or its location. Because unskilled workers were earning 10s.* per day, almost five times as much as before the war, the wages of skilled artisans were rising accordingly. Many of these, and particularly carpenters, were employed in the army departments, and perhaps Chisholm was among them. In any case this frugal Highlander would appear to have obeyed the aphorism of the time which admonished mankind to "make hay while the sun shineth." Somehow Chisholm contrived to become a merchant with at least one employee.[5]

Naturally Chisholm sought out the Highlanders of whom there were large numbers in the city. One such was Captain Normand Tolmie who commanded the volunteer company[6] in which Chisholm enrolled. Tolmie, a Highlander from the Isle of Skye, had since 1756 been resident in York as merchant trader between York, Antigua, and London. At the outbreak of the war he had fled to Long Island, joined the British troops as a volunteer, and engaged in the battle of Long Island. Upon the British occupation of York Governor Tryon had appointed him captain of an independent company known as the Highland Volunteer Militia which wore Highland dress and served without pay.[7] In 1776 Tolmie was "Enginier" in the fire company commanded by Captain Jacobus Stoutenbergh[8] who lived in Fulton Street, and the

---

* Rates of exchange for coins of various countries which passed as legal tender given in the *New-York Gazette and the weekly mercury*, May 12, 1777:

Guinea	£1.17.4 York currency
Half Johannes	3. 4.0
Moidore	2. 8.0
Spanish dollar	–. 8.–
English shilling	–. 1.9

The pound in York currency was worth half the pound sterling.

following year he was appointed superintendent in Montgomery Ward for the prevention of incendiarism. That Tolmie was explosively loyal to the Crown and would brook no nonsense from upstart Americans is clearly indicated by an affidavit he made in 1766.[9] Upon the signing of the Declaration of Independence Tolmie was immediately summoned before the Commissioners for Conspiracies and his name duly entered on the "List of Suspected Persons."[10]

Alexander Leckie, the merchant in Hanover Square, and Alexander Robertson, employed in the Barrack Office, were also to become acquaintances of Chisholm's. Robertson had been in America since 1770 and became and Indian trader on the Ohio River in Pennsylvania not far from Fort Pitt. Having become implicated in a plan to destroy a rebel magazine in 1777 he had fled within the British lines.[11]

Another man with whom Chisholm was to become acquainted was a native American with a typical Loyalist story. Charles Oliver Bruff was the eldest son of James Earl Bruff who had substantial landholdings in Maryland and who possessed lead and silver mines in the Wyoming valley of the Susquehanna in Pennsylvania. Charles became a silversmith, jeweller, and cutler, establishing himself at York in 1775. Being "a good sword cutter" he had been forced to work for rebels though unwillingly and always without pay. Because of his work he was excused from turning out with the militia, but was obliged to take duty in the city watch. When the British landed on Long Island Bruff escaped to New Jersey, joined the British army, and returned to York.[12] "Those gentlemen of the navy and army," he was advising the public through the press in 1778, "in want of swords, may be suited with all sorts" at the sign of the Teapot and Tankard, no. 196 Queen Street. He was making light-horse swords with death's head and cross-bones, and others of "the most elegant pattern that has ever made its appearance in America" : His Majesty's likeness with an ornamental guard lettered all round with "Success to British arms." This legend was also incorporated with a crown and "the Old English Rose" in a design for silver shoebuckles "suitable for all Loyalists."[13] When advertising for assistants Bruff offered "highest wages... and a quart of GROGG a day."[14]

Soon after his arrival at York, Chisholm was in touch with another Highlander, William McKenzie, a refugee from the Old England District of Tryon County. The McKenzies who had migrated from the Highlands in 1774 (see pp. ix, xi) had settled a short distance above Unadilla on a 150-acre farm in the "Scotch Settlement" in the valley of Ouleout Creek,* a tributary of the Susquehanna. Although the approaches to the settlement were steep and rough it lay on one of the main trails leading east and west,[15] but more than thirty miles of hills and dales stood between this little Tory community and the Head of the Delaware. William McKenzie had also owned seventy-five acres in the "District of Kinderhook" which was undoubtedly the township of Kinderhook laid out by Sir William Johnson on the east side of the Hudson some twelve miles above the Kaatskill Landing and about twenty miles south of Albany.[16] The holdings he was forced to abandon were valued at £457.6.7.[17]

In the summer of 1778, George Chisholm and William McKenzie's twenty-year-old daughter, Barbara, were married. Presumably the ceremony was performed by

* In the printed version of the journal kept in 1779 by Lieut. Erkuries Beatty of the Continental army the name of this settlement appears as Albout—probably a misreading of Aleout as given on the 1778 map of William Gray. Both journal and map were published in George S. Conover, ed., *Journals of the Expedition of Major General John Sullivan against the Six Nations Indians in 1779* (Auburn, N.Y., 1887), pp. 23 and 288.

Reverend John M. Mason,* minister of the "Scotch Church" which had been built in 1768 in Cedar Street near Broad Way.[18] Originally part of the Wall Street Church founded in 1757, this congregation had seceded and in 1761 had called Dr. Mason from Scotland to their pulpit. On August 28, 1779, Barbara Chisholm was delivered of a daughter, named Janet for her paternal grandmother, but this child did not survive infancy. A second daughter, Mary Christina, was born on April 24, 1782. It so happened that at this time her future husband, Ephraim Land, a lad of seven, was living in the city with his mother, Phoebe, and a brother and sister. This was the family of Robert Land, woodturner and justice of the peace at Cushetunk in Pennsylvania nearly opposite Cochecton, New York, on the Delaware River about twenty miles above Minisink. Robert was a native of Devonshire who had migrated in his youth to America and settled in the Delaware Valley. He served in the Seven Years' War and by 1772 he and his wife (Phoebe Scott of Virginia) had several children, and he had become an important man in this remote frontier community. Due to his knowledge of the country Land became a dispatch carrier for General Sir Henry Clinton, commander-in-chief of the British forces. While Land was absent in April 1777, a band of marauding Indians massacred a neighbouring family and burned the house. Phoebe and her children were saved by a friendly Indian but her second son Abel was carried away. The eldest son John and a group of settlers overtook the Indians and bargained for Abel's release. When, one by one, Robert while on a mission, Abel while serving with Joseph Brant, and John were taken and thrown into gaol, Phoebe fled with her youngest children to safety within the British lines.[19] "The bearer is the wife of Robert Land," wrote Lieutenant-Colonel Beverley Robinson on May 22, 1779. "This woman came in yesterday with three Children. I believe it would be proper to give her an order to Col^n Morris to draw provisions for herself and Children. She tells me her husband made his escape and gone to Butler. . . ." This letter bears the endorsement "Col. Morris will be pleased to give provision to Mrs. Land."[20]

The following May when under sentence of death for treason Robert Land again contrived to escape but Ralph Morden, his friend and guide through the Blue Ridge Mountains, was taken, tried, and condemned to death. It was to Morden's execution that Thomas Hughes referred when he entered in his journal on November 26, 1780, "A man was hanged this morning for piloting some people through the back woods, to the Indians. He was very old and left a wife and 9 children. His death was chiefly owing to his being a noted friend of Government."[21] Eventually Robert Land joined his family at York and attended the baptism by the rector of Trinity Church of his son Ephraim on January 21, 1781.[22] But he was soon off again to Niagara and was not destined to see his family again for many years.

By 1779 Hugh Fraser and Allen Macdonell were also in York, but just how or when they had contrived to reach it has not been discovered. The first intimation of their presence appears in a request dated November 16, 1779, and addressed to the Continental authorities that their families be permitted to join them at York because they intended to return to Scotland.[23] The story of the detention of the Frasers and the Macdonells is linked with that of such families as the Moores and the Campbells who were taken prisoner at Cherry Valley on November 11, 1778. The following

---

* Thirty-two years later, in 1810, Dr. Mason resigned to become provost of Columbia College which had been King's College until 1784 (Kenneth Holcomb Dunshee, *As You Pass By* (New York, 1952), p. 195).

March Colonel Samuel Campbell had appeared at Canaseraga near Oneida Lake to plead with the British officers for the release of prisoners held by the Indians. "As I understand it," the Commandant of Niagara reported to General Haldimand, "they wish to get back some of their Prisoners taken at Cherry Valley & have offered to exchange Mrs. Butler & family. . . . It appears to me that they [the Indians] have got some prisoners that the enemy has a much greater esteem for than any of those formerly taken. . . ."[24] Therefore, when Colonel John Butler arrived in the Indian country to prepare against Sullivan's campaign he searched out Mrs. Campbell and Mrs. John Moore and her four daughters.

It was not always possible to secure the release of captives merely by paying ransom. In cases where adopted prisoners filled the places of dead relatives much tact and discretion were required to gain them their freedom. Such was the status of Mrs. Samuel Campbell, and the family into which she had been adopted were most reluctant to part with her. She had been treated with civility bordering upon admiration. Upon one occasion when receiving the gift of a cap which was cut and stained with blood she recognized it as having been worn by her dead friend, Jane Wells, daughter of Reverend Samuel Dunlop. The strong appeals of Colonel Butler prevailed, however, and on June 18 he was able to advise the Commandant of Niagara: "I have procured the Releasement of a Mrs. Campbell, and have sent her with Mr. Seacord to Niagara; she is much in want of Cloathes & other necessaries; if there is not a more convenient Place, I have told her she might stay at my House. I expect in a few days to get Mrs. Moore & Family released likewise."[25]

Meanwhile, ever since her husband had gone to gaol as hostage for Sir John Johnson in 1775, Mrs. Allan Macdonell and her children had been detained "about Albany." Although they were not actually prisoners, they had for some time been held at Schenectady[26] where had it not been for the assistance of James Ellice, prominent merchant of that town, "they must have perished."[27] Hugh Fraser's wife was evidently living in similar circumstances east of the Hudson at Hoosick, New York,[28] only a short distance from Bennington, Vermont. The futures of both these families was made clear by Governor Clinton of the State of New York in his decree dated October 13, 1779: "No permissions will be granted to the Wives and Families of Persons who have joined the Enemy to remove from the Country until the Women and Children taken at Cherry Valley and other places on the Frontiers are returned to their Husbands and Friends."[29] Macdonell and Fraser were thus moved to make the request referred to above. This stirring appeal, which was carried from York to Albany by ladies granted passes for travelling through the enemy's territory, first expressed "the Feelings of Husbands and Parents" and disclaimed all connection with the border raids, and then continued as follows:

> We deplore, that the proceedings of Colo. Butler and the Indians under his command should be plac'd as a Bar to our most anxious wishes of meeting our unfortunate families. . . . That Mrs. Campbell and one or two more women being carried off from Cherry Valley we hope will not in any shape be imputed or resented on our innocent Wives and Children. . . . We humbly hope that the hard & unparallel'd condition of requiring detention of our families for Mrs. Campbell &ca. will not longer be insisted on. In fine, Sir, altho of opposite sentiments politically, that as Men, as Christians, and as Gentlemen we may have the honour to resemble you in wishing to relieve the distress'd and helpless Women and Children. . . . P.S. please observe that nothing detains us from retiring to Great Britain but the arrival of our Families.[30]

In February 1780, the Continental authorities were advised by the British that the Campbells and Moores had been secured with great trouble from the Indians and were then at Niagara;[31] that they would be safely conducted to any convenient place provided that Mrs. Butler were sent across Lake Champlain while the ice was still safe; and that, should the exchange be too long delayed, the Indians, already displeased, would demand the return of their prisoners.[32] The Continentals replied that Mrs. Butler would be advised of permission to go to Canada and that Mrs. Macdonell and Mrs. Fraser would have safe conduct either to Canada or to York.[33] Early in the spring the Moores and the Campbells were therefore sent down to Montreal where they were to remain until the exchange took place. There Mrs. Campbell found her fourth child, a son, under the care of Mrs. Butler. He was dressed in the green uniform of Butler's Rangers and having forgotten the English language spoke only the Indian. His grandson, William W. Campbell, was the author of that valuable source book on the New York frontier known as the *Annals of Tryon County*.

Finally, late in the summer of 1781, with other prisoners for exchange the Moores and Campbells set out in batteaux on the water route by way of the Richelieu River and Lake Champlain. Upon the arrival from enemy territory of a group of Loyalists "brought by a flag" to St. John's, the Commandant, Brigadier H. Watson Powell, wrote to a Continental officer, "I am sending by your return flag of truce, Mrs. Campbell, Mrs. Moore, and their families. . . . The attention which has been shown to Mrs. Campbell, and those in her unfortunate circumstances, as well as the good treatment of the prisoners, which it is hoped they will have the candor to acknowledge, is referred to for comparison, to those by whose orders or permission His Majesty's subjects have experienced execution, the horrors of a dungeon, loaded with irons, and the miseries of want." [34] The prisoners were then taken up the lake to Skenesborough (modern Whitehall) where they were awaited by the commissioners for exchange representing both combatants. The families of Hugh Fraser and Allan Macdonell, however, were neither permitted to leave the country nor afforded any relief, and were obliged to make out as best they could until the end of the war.

Captain John Macdonell's wife Catherine and her five children were also in great distress. The Captain appealed to Governor Haldimand,[35] and, upon hearing a report that an exchange had been effected, he went to St. John's only to find the rumour untrue. To the Governor's secretary he wrote that he knew for certain that they were both naked and starving; that his eldest daughter Mary of about sixteen was obliged to hire herself to an old Dutch woman "to spin in order to prevent starving"; and that

> I hope that you or any man of feeling may never experience what I suffered upon the occasion; If nothing can be done to obtain their speedy deliverance I beg . . . that you apply to his Excellency to send a party of Savages to bring me their six scalps, tho' it may seem unnatural, yet I assure you I would rather see, or hear them dead than to linger any longer in misery. If his Excellency has not prisoners to give in exchange, I will most cheerfully head any party he may think proper, and make out their number, or perish in the attempt.[36]

It would appear, however, that this family like the Frasers and the Allan Macdonells were obliged to remain in dire circumstances until the end of the war.

In the meantime, the refugees already at York were beset with many hardships. In the summer of 1778 another great fire swept the congested area in the lower reaches of the city. It broke out in the early hours of August 3 in a ship chandlery on Crugh's Wharf. The flames jumping across narrow Little Dock Street consumed the houses on the next block in Great Dock Street, including the handsome residence of Lawrence Kortright who had continued to remain in the city.[37] Fire fighting companies together with the salvage corps went into action. The Fire Patrol formed of citizens who volunteered to aid in removing and securing endangered property had been organized after the first fire engines had been unloaded from the *Beaver* and placed in sheds near the City Hall in December 1731. The "enjines from London" were two-cylinder, sidestroke machines mounted on solid wooden block wheels and operated by eight to ten men. Having no fifth wheel for steering they had to be lifted when turning corners.* [38] In addition to the usual salvaging equipment, the Fire Patrol carried stout linen bags in which removable property was secured. Members were authorized to wear round leather hats with black brims and white crowns bearing the painted insignia of such companies as the "Hand in Hand" (clasped hands) and the "Heart to Heart." [39] There were, of course, citizens who loudly protested that more property was lost through the pilfering of the rescuers than was ever destroyed by fire. Because this fire was looked upon as "not the effect of Accident but Design" a reward of one hundred guineas was offered for information leading to the apprehension of the arsonists.[40]

Conditions improved somewhat in 1779 because the British campaigns in the Highlands of the Hudson had opened parts of the surrounding country and refugee Loyalists were permitted to work farms on the mainland in an attempt to augment the food supply. But prices were so high as to burden the wealthy let alone those possessed of little.† Also, there was an epidemic of "very contagious distemper" brought in July by a ship from Georgia. It was said that almost every house was a hospital and that there were scarcely enough well persons to tend the sick. As to doctors the better training and wider experience of the army surgeons made them superior to private practitioners. A Dr. Dasturge at 13 Duke Street advised the public that he had trained in Paris and claimed among his many accomplishment the making of excellent artificial teeth and "bandages for all kinds of ruptures, and other pieces proper to repair defects of the human body, some of which decency will not permit him to explain...." [41] ("Any persons that are willing to dispose of their Front Teeth may hear of a purchaser by applying ...," runs another announcement of the period.[42]) For those unable or unwilling to consult physicians there were patent medicines galore such as "Dr. Ryan's Incomparable Worm destroying SUGAR PLUMS necessary to be kept in all Families ... a sovereign cure for the Whouping Cough." [43] Maredant's Antiscorbutic Drops were a remedy long renowned for scurvy.[44]

Crowded conditions and insanitary practices contributed to the rapid spread of disease. Although the authorities ordered that all filth be kept indoors until the weekly collection (at the householder's expense) for dumping in underwater swamps citizens continued as formerly to throw it in the streets. Fresh Water Pond where clothes were

---

* The largest of New York's first fire engines may be seen at the museum of the Fireman's Home in Hudson, New York.

† The price of bread though pegged by the government had risen from 14 coppers for a 3¼-lb. loaf in 1778 to 21 coppers for a 2-lb. loaf in 1779. Prices of country produce in this year as compared with 1773:

	1773	1779
Butter per pound	£ 0. 4.0	£ 1.10.7
Tallow ,, ,,	0. 3.0	1. 4.5
Cattle ,, ,,	18.18.0	115.15.0
Calves ,, ,,	7.10.0	45. 2.9
Sheep ,, ,,	4. 0.0	27.10.0
Hogs ,, ,,	3. 0.0	26. 0.0
Corn per bushel	1. 1.4	2.16.3
Firewood per cord	4.15.0	16. 0.0

(J. Almon, ed., *The Remembrancer, or Impartial Repository of Political Events for 1781*, pp. 185, 195.)

washed was also used for a dump, but by some miracle the city escaped any major epidemic (excepting the one brought from Georgia and discussed above) during the years of the war.

The winter of 1779-80 was so exceptionally long and severe as to cause great suffering among the population, both military and civil. Snow which began falling in November continued almost daily until the middle of March. In some places it lay four feet deep on the level, and ice in the rivers was too thick for boats to pass through but at first too thin for sleds to be drawn across it. Transportation of provisions and wood became impossible and the city was virtually isolated before January. All the trees in the city including ornamental, fruit, and spruce, the latter of which had heretofore been protected for making the spruce beer that helped to avert scurvy, were cut down. Old ships, sheds, shacks, fences, and anything that would serve as fuel soon disappeared. Families crowded together in one house for warmth and some poor people even resorted to burning fat for the little heat it gave. Many froze to death before wood and provisions could be brought in, and by the time the cold weather abated York Island was totally deforested and stripped of wood of any kind.[45]

The deepening ice laid the city open to attack from the mainland. "We could scarcely be said to be an insular state," wrote General Pattison to his superior in England. "The passage in the North river, even in the widest part from thence to Paulus Hook, 2000 yards, was about the 19th [January] practicable for the heaviest canon, an event unknown in the memory of man; and very soon after provisions were transported upon sleighs, and a detachment of cavalry marched from New-York to Staten Island, eleven miles upon the ice."[46] All males, firemen excepted, between the ages of seventeen and sixty were called up and within seven days of the proclamation forty companies were enrolled, officered, and armed. "The old volunteer companies," continued General Pattison, "likewise augmented their numbers, and in a very few days. I reviewed them all together under arms, [reported elsewhere as totalling 6,000] most of them cloathed in uniform at their own expense. General Knyphausen, General Tryon and all the General officers were present and expressed the highest satisfaction at so respectable a body of men."[47] The list given under the heading of "Old Companies" shows the enrolment of the New-York Highlanders commanded by Captain Tolmie to be two lieutenants, four non-commissioned officers, and a hundred privates.[48] Among them was Chisholm's father-in-law, William McKenzie.[49] Judge Jones recalled the company of Highlanders who "dressed in the habit of their country made a most respectable and warlike appearance. The officers consisted of gentlemen of the first rank and the privates composed of respectable merchants, traders, private gentlemen, and well to do mechanics."[50] The Scots clad in their clan tartans and bonnets and led by their pipers would have made a fine contrast to the militiamen clothed in the usual short coats, capes, and buckskin hats who marched to fife and drum.

The volunteer corps, equipped only with arms from the royal arsenal, served as guards, thus relieving the regular army for service outside the city. They patrolled the docks, guarded civil and military prisoners, erected fortifications, and stood ready for various other types of duty. They exercised three times weekly and before long became "as expert as any regiment in his majesty's service," according to Judge Jones.[51] McKenzie was employed in carpentering[52] and likely Chisholm as well. Though the expected attack on the island did not materialize during the thirty-six days that the ice formed a bridge to the Jersey shore the British did not relax their vigilance once the immediate danger had passed.

During these times of strain and stress, hunger and want, and above all the inactivity that masses of the citizenry were forced to endure, public entertainments of all kinds were encouraged by the military authorities. There were concerts when lanterns were strung in the trees along Broad Way, and celebrations on the birthdays of the King and Queen when royal salutes were fired from the Battery and ships in the harbour, and there were parades, feasts, balls, and fireworks. Lists of the fireworks describe such pieces as men-of-war engaged in a sea battle, illuminated air balloons, Chinese fountains, "cascades of brilliant Fire, with two Nests of Serpents, and a Swarm Box," a large illuminated tree "with several Birds flying out, and coming in again," a flight of small rockets, and of course "The King and Queen Illuminated." [53] For those who had the money for tickets of admission there was no lack of exhibits. At one time there was "a Panther, To be seen at the Sign of Rodney's Engagement . . . the most curious wild Beast that has been seen in this City these 40 years. Admission, one shilling." [54] At another time Thomas Courtney in Dock Street exhibited "a curious Magic Lanthorn . . . every Evening this Week at six o'clock precisely. . . . Tickets at Two Shillings." [55] Charity benefits were given at the Theatre Royal in John Street, when *She Stoops to Conquer, The Rivals, Richard III, School for Scandal,* and such farces as *High Life below the Stairs, Love à-la-Mode, Miss in Her Teens,* and *The Upholsterers* were acted out; sometimes "the Characters [were played] by the Gentlemen of the Army." Before performances scheduled for 7 P.M. "Ladies and Gentlemen are desired to send servants to their places at half past four to prevent mistakes. Vivant Rex & Regina." [56] In the winter of 1780 when the danger of attack was greatest, leading citizens and the garrison forces attended a ball at Hicks' tavern where portraits of the King and Queen surrounded by the legend "Britons, Strike Home" hung above the entrance. Though apt to keep many of the officers in debt such activities were encouraged by the authorities to keep up morale. The social whirl also included subscription concerts, "Little Hops," and card games. One bookseller stocked *Hoyle Improved, or New Maxims for Playing the Game of Whist.*[57] The sporting gentry supported horse-racing and cock-fighting, and lotteries were most popular. A publisher at the Bible and Crown in Hanover Square offered *A Little Lottery Book for Children . . . published with the Approbation of the Court of Common Sense.*[58] Other books in demand were *The Wonderful Life and Surprising Adventures of Robinson Crusoe, Letters of the Earl of Chesterfield to his Son . . . , The Complete Housewife, or, Accomplished Gentlewoman's Companion,* and *The Complete Letter-Writer, or Polite English Secretary,* [which] *contains familiar letters on the most common Occasions in Life.* "Also a Variety of More elegant Letters for *Example* and improvement of *style,* from the best modern Authors, together with many Originals on Business, Duty, Amusement, Affection, Courtship, Marriage, Friendship and other subjects." [59]

Coffee houses were numerous and taverns legion. Among the former were the Merchants', the London, and the Horse and Chair. Some taverns were The Sign of the Faithful Irishman and Jolly Sailors, The Black Horse Tavern, The Bunch of Grapes, the Old Punch House, The Sign of Joseph Brandt or the Indian King, the Queen's Head Inn, and the Ordinary of Charles Roubalet where "Dinner [was] on the Table precisely at three o'clock." Because the Queen's Head was to become famous as Fraunces' Tavern which is the oldest building in the city today the following description given when it changed hands in 1781 may hold some interest: "An elegant three-story and a half brick dwelling house, situated in Great Dock Street at the corner of Pearl Street . . . and ffor many years distinguished as the Queen's Head Tavern; in which are nine spacious rooms, besides five bed chambers, with three bedrooms, well furnished, an exceedingly good kitchen, and a spring of remarkable fine water therein; a most excellent cellar under the whole." [60] Built early in the century on the northeast corner of Broad and Great Dock streets as a residence by Stephen Delancey this property was purchased in 1763 by Samuel Fraunces who had there established the Queen's Head Inn.

From June to October citizens might foregather at the "Bathing Machine upon the plan of those used at Margate, and other watering-places in England" situated on the bank of the North River. (Subscribers, one guinea per season ticket, non-subscribers, five shillings.) "It is expected that Gentlemen Subscribers will rise early enough to dismiss the machine for the use of the Ladies. . . ." [61]

Taken at face value, the long lists of goods offered by merchants and tradesmen show few indications that the circumstances of the population had been much altered by the war. In point of fact many of the items were mentioned by reason of their scarcity. Periodically Alexander Leckie in Hanover Square announced "a neat assortment of dry goods" imported from London and Glasgow, "also Superfine flour, Durham mustard, Poland starch, hair powder, with perfumeries assorted, playing cards," and et ceteras almost *ad infinitum*. A merchant in Little Dock Street listed "ribbons, sailcloth, tripe in kegs"; another "Royal tooth powder, Tooth brushes of various sorts, Shoe do., Buckle do., Camel's hair do. for shaving, Common do. for do." There were "French curling irons, crapeing do., Pinching do., Tupee do., Swansdown puff, An innocent liquid to change the colour of red or grey hair, Bears grease plain, hard and soft pomatum" variously scented. For ladies there was "Liquid Bloom of Circassia [which] instantly gives a Rosy-Hue to the cheeks, not to be distinguished from the . . . animated Bloom of Rural Beauty, nor will it come off by Perspiration or the Use of an Handkerchief." [62]

The summer of 1782 was to be long remembered for the distress caused by a shortage of water. Drought dried up most of the wells in the city and what water was procurable from vendors was both prohibitive in price and poor in quality. Despite constant efforts on the part of the officials to prevent it the water became contaminated. After extensive research on all matters pertaining to this period in the history of the city of New York Dr. Oscar T. Barck reached the conclusion that the officials did their work well considering the problems with which they were confronted.

> The British officials had more to do than plan campaigns and protect their gains. They had to provide the necessities of life for the civilian inhabitants of New York as well as for their own men. . . . it is a wonder that with all the hardships endured and self-sacrifice practiced by the Loyalists, there was not more defection from the royal cause. Perhaps this could be accounted for in two ways: because the Loyalists were content to endure temporary discomfort for the sake of ultimate victory, and because there was not much else to do but stay and make the best of things.[63]

Also the Loyalists had been assured of the King's readiness to help them seek new homes once hostilities had ceased. As early as April 21, 1777, General Howe had promised that officers would receive two hundred acres and privates fifty acres of land in Canada at the end of the war. By autumn 1782 little doubt remained of the necessity of removing Loyalists from the country. Whereas it was relatively simple for the British government to provide the hundreds at Niagara with land by purchasing it from the Indians, at York the government was faced with the problem of evacuating thousands to another province by sea. To plan and execute this large-scale operation Sir Guy Carleton was appointed commander-in-chief of North America with headquarters in the city.

The land chosen for the settlement of these Loyalists was that named Nova Scotia by Sir William Alexander, the Scotsman to whom it had been granted in 1621 by King James I of England and so aptly called "the doorstep of a continent." For some years parts of the province had been settled by colonists from New England, and during the war small companies of Loyalists had found refuge in Halifax. In an effort to discover others wishing to go there a public meeting was called by a group of prominent men who had heard of Port Roseway. This fine harbour situated on the south coast of the peninsula of Nova Scotia was specially adapted to shipping, and its fisheries were capable of supporting thousands of people. At the meeting a committee was chosen, and 120 heads of families entered into an agreement to become settlers at Port Roseway. Being of the opinion that a settlement there would both promote the fisheries and trade and at the same time further the security of the province Carleton requested that lands be granted to the families anxious to go to Port Roseway.

The minutes of the proceedings of the Port Roseway Associates begin Saturday, November 16, 1782.[64] "At a meeting of the Loyalists Associated for the purpose of removing and Settling at Port Roseway in Nova Scotia [runs the first entry]—in consequence of the Encouragement of Sr Guy Carleton Commander in Chief at New York —Sr Andrew Snape Hammond, late Govr. and Commander in Chief at Nova Scotia— and the Proclamations relating to the settlement of the said Province," it was voted unanimously "that all things" relative to the settlement "be determined finally by the Majority of Votes of the Company assembled." Joseph Pynchon was chosen president for that meeting, and together with Captain Joseph Durfee, superintendent of small craft at the port of New York,[65] James Dole, formerly merchant at Albany, Thomas Courtney, Joshua Pell of Pelham Manor, and two others, was appointed to the committee in charge of arrangements. It was also voted "that no Person be allowed to subscribe their names to the Association at the place of General Meeting—But to attend for that purpose at the House of Captn. Durfee, No. 125 Water Street, New Slip *with a proper* Recommendation from one of the Associators."

On November 30 at the City Hall (built 1700 and remodelled 1763) in Broad Street where it ended at Wall Street, it was agreed that all persons other than Associates and those holding tickets of recommendation should be excluded from the meetings, and a door man was appointed for enforcement of this ruling. Any person could have his name erased from the list before December 17 but thereafter those refusing to go "should have their names transmitted to the Governor of Nova Scotia as persons forfeiting their *word & honor*."

George Chisholm, William McKenzie, and the jeweller and cutler, Charles Oliver Bruff, became Associates, but as the names were listed alphabetically it is impossible to determine at what stage of the proceedings their decisions had been reached. Chisholm is no. 6 on his list, McKenzie is no. 9, and all three men were recommended by Alexander Robertson. No McKays appear. Edward Bowlby, farmer, with whom both Chisholm and McKenzie were to become well acquainted, also joined the Associates. A native American and formerly a man of considerable property, Bowlby had, in 1773, inherited his father's land in Hanover, Morris County, New Jersey;

said to be the best land in the county. As Bowlby told his own story, "he joined the British at Hackinsack in 1776, but on returning to his family he was taken Prisn^r by the Rebels but made his escape and got into New York in 1777. He was taken Prisn^r in the Jerseys in 1778 & tryd for his life but was only flogged. He received 500 Lashes & [was] sent into the British Lines."[66]

At a meeting held December 7, 1782, the Port Roseway Associates chose Joseph Pynchon and James Dole as commissioners to go down to Nova Scotia "and to make and transmit a report thereof."[67] Upon their arrival in Halifax they were given a cordial reception by the Governor who assured them of assistance in the matters of provisions, surveys, building materials, and such. On January 23, 1783, Pynchon reported that in the opinion of Governor Parr and Sir Andrew Hammond, Port Roseway "will be one of the Capital ports in America" and that

the Surveyor General says we have chosen the best Situation in the province for Trade, Fishery, and Farming. . . . It is generally supposed that the best Grounds for farming are yet ungranted, back of Port Roseway and Jordan River . . . very few people here have any further acquaintance than the heads of the Harbours, for further Information I expect . . . to make a Journey to Annapolis—expecting to send a Surveyor with Chain and Compass across Country to Port Roseway [to make remarks on the terrain every mile or so]. . . . As to fruit in this Country—Strawberrys are in great perfection, Currants, Raspberrys, Cherrys, Gooseberrys, Plumbs, Apples & Pears and almost every other New England fruit but Peaches—at Port Roseway they raise Oats, Barley, Rye and the best of Flax, and the last year Siberian Wheat in perfection and without Blast. . . .

Pynchon recommended the purchase at York of nails:

They are scarce in this place [Nova Scotia], Also Tools for Building . . . I would strongly recommend that every Family with whom it is possible would bring with them whatever Stoves can be procured, or at least every Family one—for it may be possible that all our Chimneys cannot be built before Winter—in such case every Family with a little cooking Shed adjoining the back door, and a Stove in the Keeping Room, may be very comfortable during One Winter.[68]

With the reception of this favourable report the number of Associates increased to more than four hundred families and plans went forward for their removal. Included in this number was Hugh Fraser of Kortright who had finally brought his family into York early in March 1783.[69]

The committee was advised that from the day of landing all males and females above ten years of age would receive the full allowance of rations, a concession which had never been made heretofore, and that children under that age would be allowed half rations. Governor Carleton recommended that the Associates form themselves into militia companies and immediately appoint "proper persons as Captains, and those Captains shall be authorized as Magistrates by him, to determine, and settle all disputes that may arise in the body between Individuals or Others—until the Government of the Province of Nova Scotia takes place."[70] The captains assisted by two lieutenants would direct the distribution of provisions and the division of lands. Carleton appointed a board of agency and Lieutenant-Colonel Beverley Robinson its president to apportion government aid among the refugees.

Besides free passage to Nova Scotia the Associates were given "permission for the Shipping of any article they may find necessary to carry with them" in the ships provided by the British government.[71] The subscribers having submitted the numbers of their respective families, the committee applied for thirty tons of shipping per family (at which Commissary Watson seemed greatly surprised) and for the conveyance of eighty horses belonging to farmers. Carleton raised the question of how the horses were to exist after their arrival since to take sufficient forage for them would be impossible. This problem was left to the further consideration of the committee.

The news made public at a large meeting on March 19, 1783, that after six months no more provisions would be forthcoming caused dismay and discouragement to fly through the ranks of the Loyalists. Carleton assured the committee that although supplies for only six months had been ordered the government would certainly not allow them to starve.[72] None the less, the committee took the precaution of advising Sir Andrew Hammond of their fears on the eve of their departure. After thanking him for his interest and assistance "which we hope will have their due effect upon the Association in General, and make the name of *Hammond* dear to every Individual," and setting forth their circumstances the committee concluded: "It is needless for us to attempt to describe our feelings, nor how much we shall be at a loss. . . . In this situation we . . . are looking up to those Friends who are willing to support and relieve the distresses of a number of people suffering for their Loyalty to the King of Great Britain."[73]

On March 23 twenty-four men were nominated and voted upon to serve as captains, sixteen being chosen from the candidates. Although he received more than sufficient votes Alexander Robertson apparently declined to serve; therefore the group with which the McKenzies and Chisholms became identified is unknown. This is also true of the Frasers. After ruling that the subscription book be closed at noon on March 30 the committee requested Governor Carleton "to issue the necessary Orders for the Conveniency of Embarkation and settlement at Port Roseway."[74] The Governor replied that he wished the Associates to embark as soon as possible that they "may reap the benefit of the Season" and advised application be made to Admiral Digby for a strong convoy.[75]

On preparing to remove to the wilderness of a new country the Loyalists had packed their personal effects in chests and trunks, their china and crockery in hogsheads and casks. Placing these together with chairs, bureaus, beds, carpets, and bedding upon carts they transported their possessions to the wharves at the harbour and stowed them away in the holds of vessels. Townspeople took carriages and horses, artisans the tools of their trades, and farmers their cattle, sheep, hogs, and crates of fowls and geese. Margaret Hembrow "at No. 2 Pump Street, opposite the Wind-mill, Bowery Lane" advertized that "Persons going to Nova Scotia, &c. can be supplied on reasonable Terms" with an assortment of choice garden seeds.[76] Some took squared timbers and other materials for building frame instead of log houses, and others their dismantled houses for setting up in Nova Scotia. Almost every family was accompanied by their servants; the Bruffs had eight, the Frasers three though the McKenzies (with two daughters and son Murdoch) and Chisholms each had but one.

The Associates assembled for the last time in York on April 12, the day before embarkation, when it was moved "that meetings of this Association do adjourn until the Body arrives at Port Roseway."[77] That same day Governor Carleton wrote: "The Refugees who are going to Nova Scotia will embark tomorrow, and sail in a few days for Port Roseway and St. John's River, consisting of about four or five thousand; probably many more will follow."[78] About half of the people were bound for Port Roseway, and there were also several hundreds of "Black Pioneers," the only Negro corps enrolled for service in New York; formerly they were slaves who had sought refuge within the British lines. This corps was under the command of Colonel Stephen Bluck, a mulatto of outstanding ability. Aboard other ships were Phoebe Land and Lawrence Kortright who with their families were bound not for Port Roseway but for the St. John River.[79] The great majority of the people bound for Port Roseway were farmers, small merchants, lawyers, physicians, clergymen, and persons of various trades and no trades. "A Return of the Numbers of Loyalists gone to Port Roseway" shows that the women were greatly outnumbered by men (721 to 1,144), and that nearly one-third of the total of adults were slaves. The companies varied in size from 26 to 323 persons.[80]

Four days later the fleet of more than thirty sail of square-rigged vessels, schooners, and sloops put out to sea under the convoy of two ships of war. At the end of a fair voyage of a week the first land was sighted, Cape Sable Island, off the southwestern tip of Nova Scotia, and the ground was under snow.

CHAPTER EIGHT

PEACE BESIDE THE SEA

THE COAST LINE of Nova Scotia is deeply indented with sheltered coves, bays, and harbours, with woodland growth coming close to the water's edge. The interior is a region of wooded hills, lakes, bogs, and barrens everywhere laced by streams. This is a country of granite, spruce and fir, and foaming brown streams that come down swiftly to the sea; of rock-bound coasts and water of an intense blue in clear weather —a land of great beauty. But it is a land for fisherfolk and lumbermen. The rocky shallow soil, in places only a few inches deep on top of the underlying crust of granite, is unsuitable for agriculture except in some river valleys where the soil is deeper. The splendid harbour of Port Roseway, protected at its mouth by a large island and reaching for more than eight miles inland between wooded hills dropping directly into the water, was named Port Razoir by the French. Here they had established a fishing settlement and fur-trading post which was soon destroyed by pirates. When fishermen from New England located at the lower end of the bay the name took the Anglicized form of Port Rosaway, and finally Port Roseway. Nearby along the coast New Englanders from Massachusetts and Connecticut who were sympathetic to the Continental Congress during the war had established other fishing settlements; at Ragged Islands (now Lockeport) and Liverpool on the east and at Barrington on the west. Although Champlain's settlement of Port Royal on the shores of the Annapolis Basin was a thriving village before the Pilgrim Fathers landed at Plymouth Rock, virtually nothing was known of the inner fastnesses of the western section of the peninsula. In all of Nova Scotia there was only one road, that leading from Annapolis to Halifax.[1]

About 4.00 P.M. on Sunday, May 4, 1783, the ships from York were sighted by three surveyors who, having been sent from Halifax by Governor Parr, were now encamped on the shore. Benjamin Marston, the chief surveyor, was a man of education and formerly a merchant and leading magistrate of Marblehead, Massachusetts. "Having rendered himself obnoxious" by his Loyalist principles he had escaped from his "handsomely furnished house" with its "pretty library" and in an open boat made the hazardous voyage to Boston to join the British. The year following he had gone with General Howe to Nova Scotia and to sea in a merchant vessel. Marston was imprisoned for six months, treated with "uncommon severity," and after further varied experiences was practically destitute when appointed chief surveyor of lands for the Port Roseway Associates on April 21, 1783. His diary is valuable in the many details, not to be found elsewhere, that it gives about the Port Roseway Loyalists.

"Last night the fleet got in below," he wrote in his journal May 5, "upwards of thirty sail in all."[2] While the government engineer and Marston explored the shore of the bay to choose a town site the refugees gazed from the decks of the ships upon this land which was to be their new home. Undeterred by the bleak and forbidding aspect of the "ironbound" shore the Loyalists had visions of building a second York. The scrub bush told that the land was poor but this was of no matter for a town, although, according to Marston, there was some disagreement about the location of the town site :

> The multitude object to the place which the Captains and Chief men have chosen for the situation of their town because, say they, 'tis a rough uneven piece of land—so they propose to mend the matter by choosing three men from every company to do the matter over again. That is to commit to a mere mob of sixty what a few judicious men found very difficult to transact with a lesser mob of twenty, so this day has been spent in much controversial nonsense. This cursed republican, town-meeting spirit has been the ruin of us already, and unless checked by some stricter form of government will overset the prospect which now presents itself of retrieving our affairs. Mankind are often slaves, and oftentimes they have too much liberty. Today surveyed the shore on the Eastern side of the NE harbour, where it was determined to fix the town.
> Fri. May 9—According to the determination of Thursday, laid out the center street of the new town, and the people began very cheerfully to cut down the trees—a new employment to many of them.[3]

The soldiers were also at work across the bay opposite the town site, clearing ground upon which to build barracks. Up until this time the weather had been clear and fair, but it now changed to drizzling rain, and fog blew in from the sea. However, after three days the skies cleared, and the weather continued fair until the end of May.

Meanwhile, Marston "ran the water street line and four [parallel] blocks, and two on each side of the center street," and lined out blocks of building lots on the bank sloping up from the bay. At the same time, the street allowances were cleared by the people who were eligible to be located. Marston named the street running alongside the bay, which was to become the main thoroughfare of the town, Water Street, and those above it on the slope Mowat and Hammond streets. What he termed the centre street, which climbs up from the bay and divides the town into North and South divisions he named King Street, and those south of it St. John and Ann streets, both of which are of greatest interest to this narrative.

At provision musters families were issued their ration tickets for pork and flour. Game was plentiful and the water teemed with fish. Not far offshore is one of the finest fishing grounds in the world. "This evening," wrote Marston on May 13, "came one of our fishing sloops with 800 fish, which 5 men caught—they were out only 24 hours." The following day he remarked, "people turning very indolent, some parties not at work until 11 o'clock. Many of the people who came in this fleet are of the lower class of great towns. During the war such employments as would not cost them much labour afforded them a plentiful support. This has made them impatient of labour. They begin to be clamorous, and to have a thousand groundless rumours circulating among them to the prejudice of those to whom they ought to submit." Three days later when he began to mark out some blocks into house lots, working parties were organized by the captains.

The rectangular blocks of land above Water Street, lettered alphabetically, were laid out in sixteen numbered lots running north and south. Marston ran out the land below Water Street in long narrow blocks of warehouse or water lots, 25 by 70 feet, numbered consecutively and fronting on service lanes running down to the bay from Water Street. He prepared a location ticket for each person who was to be allowed to draw for a lot. "The Association from New York are a curious set," he commented May 21. "They take upon them to determine who are proper subjects of the King's grant. They have chosen a committee of 16 who point out who are to be admitted to draw for lots. They say only 441." The next day, May 22, the people drew their town lots. "Tis a task trying to humanity," fretted Marston. "Some grumble, some are pleased. They are upon the whole a collection of Taylors, Shoemakers, and all kinds of mechanics, bred and used to live in great towns, they are inured to habits very unfit for undertakings which require hardihood, resolution, industry and patience."

Each qualified Associate was assigned a town lot 60 feet wide and 120 feet deep, "just large enough for a good House and a Small Garden." [4] Eventually, after further surveys were made, they would receive a water (or warehouse) lot if it was required, and at least fifty acres of land in the outlying district. Hugh Fraser drew lot no. 3 in Block Letter C in the South Division situated on the east side of Water Street between Ann and St. George (now called George) streets. Setting up as merchant and trader he remained here until he sold the lot in June 1785. The house which stands there today was built by the second rector of the Church of England, Reverend John H. Rowland. George Chisholm's lot, no. 11 in Block Letter D, South Division, lies on the hill two blocks above Water Street on the west side of Hammond between St. John (now called merely John) and Ann streets. Today this is a garden which faces the Methodist cemetery situated on the north side of the Shelburne Court House which adjoins it. William McKenzie had a corner lot two blocks above Chisholm's on the "flat," no. 9, Block Letter K, South Division, on the southwest corner of Ann and Harriott streets behind the Anglican Church. His son Murdoch, now sixteen years of age, was granted the lot opposite on the northwest corner (no. 16, Block Letter I).

Although a minister who reached Port Roseway early in June noted that "our friends from York" were "just set down in the midst of barren woods, with not a single house in the town," [5] building started soon thereafter. As the settlers drew their town lots tents, huts, and other temporary shelters sprang up among the stumps. For those who could afford to buy it there was no lack of sawn lumber. Hardly had the fleet made port when merchants along the coast began shipping their lumber. "There is many people Said to be arrived at Roseway, & our people flocking there with Boards," wrote Simeon Perkins, merchant at Liverpool, on May 8. "I agree to Load Knowles Shallop and give him one Quarter," but four days later, upon hearing that "they are fallen Almost to no price" (during the first year log would outnumber framed houses almost four to one), Perkins decided "not to Ship any Boards, but Lay them on the Wharf for the present." [6]

Other matters were also tended to without delay. Wells were sunk, several families joining together for digging, stoning, and providing of windlass, rope, and bucket. To circumvent any future claim being made by one family the wells were located on the fifty-foot street allowances where a number of them may be seen today. The one in Mowat Street from which the Chisholms would have drawn their water is still complete with windlass and iron handle, as may be seen in the photograph facing page 133. Grass growing in the beaver meadows along the Roseway River was cut for hay and stacked on the outskirts of the town for the cattle. Most families had also a few sheep, hogs, fowl, geese, or goats which, if they had not brought from York, had been purchased from visiting traders, and little time was lost in planting seed among the stumps.

On May 24 a furious fire broke out. "It has ended with fewer serious consequences than might have been expected," wrote Ben Marston. "One or two families have lost their all. Some others have met with considerable losses. There is now such a damn'd noise with singing in our tent 'tis impossible to recollect any other circumstance."

Thereafter no one was allowed to start building until all brush had been cleared away.

Marston, who had been educated at Harvard, deplored the lack of adequate leadership. "These poor people are like sheep without a shepherd. They have no men of abilities among them. Their Captains, chosen out of their body at New York, are of the same class as themselves—most of them mechanics, some few have been shipmasters, they are the best men they have." To his disgust all work was interrupted on the King's birthday. "Wed June 4—No business today—'tis the King's Birthday; but any dissipation, any neglect of business ought not to be in ye least countenanced at present in this place. Ships sailed for New York this morning. Towards evening some fine showers which have come very opportunely to prevent the ill effects of a nonsensical *feu de joie*, which was performed just at dark, and would have fired the streets in an hundred places but for the rain. A Ball tonight—all our Tent over to it but myself, and I am very happy to be absent. . . . Sun June 8—Since the King's Birthday very little done. It took all the next day to get rid of the previous day' and night's excess."

With the arrival of sixty more families in three shiploads of refugees, among whom were undoubtedly John and Neil McKay, the surveyors were obliged to extend the town limits and lay out more blocks of town lots. John McKay drew no. 4 in Block Letter X, South Division, on Clements Street between Ann and George streets. A nearby landmark is the old Firth house with saltbox roof which stands on the southwest corner of George Street. Neil drew no. 4, Block Letter N, situated on Cornwallis Street between Charlotte and Thomas in the new St. John's Division adjoining the South Division. Today there are no landmarks of interest here.

By the middle of July all warehouse lots and a considerable number of fifty-acre farm lots had been surveyed and assigned. Of the group of six Scots (William and Murdoch McKenzie, Hugh Fraser, George Chisholm, John and Neil McKay) only Chisholm and John McKay secured warehouse lots. Chisholm drew the fourth lot below Water Street fronting upon the south side of Rodney Lane (no. 71, Block Letter C, South Division). Farther down the hill on the opposite side of the lane is no. 59 which was assigned to McKay. The Chief Surveyor laid out some of the farm lots, namely, those called Marston's Division along the west side of the Roseway River, but the majority were surveyed by his deputy, Charles Mason. The 236 lots in Mason's Division begin where the hydro-electric dam is now situated, follow the river to its mouth, and extend down the east side of the bay to the town. Recommencing below the town's southern boundary they continue to follow the shore line of the peninsula formed by Jordan Bay on the east and come to an end some two miles up the Jordan River which flows into the bay from the north. That all might have water frontage the lots are narrow and deep; ten chains (660 feet) in width they run $1\frac{1}{4}$ miles inland. No. 6 in Mason's Division, fronting on the Roseway River somewhat less than a mile above the northern limits of the town, was drawn by Chisholm. Nos. 18 and 22 in Marston's Division laid out on the west side of the river went to Hugh Fraser and William McKenzie respectively. The farm lots of the remaining Scots were located in Mason's Division fronting upon the northwest arm of Jordan Bay at some distance from the town. John and Neil McKay took land even farther afield and in considerably larger tracts. At a later date John secured a grant to 238 acres situated on the east bank of the Jordan River running inland to Hayden Lake. He also obtained no. 27 and Neil no. 26, lots of 200 acres each, on the east shore of Port L'Hebert upon which the small fishing community of East Port L'Hebert now stands, some twenty-five miles east of Shelburne Harbour. The McKays were unquestionably attracted by the fishing in this fine bay, the south shore of which was explored by Champlain in 1604. He named it after his apothecary, Louis Hebert, who became one of Quebec's first settlers. Although modern cartographers have chosen to show it as Port Hebert, to the natives it is, as it has been for more than three and a half centuries, Port L'Hebert.

On July 20 Governor Parr arrived from Halifax in the frigate *Sophie* to pay a visit of several days. When he landed to view the town he was welcomed ashore by a salute of cannon. Proceeding up King Street between two lines of citizens under arms the Governor reached the place appointed for his reception, and a short proclamation was read. The populace then learned of his decision to name the town and district Shelburne in honour of the Secretary of State for the Colonies. He appointed justices of the peace, administered to them the oaths of office, and returned on board the frigate to sit down to an elegant repast. The day following, the Governor and his suite dined with leading citizens, and in the evening attended a public supper and ball given by the town. "From every appearance," he wrote to Sir Guy Carleton during his visit, "I have no doubt but that it will in a short time become the most flourishing Town for Trade of any in this part of the world, and the country will for agriculture."[7]

The population, at this time 5,000, was doubled to some 10,000 by new arrivals in August. And they continued to come especially after the complete evacuation of York by the British on November 25, 1783. One of the last to leave was Ward Chipman who wrote as follows:

> I have been witness to the mortifying scene of giving up the City of New York to the American Troops. About 12 o'clock on Tuesday the 25th inst. all our Troops were paraded on the wide ground before the Provost, where they remained till the Americans about 1 o'clock marched thro' Queen-Street and Wall-Street to the Broad-way, where they wheeled to the hay-wharf and embarked immediately and fell down to Staten Island. I walked out and saw the American Troops under General Knox march in, and was one of the last on shore in the City; it really occasioned most painful sensations and I tho't Sir Guy, who was upon parade, looked unusually dejected.[8]

Upon taking possession of the city General Washington, Governor Clinton, and members of the provisional government were met at the Bull's Head Tavern in the Bowery by citizens and military who escorted them to another public house in Broad Way for the presentation of addresses and other ceremonies. A fortnight later the General then proceeded to Fraunces' Tavern where he bade farewell to his officers and left for retirement at Mount Vernon, his home on the Potomac River in Virginia.

Refugees were continuing to bring building materials with them to Shelburne. There is mention of a house frame being landed,[9] and at York there was an advertisement of "English Bricks—Six Thousand, suitable for elegantly fronting new houses, whether in this city, Port Shelburne, Annapolis Royal, &c. &c."[10] All settlers were now called upon to take the oath of allegiance to the King before magistrates newly appointed by Governor Parr. "The most liberal of the Loyalists," he wrote to Lord Sidney, "would not go to Shelburne and the River St. John, so that I had to make magistrates in these settlements of men whom God Almighty never intended for the office, but it was Hobson's choice."[11]

As he worked at enlarging the town Marston continually kept "a good look out against land speculators." He commented on August 9 that "A Capt. MacLean has this evening sent me a green turtle, but this must not blind my eyes. He must run the same chance as his neighbours who have no turtle to send." He also made provision for the "black men," who according to the Governor's orders were to be located at the head of the northwest arm of the harbour, by land about four miles from Shelburne. Upon finding that they were "well satisfied with it," Marston proceeded with the survey of "lands for Colonel Bluck's black gentry." They chose to call their settlement Birchtown after Brigadier-General Samuel Birch, commandant of the city of York or New York (as it was now generally called).

From time to time the New York newspapers reported on the progress of the Loyalists' settlements. Upon the arrival late in August of a brig from "New Scotland" the *Gazette* announced that "by the last Accounts from Port Roseway, no less than 400 Houses had been erected in the City of Shelburne, and that the Settlement of the Place went on amazingly." [12] The *Remembrancer* carried an extract of a letter dated October 9 in which a British naval officer describes the emigration of the Loyalists as being almost incredible.

> The majority are fixed at Port Roseway, where they have erected a large city (Shelburne) which contains nine thousand inhabitants, exclusive of the Black town, containing about twelve hundred free Blacks, who served during the war. This part of the country is almost level and more easy to clear than the generality of it. The small islands, and many other parts which have been cultivated some years, are as fertile as it is possible to conceive; and from the excellence of its harbour, its situation for trade and number of inhabitants (many of which are wealthy) there is every reason to suppose that it will soon be the capital of Nova Scotia.[13]

Deborah Smith who arrived from New York some weeks later in the schooner *Cherry Bounce* recounted somewhat less enthusiastic impressions upon stepping ashore at Shelburne : "The snow was about two feet deep . . . there were a number of houses building, but none finished; plenty of marquees, tents and sheds for the people to shelter under, which they greatly needed at that season of the year. It looked dismal enough. Called on some friends in their tents. . . . The servants had sheds of boards to cook under." [14]

Few settlers at Shelburne were satisfied with their locations so that the shifting of land ownerships became almost universal. Many Associates were able to dispose of their improved holdings to late-comers at a profit; farmers wanting more or better land traded their town lots for the wild land of those preferring to hold land in the town. Because a considerable proportion of these transactions, some of them quite involved, took place before the grants were issued by the Crown and the deeds in many instances remain unrecorded, the land deals are inclined to be somewhat obscure. Of the six Scots only Chisholm's transfers of land are clear enough to be cited as fair examples.

On October 13, 1783, George Chisholm bought lot no. 110, Mason's Division, of fifty acres from the grantee Kenneth McKenzie for £30 "Current Money" and sold his town lot to one Alexander Fraser for £10. Two days later he bought Fraser's town lot (no. 14, Block Letter N, North Division) for £10, an equal trade, and immediately sold it to Kenneth McKenzie for £20 "Current Money." [15] Four months later, on February 13, 1784, he acquired the adjoining lot, no. 111, Mason's Division, from the grantee, James Wilson, in equal trade for his lot (no. 6) on the Roseway River.[16] Lot 6 extends eastward from the lower section of the island situated about a mile from the river's mouth to a point a short distance beyond Black's Brook. On December 5 and 6, 1783, Marston had been employed in "Settling a mode for the Farmers to get into the country—which after all my contrivance I find a very difficult matter. . . . However they have at last broke out today, Monday the 8, Captain Wright and a party of about 14 . . . have set out to begin a road thro' the country to Annapolis." This road running inland from the north end of Water Street and named for Captain

Daniel Wright opened the way to Chisholm's land. (Annapolis or Pell's Road paralleling Wright's Road about a mile to the east was of somewhat later date.) In the spring settlers located in this area applied for grants from the Crown, electing one of their number, George Thomas, to go to Halifax as their representative. In a memorial dated at Halifax April 5, 1784, Thomas with those persons "Located on fifteen 50 Acre Lotts situated on the falls, Shelburne side," among whom Chisholm is listed, requested that their grants be approved. This was accordingly done.[17]

The grants in Nova Scotia at this period are of interest as reflecting the difficulties the Loyalists encountered in the terrain. Grantees were reserved the "privilege of hunting, hawking and fowling" whereas "all white pine trees . . . all mines of gold, silver, copper, lead and coals" were reserved to the Crown. At the end of ten years grantees were to begin paying "at the Feast of St. Michael in every year, at the rate of 2 shillings for every 100 acres" provided that the following conditions for cultivation and improvement were met within three years:

for every 50 acres of plantible land hereby granted, [the grantee shall] clear and work 3 acres, at least . . . or else to clear and drain 3 acres of swampy or sunken land, or drain 3 acres of marsh . . . and shall . . . put and keep upon every 50 acres thereof accounted barren, 3 neat cattle . . . and if there shall be no part of said tract fit for present cultivation, without manuring and improving [the grantee shall] erect on some part . . . the like number of neat cattle on every 50 acres; or otherwise, if any part of the said tract shall be stoney or rocky ground, and not fit for planting or pasture [the grantee shall within 3 years] begin to employ thereon, and continue to work for 3 years . . . in digging any stone quarry or mine, one good and able hand for every 50 acres.

If not registered within six months "this grant shall be void." Before the grantee could be "deemed the lawful Possessor" of the land he must, within a year, show proof by magistrate's certificate of having taken the oath of allegiance in the following words: "I [name] do promise and declare, that I will maintain and defend to the utmost of my Power, the Authority of the King in His Parliament as the Supreme Legislature of this Province."[18]

The only one of the group of Scots to remain on the Shelburne side of the peninsula was Hugh Fraser who was evidently satisfied with his lands. His farm lot situated on the west side of the harbour below the falls where the Roseway tumbles into the bay was little more than a mile from the town. At this period he is listed as merchant and thereafter appears as both merchant and trader in Water Street and "Roseway farmer" until 1790.[19] Evidence points to John McKay having settled on his grant on Jordan Bay. Early in April William McKenzie, having found a buyer for his Roseway River tract, bought lot no. 118 in Mason's Division a short distance above Chisholm's.

The peninsula upon which the town of Shelburne is situated stands between Shelburne Harbour and Jordan Bay. It is about 8 miles long and varies between $3\frac{1}{2}$ and $4\frac{3}{4}$ miles in width. The interior of bogs and barrens is now uninhabited, settlement hugging the shore of the peninsula. The road by which the latter is now encircled keeps to the top of the bank that slopes down to the sea, but in earlier times it followed the shore at the foot of the hill. The name of the bay, according to one authority, derives from the French "Rivière des Jardins," so called for the Indian gardens found along its lower reaches.[20] Certainly, the name as shown on Franquelin's map of 1702 is very clearly "R des Jardins,"[21] and tradition says that the Indians who were encamped at the head of the northwest arm of the bay had gardens on the hillside near Purney's Brook. Considering such variants as Cape Blowmedown for Blomidon,[22]

La Bear for L'Hebert, and Jolly for Joli,[23] it is surprising how many French names have survived.

The Jordan and Roseway rivers, brawling torrents among boulders in their lower reaches, rise in the bogs and swamps of the interior and flow southward into the northeast arms of their respective bays. They have much in common except that the Roseway broadens into a chain of lakes where the still water, reflecting the sky, appears an intense blue although in reality it is the colour of amber. In their search for better land and a way to reach Annapolis the Loyalists, by the autumn of 1783, had explored the Roseway "from lake to lake to the distance of 45 miles, done in a flat boat pushed up against the stream with poles."[24] Though they found good land it was inaccessible; today the Ohio Road leading to some of these lakes peters out in the sixteenth mile.

The bays, however, have little in common. Whereas Shelburne Harbour is deep and its shore rockbound all the way up to the town, the upper reaches of Jordan Bay are shallower and bordered by tidewater marshes. On the level land on the east shore a mile below Jordan Falls (about where the railway bridge stands today) was the home of John McKay and his wife Catherine. William McKenzie and George Chisholm were located some distance down the bay on the west shore: the McKenzies under the lee of McLean's Island* and the Chisholms about a mile farther south and close to the open sea. (Both families were within the community now known as Jordan Bay which is six miles from the town of Shelburne by the Lake Road crossing the peninsula.) Chisholm was listed as farmer[25] when Marston stated that on the fifty-acre lots round the harbour there were about thirty "Log-Houses, built of pieces of Timber framed together at the ends—and these are sometimes clapboarded over; they may be made permanent buildings to endure for years."[26]

In addition to the attractions of better land, excellent fishing grounds, and the desirability of the sheltered cove was another which had drawn Chisholm and McKenzie to so great a distance from the town: the timber, particularly white oak, growing on the banks of Jordan Bay. Nearly twenty years before Robert Rogers in *A Concise Account of North America* had written that the exports of Nova Scotia "are chiefly lumber, such as plank, staves, hoops, joists, &c., and fish,"[27] and in 1777 Simeon Perkins referred to staves made at Jordan River.[28] It may be recalled how at Kortright timber of excellent grade had been burned because it could not be got out to market, and that Chisholm had been engaged with Daniel Rose and others in making potash before the war. In Nova Scotia the majority of the trees were unsuitable for the making of potash and though smaller in size than those of New York their timber was readily available for trade because of good harbours. Timbering and stave-cutting being the winter work of farmers, it is likely that at least some of the Scots at Jordan Bay contributed squared timber to the first shipment to go from Nova Scotia to England. "On Thursday last," runs a news item in the *Royal American Gazette* of June 20, 1785, "sailed the Ship Prince William Henry, for Jordan-river, to take in a cargo of squared timber, for London. Captain Meader, who is owner as well as commander of said ship, has the honour of being the first gentleman who carries a cargo to England of the produce of this province."

The Loyalists had lost no time in setting up sawmills for cutting lumber and one was located near the mouth of the Jordan River at the head of the bay. Soon three sawmills on the river were "kept going night and day for the merchants of Port Rose-

---

* The sole evidence that a house once stood on this land is the little stoned cellar hole hidden by wild roses near the edge of the bank above the rock-strewn beach.

way who are constantly shipping off lumber to the West Indies, both from these mills and two other[s] lately erected above Shelburne." [29] In May 1785, the magistrates in special session had ordered that "all proprietors, or Lessees of Water Mills, do, by sun set, every Saturday Evening, open their respective Mill dams, and keep them open until Sun Rise on the succeeding Monday Morning." [30] In an effort to raise the standard of Shelburne's products the "Grand Jury came into Court and gave the following Presentiments . . . That as the Quality of Lumber exported must materially affect the Interest of this market, they beg leave to request that the Surveyor, or Surveyors of Lumber be particularly Ordered to pass no Lumber that is not altogether Merchantable, and that all materially damaged, be pronounced Refuse, and that all Boards, Plank, One sixth of their Length split, or otherwise damaged . . . be pronounced Refuse. . . ." [31]

Settlers in the area were confronted not only with vast quantities of rock and standing wood but also with much fallen timber covered by large tracts of moss which made it difficult to judge the soil and caused them prodigious labour.[32] But they were finding that this country was naturally productive of grass and that wherever the land was cleared a great variety of the best grasses appeared.[33] What land was brought under cultivation was producing good crops of wheat, oats, barley, potatoes, flax, and that old standby Indian corn,[34] though it would be some time before they would be able to support themselves.

That the Loyalists continued to be victualled by the British government was in some measure owing to the influence of Sir Andrew Snape Hammond. "We have been well served with the King's provisions," remarked Marston, "which have been very good of their kind, particularly the bread. There has been likewise a distribution of clothing, working tools, some boards, &c., but in what proportion I do not know, these matters being out of my line." [35] A company muster roll shows issues of tools and clothing. Each man received an axe, a spade, 2 pairs shoes, 2 pairs stockings, 1 pair mittens, 4 yards woollen cloth, 7 yards linen cloth. Each woman received 1 pair shoes, 1 pair stockings, 1 pair mittens, 3 yards woollen cloth, 6 yards linen cloth. Each child under ten years of age received $1\frac{1}{2}$ yards woollen cloth and 3 yards linen cloth.[36] Rations, "farming utensils," * and other issues were secured at Commissary Island lying close by the water front of the town of Shelburne. In September 1785, the magistrates memorialized the King through Governor Parr, asking that provisions be continued for another two years. They also requested a grant of money to open roads, explaining that the difficulty of securing land for cultivation had delayed the Loyalists in obtaining produce for their support and that their savings were now nearly exhausted.[37] The government allowed two-thirds of the former rations during 1785, and the year following one-third of a ration per person. At the end of three years the royal bounty of provisions would altogether cease.

Because of the lack of genealogical data it is impossible to know to what extent most of the Gaelic families were in need of the royal bounty. It is known, however, that settlers in large numbers were getting a living from harvests of the sea. Since white men had first come to Nova Scotia the catching and preparing of cod fish for market had been a major industry as it is still today. The salted and dried fish keeps well in the tropical climate of the West Indies where it continues to be used. Settlers traded their fish in return for necessities with merchants who in turn exchanged it

---

* This archaic Scotticism continues as current usage in this section of Nova Scotia; also the word puncheon which today is common only with historians.

for products of the West Indies. They cured their own catches in a manner then old and but little changed even now after four hundred years. The freshly caught cod is split down the back, and the head, tail, and entrails are removed. After being salted the pancake-flat fish is stacked in "stores" to await the sun. In fine weather men, women, and children along the coast "make fish," that is, spread the salted cod on "flakes" to dry. To fisherfolk, frames mounted on posts have been "flakes whereon men yeerely dry their fish" [38] since ancient times. The word signifies a wattled hurdle used to form temporary fences, sheep pens, and the like. The fish must be turned often, and stacked up and covered when it rains. In brisk, windy, sunny weather the fish dry fast and if well cured will keep for a considerable length of time.

Salmon and alewives were also salted for export. The run of alewives started the middle of April and continued for about a month when salmon began to roil the waters of Jordan Bay. The chief run of salmon which averaged between nine and thirteen pounds occurred between May 10 and June 10. Haddock caught for the settlers' own use, sturgeon of ten to twelve feet in length, very large skate, mackerel, herring, flounder, eels, and dog fish which furnished excellent oil were caught in great abundance throughout the summer in Jordan Bay, and the bottom crawled with lobsters.[39]

When Shelburne's brisk trade in fish and lumber took an upward curve early in 1785, and wharves for landing goods and warehouses for securing them increased apace, Chisholm succeeded in selling his water lot.[40] Today this land is vacant, but in nearby Charlotte Lane stands a warehouse which has survived to be preserved as a museum. Now called the Ross-Thomson House, it was built by the Aberdonian brothers, Robert and George Ross, merchants engaged in the West India trade. It occupies four water lots at the south end of which is their dwelling with separate living quarters for each brother whose slaves (so it is said) slept in the attic. This building presents an interesting study in contrasts—the square massiveness of the warehouse with its heavy door, great iron strap hinges, double lock, and ponderous bar resting in wrought iron brackets, its partitions of planks and (when sawn lumber had run out) squared timbers split lengthwise, and the classic elegance of the living quarters with their stairway, fireplaces, and panelling of exquisite workmanship and the delicately fashioned but none the less sturdy iron work. The clapboards are bevelled and lapped, and birch bark served instead of tin for flashing.

Shipbuilding was also becoming a major industry. Marston had estimated that within the first four months the number of vessels belonging to the port were "somewhere about 50 sail, or may be more. About half the number are employed in the cod fishery." He remarked that the whale fishery (being developed in Brazilian waters) was meeting with success, and that other vessels were employed in the coasting and West India trade, but that most of them, during this first summer, were making "voyages to New York, from whence, under the color of bringing the effects of Loyalists, much smuggling is carried on of Gin, Brandy, &c. But these matters will I suppose be better looked into when the bustle of settling is a little over." [41] With "at least 300 sail of all sorts . . . a vast number of vessels built . . . chiefly for the fishing business, some of them as large as 250 tons burthen," Shelburne, within three years of its founding, would rival Halifax itself.[42] Into these bottoms went planks of oak secured by trennels (treenails) of hackmatack from the shores of Jordan Bay.

Until the spring of 1785 land transportation to Shelburne was confined to an Indian path leading from their encampment at the head of the northwest arm of

Jordan Bay. In April the Court of Quarter Sessions granted two licences for public ferries: to Hugh Eagle to ply between his lot (no. 186) situated a short distance below the Indian encampment and the east shore of the Jordan River, and to John Johnston farther down the bay to ply to the opposite shore from what is still called Jordan Ferry. At the same time, a road was ordered to be cut across the peninsula from Johnston's Ferry to Shelburne. The schedule of tolls set for this ferry was two pence for one passenger or a "Kagg," three pence for a barrel, a shilling for each horse or cow, and two shillings for a hogshead.[43] This ferry considerably shortened the distance between the Scots on the west shore and the McKays on the east, but it was not until the following spring that the William McKenzies and Chisholms were connected more closely with the town of Shelburne. Although application had been made in January 1785, it was not until March 28, 1786, that the magistrates assembled in the court decreed that a road be made to Shelburne "commencing at Lots 124 and 125, and from thence to proceed to Lake Rodney."[44] Meeting the shore road close to William McKenzie's and about a mile above Chisholm's this new road called the Lake Road running through the dense forest on the upper section of the peninsula shortened by more than four miles the distance to the town. The road referred to earlier as circling the peninsula along its shore was also constructed about this time, and the Indian path, also previously mentioned, was ordered to "be recorded as a Public Road Sixty feet wide. . . ."[45] The tax book of this year shows fifty farmers, a carpenter, a mason, and a judge living along the eastern shore of the peninsula.[46]

As time passed and their herds increased the farmers were in need of extra pasturage. Owing to the topography of the so-called "farms" none were capable of supporting more than a very limited stock. Chisholm had increased his holding to 150 acres by the acquisition of the adjoining lot on the north, no. 112, but how or when does not appear because the deeds were not recorded. Oxen were the draught animals for hauling logs and sledding wood even as they are today. (Simeon Perkins at Liverpool agreed "for a Yoke of Oxen, Seven years old, to allow . . . fourteen pounds in Goods." He used the cattle for hauling long timber in winter on a "Bob Slead."[47]) The wild fresh-water grasses when cut and dried served as winter fodder for the cattle. Dried kelp was a favourite and unfailing source of winter feed for sheep which also fed on the roots of shrubs and swamp grasses, and in spring on the tender buds and "spills" (colloquialism for needles of evergreens) of the spruce trees. Though turned out the year round sheep were yarded at night as protection from the wild cats, those marauders so familiar to the Scots in the Kaatskills. Few restrictions were imposed on domestic animals except for swine which were prohibited from running at large "without being suitably yoked."[48]

Game was plentiful on the land. Porcupine, partridge, and rabbits took cover in the woods. "In this Neighbourhood," wrote Reverend James Munro, "are Rabits in great plenty so that in one Season by one person 700 hath been taken, and 400 by another."[49] Deer roamed the forest, and black bears, whose skins were valuable as well as useful and whose flesh was eaten either fresh, salted, or dried, roamed the hills. Moose whose meat when dried kept the year round were common.[50] The air teemed as richly with life as the ground. Ducks, geese, and other water fowl frequented the marshes. Pigeons, doves, and myriads of other land birds flocked in the trees. Predatory birds were abundantly represented by various species of hawks and owls, the great black raven, and the greater bald eagle.[51]

Many small fruits, in fact "all the more common berries of Europe," according to one contemporary authority, were found growing wild in this country.⁵² Those which grew in profusion and were hitherto unknown to the Scots were the blueberries found in dry places and the red cranberries in the bogs. Also flourishing in the bogs were the amber-coloured cloudberries which were unpalatable until boiled up with sugar to make what was then known as bake apple jam. Raspberry shrubs shooting up wherever the land was cleared bore fruit of particularly excellent flavour which was equally true of the wild strawberries. There were also blackberries and the trailing dewberry with its strawberry-like leaves and tiny black fruit of a deliciousnes that compensated for its size.

By 1786 Shelburne had reached the peak of its prosperity. Its meteoric rise had continued until it had become the largest town in British North America. During the first year of its existence its population had equalled the combined populations of Montreal, Quebec, and Three Rivers, and it was exceeded in size by only three cities in the United States—Philadelphia, New York, and Boston. "In this Town," Gideon White, one of the more influential citizens, had written in August 1784, "are 2700 Houses—Above 200 are framed—And business will soon be sprightly." ⁵³ Marston had earlier described "the state of buildings in this town as follows: viz., 231 Framed houses, 816 log houses, 80 on the Commons—temporary for winter only [for latecomers] ... total [inclusive] 1,157. All since the 9th May last [1783]." ⁵⁴ He found the majority of houses "most generally large, commodious, and some of them altogether elegant buildings." ⁵⁵ Still overburdened with the work occasioned by late arrivals in the "Fall fleet" Marston wrote to a relative, "I am in as perfect good health as a reasonable mortal can wish, but almost dinned to death for Town lots and Water lots, for 50 acre lots and 500 acre lots. My head is so full of triangles, squares, parallelograms, trapezias and rhomboids, that the corners do sometimes put my eyes out. However I thank God they are there. Had it not been for them I should by this time have starved to death, or, what is ten times worse, have been the burden and pity of my friends." ⁵⁶

At the south end of the town was the establishment of the jeweller from York, Charles Oliver Bruff. One of his announcements reads in part: "Charles Oliver Bruff, Goldsmith & Jeweller At the Sign of the Tea-pot, Tankard and Cross-Swords ... near the Market, at the Head of the Cove; makes & mends all sorts of Goldsmith's and Jeweller's work ... ; surveyors' and mariners' compasses; keys for padlocks of all sorts ... gun locks repaired ... makes all sorts of mourning rings, with coffin stones; mends stone buckles, sets miniature pictures. He likewise has for Sale, a valuable Fifty Acre Lot...." ⁵⁷ Nearby in Water Street stood Hugh Fraser's place of business, and in Mason Lane the tavern of James McGrath where on January 19, 1784, the Queen's birthday had been celebrated by a ball. "About 50 gentlemen and ladies," wrote Marston, "danced, drank tea, played cards, in a house which stood where six months ago there was an almost impenetrable swamp—so great has been the exertions of the settlers in this new world. The room was commodious and warm, tho' in the rough. The whole was conducted with good humour and general satisfaction." ⁵⁸ Other meeting places were the Merchants Coffee House in Water Street, and Alexander Fraser's tavern which now stood on the lot in Hammond Street that Fraser had bought from Chisholm.⁵⁹ Tavern keepers were obliged to observe the following prices as set by the Court of Quarter Sessions: for a man and wife, "lodging in a comfortable bed—6d.; breakfast of bread, butter, tea, coffee or chocolate with loaf sugar—8d."; dinner of "good wholesome meat" with bread and vegetables—10d.; supper of same—8d.;

"Sufficient Hay to Bate A Horse while his master Breakfasts or dines"—4d.; stabling and hay for same overnight—1s.[60]

A fair proportion of "gentlemen" were numbered among Shelburne's population. Beside merchants and shopkeepers, fishermen, seamen, and pilots the trades were represented by the usual complement of shoemakers, tailors, watchmakers, bakers, house and ships carpenters, masons, blacksmiths, coopers, and bricklayers. There was also a soap boiler, a coppersmith, milkman, carman (carter or carrier) and tidewaiter (customs officer who awaited the arrival of ships coming in on the tide and boarded them to prevent the evasion of custom house regulations), and a pomatum maker[61] undoubtedly employed by the "Hairdresser Nigh the Head of Mason-Lane." The latter had for sale hard and soft pomatum of all sorts; the best double-distilled lavendar-water; violet, oris, and Poland hair powders; tooth powder and brushes, razor strops, and dressing combs. "N.B.," concludes an announcement, "Ladies and Gentlemen dressed, at their own Lodgings, on the shortest notice, and in the newest fashion."[62]

It is apparent in their newspaper advertizing that the merchants and tradesmen catered to people used to a high standard of living. The long lists of articles offered for sale would almost appear to have been stocked for a clientele in either New York or Philadelphia rather than for that of an isolated community in the wilds of Nova Scotia. "Ladies Riding Habits made in the newest fashion" lately come from England; "Women's calimanco shoes"; "Women's stays, assorted." For men there were "superfine camblet cloaks, lined with green baize, beaver gloves, silk and worsted hose, "a neat choice of newest fashion London made suites of Cloathes . . . and a collection of well chosen books." In the matter of housefurnishings there were "Scotch carpets, fluted and plain four post bedsteads, with ticking and furniture compleat, elegant prints, framed and glazed." Builders were offered "H & HL Hinges for shutters & doors, a few very elegant brass knobs locks for front doors" imported from London. At the store in King Street opposite the British Coffee-house there was little that the Scots could not obtain in exchange for "fish, furs, or lumber." We read of pots of pickled walnuts, ketchup and pickles, and "a few chaldron best New Castle coals" imported from London; of Fearnaught great coats, swan skin drawers, dutch ovens, and chaffing dishes; of sliding pencils, Scotch thread, and spelling books. At the Medical Store in the block north of Hugh Fraser's place of business in Water Street could be obtained the "most approved Patent Medicines," such as "Hooper's Female Pills," the old remedy "Maredant's Antiscorbutic Drops" together with corn salve, tobacco and spices.

Concerning the religious denominations represented among the Loyalists at Shelburne, there were a few Methodists, but the majority of the settlers were members of either the Established Church or the Church of Scotland. The Presbyterians had as their minister Reverend Hugh Fraser who had officiated as chaplain to the 71st Highland Regiment except for eighteen months imprisonment in Boston. He "had been induced to go to Nova Scotia with several of his own religious tenets,"[63] and when Simeon Perkins noted his arrival at Liverpool on May 28, 1783, Fraser was already recognized as "the Port Roseway Minister."[64] The building which served as the Presbyterians' place of worship was on Hammond Street between King and John streets in the first block northeast of the Chisholms'. During the summer of 1787, however, this structure collapsed in a wind storm. In a petition for financial assistance addressed to the Chancellor of the Exchequer, William Pitt, "the Loyalists of the Church of Scotland in Shelburne" stated :

> That contented to spend together the remainder of their days, amidst desarts [sic] where they could enjoy the privileges of British Subjects, the protection of British Laws, they brought along with them a Steady & Unalterable attachment for that Religious Establishment in which they had been taught to fix . . . their principles of Loyalty to their King, and of piety to their God :—
>
> That Anxious to Secure for themselves & for their Children the ministrations of a Clergyman from their native Church, they had early entred [sic] into a bond of Association, and amidst all their straits and difficulties took care to obtain the Grant of a Lot of Ground . . . for erecting a place of Public Worship And have from the Wreck of their fortunes endowned & supported the Reverened [sic] Hugh Fraser....
>
> But obliged . . . at first to encounter all the hardships of Original settlers in this high Latitude of North America, and doomed as they have been to struggle for five long Years with difficulty and distress in every form—Numerous tho' they are,—they have found their most strenuous exertions inadequate to the expence [sic] of erecting a Church in which they could assemble with any Comfort during the Winter Months. To them, My Lord, this is an object of the most Serious Concern. In their Condition they greatly need the Consolations of Religion, and if they were enabled to procure them by the Generous Aid of Government [they would be perpetually reminded] that their services and Sufferings had not been disregarded.[65]

The Presbyterians were given the use of the court house during the winter [66] but they never achieved the erection of a church. The wreck of their flimsy structure lay on the plot on Hammond Street until after the turn of the century.

Benjamin Marston was some months gone from Shelburne, and unhappily no one replaced him as chronicler to tell of an event long awaited by the Loyalists : the advent of the commissioner appointed by Parliament to inquire into the services and losses in consequence of their loyalty to the Crown. According to the Act of Parliament passed in 1783 claimants lodged their claims in England, but it soon became evident that commissioners must be sent to meet them personally and obtain evidence on the spot. Claimants were required to state in writing the nature of their claims and swear to the truth of their statements before witnesses and a justice of the peace. Most settlers like Hugh Fraser had already filed their claims and appeared before one or another of the commissioners at Montreal, Quebec, or Halifax. Fraser had given evidence three months before at the Office of American Claims at Halifax. However, some settlers such as William McKenzie and George Chisholm did not present their claims until March 13, 1786, when accompanied by their witnesses they appeared at Shelburne before Justice Alexander Leckie who took their affidavits. McKenzie stated that the claim he had sent to London by his agent had apparently miscarried, and Murdoch McKenzie and Hugh Fraser swore that they knew him to have been possessed of what he claimed.[67] Chisholm deposed to his inability to present his claim sooner; that he "was at a Distance in the Country improving his land" when the agent from the Loyalists at Shelburne went to England.[68] William and Murdoch McKenzie "being severally sworn upon the Holy Evangelist of Almighty God" attested that they knew Chisholm was possessed of the property mentioned excepting that (valued at £20) lost when he was taken prisoner on Lake Champlain.[69]

Colonel Thomas Dundas, one of the two commissioners who went to Canada, did not start work at Shelburne until June 28. McKenzie gave his evidence on July 23, but unfortunately his claim of £457.6.8 N.Y. currency was disallowed. Chisholm's "Schedule of Losses" totalling £138.0.10 was also rejected.[70] As he himself stated, "all his Friends and the Neighbours of his former Residence before the War came to [Niagara] and he was disappointed of receiving for want of their

Evidence any Compensation from the Commissioners appointed to Examine into the Losses and Claims of American Sufferers."[71] The McKays were now gone from Shelburne and when Chisholm's property had been confiscated May 1, 1777, Hugh Fraser was a prisoner in Albany Gaol. Lacking the support of eye witnesses Chisholm had produced the best evidence possible under the circumstances, that of his wife's family. Inevitably the disallowance of their claims was a serious blow to both these Loyalists. Not long after his appearance before the commissioner William McKenzie was dead.[72]

The rosy future predicted for Shelburne during its early prosperity proved illusive and it was not long before this settlement in the wilderness was showing unmistakable signs of deterioration and decline. The gradually increasing number of properties and business enterprises put up for sale indicate a mounting discontent and unstable economy. "To be sold at Public Auction," runs the announcement of John Hughes as early as 1785, "an elegant two story House, a little above the cove, in Carleton-street, corner of Queen-street, 30 × 22 feet and a good kitchen in rear, 18 × 14 feet, with cellar under the whole; there is three fire-places besides a large fire-place in the kitchen, and a good oven."[73] Some months later Hughes announced the auctioning of another property. "At the Merchants Coffee-House, will be sold a likely strong Negro Wench, About 18 years of age; she was brought up in a genteel family, is well acquainted with all kinds of house work, and can have an undeniable character; is sold for no fault but want of employ.—The property warranted."[74] For a shilling the public bellman would announce houses and lots for sale, articles stolen or strayed, and the same amount was charged "for crying the arrival of a Vessel through the Town."[75]

After a disastrous storm swept away wharves and warehouses along the water front in 1786 and when the distribution of food by the government ended, many people began to move away to other places. These removals continued at an alarming rate, and Captain William Dyott, who accompanied Prince William Henry to Shelburne, remarked that from an account taken by the commanding engineer in the winter of 1787–88 there were 360 uninhabited houses.* Soon, too, the timber trade began to suffer. In 1791, a petition for governmental assistance addressed to the Secretary of State and signed by seventy-six "Merchants, Owners of Shipping, and Principal Inhabitants of the Town and Port of Shelburne" put forward a plan for arresting the fall of trade before it became irretrievable. This document states:

that the scarcity of proper Timber on the shores in the Vicinage of the Port, the want of Inland Navigation, and of Roads of Communication with the Interior Parts of this New Country (where only any Quantity of Lumber can be cut) so greatly enhances the price of this Article to the Shippers, as to put it out of their power to continue that trade without considerable Loss....

Your Petitioners beg leave farther to submit to Your Lordship on the Subject of their Fisheries that the very liberal indulgencies granted by the Treaty of Peace with the United States, to their Fishermen in permitting them to catch and even cure their Fish on the Coasts of this Province added to their superior experience in that business hath hitherto precluded us from becoming their Rivals in this valuable branch of Commerce....[76]

However, the merchantable timber along the shores of Jordan Bay became exhausted and two of the three sawmills stopped running, forcing the families in this neighbourhood to rely upon fishing and farming alone for a living.

* Dyott considered the situation of Shelburne "the most wretched I ever beheld. Nothing on the surface of the ground but immense large stones and stumps of trees.... in the town streets the stumps ... are not taken up" (Reginald W. Jeffery, ed., *Dyott's Diary 1781–1845* (London, 1907), p. 55).

The plight of Shelburne was heightened by the disastrous fires that swept the district during 1790 and 1791. The Grand Jury called late in the spring could not attend "for the alarming fires which surround the town." [77] Shelburne was saved but the fire running before the wind swept over the peninsula to Jordan River where nearly fifty houses were burned to the ground. The following week the Grand Jury was advised "to take into consideration the distressing situation" of the settlers who had suffered by this disaster.[78] In June and also in November of the following year the country was again laid waste by fires and on one occasion the inhabitants of Shelburne fought for fifteen days to save the town.[79]

The depopulation of Shelburne continued until by 1792 its inhabitants were reduced to less than 2,000.[80] To Reverend James Munro, who passed this way in 1795, the town "now wears a gloomy aspect . . . so many waste Houses," many of which had been left unfinished.[81] When unsalable some of the buildings, and sometimes even their contents, had been abandoned by their owners.[82] Munro also states that "upon Jordan River and Bay are 25 families mostly presbyterians who live by fishing and farming, Lumber having greatly failed." [83] By 1816, according to the Surveyor-General of the province, there were only 374 persons left in the town and suburbs, although this statement is considered an exaggeration by historians. Not only Shelburne but the province as a whole had suffered an exodus of Loyalists. Thus the land named "New Scotland" by Sir William Alexander, the Scotsman to whom it was granted in 1621, received the new name of "Nova Scarcity."

Various causes for this early decay are ascribed by later authorities: remoteness from other settlements, lack of good farm land, the preponderance of merchants, military men, and other townspeople unacquainted with settlement practices and unable to appreciate the value of the great fisheries so close at hand. However, the few contemporary documents extant in which reference to this question appears offer a somewhat different slant, and in three of them the major premise is identical: that in building dwellings and warehouses, docks and wharves the Loyalists had lavished too great a portion "of that Property which the Wreck of a Civil War had left them." [84]

In the opinion of the author, the assertions that the unsuitability for agriculture of the southwestern section of Nova Scotia was either misrepresented or ignored by the Port Roseway Associates' agents, that they were unwilling to take the trouble to make thorough investigations, and other like criticisms seem altogether unjustified because this was unknown country and the Loyalists were pressed for time. "Very few people here have any further acquaintance than the heads of Harbours," wrote Joseph Pynchon about the Port Roseway area to the Association on January 23, 1783, and several of his statements are prefixed by "it is generally supposed," "in the opinion of," and other such qualifications.[85] Colonel Robert Morse, R.E., who the following year visited this coast, wrote of the interior back of the Roseway and Jordan rivers: "Beside the vast quantity of standing wood, the surface is covered with trees which have decayed and fallen. And the moss growing upon these and running from one to another entirely covers, for large tracts together, the surface of the earth and . . . renders it difficult to judge of the soil. . . ." [86] The Surveyor-General was correct in supposing that the best farm lands, as yet ungranted, lay along these rivers, but he was obviously unaware of their limited extent and distance from the coast. He had under consideration merely the settlement of the small band of Associates (not of the unexpected thousands that were to come), and Pynchon was warned that they "must expect indifferent land in every part of the Province." [87] The unfortunate plight of the agriculturists at Shelburne would seem to have been due more to circumstances than to incapacity on the part of either their agents or the provincial government.

Among those affected by the changing circumstances of Shelburne were some of our Scots. Neil and John McKay had left the area by 1786 and had removed to join their countrymen who had gone off to Canada with John Macdonell early in the war. These people had settled in Quebec on the north shore of the St. Lawrence west of Montreal.

When the war ended Sir John Johnson and his corps, the King's Royal Regiment of New York, were stationed in forts along the Richelieu River between Lake Champlain and the St. Lawrence. Upon the regiment's disbanding Sir John had organized his men and their families for the toilsome journey overland to the St. Lawrence and up the river to their new settlement above the mouth of the Ottawa River. In after years a Highlander who had been in charge of a party enjoyed telling of his arduous journey. When a visitor remarked that the adventure compared with that of Moses leading the people of Israel into the Promised Land the old Scot rose to his feet and shaking his cane exclaimed, "Damn it, sir, Moses lost half his charges in the Red Sea, and I brought all these folk through without losing a man, woman or child." [88] The settlers who had followed Captain John Macdonell from the Head of the Delaware and others who had later joined Sir John were: John and Neil McKay, William Rose, Roderick, Allan, and other Macdonells, John and William Cameron, Thomas Shearer, John and James Dingwall, several Grants, Dr. James Stuart, the widow of James Calder who died before the close of the war, Adam Chrysler's brother Philip from New Turlach,[90] and Jacob Stoneburner and his sons.[89] After years of "skulking about" following his release from prisons Stoneburner was still in the north. He had gone to the seashore in New England in hopes of finding a boat that would take him across the sound to Long Island. He had lurked along the Hudson on the chance of getting through to the St. Lawrence. But it was late in the summer of 1783, before he finally reached York and upon its final evacuation by the British he was taken to Canada and there reunited with his four sons who had served under Sir John Johnson throughout the war.[91]

The Scots mostly concentrated in township no. 1 of the county bordering the St. Lawrence named Glengarry whose Gaelic character was intensified by further migrations under the leadership of other Macdonells from Inverness-shire. Captain John Macdonell's family seat, named New Scottos after his ancestral home in the Isle of Skye, was situated in the community of Riviere Aux Raisins (modern St. Andrew's). His son, Miles, later engaged by Lord Selkirk as manager of the North West Settlement in the Red River Valley, became the first governor of Assiniboia, the Manitoba of today. Shortly before his eighty-second birthday Captain John wrote to his eldest son and namesake, a fur-trader in the far west (later partner in the North West Company), "I wish to god you could be quitt [sic] of that Antichristian country and come to live among us." Of his youngest son William Johnson who was born on the Charlotte River in New York and at this time was employed in the Boston Customs Department he remarked: "Our William is doing well indeed, and is a great favourite with the Bostonians. I think he will never leave the place. William looks to be a very clever fellow. In short, he keeps his wife so busy getting Daughters that, if that method is continued, he will give the family Yankee connections enough in course of time. He has got four Daughters already."[92] Soon thereafter Captain John Macdonell was dead.

Hugh Fraser appears to have held out until the spring of 1790 at which time he sold out and presumably left Shelburne although further trace of him has been lost.

George Chisholm also experienced difficulty in making a living for his ever increasing family. In addition to his wife and his daughter Mary Christina, there was John who had been born on May 24, 1784, and named for his paternal grandfather. Another child, born May 20, 1786 and christened James did not survive infancy. Perhaps he succumbed to one of the children's diseases listed as causes of death on the burial register of the Church of England at Shelburne. Between 1783 and 1791 the mortality rate among infants ran high, many dying of "fits," "small pocks," "worm fever," "Plague or Infectious Distemper," and dysentery.[93] (Adults died of dropsy, consumption, and "general decay.") On October 15, 1788, another son was born to the Chisholms and named William, a popular name with Clan Chisholm. The birth of this child coincided with the visit to Shelburne of Prince William Henry, so this Loyalist family may also have intended to honour their son with the name of the brother of the king. (Upon his accession to the throne the prince became William IV, the "Sailor King.") Finally, on March 6, 1790, came the birth of another daughter named Barbara for her mother. By this time, George Chisholm was unable to hold out any longer and had to admit defeat. As he himself stated, he had done his "utmost for Seven Years to support himself and Family, but was at last obliged to abandon [his land]."[94] On April 17 he sold out to his neighbour, Edward Bowlby,* for £50[95] and made preparations to leave Jordan Bay. It may have been supposed that the Chisholms went directly to Niagara were it not for an old document handed down by descendants which reads "came to Canada 1791."[96] Of their activities between the spring of 1790 and their arrival at Niagara in 1791 nothing is known.

Except for the small meadows and orchards on the water frontage already described, the so-called farms of the Scots along the rivers and bays remain as then rough, unclaimed bush land. The holdings of the McKays on Port L'Hebert are now accessible only by water, and it would seem unlikely for anyone ever to have lived in so remote a place at so early a date were it not for the testimony of Munro. "From port Jolly to port La Bear three Miles still going westward," he wrote in 1795, "small path and much encumbered with brush wood which retards, and wets the Traveller either in dew or rain. There are 10 families also in this settlement as in the former and generally of the same religious perswasion [Presbyterian]. And live in the same manner and by the same means [fishing and farming], and settled at the same time at the end of the american war and both settlements mostly scotch."[97]

The Chisholms' homestead in the lower reaches of the bay stood close to the open sea. It was situated on a little point of relatively level land jutting on a cove sheltered by an outlying shingle beach and girded by the smooth round beach rocks so characteristic of this coast. On the west where it curves inland the shore is bordered by a salt marsh into which a stream once flowed down from the hill above. To the north where the slope becomes more gradual an old orchard climbs the hillside, and here from the vantage point of an outcropping of granite the front of Chisholm's land

---

* Chisholm's farm later passed into the hands of McKenzies. Some of the families living along Jordan Bay were descendants of Murdoch who married Isabella Johnson on March 4, 1790 (Shelburne Historical Society, Anglican Church Records, Marriage Book). It would be interesting to know whether or not John McKenzie, yeoman, who in 1842 bought lot 112, formerly George Chisholm's, for £30 at Sheriff's sale, or his successor, Edward McKenzie, master mariner, who sold it to the father of the present owner, were numbered among the progeny of Murdoch McKenzie.

spreads out below. I have stood there when the bright sunlight of a clear September day picked out the autumn colours of deciduous trees from the dark evergreens on the shore across the bay, and turned the sea a remarkably intense blue. Away on the horizon was the mass of Gull Island standing out to sea. The beach offshore in the middle distance was animated by the endless wheeling and tacking and comings and goings of herring and great black-backed or "Minister" Gulls. In the foreground the beach rocks, crowned with the yellow-brown rockweed, imperceptibly emerged with the falling tide. Reaching out into the water the wharf of crib work filled with boulders was piled high with lobster pots and their wooden markers. At its head was the weathered fish house where tubs of coiled cod and halibut trawls and other gear were kept. Close by stood rows of wooden net stakes where the nets were hung to dry. In the meadow nibbled short by the cows and lying like a soft green carpet on the point stood the house with low spreading roof and simple lines of an earlier age. Nearby the old grey barn on the slope hid the view of the beached fishing boat and the pale green marsh grass rimming the cove beyond. Spruces standing in moist land, of which Chisholm had his share, encroached slowly but surely upon the old orchard, cutting off the sight of McLean's Island away to the north. The orchard's upper boundary, beyond which the land has never been cleared, was marked by an ancient wall whose stone may well have been laid by Chisholm. Behind me the rocky lane climbing through spruce, fir, alder thicket, sweet smelling bayberry bushes, and hackmatack, as tamarack is called here, met the road on the hill above. Behind me the cows, each wearing a bell, examined with interest so curious a trespasser. I have stood in the orchard when fog rolled in from the sea; when streamers of low lying mist obscured all but the tree tops on the opposite shore; when great white billows shrouded the world and the pale green bearded lichen or old man's beard hanging from the limbs of dead trees dripped gently with the cold moisture.

One time while the cows, now my daily companions, lurked nearby among the gnarled apple trees, I sat down on the rock to consider the changes known to have come about since the Chisholms lived in this place. From a distance the forest on the hillside, though in reality much tamed, probably appears much as it did then, but below on the seaward side erosion has taken its toll. The outer beach, washed down by high tides and gales, has moved northward in a curve towards the mainland, and the passage by which it was cleft was closed long ago. The lowered barrier abreast of the low lying point allows the heavy surf of very high tides and winter storms to roll in, and eel grass hanging from the top strand of a fence bears evidence that at times the house stands on an island. Because this house was built close by the southeast corner of an earlier dwelling it is probable that Chisholm's log house occupied approximately the same site.*

Chisholm's grant on the Roseway River (lot no. 6, Mason's Division) shows no evidence of ever having been cleared for tillage. It is crossed by the Ohio Road and by a rough narrow track leading nowhere and ending abruptly which yet bears the name of Wright's Road. This timber land, covered by immense granite boulders, is now the habitat of deer, porcupine, fox, and other wild creatures, and is accessible by

---

* The present owner, Captain J. Guerdon Bower, is a son of Charles Bower who bought the property in 1861 (Shelburne Court House Records, Deed Book 11, p. 162). His forebear was Adam Bower, a Palatine German who had migrated to South Carolina about 1762 and came to Shelburne as a Loyalist (*2nd Rep. Ont. Arch.* (1904), p. 662, Evidence on the claim of Adam Bower). Captain Bower was born in this house that was built of materials brought down by trading vessel from St. John, New Brunswick.

the deer trails leading down to the river. The shady moist parts are a wonderland where beds of soft green woodland mosses spread over the great rocks and the brown carpet of dead leaves and evergreen "spills" lie on the black mould of the forest's floor. Over the moss, so deep on some boulders as to foster spruce seedlings of fair size, trails the partridgeberry with dark glossy leaves and, in autumn, bright red berries. Standing upright on its single stem the bunchberry presents its red cluster in a whorl of leaves. Everywhere are banks of ferns—some tall and majestic, others low and delicately fronded—and toadstools of spectacular shapes and stupendous size—seven inches across by actual measurement. In colour the range and combinations seem unlimited: charcoal black, chocolate brown, fawns and creams with markings and without, tomato red with white dots, and lemon yellow. The deer trails wind upward around the rocks to higher ground where wild roses and blueberries flourish in spaces timbering has laid open to the sun. Farther eastward is Black's Brook which was probably named for David Black. In 1789 he was planning to build a mill race for a snuff mill [98] and according to local tradition there was a wooden mill race near the mouth of this stream.

However, for George Chisholm and many others of the Scots, the beauty of the countryside could not compensate for the declining prosperity of the area and the attendant difficulties of providing for their families. Thus forced to move on to localities where the outlook for the future was more promising, these Loyalists would regard Nova Scotia only as a stopping-off point in their search for a return to the happiness and stability of pre-Revolution days.

CHAPTER NINE

THE BRITISH WAY OF LIFE

UPON FINALLY REACHING Niagara, George Chisholm found the Scots from the Head of the Delaware well established in the heart of a thriving agricultural community. They were now reaping the benefits of the years of hard labour that had gone into bringing their farms into production for the maintenance of themselves and the families for which all were now responsible. There was also the additional security that official recognition by the British government had been accorded to both the Loyalists and their children. The Presbyterian congregation of which they were members erected the first place of worship of that denomination in the upper country, and the Scots took a dominant part in its founding. They lived in an area now squared out into townships which were rapidly spreading inland and westward along the north shores of Lake Erie and Lake Ontario. Because these lands were being settled by Loyalists of British origin the region above Montreal had been newly set off from Quebec as the Province of Upper Canada to be governed by English law. How these and other events had come to pass were significant questions to which Chisholm gradually learned the answers while working along the river before he also became permanently settled.

Even before the disbanding of Butler's Rangers in June 1784, the settlement on the west side of the Niagara River had consisted of forty-six farmers whose clearances totalled above seven hundred acres.[1] Except for John Chisholm who had remained below the Lower Landing the Scots all lived one beside the other on the Mountain, now called Mount Dorchester. (This name was conferred in honour of Sir Guy Carleton who was raised to the peerage in 1786 as Baron Dorchester.) Here in the oak forest there was "little more for the farmer to do, than cut a sufficiency of timber to fence his fields, girdle or ring the remainder, and put in the harrow, for in few places only is it necessary to make use of the plough, till the second or third crop, there being little underbrush."[2] More than twenty years later a visitor would be "struck by sentiments of regret" at the great numbers of fine oaks consumed daily by fire.[3] Nor was any use made of the ashes for no potash was manufactured in the area.[4] During the eighteen months following the first census Daniel Rose had doubled his clearance to twelve acres and had got ten acres under wheat, oats, and Indian corn. On the adjoining farm to the south Thomas McMicking grew the same crops but had not extended his clearance. On these farms the livestock still lacked covering. Down river below the Mountain John Chisholm had succeeded not only in clearing twenty-five acres and in raising a log house 17 by 16 but also in rolling up a 20-foot-square barn for the five horses he had acquired. He had little other livestock and only three acres under the one crop of fall wheat.[5]

Upon the disbanding of the Rangers, James Park and Archibald Thomson settled side by side between McMicking and the Twelve Mile Pond, as the Whirlpool was then called.⁶ When his brothers James and John had migrated from Hawick, Roxburghshire, in 1785 Archibald had given them the portion of his land extending southward from Park's property to the rim of the pond.⁷ James Thomson had brought his wife and three small children, and John his bride, Janet Nixon of Hawick.⁸ These families all lived along the portage path which by 1788 had become part of the "good road" extending for fifteen miles from Lake Ontario to the Great Falls of Niagara.⁹ Their immediate neighbours were Peter Thomson, Jacob and Adam Bowman, Gilbert Tice, and John Burch.¹⁰ Peter Thomson was also a Loyalist Highlander from New York¹¹ who was somehow related to the other Thomsons and may well have been among those from the Head of the Delaware of whom all record is now lost. Jacob Bowman and his son Adam had been separated from the rest of their family for seven years when they came to Niagara from Quebec in 1784.¹² The story of how both had been severely wounded in their second attempt to escape from the Continentals has been told elsewhere (see pp. 49–50) and neither was ever to recover fully from his injuries. Jacob and Elizabeth lived out their lives beside Bowman's Creek on the Mountain. This stream which meandered through their lands on the Mountain to cascade down the side of the gorge into the Whirlpool appears as Bowman's Creek on a geological survey made in the twentieth century.¹³

The bank of the pond in the upper reaches of this stream was chosen by Gilbert Tice as the site of his house. He together with John Burch and Hendrick Nelles were among the first appointed to civil offices in the upper region of the Province of Quebec. Tice had been district sheriff for three years and commissioner of roads for only a few months when he died about the time that George Chisholm arrived in the community. Thereafter, his wife Christian kept the inn which would be a famous landmark for many years to come. Adjoining Tice's acres on the north were those of John Burch where the latter undoubtedly lived for a time. By the summer of 1785 he was engaged in building the grist and sawmill which made the first use for industrial purposes of the tremendous water power in the Niagara River. On the recommendation of the Commandant of the fort Burch was granted permission to erect mills at a place selected by British officers, one of whom was an engineer. The site chosen was on level ground beside the rapids between the Great Falls and the Chippawa near the overhanging ledge called Table Rock. Burch stated that he had risked more than his whole property in the undertaking because of the extravagant prices he had been forced to pay for labour and provisions.¹⁴ Logs cut on the banks of the Chippawa were conveyed one by one down to the sawmill by the current through a "species of canal" formed by a "chain of poles" held parallel with the shore by twenty-foot poles projecting from the land. So ingenious was it considered that there is no dearth of descriptions of this canal which continued in use for a considerable time. To Captain Ennys of the 29th Regiment the mills appeared to be "a very elegant piece of workmanship."¹⁵ After "Burch's Mills" went into production in 1786 patrons paid one-twelfth of the grist as the miller's dues and "a moiety" (one-half) of the sawn lumber to the sawmill operator. John and Martha Burch went to live on a new farm near the mouth of the Chippawa, whose waters, because of their colour and fluidity, were likened to West Indian molasses.¹⁶ Nearby was Thomas Cummings Jr. who had escaped with Burch from Papacunck early in the war, become a merchant, and gained distinction as "the first settler of Chippawa."¹⁷ After his appointment as justice of the peace in June 1786,¹⁹ John became Squire Burch. Though empowered to perform the marriage ceremony his appointment came too late for John Chisholm who had been married when the

Commandant of Fort Niagara (at the time Major Campbell of the 29th Regiment) was still performing this function.[19]

John Chisholm and Christine Stuart were joined in holy matrimony on September 21, 1785. Although documentary proof is lacking there is every indication that she was the daughter of Dr. James Stuart of the Head of the Delaware who, after serving as surgeon's mate in the King's Royal Regiment of New York, had settled west of Montreal.[20] Some of his children had remained in New York State, but others had followed him to Canada.[21] A son born to the Chisholms on May 26, 1787, and christened William was left motherless at the age of fourteen months when Christine died October 1, 1788. John remained a widower until the summer before he was reunited with his brother George. His second wife Catherine Fletcher, to whom he was wed July 15, 1790, was born in Glenorchy, Argyllshire, a daughter of Archibald Fletcher and his wife Flora MacNab. Catherine was eight years of age when the family migrated to America, and evidently accompanied her younger brother Alexander to Niagara after the war.[22]

Thomas McMicking's wife was also a Scotswoman. In 1787 when he and other settlers at Niagara had been obliged to appear before the Loyalist commissioners sitting at Montreal he had grasped this opportunity of returning to Scotland. There he married Isabella Gass, daughter of William Gass, grain merchant. She was also a Lowlander, a native of Annandale, Dumfriesshire, not far distant from Thomas' birth place, Stranraer. Isabella was his junior by seventeen years and was twenty when she came as a bride to Niagara.[23] Thomas' sister Janet Cooper married "Wullie Broon" (William Brown), a Scot who had come out with the 10th Regiment and later joined the Rangers. She and her sons Thomas and James then went to live on Brown's farm adjoining Philip Bender's where one day a suspension bridge would span the gorge.[24]

The wives of James Park and Archibald Thomson were American bred, the former's name of Hagar suggesting Palatine origin. Thomson married Catharine Emery, a widow from the lower Susquehanna (modern Harrisburg, Pennsylvania) who with her daughter Margaret had been captured and brought to Niagara by Indians during the war. She had witnessed the death of another child when its brains were dashed out against a tree.[25] Margaret Emery became the second wife of Archibald's brother, James Thomson. The Thomson brothers were obviously happy in their new surroundings as a letter handed down through the Thomson family and written by Archibald's fourth brother Richard attests: "we are all very happy on every occasion to see that you were all in good health and had got a settlement and are pleased with the country." [26]

With the notable exception of one year the settlers had been blessed with favourable seasons and bountiful crops. The average yield of forty bushels of wheat per acre, which would continue without manuring until after the turn of the century, compared favourably with that of the best farm land in the Mohawk Valley. Settlers both increased and improved their stock by buying cattle brought by drovers from Pennsylvania and New Jersey and ferried across the river in batteaux and Schenectady boats.[27] Their hogs throve so well on the acorn mast covering the floor of the oak forest that farmers often "killed them out of the woods, well fatted on nuts." [28] Hogs were also useful for hunting down the rattlesnakes which infested the area: the large timber rattlers six or more feet in length which like limestone cliffs and the smaller massasaugas that prefer swamps and bogs. In the Whirlpool below the Thomsons was a large den of rattlers "of uncommon size." Whereas the Indians set fire to dry leaves in order to kill the snakes when they were emerging from hibernation, the settlers made war upon the snakes with the help of their hogs. Some five hundred were killed on one day by an organized expedition in the gorge.*[29] A brooch containing rattles mounted under glass and set in gold filligree is still treasured by descendants of Daniel Rose.

Orchards of apples, cherries, and peaches were being set out [30] and McMicking is credited with having grown the first apples in his vicinity.[31] His son told how he had brought seeds from the Kaatskills, and having been advised that they would germinate better if steeped in milk he had dropped them into a cup which he placed on top of a cupboard. It was found by a cat which promptly consumed the seeds with the milk.[32]

Merchandise and necessities such as salt were bought from itinerant traders who came by boat up the Mohawk from Albany.[33] The first to arrive in the summer of 1783 had evoked a bitter protest from Hamilton and Cartwright and other merchants who cried "smugglers,"[34] but Americans continued to come and settlers continued to patronize them.

In 1787 after the harvest the mass of the male population including the Scots made the long journey down the St. Lawrence to give evidence in support of their claims before the commissioners sitting at Montreal.

John Chisholm, Daniel Rose, Archibald Thomson, and James Park appeared in that order before Commissioner Pemberton on August 29. Each acted as witness for another, and McMicking and Chisholm stood for John Burch. They produced a certificate which was signed by Joseph Brant and which verified their services under him as unpaid volunteers from 1778 until the end of the war.[35] Their evidence given under oath and duly recorded, the commissioner noted in the margin of his ledger his impressions of these claimants. He found Chisholm who estimated his losses at £82.10.0 "a fair man," Thomson and Park (who had pooled their claim of £155.10.0) "Good men—to be allowed a little," but he failed to comment on Rose † whose claim of £72 included £5 for his share in the two kettles (original cost £11) used in the potash manufactury at Kortright.[36] Like George Chisholm and William McKenzie at Shelburne, McMicking was unfortunate in having "the whole Claim [£320.10.0][37] disallowed being for Supplies furnished British Scouts and Friendly Indians,"[38] although in the light of further supporting evidence it was later reviewed. Others under examination were deemed "very good people," "a poor honest creature," a few cases appear of "Evidence feeble" and only isolated instances of "No Loyalists," "Claimant a damed rascal," or "a drunken dog." Payment of valid claims was based on a fixed scale of percentages according to the amount of the losses. The outlay by the British government to Loyalists in Canada alone would eventually reach some thirty million dollars.[39]

It is from the other commissioner, Colonel Thomas Dundas, that we learn how the settlement at Niagara was fulfilling the purpose for which it was established. He advised Lord Cornwallis that the Loyalists there were mostly thriving, in so much as to have already supplied the King's post with bread, and that before long they would

---

* That timber rattlesnakes inhabit the Niagara Gorge at the present time was reported in the *Bulletin of the Federation of Ontario Naturalists,* June 1959, p. 30.

† Although Rose's evidence appears under the name of "Donald Ross" his claim and the payment thereof show "Daniel Rose." His name is found elsewhere in various forms which can be explained by the fact that he was illiterate. Evidently his name was often written according to his Gaelic idiom.

be "a good saving to Great Britain. Canada, my lord, has surprised me very much as I had figured to myself it resembled Nova Scotia; but it is . . . equal in extent of rich country to any part of America. . . . The Loyalists . . . are a happy flourishing people. . . . The business of our branch of the Commission will be finished by the month of June, when I propose to return to England. . . ."[40] Before he returned to England, Commissioner Dundas spent some weeks at Niagara in the spring of 1788. To the Duke of Clarence he wrote that he would not attempt a description of the Great Falls, but "must mention as a curiosity a woman of 50 years old, strong and healthy, who has lived four years next house to the Falls, within 200 yards, and who never saw them. This I confess surprised me as much as the Falls. . . . The falls, the navigation, the Posts, and the New Settlements, all considered, I never spent a month in my life more to my satisfaction."[41] Dundas was presented at this time with an address dated at Niagara May 15, 1788, wherein "the inhabitants of the New Settlement" asserted that the work of the commission had "given universal satisfaction, and therefore merits our united thanks" both to the commissioners and the nation. This theme, developed in elegantly turned phrases, reaches a climax in the rhetorical flourish, "May our prayers and wishes for your welfare prove propitious, and waft you with safety to the other shore."[42]

The population of the country above Montreal was about 6,000 when Lord Dorchester's proclamation of July 24, 1788, divided it into four districts. The Niagara settlement then lay within the District of Nassau. The area along the river was resurveyed and the appointed land boards confirmed locations already granted under military authority. In consequence the Scots as early settlers no longer held their lands merely as tenants of the Crown. The official survey was made by Philip R. Frey who as a lad had escaped from the Mohawk Valley before the war. He had received instruction in surveying both from his father Hendrick, a land surveyor, and at school in Schenectady. Having served with the 8th Regiment stationed at Detroit he had been appointed to survey the lands of the new settlements at Detroit and Niagara. Later when urged by his father to come home Frey applied for leave of absence which was refused. Nevertheless he returned to his boyhood home near Canajoharie. Because he died at Palatine Hill he had evidently remained unmolested, a fact which prompted Dr. Flick, historian of New York State, to comment that "few of this character were favored."[43] Frey was replaced as surveyor by his assistant Augustus Jones.

Meanwhile working under the Commandant at Fort Niagara Frey and Jones laid out two townships along the river which were given numbers in the French manner rather than names according to the British custom. Township no. 1 lying south of Lake Ontario extended over the top of the escarpment to the northern boundary of Daniel Rose's land and township no. 2 thence to the Chippawa. Because Macdonell's survey proved inaccurate new lines struck by the surveyors[44] caused considerable discord among the settlers. Some found that land they had cleared and cultivated belonged to their neighbours, and others that their buildings stood outside their new lot lines. But the rule was established "that the oldest improvement should hold Title,"[45] and "the eldest possession kept possession."[46] A case in point is that of the land given by Archibald Thomson to his brothers. When it "came to be run over" by the surveyor it was found that "part of the lot fell to Peter Thompson and the other to John Thompson. . . . James being a Single man gave up his right to John and Peter,"[47] and removed to the banks of the Chippawa. (The name Thomson acquired its letter "p" during a land transaction, according to family tradition.) A dispute between John and James Park proved a hardy perennial for some time after Hagar Park had become a widow.[48]

Wild land on the Mountain which had sold for a shilling an acre four years before[49] was rapidly rising in price as Loyalists continued to arrive from "the States." Up the valleys they came—from New York, the Jerseys (East and West), Pennsylvania, and even from so far south as the Carolinas, bringing with them their most treasured possessions. "Five or six hundred miles is no more considered by an American than moving to the next parish is by an Englishman," an observer was led to comment.[50] They travelled by batteau to the head of the Mohawk, crossed the nine-mile portage to Wood Creek and down the Oswego; by foot, driving their cattle and leading pack horses carrying their children in baskets; by covered waggon which at river crossings served as batteaux when the bodies were caulked and removed from their wheels. It was indeed a misfortune that the year of heavy migration, 1788–89, should turn out to be the Scarce or Hungry Year, when late snow and frost followed by midsummer drought and hail ruined many crops, and numbers of people faced starvation. It so happened that some of the Scots were seriously short of flour. For the first time McMicking and others had shown a disposable surplus of wheat (in the spring of 1789), but they shipped all they could spare down by batteaux which were returning to Montreal after delivering garrison stores.[51] Established families shared their flour with newcomers to the extent that it was exhausted before the wheat was ripe, and flour brought in boats by Americans cost "8 dollars per hundred, hard cash,"[52] which few could afford. However, the McMickings and presumably others salvaged enough of their crop to tide them over the winter.[53] Game was also scarce but the fish in the river were a boon to both troops and inhabitants, who fished on stated days. Patrick Campbell saw more than a thousand, mostly white fish, taken in one haul of a seine, and learned that six times that number had been caught in one day.[54] Sturgeon averaging 30–40 pounds of which a hundred were sometimes landed in a day, were considered useless by white men although the Indians shaped the upturned snout into balls for their national game, lacrosse.

There were so many newcomers to the upper country that Lord Dorchester reached the decision that some means must be devised by which they might be distinguished from those who had actually served the cause of their King and their country during the war. At a meeting of the Executive Council of the Province of Quebec on November 9, 1789, he stated:

that it was his wish to put a mark of honour upon the families who had adhered to the Unity of the Empire, and joined the Royal Standard in America before the Treaty of Separation in the Year 1783.

The Council concurring with his Lordship, it is accordingly ordered that the several Land-Boards take course for preserving a Registry of the names of all persons falling under the description aforementioned, to the end that their posterity may be discriminated from future settlers, in the Parish Registers and Rolls of the Militia of their respective Districts ... as proper objects, by their persevering in the fidelity and conduct so honorable to their Ancestors, for distinguished benefits and privileges.—

And it is also ordered, that the said Land-Boards may, in every such case, provide not only for the *Sons* of those Loyalists as they arrive to full age, but for their *Daughters* also, of that age, or on their marriage, assigning to each a Lot of two hundred Acres more or less....[55]

The resultant registry of names is the famous "Old U. E. List." Under the heading "Alphabetical List of Loyalists settled in different Townships in the Province of

Colonel John Butler's home on Switzer Hill, Fonda, N.Y., about 1900
(Courtesy of Mrs. Eleanor M. Rockwell)

John Chisholm's house on the Portage Road, Stamford Township, Welland County, Ontario

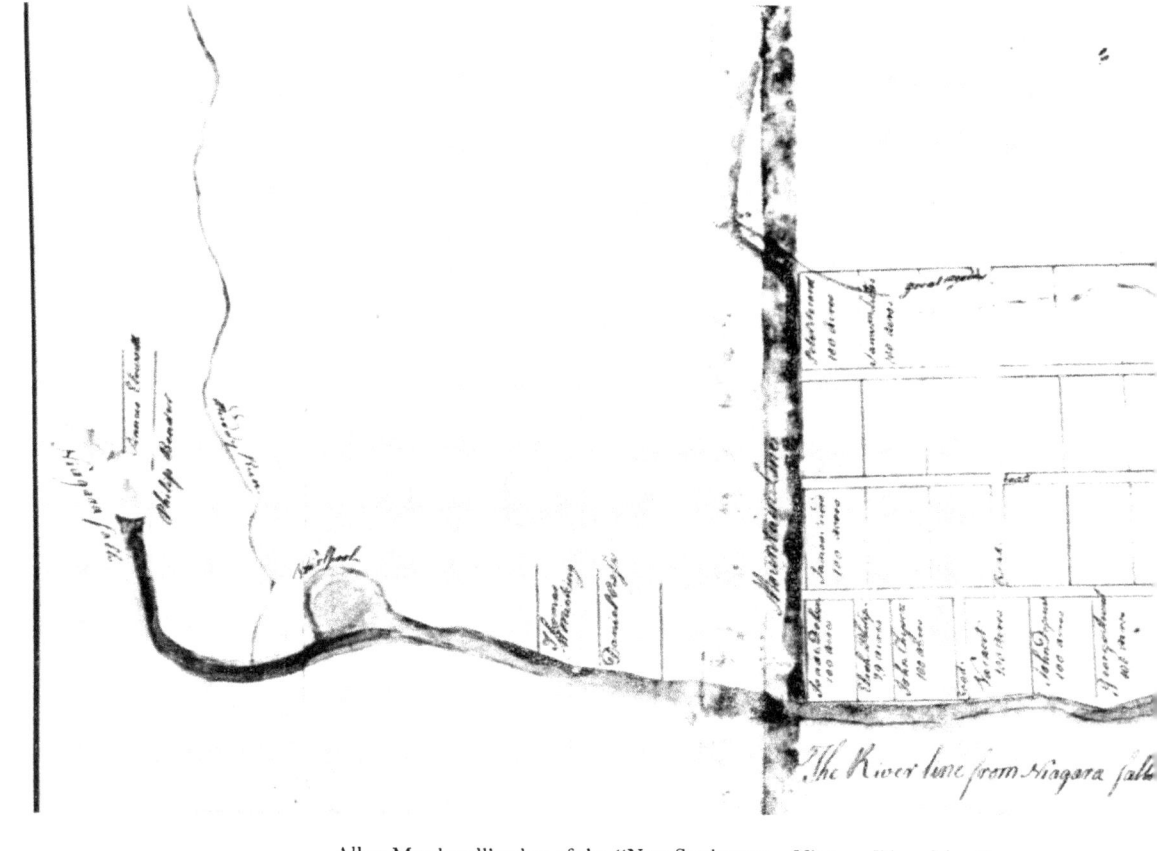

Allan Macdonell's plan of the "New Settlement—Niagara River Line,"
March-April 1783 (Courtesy of the British Museum)

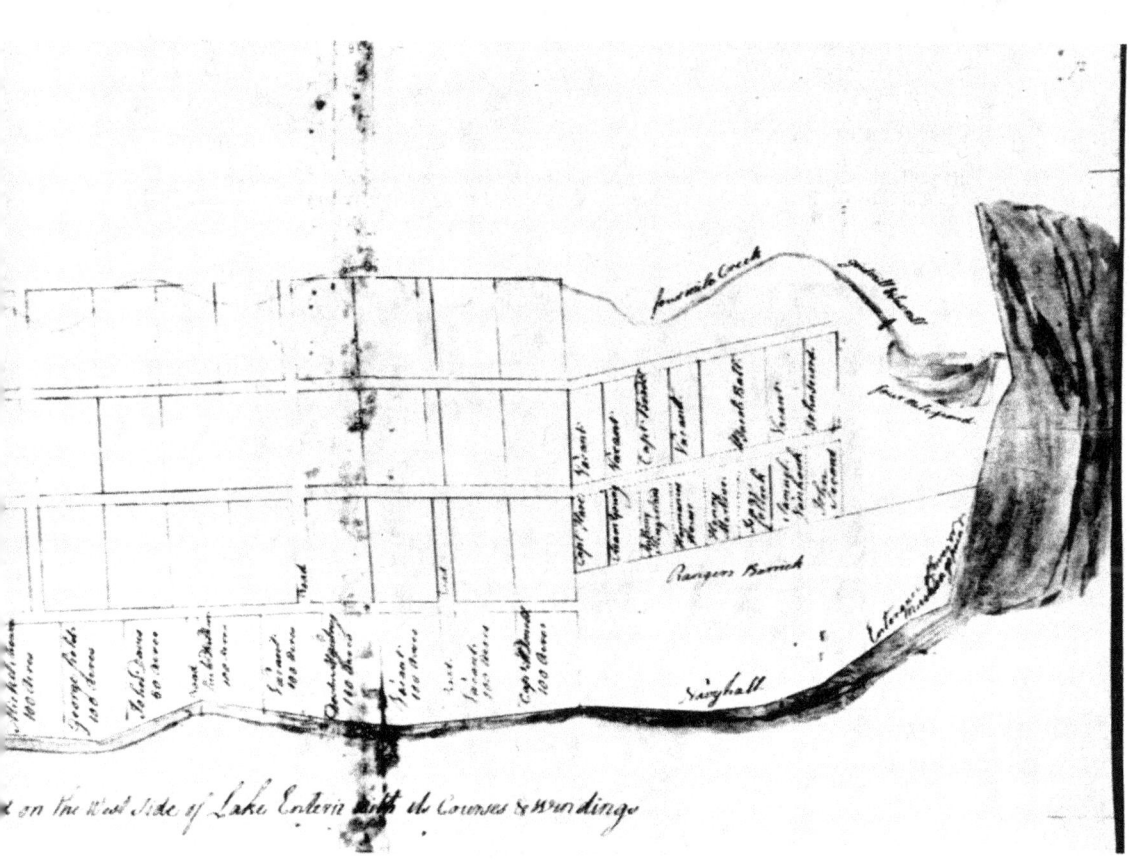

on the West Side of Lake Entern with its Courses & windings

Part of the town of Shelburne, Nova Scotia, 1789, with barracks opposite. Wash drawing by Captain W. Booth, Royal Engineers (Courtesy of the Public Archives of Canada)

Well in Mowat Street, Shelburne, from which George and Barbara Chisholm drew water

Quebec" the names together with some information relative to background and military service appear in clear copperplate handwriting on pages of heavy rag paper measuring $9\frac{1}{2}$ by $14\frac{1}{4}$.[56] The entries relating to Daniel Rose, Thomas McMicking, James Park, Archibald Thomson, and John Chisholm show that because of their services in the Indian Department they were granted land on the authority of the Surveyor-General of Quebec, and that their names are on the Provision List, Stamped Book, 1786, as having received rations issued at Niagara. The entry relative to George Chisholm, placed on the roll after his arrival in the province, shows "States carpenter in Burgoyne's army" and that he also drew rations for a time. Here was documentary proof that these men were entitled to affix to their names the Mark of Honour, U.E.

Effort was made to control the granting of lands to people from the United States who were not Loyalists and who applied without any intention of settling, wishing only to make money by their sale. To this end printed certificates were issued which could be transferred only with the sanction of the Land Board. They served as title deeds and for some time were all the holders possessed to prove ownership of their land.

For a time it appeared that the district town for Nassau with its public buildings would be situated on the Mountain. When the prospective abandonment of Fort Niagara to the United States necessitated the provision for a town on Canadian soil, among the suggested sites were "the rise of Mount Dorchester above the Landing," and "the Glebe lands on Mount Dorchester."[57] Meetings were held to determine the feeling of the people, but the Land Board chose the government lands at the mouth of the river which were vacant except for the Rangers' old barracks and a ferry house beside the river.[58] Westward near Two Mile Creek Colonel Butler lived on his farm Butlersbury, which name was applied to the surrounding area. But the town which, upon his arrival, George Chisholm saw lined out was officially named Lennox[59] in honour of Charles Lennox, fourth Duke of Richmond.

This location of the district town, though a loss to the Mountain township as a whole, was advantageous to the Presbyterians there because they were granted fifty acres of the glebe lands or public common in April 1792. It seems that surveyor Allan Macdonell had placed road allowances of one chain between every six instead of every two lots as according to law and that Frey, his successor, had laid out "as much Land as a public common to the Township as this difference would amount to," that is, 800 acres.[60] The trustees of the Presbyterian congregation appointed to administer these lands and to serve in that capacity for twenty years or longer were Peter and Archibald Thomson, Thomas McMicking, and James O'Reilly.[61] They erected a log meeting house facing the Portage Road on the east half of lot no. 44. After years of meeting in various homes for divine worship John Thomson had made inquiries of his brother Richard about securing a minister from Scotland. Richard replied that he had informed John how to apply to the Synod "but I expect my Letter has never come to your hand. . . . The principal thing that you seem to want [on the Mountain] is the Gospel; and, considering the liberal subscription you mention, it is a great pity you should want it. But I understand the young Preachers in this country are peculiarly adverse from coming to America."[62] None the less the Presbyterians on the Mountain did succeed in securing a licensed minister of the Church of Scotland, Reverend John Dun, educated at the universities of Glasgow and Edinburgh.[63] The subscription list of October 1, 1794, carries the provision that "he reside amongst us," which he did for three years.

Of the sixty-one members who bound themselves to annual pledges ranging from 8s. to £4 sterling for a period of three years a number of names are familiar: John Burch, Thomas Cummings, Thomas and James Cooper and their step-father William Brown, Samuel Montgomery, and of course the Thomsons—Peter, Archibald, and John—Daniel Rose, John Chisholm, and Thomas McMicking.[64] The first interment in the burial ground was that of Janet Mulwain McMicking who lies on the south side of the first Presbyterian church to be founded in the Province of Upper Canada.

For this was the new name for the upper country bestowed by the Constitutional Act of 1791 whereby it was given a form of government according to English Law. By the same token what remained of Quebec became Lower Canada where the old French system endured. Colonel John Graves Simcoe appointed governor of Upper Canada had first come to America with the British regulars in 1775 at the outbreak of the Rebellion. Between 1777 until Cornwallis' surrender he had commanded the Queen's Rangers, a provincial corps made up chiefly of native born Loyalists. When it became known at Niagara that the Governor and his lady had reached Lower Canada an address of welcome was drawn up and dispatched to him by Colonel Butler and Robert Hamilton. The familiar signatures on this document dated at Niagara, February 24, 1792, are those of John Burch, Daniel Servos, Philip Buck, two sons of Lewis Clement, Hendrick Nelles' son Robert, Thomas McMicking, "Donald Rosse," George Chisholm, and Peter Secord.[65]

How the Governor, his Executive Council, and the Queen's Rangers newly recruited in England for the execution of public works ascended the St. Lawrence; how the Governor arrived by schooner at Niagara to live in canvas houses first used by Captain Cook on his voyage of discovery in the South Pacific; how he set up the provincial government, opened the first Parliament, and laid plans to attract settlers from the United States to populate the new province—all these events belong to the oft-told story which need not concern us here. What seems more pertinent to this narrative is that he brought with him a brace of pistols as a gift to Joseph Brant from the Duke of Northumberland who had previously presented him with a very handsome rifle. The stock was fashioned of rosewood inlaid with fine silver scroll work and a carved handgrip. Accompanying the pistols was the following letter dated at Northumberland House, September 3, 1791:

My dear Joseph,—
Colonel Simcoe, who is going out as Governor of Upper Canada, is kind enough to promise to deliver this to you, with a brace of pistols, which I desire you will keep for my sake. I must particularly recommend the colonel to you and the nation. He is a most intimate friend of mine and . . . loves and honours the Indians. . . . He wishes to live upon the best terms with them, and, as Governor, will have it in his power to be of much service to them. In short, he is worthy to be a Mohawk. . . .
I was very glad to hear that you had received the rifle safely . . . and hope it has proved useful to you. I preserve with great care your picture, which is hung up in the Duchess' own room.
Your affectionate
Friend and Brother
Northumberland,
"Thorighwegeri" [66]

Meanwhile George Chisholm and his family were at Fort Erie. Because there could have been little else to take him to this little post in the wilderness it must be that he had found employment as carpenter on the works then in progress in connection with the carrying trade. By then the portage road between the Lower Landing and the Upper Landing at the mouth of the Chippawa had begun its rise as the principal route of travel and trade in the upper country.[67] In 1788 a group of traders headed by Robert Hamilton had undertaken to develop their own portage on the west bank of the river, employing local farmers and their teams. As the expiration of Stedman's contract and the surrender of the east bank of the river to the Americans drew near Lord Dorchester ordered that arrangements be made for carrying government stores on British soil. When Hamilton and his associates were awarded the contract in the spring of 1790 the government began the construction of wharves and warehouses for the accommodation and protection of stores and merchandise in transit. Here the cargoes brought up river from Chippawa by batteaux were trans-shipped into lake schooners. These works were being carried out at the three points of trans-shipment, the two landings and Fort Erie, the only post left to the British by the peace treaty. The buildings were all block houses and those for the garrison at Fort Erie were surrounded by palisadoes. Beyond the precincts of the fort stood four similar houses for the accommodation of workmen and their families.[68] It must have been in one of these that on September 16, 1792, Barbara Chisholm gave birth to her fourth son, who was given the name of his father, George.

The traffic passing along the portage road increased steadily in volume. Four or five yoke of oxen or from two to four span of horses were required to draw the strong heavily laden waggons up the steep gradient of the Mountain. "I have seen four vessels of sixty and one hundred tons burden unloading at the same time," wrote an observer of the Lower Landing, "and sometimes not less than sixty waggons loaded in a day.... This portage is an increasing source of wealth to farmers for many miles around, who carry from twenty to thirty hundred weight, for which they get one shilling and eight pence N. York currency per hundred weight, and load back with furs, &c."[69] It is entirely possible that at least some of the Scots were at one time or another concerned in this carrying trade passing so close to their doors.

The Governor's regiment, called briefly "The Queen's" occupied buildings close to the river at the Lower Landing. These barracks were designated as "the Queen's town" with the result that this name was soon applied to the landing as well. This was one of the many changes in names which occurred at this time. Joseph Brant was heard to remark that Governor Simcoe had "done a great deal for this province, he has changed the name of every place in it." [70] The Governor began the systematic substitution of good English names for those of Indian and French which so offended his ears, and he showed a distinct preference for those in the shires of eastern England where several generations of his forebears had lived. Thus the sister townships along the river were among those comprising the county of Lincoln, that on the north was called Newark, and the mountain township Stamford. Chippawa Creek became the Welland River. It has generally been conceded that the name Stamford originated with Governor Simcoe, but to Ernest Green, the earlier historian of the area, this seemed an unsatisfactory explanation. "There is no evidence," he wrote, "that a single person from Stamford in England had settled in the township or had any connection with it." The present writer submits that the Governor, who was well acquainted with many settlers on the Mountain and frequently visited among them,[71] sanctioned the name originating with those from the Head of the Delaware.

Several other points in the growth of the settlement along the Niagara River are worthy of note. In the spring 1789 a post office was established at Fort Niagara, and henceforth the post was to be dispatched every four weeks from Montreal, either by batteau or, if the St. Lawrence was closed to navigation, by winter express. Merchants and traders at New York and Montreal had long used this latter age-old means of Indian courier for communicating with the upper posts. The following notice appeared in a New York City newsheet in 1773: "Niagara, Detroit, &c.—Notice is hereby given, that the winter express, will set out with packets for those places, from Schenectady on the 18th day of January next, to which all persons interested in that communication, are desired to . . . forward their dispatches to their friends at Schenectady." [72] When the winter express was resumed after the war the trustworthy Mohawk chiefs, Jacob Lewis and Little Aaron Hill, were employed on the Canadian route. Travelling on snow-shoes they usually reached Niagara late in January, then went on to Fort Detroit, sometimes covering sixty-five miles in one day.[73] Upon returning to Montreal by way of Oswego they had completed a journey of at least three months. One who met Jacob and his wife wrote that they were handsome and well dressed; that she was "a very pretty woman, the only handsome woman I have seen among the Indians," and that she could work any pattern given her in beads "remarkably well." [74] Jacob, says our informant, "danced Scotch reels with more ease and grace than any person I every saw, and had the air of a prince. The picturesque way in which he wore and held a black blanket gave it the air of a Spanish cloak; his leggings were scarlet; on his head and arms he wore silver bands. I never saw so handsome a figure." [75]

Then there was the provision for trying breaches of the peace in the Court of Common Pleas. When convicted of stealing salt Abel Wilsey was ordered not only to pay the plaintiff 12s. but "to stand for half an hour before the Tavern, with a bag of salt round his neck and . . . a label pinned to his Breast, For Stealing Salt." [76] When Francis Goring, William Brown, Archibald Thomson, and James Park sat January 15, 1789, on the Petit Jury, they handed down a verdict of wilful, deliberate, and corrupt perjury against a defendant "for prying," ordered him to pay £20 to the King, "stand one hour in the Stocks on the next Court day in April, and Rendered infamous as the Law directed." Another man found guilty by the same jury of stealing pork was sentenced to "cut down One hundred Logs for the purpose of building a Gaol—The Overseers of that work to direct this." [77]

Nor was education neglected in the settlement. The Scots, for example, turned to Francis Goring to teach their sons. The association probably began with James Thomson, although Goring's note in his diary that "James Thomson began schooling with me" in September 1789 [78] refers to the adult James. After settling on his land at the foot of the escarpment where his descendants live today (lots no. 179–80, Niagara Township), Goring became a farmer-schoolmaster. The new schoolhouse built on Three Mile Creek was opened in May 1790,[79] but later removed to Queens Town. "This day commenced keeping school at the landing," he recorded December 10, 1792, and among the seventeen day scholars were three sons of Robert Hamilton and John Chisholm's son William.[80] The copy book of a later pupil, twelve-year-old James Thomson Jr. has survived to show some of the problems in arithmetic set by Francis Goring:

Divide 4876 [eggs] between 6 Old Irishmen & tell me how many the old men had a piece.
Divide 3706 bannocks between three old Scotchmen.
Divide 67676 Watter Melons between 12 Yankees & tell each man's quoto.
How many Barley Corns will reach round the globe of the earth, which is 360 Degrees, and each Degree 69 miles and a half.[81]

Francis Goring's achievements with a goose-quill pen are outstanding even in an age when penmanship was little less than a fine art. Whether embellishing with scrolls, drawing intricate geometrical patterns, or merely writing a business letter his unerring hand maintained the same degree of perfection. During the years of employment in winter as Robert Hamilton's secretary he went out to deliver five or six hundred letters of account, travelling on foot for six weeks or more. "I have in one Winter traversed over Twenty-two Townships," he wrote in his graceful script, "and have traversed to Ancaster &c twice in one Winter (I say traversed for I was seldom on the direct road.)" For his services over a period of years as Hamilton's secretary Goring arranged to take part payment in materials for a barn, but Hamilton died suddenly owing him some £400 which Goring found difficult to collect.[82]

The Niagara settlement saw an early development of municipal government. Upon the passing by the legislature of a measure "for the Nomination and Appointment of Parish and Town Officers" on July 9, 1793, the sister townships lost no time and were the first in the Province of Upper Canada to establish municipal councils. On August 1 Robert Hamilton and John Burch as magistrates fixed August 17 as the day for "a Town Meeting to be held at Newark . . . [and] the same day has been fixed for the Elections of the Township of Mount Dorchester."[83] The householders who assembled on that day elected Thomas McMicking one of two wardens to act on their behalf in all actions affecting the township as a whole.[84] The following year Archibald and James Thomson were elected to fill this office, and Peter Thomson was elected assessor. The former were succeeded by Adam Bowman and William Brown. McMicking and Archibald Thomson reappeared as wardens during the next ten years when the younger commenced replacing the older generation.

There was also local military organization. Rumours constantly reaching Niagara of attempts on the part of Americans to incite the Indians to attack forts still held by the British prompted Colonel Butler to organize a militia. His official return made in the spring of 1791 shows that the three battalions of Nassau militia totalled 835 men between the ages of eighteen and sixty, rank and file.[85] The Scots enrolled among the 200 men in the 2nd Battalion which included all settlers living along the river between the lake and Chippawa Creek.[86] Thomas McMicking's commission as ensign in this corps is dated October 27, 1788.[87] On July 26, 1794, Governor Simcoe, understanding that the officers desired uniforms, was "pleased to direct" that they provide themselves at their convenience with a scarlet coat with plain guilt buttons, blue facings, and white waistcoat.[88] Two days later Daniel Rose was commissioned captain and Peter Thomson and Thomas McMicking lieutenants.[89] McMicking's sword and pieces of his scarlet coat have been handed down through his family.

By 1795, the Scots' farms extended along the rim of the gorge for more than two miles. (John Chisholm had sold his holding below the Lower Landing, apparently to Robert Hamilton, and had settled on the 100-acre lot no. 2 in township no. 1 north of Rose.) But as their children increased in number the four Scots who had served as volunteers in the Indian Department during the war jointly petitioned the government for grants of additional lands. As the result of the first petition of July 8, 1795, certified by Colonel Butler and John Macdonell, they were recommended for 300 acres each in addition to what they had already received.[90] By the time a second petition was drawn there were only three volunteers, for James Park was dead and the representations were made on behalf of his widow Hagar. On August 15, 1796, "Archibald Thomson & Associates" averred that "unpaid, unprovisioned, and uncloathed," they had served His Majesty for seven years "with all the Zeal, and Bravery of Britons," and that since settlement they had "proven themselves good Husbandmen and members of Society," as Robert Hamilton and numerous others were willing to confirm. They stated that they had "already benefited by the Bounty of Government to a Certain Extent" but considering the loss of the whole of their former property they hoped their case would receive consideration. They had always looked forward, they continued, to the time when their services might be remembered, and because they all had rising families it seemed "that the time had now arrived." As it happened, another child was born to each family during the following year. James Park and John Chisholm each had four children (John would eventually have five), Archibald Thomson six (to which two more would be added in future), and Daniel Rose the eight children who were to complete his family. They would, concluded the petitioners, think their services well requited "in such a Grant of Waste Lands of the Crown, as will render them and their families after them Respectable and mark that *Honor* on them, recommended by the Governor General, Lord Carleton."[91]

A portion of these additional lands were located at the head of Lake Ontario in East Flamborough Township surveyed by Augustus Jones in 1791.[92] The remainder were located hither and yon in new townships scattered throughout the province. In consideration of his "steady loyalty and services to loyalists while living in the revolted colonies" Thomas McMicking also received an additional 400 acres,[93] which like those of the other Scots were widely scattered. It was in East Flamborough that George Chisholm finally settled. While his compatriots on the Mountain were all well established as yeomen George was still working for wages at the end of his second year in the province. In March 1793 he had petitioned Governor Simcoe for a grant of land, setting forth how he had been forced to relinquish his land in Nova Scotia because he had found it impossible to support his family.[94] By order-in-council dated July 11 he was granted 400 acres of the waste lands of the Crown.[95] However, he had already chosen a tract at the head of Lake Ontario which he purchased jointly with Charles King from Dr. Robert Kerr, surgeon to the Indian Department.

Charles King, a native of Morris County, New Jersey, had been six years in the province.[96] That he and Chisholm paid £150 New York currency for their 600 acres suggests that they were fellow-workers at Fort Erie because few workmen were paid in cash except by the Government. The land purchased was part of a 1,000-acre tract situated on the north shore of Burlington Bay and granted to Dr. Kerr as a portion of his allowance for services during the war.

Kerr, a Scot whose name was also spelled Karr as it was pronounced, was taken prisoner with Burgoyne's army. After being released he was surgeon in Sir John Johnson's Royal Yorkers. From October 1784, he was surgeon to the Loyalists in the upper country until appointed to the Indian Department at Niagara in April 1788. His wife Elizabeth, niece of Joseph Brant, was a daughter of Sir William Johnson and Molly Brant, and was reared at Johnson Hall. The doctor's was one of six 1,000-acre tracts taken up by himself, Philip R. Frey, Robert Hamilton, and three other persons. Augustus Jones had surveyed these tracts in the autumn of 1788 in the eastern extremity of the lands ceded by the Indians May 22, 1784.[97] In the agreement dated July 12, 1793, between himself and Charles King Dr. Kerr engaged to procure "Regular Deed of Government for the Land" within twelve months; otherwise "the Bargain shall be Null and Void, and the foresaid sum of one hundred and fifty pounds shall be duly paid to said Charles King."[98]

The joint holding of George Chisholm and King was situated in the southeast corner of the township. Chisholm took lot no. 1 in the Broken Front and concessions 1 and 2 which were set off by the Purchase Line from the land of the Missisauga Indians, and King took the corresponding lot no. 2. These lots stretched back from Burlington Bay, formerly called Lake Geneva although long before and long after the latter name appeared this bay formed by a sandy beach at the head of Lake Ontario was known as the Little Lake. Its south shore lies close to the foot of the escarpment, but on its north shore the Mountain, as it is known here as well as at Niagara, stands away to the northwest. About three miles back from the bay, the lots in concession 2 run over the top of the Mountain which forms a steep cliff near the summit. The shallow bay, navigable only for small craft, was almost land-locked. The only break in the oak covered "long Beach" was the outlet near its northern end, called Pimmebetonggonk—a creek running through the sand—by the Missisaugas.[99] Their name for the Little Lake was Wequatetong—a bay.[100] What had attracted Chisholm and King was the oak timber standing in the open woods skirting the north shore which the grantee of the adjoining tract on the west described as follows:

> It contains 600 acres—ascends gradually from the Bay with a South front—and from the distance the trees stand from each other—and the great Verdure under them [the tract] has more the appearance of an English Gentleman's Park than wild land in America . . . and you may be conveyed in your Barge from your own Door to Niagara . . . or . . . any part of the Settlements on Lake Ontario—
> You have besides close to your front great abundance of Water Wild Fowl—and the most delicious fish such as Salmon, Maskinonge, Black Bass, Salmon Trout, Pickerel, &c., & in your Rear, Deer, Wild Turkies—Pheasants—Woodcocks—Hare &c.—About four miles from this Situation . . . is one of the first mill seats in the Province. . . .[101]

Above the oak lands stood a belt of pines, thence upwards on the slope of the Mountain the timber was mixed.[102] A visitor quoted Chisholm as saying that in the wild land behind were many cedar swamps and the rattlesnakes so fond of rocky places.[103] In very dry weather they would go down to the lake to drink; seven hundred were killed near the bay during the summer of 1795, according to Augustus Jones.[104] Chisholm also told his visitor how he and others had found the wild hay in the marshes and the rushes growing in the woods "a great help in the infancy of the Settlement," though when pastured a year or two they died out.[105]

From Patrick Campbell we learn of the high grass growing on the beach which "the neighbouring inhabitants" found so useful for fodder. He saw the bay in winter and when he crossed it on ice covered by almost a foot of snow (his first encounter with snow-shoes) he saw some Missisaugas fishing in a manner which he found curious. They used fish fashioned of wood weighted with lead "so exactly formed and coloured, that it is impossible to conceive it to be any other thing than a real fish, without handling it." Through a hole cut in the ice the native, lying covered with a blanket to keep out the light, dangled the fish on a line, making it "play as if live in the water," and spearing the fish thus attracted. The Indians bartered their fish and venison for other necessary provisions.[106]

George Chisholm built his house on a knoll overlooking the bay in the southwestern corner of lot 1 in concession 1 somewhat north of the road running between this concession and the Broken Front. The twin girls born here July 18, 1795, named Christy and Nancy, completed his family. When Nancy died within two years three sons and three daughters remained.[107]

An event of significance to Chisholm, as it resulted in his appointment as magistrate, was the visit of Governor Simcoe and his lady to the Head of the Lake in the spring of 1796. Since he and Richard Beasley had been recommended by Robert Hamilton as the best men living in the area to hold office [108] the Governor took this opportunity of appraising both men. Beasley, a Loyalist from Albany and cousin of Richard Cartwright Jr. (whose mother was Joanna Beasley), had located on Burlington Heights at the opposite end of the bay for trading with the Missisaugas.

Governor and Mrs. Simcoe arrived on horseback on June 10 at the King's Head Inn where they remained for five days. Built soon after the Governor first arrived in Canada, this public house was to accommodate travellers in accordance with a plan (formulated by Simcoe in 1791 before he left England) for opening roads of communication.[109] The inn was situated at the south end of the beach at the fork in the road near a portage between the lake and the bay. "There are eight rooms in this house," wrote Mrs. Simcoe the next morning, "besides two low wings behind it, joined by a colonnade, where are the offices. It is a pretty plan. . . . From the rooms to the N.W. we see Flamborough Head and Burlington Bay. The sand cliffs on the north shore of Burlington Bay look like red rocks. The beach is like a park covered with large spreading oaks." She tells how, then, they set out in a boat, and the bay was full of Indians fishing from canoes; how they dined at Beasley's; how they looked down from the heights into Coote's Paradise where Captain Coote of the 8th Regiment had "spent a great deal of time in shooting ducks in this marshy tract . . . [which] abounds with wild fowl and tortoises." Two days later the Simcoes rode on the beach, passing the Indian encampment. "Their huts and dogs among the fine oak trees they were under, formed a picturesque appearance. Afterwards we sailed to the north shore of Burlington Bay and pitched our tents near a house, where we had the tea kettle boiled, but we found the sand flies very troublesome." (Unhappily the tradition which says that during the visit the Governor chatted with Chisholm is silent on the matter of where water was boiled for the tea.) On June 15 Joseph Brant called at the inn on his way to Niagara where his two sons, "about ten years old," who were with him attended school.[110] Were it not for Mrs. Simcoe's sketches, some made on birch bark, we would have no record of the bay and its surroundings as it was known to the early settlers. This was her last glimpse of the Head of the Lake, for shortly after approving George Chisholm's appointment as magistrate [111] the Governor and his lady left the province never to return.

During the summer of 1797 Joseph Brant was to become George Chisholm's neighbour. In the meantime, almost immediately after the war had ended, Brant had built a house at Kingston where he lived for about two years.[112] He had then removed with his family to the reserve along the Grand River granted by General Haldimand to the Six Nations as Loyalists and to which they had gone from Niagara in the autumn of 1784. In turn the Indians had made numerous grants of lands in the Grand River tract to white men who had served with them during the war. A deed dated Feb. 26, 1787, in which they agreed "that our brethren living on the same river . . . shall hold a farm each . . . to extend in length three miles back from the said River's bank," shows that Adam Young * and his sons John and Daniel, originally of Youngsfield, New York, Hendrick Nelles, his son Robert, and Hendrick and John Huff were then living among the Indians.[113] Of the Scots John Chisholm and Archibald Thom-

---

* After stating that Adam had married the sister of the Mohawk chief who had succeeded Captain David (Hill), Patrick Campbell, who visited him, wrote that "Here I for the first time played cards with a squaw" (*Travels in the Interior Inhabited Parts of North America in the Years 1791 and 1792* (Edinburgh, 1793), p. 212).

son are known to have received grants from the Indians. Chisholm willed to his son George a "block of Indian Land on the Grand River."[114] When Hendrick Nelles died here in 1791 he was buried on Young's Island in the river.[115]

Patrick Campbell who made a visit to the Grand River early in 1792 tells us something of Chief Brant's English manner of life at this place. Tea was "served up in the handsomest China plate and every other furniture in proportion. After tea was over, we were entertained with the music of an elegant hand organ," and supper was served "in the same genteel stile." Two Negro slaves attended the table, one in scarlet and the other wearing "coloured clothes" with ruffles and silver-buckled shoes. On the beds he found sheets and English blankets. However, Joseph's wife Catherine, who understood but did not speak English, had retained the manners and dress of her people. She appeared "superbly dressed" in blanket, jacket, and "scanty petticoat" of knee length made of silk and the finest English cloth trimmed with embroidered lace. Her scarlet leggings fitted "close as a stocking" and her moccasins were ornamented with silk ribbons and beads. Campbell was greatly impressed with the "elegance of her person, grandeur of her looks and deportment" and the "harmony of her expressive features" which in his estimation "far surpassed ... the fair European ladies" who were also present. He examined with interest the firearms sent to Brant by the Duke of Northumberland. For his guest's entertainment Brant arranged a war dance and Campbell's appreciation expressed in Gaelic was hilariously received by the warriors.[116]

Brant had other English habits. He had been initiated a Freemason when in England in 1776, and he was one of the original members of Barton Lodge upon its formation on New Year's Day 1796, at Smith's Tavern in the township for which it was named.* George Chisholm was also a member of this lodge; when he was initiated on July 4, 1796, his was the seventh name to be entered in the Registry of Brethren.[117] Evidently Chisholm was the only Freemason among the Scots. Other craftsmen were Richard Beasley, Augustus Jones, Peter Bowman, and Robert Land and his sons Robert Jr. and Ephraim. Although Chisholm's masonic apron worn in Inverness by his father before him was older Brant's was the more illustrious, having been presented to him by King George III.[118]

Brant continued to guard the welfare of his people, as, for example when an epidemic of small-pox visited the province, spreading from Kingston at the foot of Lake Ontario. Dr. Kerr and Dr. James Muirhead, Scottish army surgeon who had married Colonel Butler's daughter, advertised inoculation on the most reasonable terms, "the poor inoculated gratis."[119] Some months previously "sundry inhabitants of the Head of the Lake" had requested inoculation for themselves and families.[120] In consequence the two doctors were dispatched by the government to inoculate Indians as well as whites. Setting up their headquarters at the Government house, as the King's Head Inn on Burlington Beach was also known, they immunized more than 160 adults and children of the Six Nations Indians who had accompanied Brant and his family to the beach.[121] The figures relative to white settlers are not available. When writing to express his own as well as his people's "sincere and unfeigned thanks for ... the use of the Government house at the head of the Lake during [their] illness with the small pox" Brant reported that all were making "a speedy recovery."[122]

It was shortly after this epidemic that Brant settled close to Chisholm. For him-

* Smith's Tavern stood on what is now the northwest corner of King and Wellington streets in Hamilton, Ontario.

self as military claimant Brant had chosen the location at the northern end of the beach at Burlington Bay which Colonel Butler was instructed to purchase from the Missisaugas in the autumn of 1795. "It will be proper," wrote Governor Simcoe, "Captain Brant should understand the Messessague Indians should retain their customary use of the Beach &c., that a public road will be cut through it and it is probable a Bridge will shortly be built to connect the two Beaches."[123] When the Missisaugas learned that the tract was intended for "their Brother," Butler reported, they consented to part with it for the consideration of one hundred pounds payable in goods, and appeared well pleased "at the Idea of Captain Brant's Settling and Improving land so near them."[124] The treaty bearing totems of the principal chiefs of the Missisaugas also carried the signatures of George Chisholm and Robert Nelles as commissioners on the part of the province.[125] Among Nelles' papers and written in his hand is a "Memorandum of things Delivered to the Missisaga Nation for a Piece of Land" dated August 21, 1797, which lists the following:

Blankets $\begin{cases} 32 \text{ Blankets 2 points} \\ 22 \text{ Do ...... } 1\frac{1}{2} \text{ points} \\ 36 \text{ Do ...... } 2\frac{1}{2} \text{ points} \end{cases}$
49 Yards Blue Strout [Stroud—blanket material manufactured at Stroud, Gloucestershire, for trade among the Indians]
$40\frac{1}{2}$ Yards Black Strout
79 Yards Linnen
90 Yards Calico
9 Dozen of Indian Knifes
47 pound of Brass Kettles [126]

Brant's Block, as it soon came to be known, of 3,450 acres as surveyed by Augustus Jones, extended from Chisholm's land eastward to a small stream called Lamabinicon by the Missisaugas and Rambo Creek by white settlers.* On the north its boundary was the same as that of Chisholm's tract, an extension of the line between East Flamborough's concessions 2 and 3, and southward it reached to the "outlet from the Little Lake."[127] Brant chose a beautiful spot for his house overlooking the lake on the bank above the "north neck" of the beach. The first log house was soon enlarged into a handsome framed dwelling of Colonial design, and there is a letter written by him to Robert Nelles ordering lumber from the latter's sawmill on the Forty,[128] as Forty Mile Creek was known. Brant named his home Wellington Square.† To a guest, the engineer Francis Hall, this "large sash-windowed house" was "superior in appearance to most houses in the Province,"[129] even as late as 1816.

The homes of the Brants, Chisholms and Kings were outposts of the "Niagara Settlement." By now the region southward from the Head of the Lake was squared out in twenty-two townships with a population of about 6,000,[130] but isolated by forty miles of unbroken wilderness from the new capital of York. The Missisaugas, resentful after the death of their principal chief in a drunken brawl with a British soldier, refused to sell this tract except for a price which the Executive Council was unwilling to pay. In fact they appeared so unfriendly that members of the government considered a military escort necessary when travelling through this territory.[131] Joseph Brant, whom they chose for their new leader, held the opinion "that it is too much

---

* Rambo (Rambeau?) Creek enters Lake Ontario at Torrance Street, Burlington, Ontario.

† This house was incorporated in the Brant House, a summer hotel which stood until after World War I. The site is now occupied by the Brant Museum, a replica of the frame house Joseph Brant built on his estate, Wellington Square. Here on display is a section of log wall from the original house, an iron stove once used by the family and other Brant relics, and a sign carrying the portrait of King George III which once hung from the King's Head Inn.

resembling the Yankees to grasp land too eagerly, as I don't see any Necessity of making this Acquisition and I think that if they [the Executive Council] will wantonly take it they should pay a good price...."[132]

Location had been the chief factor in the choice of the seat of government. Newark, as Simcoe had renamed the town at the mouth of the Niagara River, was too close for safety to the United States, so York, which was farther inland, seemed more desirable. Once the removal was effected there was considerable dissatisfaction among officers of the Crown who were obliged to leave their comfortable houses at Niagara and build new ones at York. One member refers to "the Seat of the King's Government planted in the midst of a Desart extending near fifty miles each way, through which neither Road, Bridge, or House facilitates the . . . thousands who . . . desire access to . . . the public offices of Government."[133] In the autumn of 1797 the Executive Council ordered the construction of a bridge over the outlet at Burlington Bay so that York might be connected "with the western part of the Province,"[134] and Augustus Jones was sent out to survey a road through the Indian lands to York. When the bridge was constructed Jones reported that it appeared to be well finished. "It stands on a Block of logs at each end, with a frame of three Bends [arched span of timbers] distanced between them, it is full eighteen feet wide, rising gradually from the ends to the Center." He adds that Mr. Chisholm, who lives nearby, thinks the plans "were fully complied with."[135] But the bridge was washed out and replaced within the year, and Chisholm as commissioner with Beasley and Charles Depue (eldest son of John Depue of Niagara) reported the new bridge "by no means according to the contract."[136] Thus began the perennial battle of the early settler in this area with the force of the waters of Lake Ontario, a struggle which would be continued by generations of their descendants.

The ancient Indian trail traversing the Missisauga territory became the road from the Head of the Lake to York, although it first had to be widened and cleared of timber and the numerous streams it encountered had to be bridged. To avoid extensive swamps and bogs, it kept to the level ground at the foot of the low ridge standing a short distance inland. This road circling Lake Ontario joined one of the main roads running westward at the King's Head Inn which was leased in the summer of 1798 to William Bates from the Head of the Delaware.

From Darien Township, Connecticut, William Bates was the fourth of ten children in a family which was divided by the Revolution. In 1776 he had joined the Queen's Rangers and served for eight years under Major John Graves Simcoe, rising to the rank of serjeant.[137] He was evacuated from New York to New Brunswick and after about eight years left to join his brother Augustus at the Head of the Delaware. Augustus Bates had gone to New Stamford with the post-war influx of settlers from the coastal townships of Connecticut, and he had settled as a merchant in Paines' Dale, the community which sprang up around the mills constructed at the falls in the Delaware at Town Brook. William was in some way connected with the grist mill.[138] He had married Rebecca Murphy, and they had two sons [139] when he left New Stamford and came to Upper Canada in 1798 as "a reduced Loyalist."[140] Being known to members of the Executive Council who had served as officers in the Queen's Rangers he was acceptable as lessee of the King's Head Inn at the head of Lake Ontario.

Considering his war service William Bates had had small chance of living peaceably among the Yankees who now occupied the lands confiscated from the Scottish Loyalists. Soon after taking over the King's Head he wrote to Augustus: "I have nothing to say about politics, as they are scarcely heard of here. We have peace and plenty." [141] Because Augustus also contemplated leaving Harpersfield William encouraged him to come to the Head of the Lake.

> It is my opinion you can't do better than to come here and see for your own satisfaction. If you should come and like to move by sleighing, I have room enough, and will provide you with provisions for a year. . . . Tell your wife I am sure she would be pleased with this situation. . . .
> I think I may expect to see you here soon, and will lay in salmon for your family, as now is the season. I am going to the Credit to get my winter store, never was finer at ten for a dollar, that weigh fifteen pounds each. If you come this fall I shall be able to treat you to roast duck till you are tired. They have just come, and the rice is just ripe, which will make them very fat. . . . I send you a sample of the wild rice, which is plentiful here. There are 50 acres within one mile of this that would produce 20 bushels per acre if it could be saved. If what I have said won't move you, I don't know what will.

William suggested that his brother bring with him the horse Brazon.

> I have plenty of grain and hay, and must have him by all means, but the trick is to get him here. . . . If you haven't sold your horses, and they are in good order, they will fetch £70 . . . I have keeping, and will keep them till you can make a sale of them, for nothing. Cattle are still high. Cows fetch £10. I sold a yoke of oxen a few days ago for $100 in hand. . . . Should you come bring a good beef or two, and I will pay you well for them. I will engage you £10 at least. . . . I want you to get my mill irons and still to Schenectady, and I can get them from there any time. . . . The mill irons will fetch £80 a set. The still can be put to immediate use. They would clear £100 this season. . . .[142]

Augustus arrived within the year to purchase a strip of land from Joseph Brant and turn innkeeper like his brother. The spacious two-storey building with double verandahs which he constructed overlooked the lake from the north side of the road paralleling the shore three-quarters of a mile east of Brant's home.*

The arrival of William and Augustus Bates was no doubt of great interest to George Chisholm, paticularly because they had come from the very section of the Delaware River valley where he, Dr. James Stuart, Jacob Stoneburner, and the Roses had lived before the war. The Bates would have brought news of how newcomers were reaping the benefits of the Loyalists' toil; how the settlement had prospered and was once more a thriving community far removed from the frontier; how the country of the Six Nations Indians now belonged to the white men who were pushing westward towards the Niagara River. Augustus Bates had travelled this latter territory when visiting the Head of the Delaware in the winter of 1801-2, so that Chisholm would have been somewhat prepared for the changes he encountered when he himself returned to the Head of the Delaware.

* West of Brant Street in Burlington, Ontario.

CHAPTER TEN

A JOURNEY TO KORTRIGHT, 1804

TOWARDS THE END of 1803, about the time that George Chisholm was planning his visit to the Kaatskills, he received a letter from Lord Selkirk requesting him to undertake a commission in Montgomery and Delaware counties, New York. Thomas Douglas 5th Earl of Selkirk, was a Scottish landowner who sympathized with the hard lot of his countrymen, the Highlanders. He was born on St. Mary's Isle, Kirkcudbrightshire, the youngest of seven sons, and at the age of fifteen entered the University of Edinburgh to study law. He soon became absorbed in social and political conditions, particularly those of the Scots, and reached the belief that they would be better off to emigrate to British North America. When the last of his brothers died in 1797 and he fell heir to the estates the young earl laid plans for establishing two colonies, one in Prince Edward Island and the other in the Western District of Upper Canada. In August 1803, he arrived in Prince Edward Island with emigrants from Inverness-shire, Argyll, and the Isle of Skye. A month later he started for Upper Canada, travelling by way of New York to view a land purchase made some years earlier in the Genesee area, and reached Queens Town November 15. The land granted to Selkirk in Upper Canada lay between Lake Erie and Lake Huron in the townships of Dover and Chatham. Here, he planned a national Gaelic-speaking settlement of Highlanders because "in teaching our people English," he wrote, "we teach them to become Yankees."[1] His personal farm situated on Lake St. Clair in the centre of the colony was to be its mainstay, and according to the "Plan and undertakings" for the settlement, sheep were to be considered the "staple article upon which the profit will depend."[2] The Earl's agent, a young sheep farmer, William Burn, and Alexander Brown, "Shepherd to Lord Selkirk in America," with the help of two dogs had driven a flock of 400 sheep, Spanish Merino rams sent from Scotland and ewes collected along the way, throughout the breadth of New York State. At Queens Town Selkirk found his flock "in very good order having taken about a month to travel from Albany."[3] He met with his countrymen, Robert Hamilton and Thomas Clark, before embarking in a schooner on November 20 for York.

During the six weeks he remained at York Lord Selkirk became acquainted with a number of men to whom George Chisholm was known, notably Alexander Macdonell, sheriff of the Home District. When at Johnstown, New York, in November he had encountered Peter Stewart, waggonmaker, who told him that very few of the party with whom he had migrated had purchased land, "the neighbourhood being so much taken up & land dear.... The Highlanders here and at Breadalbane—adjoining have no Gaelic preacher & some of them complain of the want."[4] Being anxious to secure Highlanders who were dissatisfied with the United States, both newcomers and experienced settlers, the earl made use of the opportunity Chisholm presented of advising those in the Mohawk Valley of the projected settlement in Upper Canada.

It was probably from Macdonell that he learned of Chisholm's familiarity with this area which was continuing to attract immigrants from the Highlands; of Chisholm's dependability, judgment, and other matters pertinent to his purposes. Lord Selkirk wrote to Chisholm as follows:

York Decr 22^d, 1803

Sir

I am informed that you will soon have occasion to take a journey into the State of New York —If your business should lead you thro' the counties of Montgomery or Delaware you may have an opportunity of seeing some of your countrymen who are settled in that neighbourhood: I imagine that many of them are unacquainted with the advantages of this Province & might be inclined to settle in it if they knew the liberal terms on which Land may be had—Tho' the King's grants are not so easily obtained now as they were some years ago, yet I have the Governor's assurance that the persons I recommend shall have every advantage as I propose to bring a settlement of Highlanders to a Township near Lake Erie, I should like very well that a few of their countrymen who have been long in America, & can instruct the newcomers in the methods of the country, should settle among them & if you find any of this description & respectable characters who would incline to come into the province you may send me a list of their names—I can make them certain of a grant of excellent land; but I beg you will make particular enquiry as to their character. The people who are coming out are respectable & substantial farmers from several parts of the Highlands, & I would not chuse [sic] to bring among them any people but such as are worthy of associating with them & I would not for any consideration that any whom I recommend to the Governor should disgrace themselves & me by misconduct.—

The Governor promises that my settlers shall get their deeds without being required to attend at the Land Board in person—this will save a great deal of time & trouble—my friend Sheriff MacDonell will transact the business of getting out their papers—all they will have to do will be to send some person to pay the Patent fees, & to shew [sic] a certificate of their arrival in the Province.

If you write direct—"care of Mr. Dudley Walsh at Albany."

Your &c.
Selkirk [5]

Before leaving York for Lower Canada on January 4 Lord Selkirk apparently left instructions that Chisholm was to be supplied with a horse. An "Account of Wm. Burn for Sundries for Lord Selkirk to Thomas Clark" shows an entry on January 7, 1804, of "a Horse to Mr. Chisholm, 40 Dollars—£16." [6] Presumably Chisholm was soon on his way eastward.

Had he been able to cross the frontier at Queens Town on the ice in the Niagara River Chisholm could have taken the Niagara Road running between Lewistown and Batavia. But this horse-road which lay below the escarpment to Eighteen Mile Creek and then climbed over the Mountain ridge and turned southeast towards Batavia, though shorter, was newly constructed. It was low, swampy, and full of holes, and ran through country almost uninhabited except by scattered fur traders. Indians still trapped the marshes lying between the ridge and the lake, and the ponds of the Four, Six, Twelve, and Eighteen mile creeks (here more frequently called "Runs") for beaver, otter, mink, and muskrat.

It was on this road at a spring a mile west of Warren's (now Warren's Corners) that John Street, trader at Fort Niagara and father of Samuel, had been robbed and murdered by white men in 1790. The body was discovered when the dog of some travellers stopping at the spring brought them a leg with a boot upon it. Friends gathered up the fragments of the body and carried them home to Massachusetts for burial.[7]

If Chisholm like most travellers took the older route he rode up the Niagara River to about two miles below Fort Erie where he would take the ferry which crossed to Black Rock in New York State. The flat-bottomed boat was large enough to carry five horses, and the charge was half a dollar for man and horse.[8] Upon landing and passing about two miles north of the village at the mouth of Buffaloe Creek, recently named New Amsterdam, Chisholm travelled the old road (now N.Y. State Highway no. 5), originally the main trail of the Indians. For sixty miles to the Genesee River this road ran through groves of white oaks called Oak Plains which like those at Burlington Bay and on the Mountain in Stamford appeared like the grounds of an English park. In some sections, however, it passed through swamps which were often impassable. In one place a corduroy road, composed of layer upon layer of logs "till a solid platform" was elevated above the marsh, was frequently completely submerged. Every spring for years, in the time of freshets, a pathmaster was obliged to draw the log causeway back into place with several yoke of oxen.[9] In other places where branching trees darkened the swamp wolves followed travellers, and many a lone horseman was compelled to take to the trees for safety and remain there until daylight.[10] Fragments of these swamps, the remains of a glacial lake, have been preserved as wildlife sanctuaries. In the interior of Bergen Swamp persist Arctic flora pushed south by the glacier, and included among its fauna are three reptiles rare in upper New York State: the massasauga rattlesnake, Muhlenberg's turtle, and the coal skink.

Farther east Chisholm would have found the road improved. Between Cayuga and Whitestown on the Mohawk the Seneca Turnpike was being built by subscription and within eight years would reach to the Niagara frontier. Like those of New England the New York turnpikes were made by clearing out stumps, ditching on each side of the road, and elevating it in the centre with dirt thrown out of the ditches.[11] Levelling and cutting down hills was done with a scraper, a large wooden scoop with handles and edged with iron dragged by a team hitched with chains.[12]

Chisholm would surely have been amazed at the tide of white settlement which was now engulfing the country through which he was travelling. The ancient homeland of the Indians of the Six Nations was in a state of transition between a vast wilderness and the "Bread Basket of the Nation" which it was soon to become. After the campaign of 1779, General Sullivan's soldiers carried home tales of this fabulous country. To farmers who had known only the thin rocky solid of New England the rich fertile mould lying as deep as fifteen feet in river bottoms[13] seemed almost incredible. Nowhere along the northern coast was there anything to compare with this land, and once the war was ended settlers began flocking to the Genishaau, the "clear shining land" of the Senecas.

The greater part of northwestern New York was being developed by land companies. The tract called the Holland Purchase, acquired from the United States government in 1793 by a group of Dutch financiers known as the Holland Land Company, extended from the Niagara to the Genesee and from Lake Ontario to the Pennsylvania line. Joseph Ellicott, engaged to survey it, was a Quaker from Maryland who had gained experience while assisting his brother in surveying the site of Federal City, seat of the United States government in the District of Columbia. When preparing to survey the western section of the Holland Purchase Ellicott had come to Niagara in June 1798, and had secured two yoke of oxen and a stout lumber waggon from Clark and Street, merchants at Chippawa.[14] "Mr. Holland Purchase," as Ellicott came to be known, chose the Big Bend of the Tonewanta for the site of his land office, naming the town in honour of Holland, then the Republic of Batavia. Land sold for two to four dollars per acre on long-term credit, instalments payable in wheat. In the land office hung a large-scale survey plan divided in three sections, each mounted on ten-foot rollers and enclosed in a glass case. When the rollers were turned the map sections moved from side to side and "landlookers" were enabled in "a minute's time" to find any particular tract in the three-million-acre Purchase.[15] In November 1803, Lord Selkirk had found the tavern at Batavia "full of Viewers."[16] It was in the third land office, built 1815, a handsome stone building with high pedimented portico supported by four Doric columns and now preserved as a museum, that the saying, "doing a land office business" is claimed to have been coined. Because Ellicott had established company stations every ten miles between New Amsterdam and Batavia travellers were no longer obliged to bivouac in the snow.

In 1791 another land company, the London Associates, had appointed Captain Charles Williamson, a Scot from Balgary, as manager of their tract adjoining the Holland Purchase on the east. Williamson planned to trade with Baltimore and Philadelphia by shipping Genesee produce southward by way of the Chenango and the Susquehanna; with New York via the Mohawk and Hudson; with Montreal and Quebec by Lake Ontario and the St. Lawrence. His plans for using the last mentioned route were jeopardized when an error in the survey involving 84,000 acres, a strip reaching from the Pennsylvania line to Lake Ontario, had cut off the southern outlet and the fine natural harbour of Sodus Bay on the north. Settlement was in progress and numbers of deeds had been issued before the error was detected, but the matter was amicably settled with the owner of the adjoining tract.[17] Upon Governor Simcoe's arrival in Upper Canada Williamson had made representations relative to opening communication between Niagara and the port of New York through his settlement. He suggested that every fortnight an Indian be dispatched from Niagara to his home, bringing "the letters to be forwarded to York, England, &c." and returning to Niagara with letters for Upper Canada.[18]

Williamson laid out the towns of Bath and Geneva around public squares. Geneva, situated at the foot of Seneca Lake, was only a short distance east of the site of the Seneca castle of Canadasaga. On the plain crowning the high bank of the lake Williamson laid out the Upper Town; the Lower Town on the margin of the lake had already grown up for trade. "The Yankees," commented Lord Selkirk while at Geneva, "have not the same attraction for water that the Highlanders have."[19] Williamson built a three-storey inn, the Geneva Hotel, which had opened with a grand ball. Under the management of a famous innkeeper imported from London this hotel soon gained the reputation of the "Astor House of the West." It was the western terminal of the stage coach service (at five cents per mile) inaugurated in 1803 between Whitestown (on the Mohawk) and Geneva. Stage-waggons drawn by four horses leaving Albany every Tuesday and engaging to carry passengers to Niagara for two hundred dollars[20] also stopped at the inn. That five lawyers were all making a good living in Geneva prompted Lord Selkirk to remark: "Everybody agrees that New Englanders are very litigious."[21]

Within seven years Williamson had built three grist and seven sawmills, opened 300 miles of road, and bridged the Genesee.[22] Poorer families he supplied with an ox, a cow, and even a house, taking care "to secure a constant supply of provisions for the settlers," and supplying them "from his own store."[23] He visited each settlement once a year.[24] As prevention against fever and ague he insisted upon houses being "tight and close" and did his utmost to convince settlers that dwellings with log floors "like a causeway—earth above and open below" were dry and wholesome.[25] The Scots at Caledonia were allowed ten years' credit, one year's provisions, teams of horses, and a few cows, the cost of which they paid in wheat. The dozen families of Atholl Highlanders who five years before had travelled two hundred miles on foot from Johnstown had settled at the Big Springs, calling their settlement first Inverness and lastly Caledonia. They had prospered, having in operation the only grist mill east of Chippawa.[26]

John Maude, a Scottish traveller who spent some time with Captain Williamson in 1800, states on good authority that the earliest settler on the Genesee was "Indian Allan." This is none other than Ebenezer Allan who served with Butler's Rangers and as lieutenant in the Indian Department. He was also one of the volunteers who with George Chisholm's brother John had fought under Joseph Brant at the battle of Minisink (see pp. 64–65). Before being released from active duty Allan had come as agent to feel out the Indian situation for the British officers at Niagara. When dismissed in 1783 for reasons irrelevant to this narrative, he had become trader and farmer at the Genesee. His nickname was due to his preference for the Indian way of life and for Indian women. When he was given one hundred acres at the falls of the Genesee * on condition that he build a grist mill for the accommodation of new settlers the Indians wondered why so much land should be needed for so small a mill. An answer was soon provided. Upon marrying Allan Miss Lucy, daughter of an emigrant headed for Canada, found herself joint tenant with his Seneca squaw and her two daughters. Miss Lucy resolved to make the best of being "co-partner in bed and board," and when Allan brought home a third wife, Mille McGregor, she and Sally whipped the newcomer. Mille was provided with a separate residence. In 1794 Allan had removed to the Western District of Upper Canada where he promoted a colony in Delaware Township on the upper reaches of the Thames and became involved in a number of fraudulent transactions. When passing through the township Lord Selkirk wrote: "Allen [sic] who began the settlement lives much with the Ind[ian]s of whose women he has a Seraglio—formerly very numerous. . . ."[27] Upon being asked how he managed the members of his large household Allan replied that he "ruled them with a rod of iron."[28]

Captain Williamson established trade between Geneva and Catherine's Town at the head of Seneca Lake by running a four-ton sloop as packet. Arks † navigated by four or five men and carrying 12,000 bushels of produce were floated downriver to be broken up at Baltimore. In 1793 he advertised the first fair held west of the Hudson, the "Williamsburg Fair and Races at the Great Forks of the Genesee," which attracted not only yeomen from the frontier but many of the sporting gentry from the seaboard as well. Perhaps nowhere else in the state were new settlers and industries encouraged as were those under the promotion of Captain Williamson. But his policies resulted in losses for the London Associates and in 1807 Williamson was relieved of his position.

Once established, settlers in the area, who had brought all the necessities of life on pack horses from Whitestown, found that the fertile soil yielded fantastic amounts of wheat and Indian corn per acre. Wheat from Dansville, the new name for the

---

* Ebenezer Allan was the first settler on the site of Rochester where there was no settlement until after 1810. This man is not to be confused with Ebenezer Allen of the Green Mountain Boys.

† "An ark," wrote Judge William Cooper in *A Guide in the Wilderness* . . . (Dublin, 1810), p. 13, "is neither strictly a boat nor a raft, but partakes of the nature of each; it is of the form of a lozenge, so that each angle operates as a wedge; this figure is found convenient, as it admits more rapidly of lateral deflection, and in case of sudden interruption in its course by shoals and other obstacles." Arks were hastily and cheaply constructed and not even water tight. Their bottoms were fitted with light timbers which made them buoyant enough to keep grain and other perishable produce from getting wet. A surprising quantity of wheat was annually conveyed to Baltimore in arks.

Canaseraga so familiar to Butler's Rangers, sold for the highest price on the New York market, notwithstanding the greater distance of carriage.[29] A settler who bought land on the site of an old Seneca town south of Geneva made, during the first year's occupation, enough cider from apples growing on trees planted by Indians to bring fivefold returns on his investment.[30] Originally the trees in this area had been grown from seed brought to the natives by Jesuit missionaries. On the renowned Genesee Plain bordering the river, grass in its natural state had grown ten feet high so that men could tie it over their heads while on horseback.[31] But the region was also fraught with danger. Endemic fevers in the swamps were so prevalent as to become known as "Genesee fever."

The need for a bridge across Cayuga Lake became manifest when fifty to one hundred teams crossed daily on the ferry—with upward of 10,000 bushels of grain in one week.[32] Begun in 1797 the bridge had been completed in eighteen months at a cost of $150,000. This marvel of engineering, acclaimed as the longest bridge in the world, was $1\frac{1}{4}$ miles long and wide enough to admit three grain waggons travelling abreast. Not long after George Chisholm passed over it the bridge was carried away by ice.

Already the need was apparent for linking the Great Lakes and the St. Lawrence with the Hudson. As William Cooper, founder of Cooperstown (see p. 13fn.) stated, the trade of this region must be divided between Montreal and New York, and about half of it would be lost unless a canal "be formed from Lake Erie to the Hudson. This project ... has been for some time meditated by individuals. ... I doubt not that it will one day be achieved." * [33]

During his travels through northwestern New York Chisholm would have stopped over at the various wayside inns and taverns. Although styled inns by their signs and the laws of the state, these hostelries were so unduly wretched, and the subject of such bitter complaint by native Americans as well as travellers from abroad, that their titles were often challenged. Most travellers concurred with Dr. Dwight who claimed that "the law has nicknamed them, and the signs are liars. ... Too many of them are mere dram-shops ... which spread little circles of drunkenness throughout the state" (and here the president of Yale College launches into a learned dissertation on the evils of such).[34] Privacy being regarded as undemocratic by the sons of liberty, wayfarers slept, washed (using a common towel), shaved (before the bar-room mirror), and ate their meals in common. It was universal practice to crowd in as many beds as room or garret would hold, and for strangers to sleep three or even four in a bed, paying a quarter of a dollar for the privilege. The better regulated hostelries posted such rules as "No boots to be worn in bed," and "No more than five to sleep in one bed." An American traveller told of being disturbed by "the noise of drunken people in an adjacent room, of crickets on the hearth, of rats in the walls, of dogs under the beds, by whizzing musquitoes about our heads, and the flying of bats about the room," by women entering for plates and cutlery, and lastly by vermin. Upon examination he found that he "had been assailed by an army of bedbugs, aided by a body of light infantry in the shape of fleas, and a regiment of musquito cavalry. I retreated from this disgusting scene ... and took refuge in a segar."[35] Upon finding a tavern in

---

* The Erie Canal was opened in 1825. Among the situations in nothwestern New York pointed out by Judge Cooper as those which "must become important places of trade" were "the mouth of Buffalo Creek" (now Buffalo), "the straits of Niagara below the falls" (now Lewiston, named for Governor Morgan Lewis), "the first falls of the Genesee" (now Rochester), and "the mouth of the Oswegarchie" (now Ogdensburg). (*A Guide in the Wilderness....*)

Canandaigua, "a house in which filth and famine strive for mastery," John Maude had slept in boots and gloves.³⁶ Breakfast, including the inevitable buckwheat cakes and maple syrup, usually cost a quarter of a dollar; other meals were somewhat more.

    Chisholm would also have witnessed the making of salt at the salt springs rising at the head of Salt Lake (later named Onondaga), a sight rarely missed by travellers at this period. The Indians, taught by Jesuit missionaries, had been manufacturing salt here for more than a century, but it was not until 1788 that white men were permitted access to the salt springs.³⁷ Asa Danforth * and Comfort Tyler boiled down the first salt manufactured by white men; they used an iron kettle hung on crotched sticks, obtaining thirteen bushels in twelve hours. In 1788 Danforth had brought his family by batteau from Mayfield northeast of Johnstown to Onondaga Hollow where he built a grist and sawmill, organized the militia, and became known as the "father of Onondaga County."³⁸ Soon settlers from far and near were bringing their kettles and securing the precious salt.³⁹ At first the brine was dipped and carried to the kettles, but in 1790 a pump was fixed to a platform over the spring and the water conveyed through log pipes directly to the kettles. In 1795 the state acquired ten square miles of land around the salt springs and two years later commenced leasing lands on a royalty basis.⁴⁰ Anyone paying a tax of four cents on each bushel carried away was privileged to cut wood and make salt on this reserve. In eight hours' time fifty gallons of brine boiled down in cast iron potash kettles was converted into a bushel of salt weighing fifty-six pounds. Tremendous quantities of fuel were required to stoke the fires. By 1804 blocks of six ninety-gallon kettles set close together over two fires were being boiled off three times in twenty-four hours. The weekly production of one kettle during which two cords of wood were consumed was twenty-five to thirty bushels of salt, a total of about five hundred cords per week. All the trees in the vicinity of the works had long since disappeared and wood was being brought from considerable distances at increasing cost. The year after Chisholm passed this way one manufacturer introduced horsepower at the pump and conveyed the brine some four miles by log pipes to his furnace which he established close to the fuel supply, but numbers of pumps were still being operated by manual labour. The salt was packed in barrels holding five bushels (costing three dollars), and the price was pegged by law at sixty cents per bushel. Shipments destined for the south were conveyed to the "salt landing" on the navigable waters of the Chenango, but the principal outlet was westwards towards Detroit, Pittsburgh, and Upper Canada.⁴¹ Barrels loaded in open boats at the wharf of the works were conveyed to Oswego and thence by schooner. In 1804 about 12,000 barrels were exported to Upper Canada. Known as Oswego Currency, salt passed as "a kind of currency at Niagara at about 1$ pr. Bushel, i.e. Onondaga."⁴² The spreading village at Salt Point, called Salina, traveller Charles Prentice found a "poor looking place & inhabited by a Rough Sett of People,"⁴³ and Selkirk called the salt works the refuge of all the greatest vagabonds in the country.

    The townships in the area are among those of the Military Tract, or lands given to Revolutionary soldiers by the state of New York. The choice of such names as Aurelius, Scipio, Ovid, Sempronius, Brutus, Lysander, Pompey, Fabius, Rurabella, Hybla, Pomona, and others harking back to ancient times are attributed to a classical

---

    * This Asa Danforth was born at Dunstable, Massachusetts, in 1746 and died at Onondaga Hollow in 1837. There were several of that name in the Massachusetts family, but the author has failed to identify the one who contracted in 1789 to cut a road along the front of Lake Ontario from York to Kingston in Upper Canada.

scholar holding the office of deputy secretary of state under Governor Clinton. These names contrast oddly with those of Puritan flavour in the adjoining area on the east; Unanimity, Frugality, Perseverance, Sobriety, Industry, Economy, Regularity, and so forth.[44] But these latter names did not long endure and were eventually changed.

Riding up hill and down dale over increasingly rolling country then descending the beautiful valley of the Mohawk lying deep between the hills, George Chisholm finally entered Montgomery County which he had known as Tryon County. In 1784 the name of the Royal Governor had been discarded in favour of the Continental hero, General Richard Montgomery, who had died in the unsuccessful attempt to seize Montreal in 1775. Chisholm had now reached familiar territory. He passed close by such landmarks as the stone homestead erected 1750 (and still standing as a museum east of St. Johnsville) by the Indian trader Johannes Klock and used as a fort during the war, the Palatine Church, and the residence of John Frey. Built 1739 by another fur trader, Hendrick Frey, this latter stone homestead (now a private residence at Palatine Bridge) had been used in earlier times by the English as a fort during the Seven Years' War. Nearby the new Palatine Bridge, constructed the previous year, spanned the Mohawk at Canajoharie. From there the horse trail Chisholm had known so well was now a well-travelled waggon road to Cherry Valley. In this area the snow lay so deep and fodder was so scarce that cattle were perishing of starvation, and those contriving to survive would look like skeletons until late spring.[45] Turning north into the hills towards Johnstown and climbing the ridge which here stands close to the river Chisholm passed within a short distance of the grey weatherbeaten walls of the homestead in Butlersbury where Colonel Butler and his family had lived before the war. It stood (as it still stands) on the crest of Switzer Hill commanding an expansive view of the broad sweep of the Mohawk Valley.* And he met with other familiar sights as he rode into Johnstown; the brick court house, the stone gaol, the Episcopal Church, and Johnson Hall, by then the home of the Alison family. Excepting the church, these buildings stand today; the court house is the only Colonial one in the State of New York and the gaol is used as such at the present time.

Though the outlying area of early settlement had been carved up into townships and thus lost its identity as Johnson's Bush Chisholm found here some of the Scottish families he had known before the war. During his sojourn in Johnstown he collected for the Earl names of twenty-two prospective settlers including a wheelwright, a millwright, the waggonmaker Peter Stewart, and three Elliotts—William, James and Walter.[46] It would be interesting to know if the latter were related to the Walter Elliott of Harpersfield who was concerned in Brant's capture of Captain Alexander Harper and his men in the sugar bush in April 1780 (see p. 70).

Upon taking leave of Johnstown and returning to the Mohawk Valley Chisholm crossed the river where it bends southward in a beautiful curve as if to receive the waters of the Schoharie. Queen Anne's Royal Chapel of the Mohawks at nearby Fort

---

* When visited by the author in September 1960, the Butler house was undergoing such restoration by its owner, Mrs. Eleanor M. Rockwell, as to make it impossible to secure photographs. However, it was interesting to see the pine timbers laid bare and the filling of handmade brick between the cherry uprights of the frame (called brick nogging) opened to view in places where it was necessary to remove the old lath and plaster. The house stands on the south side of the Old Trail at Switzer Hill Road to the east of the Old Johnstown Road to Fonda, and at the time of writing is open to the public. (A view of the house before it was restored is shown facing page 132).

Hunter which had served as a fort during the war and as a tavern thereafter would be used as a stable before being demolished in 1829 to make way for a lock of the Erie Canal.[47] The manse built 1734 still exists today. About six miles south of the Mohawk Chisholm entered Corry's Bush (see Glossary). Here the gently rolling country, in some places almost flat, is quite different from the high hills and deep valley lying only a few miles to the south. In Corry's Bush Chisholm found sixteen Scots whose names he listed for Lord Selkirk, among them six McIntoshes, three Campbells and two McMillans.[48]

As Chisholm continued his journey southward, making the long descent into the Schoharie Valley, he beheld the sweeping panorama of hills standing rank upon rank in the distance. Near the junction of Foxes Creek with the Schoharie he passed close by the "Brick House at the Forks of the Road." Before the war this two-storey building with basement kitchen was George Mann's tavern, the meeting place of Adam Chrysler and other Tories with whom Chisholm had served. (It yet sits on its knoll overlooking Foxes Creek at the meeting of N.Y. routes 30 and 43 as does the Becker stone house some $2\frac{1}{2}$ miles farther upstream on route 43 which Chrysler with a band of Indians had raided towards the end of the war.) Chisholm rode close to the stone church which had been erected by High Dutch Protestants in Schoharie and which had served as the Lower Fort during the conflict.* As he traversed the flat farm land in the wide valley of the Schoharie Chisholm would certainly have recalled the battle of The Flockey, the first action fought on the frontier, in which he had taken part twenty-six years before. He would have remembered the day when Captain John Macdonell had led his countrymen against the rebels near "Fort Defeyance" which thereafter became the Middle Fort in the valley (at modern Middleburg but the fort is no longer standing). Ten miles farther south he crossed the small stream upon which Chrysler had located his home and mills and where the community of Fultonham was now growing up. Surely to Chisholm this valley where Vrooman's Nose and other high promontories bear in upon the flats would not have appeared as it did to Dr. Dwight, "singularly shaggy, wild and horrid." [49] Above Breakabean Creek Chisholm struck westward over the divide between the Schoharie and the Delaware through unbroken forest covering the townships of Jefferson and Stamford. ("I can hardly conceive that an agreeable residence will ever be found in either of these places," declared Dwight.[50]) After skirting little Lake Utsayantha and descending into the valley of the Delaware, Chisholm crossed the old east–west thoroughfare reaching from Kaatskill Landing on the Hudson to Wattles' Ferry on the Susquehanna which had recently been improved as the Catskill Turnpike. (Since the war Dutch names were rapidly becoming Anglicized.) He was now at the end of the four-hundred-mile journey which, according to the thirty-mile average of other travellers who covered the same ground at this period, had taken him about two weeks.

At the Head of the Delaware Chisholm found few settlers whom he had known before the war. The percentage of Loyalists having been high, the greater number of dwellings had stood vacant until sought after by New Englanders who had populated this like other areas of northern New York upon the return of peace. They had come in large numbers from Fairfield County, Connecticut, the same district as the earliest settlers of New Stamford on Town Brook who had been there a decade when Chisholm

* Today it is the Old Stone Fort Museum which houses an outstanding collection of historical relics.

had first come with the Macdonells to the Delaware. With this new influx the area between the Delaware and the Charlotte was set up as Harpersfield Township in 1787, and for years the town meetings were held at the home of Alexander Harper. Five years later the Kortright and Banyar patents were included in the new township of Kortright. The southern boundary of both townships was the Delaware River which divided them from Stamford Township, incorporated in 1792. (The recurrence of "Delaway" in contemporary documents shows this to have been the New Englanders' pronunciation.) Originally in Tryon County, the townships of Harpersfield and Kortright had belonged in Montgomery and Otsego counties before a further division in 1797 had placed them together with Stamford Township in the new county of Delaware.

Of all Chisholm's former neighbours on the east side of the Delaware (now within Stamford Township), only Hugh Rose is known to have weathered the storm of the Revolution. "As far as appears," wrote the county historian, "he was the only settler on the West Branch of the Delaware to continue throughout the Revolution."[51] Around his mill on Rose's Brook was clustering a community which would be shown on later maps as Roseville.[52] Upstream at the falls in the Delaware above the mouth of Town Brook was the settlement spreading out from Paine's grist and sawmill built soon after the war. In 1785, before any attempt had been made to clear the river of debris, John and Joshua Paine had succeeded in carrying five barrels of their flour forty miles down river to Cookhouse (Americanized name for Cookoze) in a canoe made at the mill. At the same time they had sent down five rafts containing some 11,000 feet of boards to the same place.*[53] In this community known as Paines' Dale,[54] not long since the home of William and Augustus Bates, the first store and inn near "the Mills" were kept by Ezra Paine.[55]

Once very Presbyterian this settlement was now almost solidly Episcopalian under the leadership of Reverend Ebenezer Diblee from Stamford, Connecticut. The Bates, particularly Augustus, had been active members of this congregation. The first entry in the baptismal register of the parish is the birth of Richard Waldron, son of Augustus and Elizabeth Bates, on August 10, 1793. When Mr. Diblee convened his congregation December 8, 1794, Augustus had been elected clerk of "St. Peter's Episcopal Church in Stamford, Harpersfield and Kortright."[56] He officiated for several years, and at a meeting of the trustees held at his home July 13, 1795, the building of a 50 by 40 foot frame church was projected and lumber contracted for. Bates was appointed to the committee for the erection of a rectory in July 1798, but before the necessary funds were collected (the estimated cost of both buildings being $529.66[57]) he had removed to Upper Canada. Upon a unanimous vote on July 6, 1801, that the church be located on Pine Hill overlooking the mills construction went forward,[58] and upon his return the following year Bates had seen the new church standing above the Delaware. St. Peter's Episcopal Church is still used today and is little changed except for the removal of blinds from its windows. When the community grew to be a village it was named Hobart in honour of an Episcopal bishop in 1828.

George Chisholm visited George Grant, son-in-law of Dr. James Stuart, and other Grants in New Stamford whose situation in the valley of Town Brook was one of

---

* Being so convenient a place for depositing lumber and timber preliminary to rafting it down to Philadelphia on the spring freshets, Cookhouse was incorporated in 1811 as the village of Deposit.

the most beautiful in Delaware County.* It lay where the Indian trail so familiar to Chisholm and his compatriots crossed the notch in the mountains and dropped down to the brook some five miles from its mouth. Because the lines of the first survey were lost during the war the tract was resurveyed and a township one mile square laid out in 1787. The "township of New Stamford" boasted eight streets bearing the names English, Irish, Scotch, Dutch, North, South, East, and West, and a parade ground for the militia.[59] But Paines' Dale on the Delaware became the place of business rather than New Stamford which remained as it had begun, an agricultural community. John More had long since left this settlement to found Moresville in the valley of the East Branch of the Delaware and become the first settler in Roxbury Township.[60]

Harpersfield and Kortright, the communities that had grown up around the churches, were called "centers" according to the custom in New England. In Harpersfield Center Chisholm found several growing industries: an oil mill for making linseed oil, a scythe and axe factory where a trip hammer was used to assist in the forging of products shipped to adjoining counties, and a manufactury of spinning wheels and reels. John Harper had rebuilt his house and grist mill on their old sites and for a time Alexander Harper had conducted a tavern at the Center. Numerous other taverns and at least four distilleries were spread over the district. "Harpersfield," wrote Dr. Dwight, "is a settlement of some standing. . . . The homes are comfortable; and the inhabitants have built themselves a decent church, added to it a steeple, in this region a singularity, and settled a clergyman . . . a man regularly educated for the ministry, and regularly inducted into that office."[61] Reverend Stephen Fenn was a native of Watertown, Connecticut, and a graduate of Yale College (1792) two years before Dr. Dwight had become its president. However, other missionaries had officiated in the log church built upon the organization of the Presbyterian congregation of Harpersfield at a meeting held in 1787 at the home of John Harper. The five Harper brothers † and Freegift Patchin were members of this congregation by 1794 when a frame church replaced the log building.[62] Subscriptions were payable in labour, materials, and so forth, and when George Chisholm came to visit Harpersfield Mr. Fenn was beginning the ninth of his thirty-five-year ministration to the Presbyterians in the area.[63] William Harper was now assistant judge of Otsego County, William Cooper of Cooperstown being the first judge.[64] But by 1804 Alexander and Joseph Harper were no longer in Harpersfield. Being true borderers and finding the approach of civilization uncongenial, they had removed to a grant of land they had received in western Ohio.[65]

At Cherry Valley Chisholm found that a few remnants of the former inhabitants including the Samuel Campbells had returned in 1784 and that funds for a new church had been raised by selling pew space. In March 1785 they had advertised:

---

* In the cemetery on the hillside above Township Methodist Church, built 1833, at the crossroads in New Stamford many Grants lie buried. Some of their gravestones are among the earliest that are still legible. By 1870 numerous families of that name lived on farms spread over the hills of this area (*Atlas of Delaware County, New York* (1869)). Abraham Gould, one of the Connecticut settlers of the post-wwar migration to New Stamford, married Mary, daughter of one of the Scottish Mores of the Moresville settlement and became the grandfather of Jay Gould. While surveying for his map of Delaware County Jay Gould became interested in the stories of old-timers and wrote his *History of Delaware County and Border Wars of New York*. Upon their publication in 1856 he was but twenty years of age. Three years later he entered upon a career of railroad magnate during which he amassed one of the great fortunes of the United States.

† Four sons of one of these brothers carried on the publishing firm which in 1833 adopted the name of Harper and Bros. whose *New Monthly Magazine* first appeared in June 1850.

"We, the *ancient* inhabitants of Cherry Valley ... having returned from exile ... give notice to all former inhabitants ... to meet at the *meeting-house* yard ... to choose trustees [of a] Presbyterian congregation...." At this gathering held in the open each person agreed to pay for his pew space in money, produce, and labour, and soon a new church had risen on the old site.[66] Chisholm may also have heard of General Washington's visit to Cherry Valley during the previous summer. The Campbells had entertained the general when, accompanied by General Clinton, he had come to the Mohawk Valley on a tour of inspection.

As in Harpersfield the nucleus of settlement in Kortright had remained unchanged. It clustered around the pre-war burying ground and spread down the valley of Banyar's Brook which was losing its identity in the new name of Wright's Brook.* The grist mill built by Hugh Alexander was again in operation though furnished with new irons because those Alexander had hidden during the war had never been found.[67] The point at which the road down this valley crosses the road along the west bank of the Delaware was called the "Four Corners." † This was the scene of a tale of buried treasure with which Chisholm was surely familiar or may in fact have had a part. The story, as related by Jay Gould half a century later, concerns "Two or three families of Scotch" settlers in Kortright, who "becoming affected with what is commonly called 'toryism,' sought asylum in Canada." They boxed and buried their goods, marking the spots that they might retrieve their possessions once peace was restored. One man who was considered wealthy "if indeed gold could have constituted wealth in so isolated a spot," feared to take 500 guineas with him in his "flight." He buried the money under the roots of a hollow tree at the junction of Banyar's Brook with the Delaware. The party "took refuge in Canada" where the wealthy man's family succumbed to a fatal disease. On his death bed the Scot revealed to his physician the secret of the hidden treasure. After peace was declared the physician journeyed to the Head of the Delaware and pretended to search for medicinal herbs at the "Four Corners." He found the line of marked trees, but the new settler in occupation had sown the fields in wheat, and while ploughing had unearthed nothing more interesting than a broken box of clothing, a set of harrow teeth, and an iron wedge. After a week, the doctor abandoned the search and, though many have hunted since, the gold continues to remain undiscovered.[68]

Upon returning to Kortright once the war had ended Alexander Leal and Alexander Mills and other Presbyterians joined with those in Stamford Township including Hugh Rose and Alexander Grant in applying to the Associate Presbytery of New York and Pennsylvania for ministerial service. On April 7, 1789, the Corporation of the Presbyterian Church of the Township of Kortright had been organized, and in the log "barn" used as a church at Kortright Center various missionaries officiated before the advent in October 1794 a resident minister, Reverend William McAuley, an Irishman with a University of Edinburgh education.[69] For years on Sabbath afternoons he and the elders, among them Alexander Leal, walked down to the Delaware to hold services at Rose's Brook after which they made the eight-mile climb over the hills back to Kortright Center. Until Leal was well on his way down to the valley no hunting or fishing was attempted by members of the congregation for if caught they were sure to be fined for breaking the Sabbath.[71] Mr. McAuley went blind before the end of his

---

* Banyar's Brook in David H. Burr's *An Atlas of the State of New York* (New York, 1829).
† The Four Corners are now Bloomville. How or when this latter name originated has not been discovered.

fifty-six years of service and died in 1857.[71] His brother Thomas McAuley was the first schoolmaster in the log schoolhouse situated at the Four Corners.

The little group of Presbyterians travelled to and from the Delaware by a road constructed to connect Paines' mills with the Susquehannah Turnpike. Subsequent to an act of 1787 which made it the duty of commissioners of highways to widen existing roads and open new ones, the first application for a new road was made in the spring of 1787 by the inhabitants of the east end of Kortright in the vicinity of the mills. John Harper, Alexander Leal, Sluman Wattles, and Levi Gaylord as commissioners promptly opened a road connecting the mills with "the publick road leading to the Susquehanna" which passed through Kortright Center and which later became the turnpike. From its description [72] which gives lot numbers and some names of residents this route is clearly the southern section of what is now McMurdy's Brook Road and the northern section of Betty's Brook Road. The part described as crossing Betty's Brook "on the Beaver Dam & slanting the hill as the ground will best admit" to meet the "publick Road" west of Leal's farm is now closed to traffic. The commissioners were diligent in widening existing roads (originally the paths of the Indians and secondly the horse trails of the Scots) and in connecting them with crossroads. Though required by law to explore the terrain and lay out the courses of new roads the commissioners found it well nigh impossible in this country of rocky slopes, countless springs, and patches of "moistey ground" to issue detailed instructions. They continually resorted to the phrase "along as straight a direction as the ground will best admit." [73] Close beside the roads sat the frame houses which replaced the temporary log dwellings and which in turn would gradually give place to those simple adaptations of the Greek Revival now so numerous on the farms in this region.

Some of these old roads have proved too winding and precipitous for the automobile and have been abandoned, in part if not in entirety. But farmers still use them to reach bordering fields and whoever climbs them on foot is rewarded by the delight of the natural beauty of an old mountain road left untouched by modern highway machinery. High overhead tall maples form a leafy archway and in their cool shade ferns, mosses, and mountain wild flowers hang from the banks in variety and abundance below the stone walls which line the open fields.

Upon concluding his business and leaving the Head of the Delaware to return to Upper Canada, Chisholm would have set out along the western section of the new Catskill-Susquehanna Turnpike. From Kortright Center it followed the valley of Kortright Creek for some distance before starting the long ascent into Meredith. This township had been carved out of Kortright in 1800 and on the western edge of the high plateau where there is a deep drop into the valley of Ouleout ((pronounced owl-ee-out) Creek a village was being laid out around a public square. Here in September 1804, Dr. Dwight * paused to admire a "magnificent" growth of white pines, noting that one which had fallen measured nearly 247 feet in length. "It is not improbable," he reflected, "that the next generation may never see a white pine of full size; and may regard an exact account of this noble vegetable production as a mere fable." [74] Some of these pines undoubtedly survive in the early frame houses of which this little community of Meredith Square is almost exclusively composed.

From Meredith, along the Indian trail that had led over the hills from the Char-

* For nine years Timothy Dwight, theologian, had been president of Yale College and one of its ablest. To escape the burdens of his heavy duties he took long journeys on horseback throughout the land, and this year, like Chisholm, he was bound for Niagara.

lotte, the road then followed the Ouleout through the valley where William McKenzie and his family, including Chisholm's wife Barbara, had settled after migrating from Scotland in 1774. Dr. Dwight describes the area thus:

> As soon as we left Meredith the hills began to be steep and rough, and the country loses its beauty. From this forbidding tract we entered a settlement on the Ouleout, a handsome millstream, which is a branch of the Susquehanna. The valley through which it runs extends from east to west a considerable distance. The borders of the Ouleout are in a long succession formed by rich intervals, divided into meadow and arable, and covered with a lively verdure, and good crops of maize, and other species of corn; the river winding through them with a course elegant and delightful. The settlement is for some miles a thinly built village, composed of neat, tidy houses. . . . From Meredith to this settlement the road descended with a disagreeable rapidity. Here we found it very pleasant. When we left this village it became again disagreeable [down to the Susquehanna].[75]

When the Continentals had destroyed the Scotch Settlement in this valley in the autumn of 1778, the McKenzies were safely within the British lines at New York. The first settlers to come to the area after the peace were the Wattles brothers, of Scottish descent from Lebanon, Connecticut, who had joined the post-war migration to the Head of the Delaware. During the first years of settlement, 1784–86, Sluman Wattles had first occupied a log house abandoned by a Scottish Loyalist family in Kortright which had survived the war,[76] and evidence points to that of James Calder.[77] While engaged in surveying the area between the Delaware and the Susquehanna into farm lots Sluman Wattles had chosen for himself one of the improvements made earlier by the Scots.* To escape the spring floods he had soon moved a short distance upstream, and Chisholm passed close by his log house standing somewhat above the eighty-second milestone on the turnpike.[78]

After descending the valley of the Ouleout Chisholm crossed the Susquehanna on the ferry established two decades before by Nathaniel Wattles,[79] and like other travellers would have stopped awhile at his inn standing at the western terminus of the Catskill-Susquehanna Turnpike.† From there Chisholm struck northward along the route well known to his compatriots who had travelled it with the Indians during the war; up the Unadilla along the border of what was once the Old England District and up the Chenango to the Genesee Pike where he turned west, heading for Upper Canada. Within ten days of leaving Kortright he would have reached Niagara, and another day's journey would then have brought him home to Burlington Bay.

Meanwhile, in February 1804, Lork Selkirk had journeyed to Albany, arriving from Quebec on the twenty-sixth. He came by the ancient north–south route which had been confined to the water for hundreds of years. But times had changed and now he was able to travel by road in a sleigh. It was at Albany that Selkirk received Chisholm's lists (dated February 7) of prospective settlers. The Earl left Albany in the early spring, visiting New York City, and in April set out for Upper Canada by the same route Chisholm had travelled to the Delaware three months before. When

---

* At Bartlett Hollow above the Flood Control Dam on N.Y. route 7B. The Scotch Settlement had spread up the valley somewhat above the town of Franklin.

† In present-day terms the old Catskill-Susquehanna Turnpike passed through the villages and hamlets of Stamford, Harperfield, Kortright, Meredith, Meridale, Franklin, and ended at Wattles' Ferry. On N.Y. route 7B below Franklin stand several of the old milestones bearing legends such as "83 Miles to Catskill" cut into the red stone of the district in the elegant lettering of an earlier age. In the summer of 1804 the turnpike was extended westward over the hills, passing through Bainbridge, Greene, Triangle, Whitney Point, then over what is now N.Y. route 79 to Ithaca and onward to Bath, the town founded by Charles Williamson. Here on the shore of Lake Salubria he lived in a large frame residence which was demolished only a few years ago and its timbers used in the construction of a new house.

passing through Geneva he met several Scots from Johnstown whose names Chisholm had sent to him, one of them Peter Stewart the waggonmaker, who were also on their way to Canada.[80] Arriving May 20 at Queens Town (now frequently called Queenston) the Earl examined his flock of sheep. From accounts of pasture, grain, and so forth, and from brief notes in Selkirk's diary it would seem that the sheep had wintered on the land of Archibald Thomson. Selkirk noted: "directed A. Brown to shear soon, & deposit wool in T. Clarke's Store . . . to leave the weakest and latest lambed at Thomsons, go with rest to plains. . . . Went forward to see the Whirlpool formed by a great bend of the St Lawce which is very grand—the whole banks from Queenston are very fine from the sublime scale of every part of the scene.—Dined with Mr. Hamilton. . . ."[81] Three days later, because no vessels were available, Lord Selkirk set out on horseback for York, reaching Bates' King's Head Inn at Burlington Bay on the second night, but no mention is made of seeing George Chisholm. Continuing, he was obliged to ride "thro' horrible roads—all unsettled except toward York—Road half of it thro' Swamps & that often close beside dry ridges. . . . Reached York in about 11 hours with $\frac{1}{2}$ hours stop at the Sixteen for Breakfast."[82]

Upon learning that some Highlanders from New York, attracted by his representations, had already arrived in the province and that a few had been settled on good lots near York by Chief Justice Allcock, then "in command of the land office," Selkirk made the proposal of some Stamford Highlanders (unidentified) "settling on the continuation of Yonge Street," remarking that this was "no part of my land or concern, but for the benefit of the province recommended Chisholm" as government agent. He discussed the matter in detail with the Chief Justice, but the notations in his shorthand are of uncertain meaning. Evidently nothing came of the matter, the Chief Justice being "not very keen of public advantage."[83] It was at this time that Selkirk proposed to Sheriff Macdonell that the latter assume the management of his new settlement in the Western District.[84]

After three days at York, accompanied by Macdonell, he started on May 28 back to the Head of the Lake, being met at the Etobicoke by an open boat manned by four Canadians who proved "clumsy hands." He observed that "the land appears along the shore to have a considerable mixture of pines at the mouth of the Credit R. & 12 or 16 mile Creek—pretty spots."[85] Landing late in the afternoon he again put up at Bates' and spent some time conversing with George Chisholm, discussing the proposals and recommendation that he had made to the Chief Justice.[86] Next day the Earl and his companion set off again, pausing at Richard Hatt's in East Flamborough where he met Joseph Brant. The remainder of Selkirk's and Macdonell's journey westward is of little interest to this chronicle except for the fact that the Earl briefly mentions the arrival of some Scots from the Head of the Delaware. "July 8. Grant and Turnbull from Stamford, Delaware Co., N.Y. arrived to see the country—with letter from James Grant." Turnbull, newly out from Cheviot, and Grant, son of an old settler, had ridden from Fort Erie, secured passage in a boat to Port Talbot, and "thence came thro' woods $2\frac{1}{2}$ days—but without fire or axe" and were often taken ill. Although they had liked some of the land they had seen they refused the offer of lots below Little Bear Creek at a dollar per acre. "They seemed to expect it at King's fees—& said Chisholm had promised—which is certainly false—but their expectations were too high wound up, talked much of distance . . . they went away without looking at the Land."[87]

Towards the end of July Selkirk left the settlement which, after its survey by

Augustus Jones, he had named Baldoon for one of his properties in Scotland. He journeyed to Nova Scotia and then returned to England. In the accounts paid in 1804 familiar names appear : to John and Mathew Dolson for labour and to Thomas Cummings of Chippawa for provisions furnished to the new settlers.[88]

The site of Baldoon (near modern Wallaceburg) had been chosen because it was strategically situated on the navigable water between Lake Erie and Lake Huron and required little clearing. But the land was low and swampy, and of the Scots who landed there during the autumn rains many soon sickened with malaria and some died. William Burn was dead on September 15 before a doctor arrived from Detroit.[89] By the time McDonell hurried over from York there were few settlers who were not ill and a number of children had been left father- and motherless.[90] Continued rains destroyed crops and delayed the driving in of two flocks of sheep thereby causing a shortage of food. The middle of December Robert Hamilton wrote from Queenston to his father-in-law at Detroit :

> The reports we hear of the Melancholy condition of Lord Selkirks Settlers is distressing to humanity. The i[n]discreet Choice of a Situation so unpleasant & so unhealthy seems completely of a piece with the other parts of the Speculation entered into with rashness & conducted without Consideration. It is said here that 20,0000£ have allready been expended. As much more may be thrown away with equal Success, for when is one Shilling to be expected back? Say that remuneration or Profit were only secondary Considerations with his Lordship, how much has Benevolence been Counteracted by the unfortunate Choice of the Situation. We have not heard a Word of his Lordship since he left us. Some hundred more Sheep & 10 or 12 Brood mares winter in this Vicinity, on their way upward.[91]

This discouraging beginning together with lax and inefficient management caused the decline of the colony that Lord Selkirk had so carefully planned down to the smallest details. Baldoon struggled on until it suffered devastation by American troops during the War of 1812. Owing to the preponderance of names common in the Highlands, both surnames and Christian, it has been impossible to determine who among the Scots who settled there had come from the Head of the Delaware. Yet a village standing today on the east shore of the St. Clair River bears the significant name of Courtright.

CHAPTER ELEVEN

A CHERISHED LEGACY

As our story now draws to a close it would indeed be gratifying to take leave of the Scots knowing that they had lived out their days in the peace and contentment to which they were so justly entitled. But the facts are inconsistent with the pattern usual to a final chapter in fiction, for the group again experienced the death and destruction contingent to another war. Their sons willingly fought to uphold the principles to which they had fallen heir, and the farms of those at Niagara became a famous battle ground.

By 1805 the two Thomsons and John Chisholm were living in stone houses which were uncommon along the Niagara River where the majority of settlers still clung to log. Though Thomas McMicking had opened a stone quarry near the bank of the river on his farm he continued to occupy the second larger log house to whose rear he added a stone kitchen.[1] Upon his visit in 1804 Dr. Dwight was surprised that such large numbers of the Niagara settlers should be content with these uncomfortable habitations which in New England were considered as merely temporary. Because they were "the nurseries of vermin in great numbers, subjected to speedy decay, gloomy to the sight, offensive to the smell, and, unless continually repaired, are both cold and leaky," Dwight deplored the effect of such surroundings on "the taste, the manners, and even the morals of the inhabitants."[2]

The characteristically Scottish stone house of Archibald Thomson was built by William Sutherland of the town of Newark. John Thomson found it so pleasing that he contracted with Sutherland to build for him "a dwelling house, of the exact size, and every way the same, as the house in which Mr. Archibald Thomson of Stamford now dwells, excepting only, that the gable ends are to be two feet thick whereas the other are only one foot and a half." Construction was to begin May 1, 1803, and continue until the building was finished, provided that Sutherland could find a suitable mason to work with him; otherwise he would be permitted to take time off to gather in his harvest, then to finish the building. Other terms of the contract are as follows: that plastering be done at Thomson's convenience; that over a period of three years from the time the building was finished he pay Sutherland in "good merchantable lime" to the amount of £46.17.6 currency; that should Sutherland not stand in need of the quantity of lime mentioned the balance be paid in wheat over a period of five years; that Thomson keep Sutherland and his employees "in sufficient victuals, drink, and lodging" during the time of their employment and find all "necessary materials and labourers enough to attend said mason, or masons."[3]

This home was described by a descendant of Archibald Thomson who had been familiar with it since childhood. It was 40 by 60 feet and built on a rise of ground so that the front was of two storeys whereas the rear was of three to accommodate a basement kitchen running across the width of the house. Its stone walls, three feet thick at the foundation, narrowed to two feet above the ground. Built of boulders from the fields, the chimneys at each end were for large fireplaces and a bake oven in the kitchen. A favourite pastime of succeeding generations of boys was climbing to the roof by way of the wide chimneys. The fan-lighted front door upon which hung an iron knocker with angels in relief admitted to a centre hall from which rooms opened on each side and the stairway rose to the floor above. This house of Archibald Thomson's stood firm until its demolition in the 1940's.[4]

John Chisholm's farm house, as will be seen by the photograph shown facing page 132, was also traditionally Scottish in design and was probably also built by Sutherland. Set in the wall was a stone bearing the date 1804. It was here that the Chisholms' elder daughter Jane was married March 17, 1807, to Joseph Silverthorn, son of John Silverthorn and Esther Corwin, Loyalists from New Jersey where they had lived near Great Meadows in Sussex (now Warren) County. Joseph was an infant in arms when his parents and grandparents had migrated in 1786 to settle in Stamford Township near his mother's family, the Corwins.[5] A month after their marriage Joseph and Jane Silverthorn crossed Lake Ontario to make their home on lot 11 on the north side of the Dundas Street in Toronto Township granted to him as the son of a Loyalist. In 1822 they replaced their log cabin with a frame farm house where they brought up a large family and celebrated their seventieth wedding anniversary. They named the farm Cherry Hill for the Silverthorn cherry brought to America early in the eighteenth century by the original emigrant from England and introduced into Canada by John.[6] The house still standing near Cooksville remained complete with all its original furnishings until the late 1930's but became bereft when no longer owned by descendants of the family.

When another war was in the making with the neighbouring democracy to the south Major-General Isaac Brock was appointed lieutenant-governor of Upper Canada to prepare for its defence. But so strong was the opposition of recent American immigrants that he did not secure a military appropriation until two months after the United States had declared war. The vote was finally carried by the Loyalist majority in the House of Assembly who expressed the hope that the enemy might be taught that a country defended by free men devoted to the cause of their King and Constitution can never be conquered.

Although most of them had held commissions in the militia since its founding by Colonel Butler the Scots were too old to take the field when the United States declared war upon Great Britain in June 1812. George Chisholm was captain in the 2nd Regiment of York militia in which his sons John, William, and George Jr. also held commissions. Regardless of his age, in 1812 he marched with them from Burlington Bay to the Niagara frontier, but he and his contemporaries were soon forced to return home and leave the defence against the aggressor to the younger generations.

George Chisholm's friend and neighbour Charles King wrote to his own sons, James and George, who were serving in the 1st Flank Company commanded by Captain John Chisholm stationed at Queenston. By then the Kings and Chisholms were even more closely connected through the marriage of Barbara Chisholm to George King. The letter dated at Flamborough, September 6, 1812, reads:

My Dear Sons

I rec^d your letter of the fourth instant wherein you mentioned that the americans had sent word to our Commander that they were ready to attack us, and it might be expected in four days after the notice agreeable to the sasation of arms—you mention that this information prevented your return home agreeable to our fond expectations. We are equally sorry with you for the disappointment, as it is far more agreeable to have you all together than to be separated—but to have any apprehention of your being cut off I assure you I have none, and I beg of you not to entertain any on your part, for I cannot believe anything be done searious as yet. And if it should, you will s[t]and as good chance to escape as any other—should disturbance actually take place. . . . At any rate I wish you to keep up your spirits. Do your duty shurly, and mind to reserve your clothing and pay, and make yourselves as comfortable as you can with it; We are all well and having nothing more to add, I remain your aff
                                                                    Father
                                                                                CHARLES KING

P.S. I hope you will be careful what you may write in future, as I believe your letters to us have been opened.

But all did not "turn out well" as Charles had hoped for this company saw action on Queenston Heights in the battle that cost their commander, General Brock, his life. Before the year was out Lieutenant George King was dead of an illness "contracted on said service," leaving Barbara a widow with two infant sons.[8] Another casualty was John Chisholm's son John Jr. who served as private in Captain James Crooks' Flank Company of the 1st Regiment of Lincoln Militia[9] and who was severely wounded in the battle of Queenston Heights. Some time after the peace had been restored, he died of his wounds and was buried beside the Presbyterian Church in Stamford three months before reaching his twenty-first birthday.[10]

When a monument was erected in 1824 by the people of Upper Canada to their great hero, Major-General Sir Isaac Brock, the land on Queenston Heights, according to tradition, was given by John Chisholm.[11] The gracefully proportioned Tuscan column of Queenston limestone stood on the rocky promontory high above the Niagara River. The engineer Francis Hall was in charge of the work and his account for £255, being the total amount for "Plans and superintendence," suggests him as the designer of the monument.[12] It was still under construction on the twelfth anniversary of the battle on the Heights when the General's remains were transferred to its vault. The fine view from the top of the column of the windings of the river and the shining lake beyond was popular; one summer the keeper took in above £35.[13] It is well that Chisholm never lived to see this handsome column damaged beyond repair by a charge of gunpowder set off by a malcontent.

Considering their location, the Scots fared not too badly during the War of 1812 when the Americans were driven victoriously back and over the precipice of the Niagara River. Loading some household necessities onto waggons the Chisholms and McMickings found asylum away from the frontier at the home of one of the MacGlashans in the Short Hills near the Beaver Dams.[14] Because their forebears were originally from Inverness John and James MacGlashan[15] may well have been connections of Chisholm's through his mother Janet MacGlashan. Upon returning some time later the McMickings and Chisholms found their homes in "dreadful disorder." The former, greeted by their joyful cat, found a plank shoved through a window, furniture wantonly broken, and sitting in the middle of a ripped feather bed a churn which had been tarred and feathered.[16]

While their men were absent from home for weeks at a time the women carried on the work of the farm. At the Roses' they planted and harvested the grain with a sickle, sending fourteen-year-old Margaret (Daniel's daughter who was to become the wife of Archibald Thomson's son Benjamin) and a smaller child on horseback to have it ground at DeCou's mills at the falls of Twelve Mile Creek. On the same day all the women in the neighbourhood baked in the Roses' outdoor bake oven, sealing the iron door with mud. One day when Jane Rose was carrying her five loaves indoors four Americans appeared and demanded them, but one man returned half a loaf when she insisted upon having some for her small grandson.[17] The American term for the Loyalists at this period was "skedaddlers."

The families at Niagara experienced the worst plundering during the fortnight in July 1814, between the battles of Chippawa, in which Archibald Thomson's son John died and two of Rose's were wounded, and Lundy's Lane when the Mountain was overrun by the victorious Americans. Thomson's losses reached more than £500 [18] and Daniel Rose, who lost ten acres of wheat (about 150 bushels) when the enemy pastured horses in his ten-acre field, estimated his as £343. He attributed "the heavy depredations committed on his property by the Americans, to his having served as a soldier in the British Service in America, during the former war and his having ... 5 sons in the Militia." [19] John Chisholm suffered to the extent of £240 and McMicking £154.[20] During the eight months that Hugh Rose was detained as prisoner in the United States his wife Eunice was helpless when parties of Americans loaded waggons with their possessions.[21]

Sons of the Indian Loyalists fought and died side by side with those of the white. True to the tradition of their ancestors, warriors of the Six Nations rallied to serve with distinction under William Johnson Kerr at Beaver Dams and under his cousin John Brant at Queenstown Heights. The latter had succeeded his father, Joseph Brant, when the gallant old Mohawk chieftain, the most eminent and powerful of his race, had died at the age of sixty-five on November 24, 1807. Although Brant's widow Catherine preferred the life in a wigwam among her own people at the Grand River,[22] his son John, "an accomplished gentleman" educated in England, and daughter Elizabeth continued in residence at Wellington Square. When on a tour one summer to escape the yellow fever at New York a British consul and his daughters were so charmingly entertained here that six pages of his book were devoted to describing the appearance, home and manner of living, all in the English tradition, of "the Indian Prince and Princess." [23] In 1828 Elizabeth became the wife of William Johnson Kerr, who was a son of Dr. Kerr of Niagara and who became a prominent man in the government of Upper Canada. Elizabeth and her husband lived at Wellington Square. John Brant, shortly after being elected member of Parliament, the first Indian to hold such an office, died of Asiatic cholera at the Mohawk Village on the Grand River at the age of thirty-eight.[24] Catherine Brant died thirty years to the day after her husband Joseph.[25]

Brant's funeral, attended by brethren of Barton Lodge, was one of the few occasions when George Chisholm wore his singular masonic apron in public.[26] It was Chisholm's daughter Mary Christina who took good care of the records of Barton Lodge during the war when her husband Ephraim Land* was on duty with the militia. On the morning of June 5, 1813, when the Americans were approaching from the Niagara frontier the inhabitants evacuated their homes. With the help of her

---

* Ephraim Land's mother Phoebe had brought her family from New Brunswick and found her husband Robert, whom she had thought long since dead, at the Head of the Lake. About 1802 Ephraim Land had married Mary Christina Chisholm, and at the time of the war they were living on his 400-acre farm in Barton Township. In present-day terms, this farm lay east of Wellington Street and south of Main Street in Hamilton, Ontario.

children Mary Land carefully wrapped and carried the masonic records together with some of her own treasures to the garden and there burried them, marking the spot with a large peony plant. But the Americans were stopped on the south at Stoney Creek and the battle proved a British victory.[27]

The King's Head Inn at Burlington Bay, of which William Bates was still proprietor, had been occupied by British troops almost from the opening of hostilities.[28] After their descent on York the American fleet sailed for Niagara, and two ships detached by Commodore Chauncey ruined the building by bombarding it with hot shot.[29] The garrison of militiamen was obliged to retire until the arrival of reinforcements from Burlington Heights when the enemy who had landed were driven back to their boats. "When the Enemy's fleet appeared off Burlington Heights," wrote the officer in command of the 2nd Regiment of York Militia relative to George Chisholm, "he again shouldered his musket, headed a number of Volunteers and marched them to Burlington where he remained until the fleet disappeared." [30]

Settlers at the Head of the Lake suffered spoliation at the hands of the western Indians attached to the British army. They killed livestock, grazed their horses in uncut grain (George Chisholm had twenty acres of wheat ruined), and burned whatever lay at hand for firewood. They felled trees in fantastic numbers, 200 apple trees on the Chisholm farm and 1,275 of various kinds on Asahel Davis' land, burned up thousands of fence rails, and demolished whole buildings to secure fuel to feed their fires. Damage to the Chisholm homestead came to £474.[31]

When John Chisholm "departed this life" on March 7, 1830, within four days of his eighty-fifth birthday, he was the last of our group of Loyalist Scots living on the Mountain. Archibald Thomson who reached the age of seventy-two had been dead for nine years, Daniel Rose was about seventy when he died some seven years before, but Thomas McMicking, also an octogenarian, had predeceased Chisholm by only sixteen days. These men, their wives, and many of their children lie at rest in the burial ground of the Presbyterian Church in Stamford, one of the oldest in the country.

Two wills contain provisions of note. In that drawn December 18, 1819, by Archibald Thomson, the "Home estate" was left to his eldest son Benjamin and 400 acres lying near the Grand River were "to be drawn by lot" by his remaining three sons, James, Archibald, and Richard. Samuel Montgomery,[32] an Irishman who had emigrated from County Down in 1768 and worked for the Thomson family since 1788,[33] was given a home during the rest of his lifetime; he outlived his employer by seventeen years. John Chisholm also made provision for a faithful retainer, his slave Diana Green, in a document dated April 25, 1828, of which the preamble is so characteristic of the last wills and testaments of the time. It reads:

> In the name of God, Amen. I John Chisholm of the Township of Niagara in the County of Lincoln, in the district of Niagara and in the Province of Upper Canada Yeoman, do make and declare this my last will and testament in manner and form following: First i resign my soul into the hands of Almighty God hoping and believing in a remission of my Sins by the merits and mediation of Jesus Christ and my body I commit to the Earth to be buried at the discretion of my executors hereinafter named, And my worldly estate I give and devize as follows
> First I give and devize to my youngest son George Chisholm his heirs and assigns for ever the homestead or farm whereon I now live.... Also I do will, order, and direct, that my said Son George shall comfortable keep, and maintain, in meat, drink, clothes, washing, and lodging Diana Green during her natural life provided the said Diana shall continue in the family....[3]

The death of his brother left George Chisholm of Burlington Bay the sole survivor of the Scottish Loyalists from the Head of the Delaware. Because he attained the great age of four score years and ten George saw the rapid development of the area at the Head of Lake Ontario in which his sons, particularly William, had no small part. John collector of customs, William the merchant and member of Parliament, and George Jr. the farmer of the East Flamborough homestead property, all of them colonels in the militia, are typical of the second generation of Loyalists in Upper Canada even as the Scots from New York were representative of the first. In 1801 John Chisholm kept a tavern and two years later established a forwarding business near the outlet of Burlington Bay.[35] About this time, he married Sarah, daughter of William Davis of Saltfleet and his wife Hannah Philipse, Loyalists from North Carolina, and went to live on Burlington Beach. In 1816 he bought land on Indian Point from John Brant for the expansion of his business (from which he was realizing £300 yearly by 1820) and on April 1 of the following year was appointed customs officer at the Beach.[36] The association of this family with their neighbours the Brants was close : one of their children they named John Brant Chisholm. When called out with the militia in 1812 William Chisholm was newly wed to Rebecca, one of the nine children of Loyalist John Silverthorn and Esther Corwin and sister of Joseph who had married Jane Chisholm of Stamford. In 1816 William and Rebecca removed to the Dundas Street in nearby Nelson Township adjoining East Flamborough at the Purchase Line.

When finally secured by the government in 1805 the Missisauga tract had been squared out in the townships of Nelson, Trafalgar, and Toronto which completed the colonization along the north shore of Lake Ontario. Settlement was concentrated along the Dundas Street stretching the length of the province, and in compliance with the promise made by Lord Dorchester the lots had been granted largely to sons and daughters of Loyalists. The settlement duties imposed upon these Loyalists form a striking contrast to those encountered by an earlier generation in Nova Scotia and show how different are the two terrains. Here there was no mention of draining swampy or sunken land, of stone quarries or barren land (see p. 113). Emphasis was placed on the clearance of road allowances. Not until half of the road adjacent to their lots had been cleared, five acres cleared and fenced, and a house approximately sixteen by twenty feet built, all within two years, could settlers procure patent to their land,[37] whereas in Nova Scotia they were allowed three years in which to clear and work three acres and neither house nor road was mentioned.

Among the Loyalists who received land grants in Nelson, Trafalgar, and Toronto townships were Hugh and William, sons of Daniel Rose; Archibald Thomson's sons Benjamin and James; George Chisholm's children, John and Mary Christina; Robert Land's son Abel. Other familiar names are those of families from the valleys of the Mohawk and Susquehanna; Clement, Buck, Bradt, Secord, Vrooman, and several Youngs.[38] In 1810 James Gage, Loyalist nephew of Augustus Jones and brother-in-law of John Chisholm through his marriage to Sarah Davis, purchased from Catherine Brant above 300 acres of Brant's Block in the southwestern corner of Nelson Township and laid out the village of Wellington Square. The townships of Nelson, Trafalgar, and Toronto were in York County until the formation of the Gore District in 1816 when they together with the two Flamboroughs (East and West) became part of the new county of Halton. In 1820 William Chisholm, general merchant and buyer of wheat, oak staves, and timber, and popularly known as "White Oak Chisholm" was elected member for the East riding of Halton in the House of Assembly of Upper Canada. How in his career as politician, colonel of Gore militia, and founder of the town of Oakville he stood steadfastly by Loyalist principles has already been told at length.* As fellow commissioner with William Johnson Kerr on the first canal project undertaken in Upper Canada, the Burlington Bay Canal, Chisholm made an important contribution to the development of the Head of the Lake area.

The canal, for which plans and specifications were drawn in April 1824 by Francis Hall,[39] the engineer employed on Brock's monument, was cut through the beach a short distance south of the outlet. Construction was nearing completion when opened to traffic by the Lieutenant-Governor on Saturday, July 1, 1826, and this proved a day long to be remembered. "'Twas a charming morning," reported the *U.E. Loyalist*, "and ere the day had scarcely dawned the roads for many miles around were literally covered with vehicles and pedestrians hieing to the 'scene of action.'" Sir Peregrine Maitland and his suite were conducted aboard Colonel Chisholm's sixty-ton schooner *General Brock* which unfortunately grounded midway through the canal. However, the party embarked in a six-oared barge and with the Union Jack flying at the mast crossed the bay to a warf where they were met by a guard of honour and conducted to the top of Burlington Heights lined with the 1st, 2nd, and 3rd regiments of Gore Militia. "In addition to the militia," continues the *U.E. Loyalist*, "an assemblage scarcely less numerous, certainly more gay, and far more interesting, seeing that it numbered in its ranks all the 'beauty and fashion' of the Gore District, were seen promenading in front of the brigade." About 4.00 P.M. dinner was announced, and about a hundred persons "sat down to an excellent repast" prepared by Messrs. Burley of Ancaster and Spaun of Hamilton, tavernkeepers, and served "in a spacious apartment, fitted up for the purpose." Many toasts were drunk and songs were sung including "The Meeting of the Waters" and the old favourite "Hearts of Oak." "The delightful varied scenery which at all times presents itself to the neighborhood of Burlington Heights," concludes the *Loyalist*, "can never be viewed with indifference by the most poetic imagination; but when taken in connection with the scenes of busy life, which were enacted on this occasion, become truly animating, when nature exhibited herself in her gayest attire, and every living thing appeared in holiday humour."[40]

The town of Hamilton had shown little progress since laid out just over a decade before and named for a son of Robert Hamilton of Queenstown, but the lake vessels brought to its door by the canal made it a flourishing port. In reporting the departure of the *General Brock* from the Burlington Canal for York laden with "whiskey, pork, &c., and a number of passengers on board" before the middle of March 1832, Hamilton's new newssheet, the *Western Mercury*, points to "the great and decided advantages this section of the country enjoys by a harbour, which remains open at all seasons of the year while every other is shut up, particularly in the Spring and Fall when the roads are so bad, and carriage of goods by land so expensive. Though Burlington Canal remains open, the Bay will not be navigable for some time, the ice being about $2\frac{1}{2}$ feet thick. On Friday last a house 28 by 20 was drawn across it upon the ice by 10 yoke of oxen without any apparent danger."[41] Trotting races in midwinter on the ice of Burlington Bay, which soon became so popular, were beginning at this period.[42]

Of all the Scots only George Chisholm lived to see the Rebellion of 1837 which

* See this author's *Oakville and the Sixteen* (University of Toronto Press, 1953).

was instigated by advocates of republicanism, but which, hardly before it had begun, was snuffed out by upholders of Loyalist principles. While Chisholm's sons as colonels in the Gore Militia were searching the countryside for the escaping leader, William Lyon Mackenzie had found refuge next door at the Kings'. Charles King having died five years before, the homestead was now occupied by one of his sons. When escaping to the American frontier after his supporters had been scattered north of Toronto Mackenzie reached the village of Wellington Square at 4.00 A.M. of a cold December day. At dawn when it began to snow he hid in a pea stack on a knoll from where he watched Sheriff Alexander Macdonell and his posse search all the surrounding buildings. In his narrative of his escape Mackenzie stated that he went "to Mr. King's, who lived on the next farm to Col. John Chisholm's, which was then headquarters for our Tory militia. . . . I had supper with Mr. King's family, rested for an hour, and then walked with him toward my early residence, Dundas village, at the head of Lake Ontario. . . . Mr. King returned and I entered the village alone in the night. . . ."[43]

So long as Mackenzie was attempting to gather more forces at Navy Island in the Niagara River the militia was stationed along the Canadian frontier. Indians of the Six Nations rallied as formerly, and though lamed by wounds received in 1812 William Johnson Kerr led out 200 braves of the Six Nations.[44] Of the burning of the American steamer *Caroline,* we have a first-hand account by Hiram Smith, merchant and postmaster at Wellington Square and husband of John Chisholm's daughter Hannah, from a letter he wrote to his wife.

CHIPPAWA 30th Dec 1837

MY DEAREST WIFE
  Since writing you there has been nothing of importance transpired with the General Movement of our forces, except last evening a party of about 50 men with Boats, armed with Pistols and Cuttlasses, set out for Navy Island in search of the Steam Boat which for some days [has] been employed, in their service conveying Men, Provisions &c between the American shore and the Island, they went round the Island, found the Boat was at Fort Slougher, they followed on for her, and when in a few yards of her was hailed by the Centry, and asked for the Countersign, when they reached her. The word was on Board. All hands followed, and took the boat, killed some of the persons on Board, they then fired the Boat and towed her out in the River and in a few Minutes she was in flames, and so down the River until at last down the falls she went. . . . Geo. Land was with the party who fired the Boat—I should like to hear from you if an opportunity serves. . . .
  We are all well and in haste

I remain
my Dear Hannah
Yours forever
HIRAM SMITH [45]

Hannah replied :

MY D HIRAM,
  I this day received two letters from you by D King, which has given me much satisfaction. . . . I heard you were to attack the Island and some said they heard great guns, and I supposed it to be true, and why I could never hear . . . my imaginations put everything in the worst light, I always borrow trouble but never mind we will talk all this over when you come home . . . and am very glad to hear you stand fatigue so well, you no doubt enjoy your hard bed better, than our rebels here do their downy pillows, goodbye and may God bless you and bring you safe home to your ever affectionate

HANNAH [46]

At this time George Chisholm was eighty-five years of age although he believed that he was past ninety. Might it have been that this uprising conjured up such vivid recollections of the rebellion in Scotland as gave rise to the fancy that he was born in 1745? Certainly he had outlived all those who could prove him in error and died in the conviction that he was nearly one hundred. Four and one-half months after his ninetieth birthday George Chisholm died at the old homestead in East Flamborough. Three days later thirty-four members of his masonic brethren attended his funeral when the remains were placed in the family burial plot beside those of his wife Barbara.[47]

> In
> memory of
> George Chisholm Sen
> who died Dec. 5, 1842
> aged 98 years
> also of
> Barbara Chisholm
> his wife
> who died June 10, 1824
> aged 65 years

So reads the tombstone which was erected by George Jr. and which was to stand on the little point of land reaching out into Burlington Bay long after it took the name of Filman's Point from the homestead's new owners.*

Few mementos of the Loyalist Scots other than those previously mentioned have survived till the present day. The only likenesses discovered are the portrait of George Chisholm in his old age and a silhouette of Catherine Fletcher, wife of his brother John. Besides a few bits of her china there is a table of black walnut cut on John's farm on the Mountain which was fashioned from the remains of a four poster bed damaged by fire.†

The brick house of the Kings standing on the west side of highway 2 (no. 736 King Road) exists as the only known survivor of the era when the Kings and Chisholms occupied their farms on Burlington Bay. Virtually the last vestiges of pioneer times were erased from the area by the construction of new highways, the Skyway reaching across Burlington Beach, and the housing necessary to accommodate a rapidly rising population. At Niagara obliteration is even more complete. The face of the "oak plains" has been changed almost beyond recognition by the expansion of the Ontario Hydro facilities. Of the stone houses built by the Scots Archibald Thomson's was the first to go, although some of his descendants were still on the land in 1929. The stone farm house that Thomas McMicking eventually built, which remained in his family until 1870, was still solid and comfortable when its thick walls were flattened by bulldozers in 1954. By the following summer when the storage lake straddling the portage

---

* George Chisholm's age of ninety-eight as given in the "Address to the Chief" quoted on page 109 of Alexander McKenzie's *The History of the Chisholms* published at Inverness, 1891 (the copy of this document brought from Scotland by Sir Allan MacNab as a gift for one of George's grandsons is in possession of the author), was considered authentic when *Oakville and the Sixteen* was published. Since then a perplexing variety of birth dates has come to light, but that date given in the Dalcross section of the Parochial Register of Croy and Dalcross at New Register House, Edinburgh, is of course unquestionable. This date, July 19, 1752, also appears on an ancient document formerly in possession of the late Mrs. W. A. Chisholm, Oakville, in H. H. Robertson's *The Gore Militia* (Wentworth Historical Society, 1904) and in W. D. Reid's "Data on U.E.L.'s" at the Ontario Archives. The tombstone of George and Barbara Chisholm remained upon the burial plot until about 1950 when upon the building of a house upon the land it was placed in Greenwood Cemetery, Burlington. Some years later permission was granted for its removal to the Chisholm plot at Oakville. Surprisingly enough a second tombstone identical to the first but broken into several pieces, which had lain underwater for many years as the underpinnings of a boathouse on the homestead property, came to light in 1958 when the building was demolished.

† These heirlooms are in the possession of a descendant, Miss Helen Bishop, Owen Sound, Ontario.

road was nearing completion, the area had become almost unrecognizable. Houses, barns, extensive orchards had vanished. Gaining the top of the great dike which now confines the water I looked down over the 750-acre enclosure, where in the midst of this vast desolate sandy waste, splendid in its isolation, the stone house of John Chisholm stood proudly as for 150 years it had stood beside the Portage Road. Only it could attest to the presence of those original Loyalists who "after striving dauntlessly to maintain the unity of the Empire, and sacrificing all their worldly possessions . . . came as exiles into the wilderness, to find new homes in this peninsula, and to be the founders of a new province under the British flag." [48]

APPENDIX A

SOME LOYALISTS OF KORTRIGHT, NEW STAMFORD, AND THE HEAD OF THE DELAWARE IN THE PROVINCE OF NEW YORK*

Name	Place of origin	Date of migration	Location of settlement	Acres secured L(ease) or P(urchase)	Acres cleared when abandoned	Provincial regiment or corps	Location of settlement in Upper Canada
Alexander, Hugh	Scotland		Banyar Patent, lot 51 on Banyar's Brook				
Beatty, James			Harpersfield				
Bennett, Daniel			New Stamford, on Town Brook				
Bennett, Obijah			New Stamford, on Town Brook				
Calder, James	Inverness-shire	1773	Kortright Patent, lot 89				
Calder, William	,,	,,	Kortright Patent				
Cameron, James	,,	,,	Arent Bradt Patent	150 L	15		
Cameron, John	,,	,,	Kortright Patent			private, K.R.R.N.Y.†	Cornwall Twp.
Cameron, William	,,	,,	Kortright Patent	150 L	3	private, K.R.R.N.Y. (1st Batt.)	,,
Campbell, Alexander	,,	1773	,,	150 L	3	private, K.R.R.N.Y.	,,
Carson, Alexander	,,	,,	,,			lieutenant, K.R.R.N.Y.	,,
Chisholm, George	,,	,,	Delaware River, south side (Arent Bradt Patent?)	100 P		recruit, Capt. John Macdonell; private, Highland Volunteer Militia, N.Y.C.	East Flamborough Twp.
Chisholm, John	,,	1774	Kortright Patent	150 L	6-7	Volunteer, Indian Dept., Butler's Rangers	Stamford Twp.
Clarke, Hugh Sr.	Scotland	,,	,,	300 L	12	private, K.R.R.N.Y. (1st Batt.)	
Clarke, Hugh Jr.	,,	,,	,,				

* Compiled from: (1) *New York in the Revolution as Colony and State* (New York, 1904), vol. II, pp. 246-47, "Rent Roll of Farms ... Forfeited to U.S."; (2) New York Public Library, MSS. Division, "List of New York Loyalists against Whom Judgements Have Been Rendered under the Confiscation Act of 1783"; (3) P.R.O., Great Britain, Claims of American Loyalists; (4) *2nd Report Ontario Archives* (1904), Evidence on claims of American Loyalists; (5) Frederick Cook, ed., *Journals of General Sullivan's Indian Expedition 1779* (Auburn, N.Y., 1887), p. 283, "Map of Captain William Gray, 1778"; (6) P.A.C., Haldimand Transcripts, B. 158, pp. 352-73; (7) J. F. Pringle, *Lunenburgh, or the Old Eastern District: Its Settlement and Early Progress* (Cornwall, 1890), Appendix D.
† King's Royal Regiment of New York.

APPENDIX A (continued)

Name	Place of origin	Date of migration	Location of settlement	Acres secured L(ease) or P(urchase)	Acres cleared when abandoned	Provincial regiment or corps	Location of settlement in Upper Canada
Cummings, James	Scotland						
Cummings, Thomas	,,	1775	New Stamford	Joint L	5	grenadier, K.R.R.N.Y. (1st Batt.)	Charlottenburgh Twp.
Dingwall, James	,,					K.R.R.N.Y.	
Dingwall, John	,,	,,	,,				,,
Fraser, Hugh	Inverness-shire	1773	Kortright Patent	300 L	above 40		
Fraser, James	Scotland		New Stamford				
Fraser, Simon (son of William)	,,		Delaware River, at Town Brook				
Fraser, William	,,		Delaware River, at Town Brook			captain, K.R.R.N.Y.	
Gentle, George			(Kortright Patent?)				
Gordon, William			(Kortright Patent?)				
Livingston, John	,,	1774	Kortright Patent	150 L	8	sergeant, K.R.R.N.Y. (drowned 1783)	(Widow Flora) Charlottenburgh Twp.
Livingston, Neil (son of John)	,,	,,	,,				
McAlister, Terence	Ireland	,,	,,	150 L		K.R.R.N.Y.	(near Sydney, Cape Breton, Nova Scotia)
McAslin, Dougal			Banyar Patent, lot 10, on Banyar's Brook Harpersfield				
McBride, Alexander	Scotland	1773	Charlotte River, north side, lot 15	150 L	6	captain, K.R.R.N.Y.	Cornwall Twp.
Macdonell, Alexander	Inverness-shire						
Macdonell, John	,,	,,	Charlotte River, north side, undoubtedly lots 12, 13, 14 (modern Fergusonville)	491 P	60	captain, Grenadier Co., K.R.R.N.Y. (1st Batt.)	
Macdonell, Roderick	,,	,,	Charlotte River, south side, lot 17	100 L	10	private, K.R.R.N.Y.	,,
McIntosh, Alexander	Scotland	1774	Kortright Patent	150 L	12		,,
McKay, Hugh	,,	1771	,,	150 L	9		
McKay, John	Inverness-shire	1773	Kortright Patent, lot 81	150 L	16		Lancaster Twp.
McKay, Neil (son of John)	,,	,,	Kortright Patent	150 L	15		Cornwall Twp.

APPENDIX A (continued)

Name	Place of origin	Date of migration	Location of settlement	Acres secured L(ease) or P(urchase)	Acres cleared when abandoned	Provincial regiment or corps	Location of settlement in Upper Canada
McKee, John	Inverness-shire	1773	Harpersfield	150 L	15	sergeant, K.R.R.N.Y.	Osnabruck Twp.
McKenzie, Duncan	Scotland	1774	Kortright Patent	150 L	9	private, K.R.R.N.Y.	Charlottenburgh Twp.
McKenzie, John	,,	,,	,,			,,	,,
McLeod, Donald	Wigtownshire	,,	Banyar Patent, on Delaware River				
McMicking, John	,,	,,	Banyar Patent, on Delaware River			Butler's Rangers	Stamford Twp.
McMicking, Thomas	Scotland	,,	Kortright Patent				
McMullin, Hugh	,,		,,				
McMullin, Dougall	,,		,,				
McMullin, Hugh			,,				
Mill, Hugh			,,				
Mills, Alexander	,,		,,				
Morrison, Hector	,,		Harpersfield				
Murray, John						quartermaster, K.R.R.N.Y.	
Park, James	,,	1773	,,	L, joint with Archibald Thomson		Indian Dept., Butler's Rangers	Stamford Twp.
Park, John	Scotland						
Rose, Daniel	Inverness-shire	1774	Banyar Patent	100 L	8–9	Indian Dept., Butler's Rangers	Stamford Twp.
Rose, James	,,	1773	Arent Bradt Patent	60 L	5		
Rose, William	,,	,,	Arent Bradt Patent, on Delaware River at Betty's Brook, lot 47	200 L	8	private, K.R.R.N.Y.	
Servos, Christopher	New York		Charlotte River, both sides, partly in Harpersfield			(killd 1778)	
Servos, Daniel	,,	,,	Charlotte River, both sides, partly in Harpersfield			captain, Indian Dept., Butler's Rangers	Niagara Twp.
Servos, John	,,	,,	Charlotte River, both sides, partly in Harpersfield			captain, Indian Dept., Butler's Rangers	,,
Shearer, Thomas	Scotland	1774	Banyar Patent	200 L	above 30		,,

APPENDIX A (continued)

Name	Place of origin	Date of migration	Location of settlement	Acres secured L(ease) or P(urchase)	Acres cleared when abandoned	Provincial regiment or corps	Location of settlement in Upper Canada
Stoneburner (Steenbrander), Jacob	Germany		Delaware River, near Town Brook	500 P	25		
Stoneburner, Jacob Jr.	New York		Delaware River, near Town Brook			private, K.R.R.N.Y.	Cornwall Twp.
Stoneburner, John	New York		Delaware River, near Town Brook			private, K.R.R.N.Y.	Osnabruck Twp.
Stoneburner, Joseph	,,		Delaware River, near Town Brook			corporal, K.R.R.N.Y.	Cornwall Twp.
Stoneburner, Leonard	,,		Delaware River, near Town Brook			drummer, Grenadier Co., K.R.R.N.Y. (1st Batt.)	Osnabruck Twp.
Stuart, Dr. James	Scotland	1774	Delaware River, at Town Brook	100 P	above 50	surgeon's mate, K.R.R.N.Y.	,,
Thomson, Archibald	Roxburghshire	1773	Harpersfield	L, joint with James Park		Indian Dept., Butler's Rangers	Stamford Twp.
Trumbull, Robert			Kortright Patent				
Trumbull, Robert Jr.			,,				
Trumbull, Walter			,,				

APPENDIX B

A LIST OF OFFICERS EMPLOYED IN THE INDIAN DEPARTMENT WITH THEIR RANK AND PAY, JUNE 15, 1777*

Peter Ten Broeck
John Johnson
James Wilson   } As Captains at 10/ Sterling per day
Charles Reaume
Thomas Butler

William Caldwell
John Powell
John Joos Harcamier [Herkimer]
Lewis Clement
Frederick Yonge   } As Lieutenants at 4/6 Sterling per diem
Barent Frey
Andrew Thompson
William Ryer Borvin
George McGinnis

Edward Smith Secretary to the Department with 12/ York Currency p. diem. James Bennit Indian Commissary of stores and provisions at 10/ York Currency p. diem.

A LIST OF PERSONS EMPLOYED IN THE INDIAN DEPARTMENT, AS OF USE WITH THEIR PAY*

James Seecord   at 8/ New York Currency p. diem

Phillip Frey
Samuel Thomson
John Depue   } at 6/ New York Currency per diem
John Yonge

                                                            [signed] JOHN BUTLER

---

*P.A.C., Colonial Office Records, M.G.11, "Q" ser., vol. 13, p. 329. The men named on these lists were serving for three months before the formation of the corps called Butler's Rangers.

APPENDIX B

A LIST OF PERSONS EMPLOYED AS RANGERS IN THE INDIAN DEPARTMENT, JUNE 15, 1777*

Pay New York Currency

at 4/ per day	*at 4/ per day*	*at 4/ per day*
1 Michl. Morin	26 Peter Seamon	51 Peter Miller
2 Thomas Sutton	27 Nicholas Phillips	52 Abraham Wartman
3 George Steward	28 John Phillips	53 Adam Bowsman Junr
4 Emanuel Humphrey	29 Nicholas Phillips Junr	54 Jacob Bowsman
5 Benjamin Davis	30 Hend^r Windeke	55 Casper Hubért
6 Daniel Young	31 John Younger	56 John Hubér [sic]
7 Hermanus House	32 Jacob Engush	57 Stephen Farrinton
8 Jacob Frederick	33 Joseph Sern	58 Hand Olderickstratt
9 Joost J. Patre	34 Conrad Sels	59 George Cintner
10 Dirk Bell	35 Jacob Druner	60 August Encar
11 John Riley	36 Redman Parry	61 Nathaniel Hicks
12 Moses Mounteen	37 Robert Farrington	62 Charles Depue
13 Partial Terry	38 Joseph Page	63 Peter Secord
14 ?	39 Joshua Beebe	64 John Parks
15 Pater Danes	40 Adin [?] Beebe	65 Thomas Griffis
16 Josm Jole [?]	41 Jacob Take	66 Hendrick Winter
17 John Secord Junr	42 Jnr. Adam Bowman	67 Jacob Huber
18 David Secord	43 Charles Encor	*at 2/ per day*
19 Silas Secord	44 Hend^k Smith	68 Isaac Van Valken Burg
20 John Secord	45 Hend^k Bowin	*at 8/ per day*
21 Solomon Secord	46 Lewis Maybie	Damange Interpreter
22 Stephen Secord	47 John Lord	*at £100 per annum*
23 Adam Wartman	48 Levi Green	Irving Murph blacksmith
24 Jacob Bowman	49 John ?	
25 Henry Seamon	50 Frederick Winter	

* P.A.C., Colonial Office Records, M.G. 11, "Q" ser., vol. 13, p. 331.

APPENDIX C

FROM THE "BOSTON CHRONICLE," MARCH 12, 1782*

EXTRACT OF A LETTER FROM CAPT. GERRISH, OF THE NEW-ENGLAND MILITIA, DATED ALBANY, MARCH 7

The Peltry, taken in the expedition will, you see, amount to a good deal of money. The possession of this booty at first gave us pleasure; but we were struck with horror to find among the packages eight large ones, containing scalps of our unhappy country folks, taken in the three last years by the Seneka Indians from the inhabitants of the Frontiers of New-York, New-Jersey, Pennsylvania and Virginia, and sent by them as a present to Colonel Haldimand, Governor of Canada, in order to be by him transmitted to England. They were accompanied by the following curious letter to that gentleman:

"TEOGA, Jan. 3d, 1782

"MAY IT PLEASE YOUR EXCELLENCY,

"At the request of the Senneka Chiefs, I send herewith to your Excellency, under the care of James Boyd, eight packs of scalps, cured, dried, hooped, and painted with all the India[n] triumphal marks, of which the following is invoice and explanation:

"No. 1. Containing 43 scalps of Congress soldiers killed in different skirmishes; these are stretched on black hoops, 4 inch diameter; the inside of the skin is painted red, with a small black spot, to note their being killed with bullets. Also 62 of farmers killed in their houses; the hoops red; the skin painted brown, and marked with a hoe; a black circle all round, to denote their being surprised in the night; and a black hatchet in the middle, signifying their being killed with that weapon.

"No. 2. Containing 98 of farmers killed in their houses; hoops red; figure of a hoe, to mark their profession; great white circle and sun, to shew they were surprised in the day-time; a little red foot to shew they stood upon their defence, and died fighting for their lives and families.

"No. 3. Containing 97 of farmers; hoops green, to shew they were killed in their fields; a large white circle, with a little round mark on it for the sun, to shew that it was in the day-time; black bullet mark on some, hatchet on others.

"No. 4. Containing 102 of farmers, mixed of the several marks above; only 18 marked with a little yellow flame, to denote their being of prisoners burnt alive, after being scalped, their nails pulled out by the roots, and other torment; one of these latter supposd to be of an American clergyman, his band being fixed to the hoop of his scalp....

"No. 5. Containing eighty-eight scalps of women; hair long, braided in the Indian fashion, to shew they were mothers; hoops blue; skin yellow ground, with little red tadpoles, to represent, by way of triumph, the tears or grief occasioned to their relations; a black scalping-knife or hatchet at the bottom, to mark their being killed by those instruments....

"No. 6. Containing one hundred and ninety-three boys scalps, of various ages; small green hoops; whitish ground on the skin, with red tears in the middle, and black bullet marks....

"No. 7. Two hundred and eleven girls scalps, big and little; small yellow hoops; white ground; tears, hatchet....

"No. 8. This package is a mixture of all the varieties abovementioned, to the number of one hundred and twenty-two; with a box of birch bark, containing twenty-nine little infants scalps of various sizes; small white hoops; white ground; no tears, and only a little black knife in the middle, to shew they were ript out of their mothers bellies....

[signed] "JAMES CRAUFORD."

---

* *The Remembrancer, or Impartial Repository of Political Events for 1782*, vol. X, pt. II, pp. 135–36.

APPENDIX D

EXTRACT FROM ALBANY NEWSPAPER, MAY 26, 1783*

As Hannibal swore never to be at Peace with the Romans, so let every Whig sware—by the abhorence of Slavery—by the liberty and religion—by the Shades of those departed Friends who have fallen in battle—by the ghosts of those our Brethren who have been destroyed on board of Prison-ships and in loathsome dungeons ... by everything that a freeman holds dear—never to be at peace with those fiends the Refugees, whose thefts, murders, and treasons, have filled the cup of woe; but shew the world that we prefer War, with all it's dreadful calamities, to giving those self destroyers of the human species a residence among us.—We have crimsoned the earth with our blood to purchase peace, therefore are determined to enjoy harmony uninterrupted with the Contaminating breath of a Tory.

At a meeting of the Inhabitants of the District of Saratoga (in the County of Albany) held on Tuesday the 6th day of May, 1783, the following Resolutions were unanimously voted, and ordered to be published in the New York Gazetteer.

Whereas, in the course of the late glorious contest for liberty and independence, many persons residing in this, and other of the United States, regardless of their duty, have basely deserted the cause of their country, and voluntarily joined the Enemy, thereof, to aid and assist in subjugating it to tyrany and slavery. And progressing from one species of villany [sic] to another, these diabolical miscreants, became the voluntary instruments of those barbarous Massacres in which neither age, or sex, or condition were spared, and in which the horrid spectacle was exhibited; of harmless infants expiring on the mangled bodies of their butchered Parents. And Whereas, wretches so disgraced with infamy and Crimes, ought not to participate of the blessings of a free Government.

Resolved therefore, That if any person who hath voluntarily joined or attempted to join, the late Enemy of the United States, and who shall hereafter return to this District, such person will be treated with the severity due to his crimes and infamous defection.

Resolved, That if any such person has already returned, since the first day of January last, and shall not remove before the tenth day of June next, he shall be treated in like manner as those who shall presume to return hereafter.

Resolved, that it be, and is hereby earnestly recommended to the Militia Officers of the District in their several beats, to make diligent Enquiry after such persons as are above described; and if any are found, to give notice to the Inhabitants of this district, that effectual measures be taken for their expulsion.

Resolved, that we will hold in contempt every inhabitant of this District, who shall countenance, comfort, aid or abet, any person who has voluntarily join'd the Enemy, or attempted so to do.

By order of the meeting

                                                                  SAM BACON   Clerk

---

*P.A.C., Haldimand Transcripts, B. 103, pp. 183-84. This was mentioned by Captain William Potts of the 8th Regiment as having been seen at Fort Niagara. A month later, June 7, 1783, the inhabitants of Harpersfield, Kortright, Cherry Valley, and other settlements in the Conajoharie District met at Fort Plain and passed six resolutions of the same purport which are quoted in William L. Stone, *Life of Joseph Brant-Thayendanegea including the Indian Wars of the American Revolution* (2 vols., Cooperstown, N.Y., 1845), II, Appendix V.

NOTES

Abbreviations used in these notes are as follows: P.A.C.—Public Archives of Canada; P.A.N.S.—Public Archives of Nova Scotia; P.R.O.—Public Record Office of Great Britain.

INTRODUCTION

1. "A narrative of the early life of Colonel John M'Donell, of Scottos, written by himself, after he came to Canada, at the urgent request of one of his particular friends," *Canadian Magazine and Literary Repository*, vol. IV, nos. 22 and 24 (1825).
2. *Ibid.*
3. Ernest Green, "Notes on the Empey (Impey) family of Stormont," *Ontario Historical Society, Papers and Records*, vol. XXVII (1931), p. 398.
4. P.R.O., Great Britain, AO 13/15.
5. Kirk Session Minutes, Parish of Croy, Inverness-shire, Aug. 12, 1762.
6. Data supplied to the author by the Session Clerk of the Parish of Croy.
7. John Ross Robertson, *The History of Freemasonry in Canada* (2 vols., Toronto, 1900), I, p. 649.
8. R. W. Chapman, ed., *Johnson's Journey to the Western Islands of Scotland and Boswell's Journal of a Tour of the Hebrides with Samuel Johnson, LL.D.* (Oxford University Press, 1951 ed.), p. 25.
9. *Ibid.*, p. 33.
10. *Scots Magazine*, vol. XXXV (Sept. 1773), p. 499.
11. W. L. Scott, "The Macdonells of Leek, Collachie and Aberchalder," *Canadian Catholic Historical Association, Report* (1934–35), p. 9.
12. Viola Root Cameron, comp., *Emigrants from Scotland to America 1774–5: Copied from a Loose Bundle of Treasury Papers in the Public Record Office, London, England* (mimeo., London, 1930). On these lists no mention appears of eviction for sheep pasture which was so important a cause of Scottish emigration after 1790.
13. *Ibid.*, pp. 76–77.
14. *Ibid.*, p. 54.
15. *Ibid.*, pp. 30–31.
16. *History of Delaware County, New York, 1797–1880* (New York, 1880), p. 234.
17. Ian Charles Cargill Graham, *Colonists from Scotland: Emigration to North America, 1707–1783* (Cornell University Press, 1956), p. 81.

CHAPTER ONE

1. John F. Watson, *Historic Tales of Olden Time: concerning the early settlement and advancement of New York City and State for the use of families and schools* (New York, 1832), p. 103.
2. William Smith, *History of New York from the first discovery to the year M.DCC.XXXII with a continuation from the Year 1732, to the Commencement of the Year 1814* (Albany, 1814), p. 325.
3. *Ibid.*, p. 326.
4. *New-York Gazette and the weekly mercury; Rivington's New-York Gazetteer,* issues for Sept. and Oct. 1773.
5. *New-York Gazette....*, Oct. 25, 1773.
6. *Ibid.*
7. John D. Monroe, *Chapters in the History of Delaware County, New York* (Delaware County Historical Association, 1949), p. 9.
8. George Morgan, *The Life of James Monroe* (Boston, 1921), pp. 143–44.

9. *Ibid.*, p. 144; Monroe, *History of Delaware County*, p. 9.
10. Morgan, *Life of James Monroe*, p. 144.
11. Oscar T. Barck, *New York City during the War for Independence with Special Reference to the Period of British Occupation* (Columbia University Press, 1931), Appendix B, "Residences and Points of Interest"; Appendix C, "A List of Farms on New York Island, 1780, from a Small Note-book kept by Evart Blancker, surveyor in New York," shows Kortright's farm on lots 98 and 100.
12. Arthur Styron, *The Last of the Cocked Hats: James Monroe and the Virginia Dynasty* (University of Oklahoma Press, 1945), p. 107fn.
13. *Rivington's New-York Gazetteer*, Nov. 4, 1773.
14. *Ibid.*
15. Francis W. Halsey, ed., *A Tour of Four Great Rivers, the Hudson, Mohawk, Susquehanna and Delaware in 1769, being the journal of Richard Smith of Burlington, New Jersey* (New York, 1906), p. 4.
16. John Stuart, *Three Years in North America* (2 vols., New York, 1833), I, p. 33.
17. Halsey, ed., Smith's *Journal*, p. 17.
18. *Ibid.*, p. 22.
19. Francis Parkman, *The Jesuits in North America in the Seventeenth Century* (Boston, 1896), p. xlvii.
20. Francis Parkman, *The Conspiracy of Pontiac* (2 vols., Boston, 1896), I, p. 16.
21. *Gentleman's Magazine* (London), Sept. 1755, quoted in O. Turner, *Pioneer History of the Holland Purchase of Western New York* ... (Buffalo, 1849), p. 248.
22. E. B. O'Callaghan, ed., *The Documentary History of New York* (4 vols., Albany, 1850), IV, p. 1088.
23. Monroe, *History of Delaware County*, p. 12.
24. *Ibid.*, pp. 10–11.
25. Halsey, ed., Smith's *Journal*, p. xviii.
26. Thomas Jones, *History of New York during the Revolution* (2 vols., New York, 1879), II, p. 313.
27. Turner, *Pioneer History of the Holland Purchase*, p. 246; Francis W. Halsey, *The Old New York Frontier* (New York, 1901), p. 120.
28. R. A. Preston, ed., *Kingston before the War of 1812* (Champlain Society Publication, Ont. ser. III, Toronto, 1959), p. 112.
29. Halsey, ed., Smith's *Journal*, p. 60.
30. Herbert F. Gardiner, "Centenary of the Death of Brant," *Ontario Historical Society, Papers and Records*, vol. IX (1910), pp. 33–54.
31. Halsey, ed., Smith's *Journal*, pp. 68–69.
32. *Ibid.*, p. 84.
33. *Ibid.*, p. 54.
34. *Ibid.*, pp. 44–45.
35. *History of Delaware County, New York, 1797–1880* (New York, 1880), p. 220.
36. New York State Archives, Manuscripts of Sir William Johnson, vol. XXII, p. 158, Allan Macdonell to Johnson, Nov. 14, 1773.
37. *Ibid.*
38. Ulysses P. Hedrick, *A History of Agriculture in the State of New York* (Albany, 1933), p. 57.
39. *2nd Report Ontario Archives* (1904), Evidence on the claims of American Loyalists—numerous entries under the names of landholders in Harpersfield, Kortright, and Head of the Delaware.
40. *History of Delaware County, 1797–1880*, p. 434.
41. P.R.O., Great Britain, AO 13/25.
42. *New-York Gazette and the weekly mercury*, Feb. 22, 1773, "An Act to settle a Line of Division between the Counties of Ulster and Albany": Holland's Map, "The Provinces of New York and New Jersey; with a part of Pennsylvania . . . drawn by Major Holland, Surveyor General, of the Northern District of America, 1776."
43. Parkman, *Pontiac*, I, p. 147.
44. H. A. Haring, *Our Catskill Mountains* (New York, 1931).

CHAPTER TWO

1. C. W. Dunn, *Highland Settler* (Toronto, 1953), p. 64.
2. William Cooper, *A Guide in the Wilderness or the History of the First Settlement in the Western Counties of New York, with useful Instructions to Future Settlers. In a series of letters addressed by Judge Cooper, of Coopers-Town, to William Sampson, Barrister, of New York* (Dublin, 1810), pp. 32–33.

NOTES

3. *2nd Report Ontario Archives* (1904), Evidence on claims for losses during the Revolution by American Loyalists.
4. Francis W. Halsey, ed., *A Tour of Four Great Rivers, the Hudson, Mohawk, Susquehanna and Delaware in 1769, being the journal of Richard Smith of Burlington, New Jersey* (New York, 1906), p. 39.
5. Francis Parkman, *The Jesuits in North America in the Seventeenth Century* (Boston, 1896), p. xlix.
6. P.A.C., Lord Selkirk's Diary, Jan. 19, 1804.
7. Mrs. Anne Grant, *Memoirs of an American Lady: with sketches of the manners and scenery in America, as they existed previous to the revolution* (2 vols., London, 1808), II, pp. 111–12.
8. Harold R. Shurtleff, *The Log Cabin Myth* (Harvard University Press, 1939), pp. 3–4.
9. *2nd Rept. Ont. Arch.*, p. 977.
10. *Ibid.*, under names listed.
11. Silas Wood, *Sketch of Long Island*, quoted in Ulysses P. Hedrick, *A History of Agriculture in the State of New York* (Albany, 1933), p. 34.
12. Halsey, ed., *Smith's Journal*, p. 21.
13. John Maude, *Visit to the Falls of Niagara in 1800* (London, 1826), pp. 32–33.
14. John Bartram, *Observations on the Inhabitants, Climate, Soil, Rivers, Productions, Animals, and other matters worthy of Notice . . .* (London, 1751), p. 67.
15. Hedrick, *History of Agriculture in New York*, p. 335.
16. Patrick Campbell, *Travels in the Interior Inhabited Parts of North America in the Years 1791 and 1792* (Edinburgh, 1793), p. 42.
17. Dunn, *Highland Settler*, p. 29.
18. *2nd Rept. Ont. Arch.*, pp. 356, 358.
19. *Ibid.*, p. 357.
20. P.R.O., Great Britain, AO 13/25.
21. *Ibid.*, AO 13/15.
22. J. Paul Hudson, "Potash and Soap Ashes," *Better Crops with Plant Food* (American Potash Institute, Washington, D.C., 1957), pp. 30–31.
23. Quoted in Hedrick, *History of Agriculture in New York*, p. 141.
24. Halsey, ed., *Smith's Journal*, p. 33.
25. Maude, *Visit to the Falls of Niagara*, p. 121.
26. Halsey, ed., *Smith's Journal*, p. 41.
27. *2nd Rept. Ont. Arch.*, p. 960.
28. P.R.O., AO 13/15.
29. *Ibid.*, AO 13/25.
30. Halsey, ed., *Smith's Journal*, pp. 26–27.
31. Maude, *Visit to the Falls of Niagara*, p. 121.
32. Halsey, ed., *Smith's Journal*, p. 33.
33. *Ibid.*, p. 32.
34. *Ibid.*, p. 11.
35. William E. Roscoe, *History of Schoharie Co., New York* (Syracuse, 1882), p. 170.
36. George S. Conover, ed., *Journals of the Expedition of Major General John Sullivan against the Six Nations Indians in 1779* (Auburn, N.Y., 1887), p. 288, "Map of Captain William Gray, 1778"; J. H. French, *Historical and Statistical Gazetteer of New York State* (Syracuse, 1860), p. 263.
37. Jay Gould, *History of Delaware County and Border Wars of New York* (Roxbury, N.Y., 1856), p. 155; Mr. Ralph Rose of Rose's Brook informed the author in an interview in 1955 of this family tradition.
38. Halsey, ed., *Smith's Journal*, p. 21.
39. *Ibid.*, p. 33.
40. P.R.O., AO 12/109.
41. Halsey, ed., *Smith's Journal*, p. 33.
42. *2nd Rept. Ont. Arch.*, Evidence on claims under names listed.
43. Maude, *Visit to the Falls of Niagara*, p. 121.
44. Levi Beardsley, *Reminiscences* (New York, 1827), p. 29.
45. *Ibid.*
46. Richard Parkinson, *A Tour in America in 1798, 1799, and 1800* (London, 1805), pp. 290–91.
47. Maude, *Visit to the Falls of Niagara*, p. 42.
48. P.R.O., AO 13/15.
49. William Cooper, *A Guide in the Wilderness*, p. 23.
50. *Ibid.*, p. 36.
51. Dunn, *Highland Settler*, pp. 38–39.
52. P.R.O., AO 12/32.

53. Beardsley, *Reminiscences*, p. 26.
54. *Rivington's New-York Gazette*, Oct. 28, 1773.
55. Dunn, *Highland Settler*, p. 31.
56. Beardsley, *Reminiscences*, p. 23.
57. *2nd Rept. Ont. Arch.*, Evidence on claims of Loyalists.
58. *History of Delaware County, 1797-1880* (New York, 1880), p. 241.
59. *Ibid.*; David Murray, ed., *Centennial History of Delaware County* (Delhi, N.Y., 1898), p. 223.
60. Murray, ed., *Centennial History*, p. 224.
61. *Ibid.*
62. Timothy Dwight, *Travels in New-England and New-York* (4 vols., London, 1823), IV, p. 513.
63. Conover, ed., *Journals of Sullivan Expedition*, p. 288.

CHAPTER THREE

1. Francis W. Halsey, ed., *A Tour of Four Great Rivers, the Hudson, Mohawk, Susquehanna and Delaware in 1769, being the journal of Richard Smith of Burlington, New Jersey* (New York, 1906), p. 31.
2. William W. Campbell, *The Border Warfare of New York during the Revolution or, the Annals of Tryon County* (New York, 1849), 2nd ed., p. 374.
3. Edward Augustus Kendall, *Travels through the Northern Part of the United States in the Years 1807 and 1808* (2 vols., New York, 1808), II, p. 87.
4. Patrick Campbell, *Travels in the Interior Inhabited Parts of North America in the Years 1791 and 1792* (Edinburgh, 1793), p. 193.
5. P.A.C., Haldimand Transcripts, B. 100, pp. 183-87, letters of Colonel John Butler, May and June 1779.
6. Patrick Campbell, *Travels*, p. 193.
7. P.R.O., Great Britain, AO 12/32, AO 13/91.
8. P.A.C., Upper Canada Land Petitions, 1791-1796, B 1, no. 116, Petition of Joseph Brant, Feb. 1, 1796.
9. William L. Stone, *Life of Joseph Brant-Thayendanegea including the Indian Wars of the American Revolution* (2 vols., Cooperstown, N.Y., 1845), I, p. 23.
10. Rev. John Stuart's account of Joseph Brant quoted in James Strachan, *A Visit to the Province of Upper Canada in 1819* (Aberdeen, 1820), p. 152.
11. Halsey, ed., Smith's *Journal*, p. 60fn.
12. J. Howard Hanson and Samuel L. Frey, eds., *The Minute Book of the Committee of Safety for Tryon County, the Old New York Frontier* (New York, 1905), pp. 1-4.
13. *Ibid.*, p. viii.
14. *Ibid.*, pp. 108-10.
15. *Ibid.*, p. 17.
16. *Ibid.*, p. 39.
17. Stone, *Life of Brant*, I, pp. 89-90.
18. *Ibid.*, p. 153.
19. *Ibid.*, p. 170fn.
20. E. B. O'Callaghan, ed., *Calendar of Historical Manuscripts relating to the War of the Revolution, in the office of the Secretary of State, Albany, N.Y.* (2 vols, Albany, 1868), I, pp. 33-35.
21. New York Historical Society, Tryon County Committee of Safety, June 8, 1775.
22. Francis W. Halsey, *The Old New York Frontier* (New York, 1901), p. 149.
23. Hanson and Frey, eds., *Minute Book*, p. 74.
24. *2nd Report Ontario Archives* (1904), pp. 965-67, Evidence on claims of Elizabeth Clement and sons.
25. New York Historical Society, Tryon County MSS., Lewis Clement to Committee of Public Safety, Sept. 6, 1775.
26. Hanson and Frey, eds., *Minute Book*, pp. 74-75.
27. *Ibid.*, pp. 91-97.
28. *2nd Rept. Ont. Arch.*, p. 85, Evidence on claim of Terence McAllister (McAlister).
29. Hanson and Frey, eds., *Minute Book*, p. 80.
30. Viola Root Cameron, comp., *Emigrants from Scotland to America 1774-5: Copied from a Loose Bundle of Treasury Papers in the Public Record Office, London, England* (mimeo., London, 1930), p. 73.
31. McMicking Papers in possession of Miss Beatrice Dennis, Stamford, Ontario.
32. Haldimand Transcripts, B. 215, pp. 196-202, Narrative of the Service of Lieut.-Col. John Butler, May 1785.

33. *Ibid.*
34. Stone, *Life of Brant*, I, p. 149.
35. P.A.C., Claus Papers, May 6, 1779.
36. Ernest Green, "Frey," *Ontario Historical Society, Papers and Records,* vol. XXXIII (1939), pp. 45-74.
37. Stone, *Life of Brant*, I, p. 141.
38. J. Watts de Peyster, ed., *Miscellanies, by an Officer (Colonel Arent Schuyler de Peyster, B.A.), 1774-1813* (New York, 1888), pt. II, pp. xlix-li, Sir John Johnson to Daniel Claus, Jan. 20, 1777.
39. O'Callaghan, ed., *Calendar of Historical Manuscripts* I, p. 375, Petition, July 1, 1776.
40. Tryon County MSS., John Harper to Committee of Safety, July 12, 1776.
41. *Ibid.*, Oath of John Thompson, undated.
42. *New York in the Revolution as Colony and State* (2 vols., New York, 1904), II, p. 245.
43. John D. Monroe, *Chapters in the History of Delaware County, New York* (Delaware County Historical Association, 1949), p. 64.
44. *Ibid.*, p. 42.
45. New York Historical Society, MS. Minute Book, Tryon County Committee of Safety, Dec. 18, 1776.
46. Dorothy C. Barck, ed., "Minutes of the Committee and the First Commission for Detecting Conspiracies, 1776-1778," *New York Historical Society Collections* (1924-25), p. 28.
47. *Ibid.*, p. 51.
48. Stone, *Life of Brant*, I, p. 177.
49. O'Callaghan, ed., *Calendar of Historical Manuscripts*, I, p. 629.
50. *Ibid.*, p. 654.
51. Stone, *Life of Brant*, I, p. 182.
52. Tryon Co. MSS., Johannes Bell to Isaac Paris, April 25, 1777.
53. Hugh Hastings, ed., *Public Papers of George Clinton, First Governor of New York, 1777-1795* (8 vols., Albany, 1899-1904), no. 713, John Harper to Committee of Safety, Aug 20, 1779.
54. Ian Charles Cargill Graham, *Colonists from Scotland: Emigration to North America, 1707-1783* (Cornell University Press, 1956), p. 81.
55. Jeptha Root Simms, *History of Schoharie County and Border Wars of New York* (Albany, 1845), p. 210, "Record of Peter Swart."
56. New York Public Library, MSS. Division, American Loyalist Transcripts, vol. 17, pp. 317-21, Evidence on Claim of Hugh Fraser, late of Courtright Township . . . March 25, 1786.
57. *New York in the Revolution*, II, pp. 246-47, "Rent Roll of the Farms left by persons gone to the Enemy. . . ."
58. George H. Warner, ed., *Military Records of Schoharie* (Albany, 1891), p. 57; New York Public Library, MSS. Division, Emmet Collection no. 4597, John Harper to Peter Curtenius, March 30, 1791.
59. *Ibid.*
60. American Loyalist Transcripts, vol. 17, pp. 317-21, Evidence on the Claim of Hugh Fraser . . . March 25, 1786.
61. P.R.O., AO 13/15.

CHAPTER FOUR

1. P.A.C., Haldimand Transcripts, B. 162, p. 135, Captain John Macdonell to Major Mathews, Dec. 12, 1783.
2. *Ibid.*
3. John D. Monroe, *Chapters in the History of Delaware County, New York* (Delaware County Historical Association, 1949), p. 65.
4. *Ibid.*
5. J. J. Talman, ed., *Loyalist Narratives from Upper Canada* (Champlain Society Publication no. XXVII, Toronto, 1946), p. 56, "Journal of Adam Crysler."
6. *Ibid.*; Jeptha Root Simms, *History of Schoharie County and Border Wars of New York* (Albany, 1845), p. 210, "Record of Peter Swart."
7. George H. Warner, ed., *Military Records of Schoharie* (Albany, 1891), p. 6.
8. Old Stone Fort Museum, Schoharie, exhibit no. 1350.
9. Monroe, *History of Delaware County*, p. 66.
10. Simms, *History of Schoharie County*, p. 248.
11. Talman, ed., *Loyalist Narratives*, p. 57.
12. *Ibid.*
13. William L. Stone, *Life of Joseph Brant-Thayendanegea including the Indian Wars of the American Revolution* (2 vols., Cooperstown, N.Y., 1845), I, p. 229; A. C. Flick, *The American Revolution in New York* (Albany, 1926), p. 157; numerous other authorities.

14. J. Almon, ed., *The Remembrancer, or Impartial Repository of Political Events* (17 vols., London, 1775–84), V, p. 392.
15. John Romeyn Brodhead, ed., *Documents relating to the Colonial History of the State of New York* (15 vols., Albany, 1853–87), VIII (1857), pp. 718–23, Claus to Knox, Oct. 16, 1777.
16. P.R.O., Great Britain, AO 13/14.
17. New York Public Library, MSS. Division, American Loyalist Transcripts, vol. 17, pp. 317–21, Claim and Eidence on claim of Hugh Fraser, March 25, 1786.
18. Talman, ed., *Loyalist Narratives*, p. 57.
19. *2nd Report Ontario Archives* (1904), p. 1056, "case of Philip Crislor."
20. P.A.C., Colonial Office Records, M.G. 11, "Q" ser., vol. 14, p. 159, Beating Order, Sept. 15, 1777.
21. Carroll Vincent Lonergan, *The Northern Gateway: A History of Lake Champlain* (Ticonderoga, N.Y., 1939), p. 31.
22. Ira Allen, *The Natural and Political History of the State of Vermont* (London, 1798), pp. 103–4.
23. *Ibid.*, p. 105.
24. Ontario Archives, Canniff Papers, Notes on the Goring family, Clunes to Goring, March 26, 1779.
25. Colonial Office Records, M.G. 11, "Q" ser., vol. 14, p. 169, Powell to Carleton, Sept. 18, 1777.
26. *Ibid.*, p. 174, Powell to Carleton, Sept. 23, 1777; p. 293, "Return of Artificers killed and taken Prisoners by the Rebels the 18th September, 1777."
27. P.R.O., AO 13/25.
28. Canniff Papers, Notes on the Goring family, Clunes to Goring, March 26, 1779.
29. Hugh Hastings, ed., *Public Papers of George Clinton, First Governor of New York 1777–1795* (8 vols., Albany, 1899–1904), no. 725.
30. *Ibid.*, no. 713.
31. *Ibid.*, no. 744.
32. *2nd Rept. Ont. Arch.*, pp. 1101 and 662, Evidence on claims of Jacob Stanburner [sic] and Hugh Clarke.
33. Monroe, *History of Delaware County*, p. 122, Evidence on claim of Neil McKay.
34. *2nd Rept. Ont. Arch.*, pp. 85–86; 357–58.
35. Hastings, ed., *Clinton Papers*, no. 747.
36. *Ibid.*, pp. 998–1,000, Evidence on claim of Adam Young.
37. Haldimand Transcripts, B. 167, p. 371, Return of Officers in the Indian Department.
38. New York Public Library, MSS. Division, Emmet Collection no. 4598, John Harper to Peter Curtenius, March 30, 1791.
39. *Ibid.*, no. 4661.
40. Brodhead, ed., *Documents*, VIII, pp. 718–23, Claus to Knox, Oct. 16, 1777.
41. Colonial Office Records, M.G. 11, "Q" ser., vol. 14, p. 159, Beating Order, Sept. 15, 1777.
42. *2nd Rept. Ont. Arch.*, p. 1112, Evidence on claim of John Glassford,
43. P.A.C., Upper Canada Land Petitions 1791–1796 B. 1, Aug. 17, 1795 (R.G. 1, L 3, vol. 27, no. 50).
44. Haldimand Transcripts, B. 105, pp. 236–42, Lists of prisoners taken by the enemy.
45. Almon, ed., *The Remembrancer ... for 1779* (vol. VII), p. 515.
46. Egerton Ryerson, *The Loyalists of the American Revolution and Their Times* (2 vols., Toronto, 1880), II, pp. 265–67, "Narrative of Elizabeth Bowman Spohn"; J. H. Mather and L. P. Brockett, *A Geographical History of the State of New York ...* (Utica, 1848), p. 199.
47. Ryerson, *Loyalists*, II, pp. 265–67.
48. *Ibid.*; *Ontario Historical Society, Papers and Records*, vol. XXV (1929), p. 28.
49. Upper Canada Land Petitions, 1793–1795, C 1, no. 97, July 8, 1795 (R.G. 1, L 3, vol 423).
50. Hastings, ed., *Clinton Papers*, no. 1578.
51. *Ibid.*
52. *Ibid.*
53. J. Watts de Peyster, ed., *Miscellanies, by an Officer (Colonel Arent Schuyler de Peyster, B.A.), 1774–1813* (New York, 1888), pt. II, p. li, Sir John Johnson to Daniel Claus, June 18,1778.
54. P.R.O., AO 12/32.
55. Upper Canada Land Petitions, 1793–1795, C 1, no. 97, July 8, 1795 (R.G. 1, L 3, vol. 423).
56. C. E. Cartwright, *Life and Letters of the Late Hon. Richard Cartwright* (Toronto, 1876), p. 31.
57. Almon, ed., *The Remembrancer ... for 1779* (vol. VII), p. 51.
58. Stone, *Life of Brant*, I, p. 338fn.
59. Brodhead, *Documents*, VIII, p. 752, Johnson to Lord Germain, Sept. 10, 1778.
60. Hastings, ed., *Clinton Papers*, no. 1527, Klock to Clinton, June 22, 1778.
61. *Ibid.*, no. 2666, Stark to Ballard, July 4, 1778.

62. *Ibid.*, Alden to Ballard, Aug. 7, 1778.
63. *Ibid.*
64. *Ibid.*, no. 1750, Commissioners on Conspiracies to Clinton, Sept. 10, 1778.
65. *Ibid.*, no. 2666, Alden to Stark, Aug. 7, 1778.
66. Victor Hugo Paltsits, ed., *Minutes of the Commissioners for Detecting and Defeating Conspiracies in the State of New York* (Albany, 1909), p. 212.
67. Francis W. Halsey, *The Old New York Frontier* (New York, 1901), p. 224, Account of Captain Benjamin Warren.
68. Talman, ed., *Loyalist Narratives*, p. 58.
69. Jeptha Root Simms, *Frontiersmen of New York* (2 vols., Albany, 1882), II, p. 202.
70. *2nd Rept. Ont. Arch.*, pp. 992–93, Evidence on claim of John Burch.
71. *Ibid.*
72. Paltsits, ed., *Minutes of Commissioners for . . . Conspiracies*, p. 191.
73. Talman, ed., *Loyalist Narratives*, pp. 45–53, "A Journey to Canada."
74. *2nd Rept. Ont. Arch.*, pp. 992–93, Evidence on claim of John Burch.
75. *Ibid.*
76. J. H. French, *Historical and Statistical Gazetteer of New York State* (Syracuse, 1860), p. 263.
77. E. A. Cruikshank, ed., *Records of Niagara* (Niagara Historical Society Publication no. 40, n.d.), p. 9.
78. Hastings, ed., *Clinton Papers*, no. 1513, June 16, 1778.
79. *2nd Rept. Ont. Arch.*, p. 957, Evidence on claim of Daniel Servos.
80. Hastings, ed., *Clinton Papers*, no. 1650, Butler to Clinton, Aug. 13, 1778.
81. Paltsits, ed., *Minutes of Commissioners for . . . Conspiracies*, p. 234.
82. *2nd Rept. Ont. Arch.*, p. 957, Evidence on claim of Daniel Servos.
83. *Ibid.*
84. Hastings, ed., *Clinton Papers*, vols. III and IV, numerous entries.
85. *Ibid.*, no. 1299.
86. *Ibid.*, no. 1438.
87. *Ibid.*, no. 1639.
88. *Ibid.*
89. *Ibid.*, John Taylor to Clinton, Aug. 9, 1778.
90. Paltsits, ed., *Minutes of Commissioners for . . . Conspiracies*, p. 214.
91. *New-York Gazette and the weekly mercury*, Sept. 14, 1778.
92. Hastings, ed., *Clinton Papers*, no. 1885, Journal of Colonel William Butler, October, 1778.
93. Haldimand Transcripts, B. 96-1, p. 230, Bolton to Haldimand, Nov 11, 1778.
94. *Ibid.*, B. 100, p. 82, Butler to Bolton, Nov. 17, 1778.
95. Hastings, ed., *Clinton Papers*, no. 1952–53 Nov. 17, 1778.
96. Haldimand Transcripts, B. 100, p. 82, Butler to Bolton, Nov 17, 1778.
97. *Ibid.*
98. *Ibid.*
99. Hastings, ed., *Clinton Papers*, no. 1952–53, Nov. 11, 1778.
100. Francis Parkman, *The Jesuits in North America* (Boston, 1896), p. lxvi.
101. Hastings, ed., *Clinton Papers*, no. 1999, Wm. Harper to James Clinton, Dec. 2, 1778.
102. *2nd Rept. Ont. Arch.*, p. 996, Evidence on claim of James Ramsey.
103. *Ibid.*, Evidence on claim of William McClellan.
104. Hastings, ed., *Clinton Papers*, no. 1970, Dec. 13, 1778.
105. Upper Canada Land Petitions, 1795–1797, T 2, no. 12.
106. *History of Delaware County, New York, 1797–1880* (New York, 1880), p. 234.

CHAPTER FIVE

1. Patrick Campbell, *Travels in the Interior Inhabited Parts of North America in the Years 1791 and 1792* (Edinburgh, 1793), p. 274.
2. Francis Parkman, *Montcalm and Wolfe* (2 vols., Boston, 1896), p. 506.
3. Parkman, *The Conspiracy of Pontiac* (Boston, 1896), p. 229.
4. Quoted in Parkman, *La Salle and the Discovery of the Great West* (Boston, 1896), pp. 12–13.
5. E. A. Benians, ed., *A Journal by Thomas Hughes for his amusement, & designed only for his perusal by the time he attains the age of 50 if he lives so long (1778–89)* (Cambridge University Press, 1947), p. 182.
6. P.A.C., Haldimand Transcripts, B. 105, p. 217, Butler to Mathews, July 24, 1780.
7. New York Public Library, Rare Book Room, Josiah Priest, *The Captivity and Sufferings of Gen. Freegift Patchin of Blenheim, Schoharie County, among the Indians, under Brant, the*

noted chief, during the Border Warfare in the time of the American Revolution (Albany, 1833), p. 13.

8. Francis W. Halsey, ed., *A Tour of Four Great Rivers, the Hudson, Mohawk, Susquehanna and Delaware in 1769, being the journal of Richard Smith of Burlington, New Jersey* (New York, 1906), p. 58.

9. J. Almon, ed., *The Remembrancer, or Impartial Repository of Political Events for 1780* (vol. IX), p. 158, "Report to Congress of General James Sullivan."

10. Narrative of Captain Jeremiah Snyder as related to Charles G. De Witt, editor of the *Ulster Sentinel*, 1827, quoted in William L. Stone, *Life of Joseph Brant–Thayendanegea including the Indian Wars of the American Revolution* (2 vols., Cooperstown, N.Y., 1845), II, p. 67.

11. P.A.C., Upper Canada Land Petitions 1793-1795, C 1, no. 97, July 8, 1795 (R.G. 1, L 3, vol. 423).

12. *New-York Gazette and the weekly mercury*, April 12, 1779.

13. *Ibid.*

14. Victor Hugo Paltsits, ed., *Minutes of the Commissioners for Detecting and Defeating Conspiracies in the State of New York* (Albany, 1909), p. 360.

15. *Ibid.*

16. *Ibid.*, p. 372.

17. P.R.O., Great Britain, AO 12/32; 13/91.

18. Ontario Archives, Canniff Papers, Notes on the Goring Family, "Copy of a letter," July 1, 1779.

19. *Ibid.*, Cartwright to Goring, July 1, 1779.

20. P.A.C., William Merritt Papers, vol. 19, Goring Papers, Cartwright to Goring, Aug. 2, 1779.

21. General James Clinton to Governor George Clinton, July 6, 1779, quoted in Stone, *Life of Brant*, II, p. 13.

22. Historical marker on site Otsego Lake, New York.

23. Stone, *Life of Brant*, II, p. 17.

24. *Ibid.*, p. 18.

25. William Merritt Papers, vol. 19, Goring Papers, "Copy of a Letter to Mr. Hamilton, 1779."

26. General James Clinton to Mrs. Clinton, July 6, 1779, quoted in William W. Campbell, *The Border Warfare of New York during the Revolution or, the Annals of Tryon County* (New York, 1849), p. 140.

27. Hugh Hastings, ed., *Public Papers of George Clinton, First Governor of New York 1777-1795* (8 vols., Albany, 1899-1904), no. 2452, July 29, 1779.

28. New York Public Library, MSS. Division, British Headquarters (Carleton) Papers in America, "Extracts from Letters from the Upper Posts and Indian Country, July 29, 1779."

29. J. H. Mather and L. P. Brockett, *A Geographical History of the State of New York* (Utica, N.Y., 1848), p. 196.

30. Hastings, ed., *Clinton Papers*, no. 2477, James Clinton to George Clinton, Aug 10, 1779.

31. *New-York Gazette and the weekly mercury*, Aug. 23, 1779.

32. William Merritt Papers, vol. 19, Goring Papers, Cartwright to Goring, Aug. 15, 1779.

33. Canniff Papers, Notes on the Goring Family, Goring to Cruikshank, Sept. 1, 1779.

34. *Ibid.*, Sept. 14, 1779.

35. Hastings, ed., *Clinton Papers*, no. 2501, James Clinton to George Clinton, Aug. 31. 1779.

36. *Ibid.*

37. Butler to Bolton, Aug. 31, 1779, quoted in *The Sullivan-Clinton Campaign* (Albany, 1929), pp. 135-38.

38. Thomas Jones, *History of New York during the Revolution* (2 vols., New York, 1879), II, p. 333.

39. P.A.C., Colonial Office Records, M.G. 11, "Q" ser., vol. 16-2, p. 611, Butler to Haldimand, Sept. 20, 1779.

40. Almon, ed., *The Remembrancer... for 1780* (vol. IX), pp. 158-66.

41. Arthur Pound, *Lake Ontario* (New York, 1945), p. 126.

42. Claude H. Hultzén, *Old Fort Niagara* (Buffalo, 1939), p. 34.

43. Stone, *Life of Brant*, II, p. 67.

44. Upper Canada Land Petitions, 1793-1795, C 1, no. 97, July 8, 1795 (R.G. 1, L 3, vol. 423).

45. *Ibid.*

46. *Ibid.*, 1795-1797, T 2, no. 12, Oct. 1796.

47. Haldimand Transcripts, B. 96-1, pp. 148-50.

48. *2nd Report Ontario Archives* (1904), p. 984.

49. *Ibid.*

50. Haldimand Transcripts, B. 110, p. 31.

51. *Ibid.*, B. 109-2, p. 31.
52. R. Janet Powell, *Annals of the Forty*, no. 6 (Grimsby Historical Society, 1955), pp. 56–57.
53. Haldimand Transcripts, B. 105, pp. 432–33.
54. *2nd Rept. Ont. Arch.*, pp. 989–90.
55. *Ibid.*, pp. 979–80. In a proclamation, dated Oct. 30, 1778, and issued by the Supreme Executive Council of the Commonwealth of Pennsylvania, the Fields and Dolsons "late of the twp. of Wioming" were enjoined to give themselves up before Dec. 15 and stand trial "or be attainted of high treason" (Almon, ed., *The Remembrancer . . . for 1778*, pp. 340–42).
56. William Merritt Papers, vol. 19, Goring Papers, Goring to Samuel Street, March 15, 1780.
57. William W. Campbell, *Annals of Tryon County*, p. 251; Stone, *Life of Brant*, II, p. 55.
58. Haldimand Transcripts, B. 109, pp. 40–76, Accounts of the Indian Dept. at Niagara, Marh 24. 1780.
59. P.A.C., Partnership Accounts, Messrs, Taylor and Duffin, Niagara, May 7, 1779.
60. Haldimand Transcrips, B. 109, p. 80.
61. *Ibid.*, p. 92, "Return of the Several Indian War Parities . . . that marched from Niagara between the third of Feb. and that of Sept. . . . 1780. . . ."
62. Quoted in John D. Monroe, *Chapters in the History of Delaware County, New York* (Delaware County Historical Association, 1949), p. 81.
63. Jay Gould, *History of Delaware County and Border Wars of New York* (Roxbury, N.Y., 1856), p. 110.
64. Hastings, ed., *Clinton Papers*, no. 2774.
65. Draper Collection of Brant MSS., quoted in Francis W. Halsey, *The Old New York Frontier* (New York, 1901), p. 290; Facsimile of Brant's letter, *Schoharie County Historical Review*, vol. XVII, no. 1 (May 1953), p. 24.
66. Hastings, ed., *Clinton Papers*, no. 2818, April 12, 1780.
67. Munroe, *History of Delaware County*, p. 79. The copy of Priest's narrative, *The Captivity and Sufferings of Gen. Freegift Patchin . . .*, in the New York Public Library is endorsed: "As far as can be traced only 3 perfect copies exist."
68. Munroe, *History of Delaware County*, p. 79.
69. Haldimand Transcripts, B. 104, p. 146, Haldimand to Butler, July 24, 1780.
70. Stone, *Life of Brant*, II, p. 80.
71. Haldimand Transcripts, B. 109, p. 92.
72. Hastings, ed., *Clinton Papers*, no. 3170, Lewis R. Morris to Clinton, Aug. 24, 1780.
73. Almon, ed., *The Remembrancer . . . for 1781*, pt. I, p. 81, "Extract of a Letter from Gen. Haldimand . . . to Lord Germain," Oct. 25, 1780.
74. *Ibid.*, "for 1779" (vol VII), p. 51.
75. Stone, *Life of Brant*, I, p. xvi.
76. *Ibid.*, p. xvifn.
77. Monroe, *History of Delaware County*, p. 77.
78. Gould, *History of Delaware County*, p. 80.
79. Haldimand Transcripts, B. 158, pp. 170–78, Sir John Johnson to Haldimand, Oct. 31, 1780.
80. P.R.O., AO 12/32; Memorial of Thomas McMicking, May 12, 1788, AO 13/91, claim of same, Sept. 18, 1784; McMicking Papers in possession of Miss Beatrice Dennis, Stamford, Ontario.
81. McMicking Papers.
82. New York Public Library, MSS. Division, American Loyalist Transcripts, vol. 17, p. 311, Estimate of losses of Neil McKay; pp. 317–21, Memorial of Hugh Fraser, March 25, 1786.
83. *2nd Rept. Ont. Arch.*, p. 357, Evidence on claim of John McKay.
84. Paltsits, ed., *Minutes of the Commissioners for . . . Conspiracies*, pp. 603, 613, 622.
85. McMicking Papers.
86. *Ibid.*
87. P.R.O., AO 12/32.
88. Haldimand Transcripts, B 109-1, p. 39ff.
89. Stone, *Life of Brant*, II, pp. 161-62.
90. *Ibid.*, p. 186.
91. "Captain Tice's Journal from 5th October 1781" quoted in Ernest Green, "Gilbert Tice, U.E.," *Ontario Historical Society, Papers and Records*, vol. XXI (1924), p. 196.
92. *Ibid.*
93. Stone, *Life of Brant*, II, p. 191fn.
94. Green, "Tice's Journal," p. 196.
95. Halsey, *The Old New York Frontier*, p. 305; Historical marker at site on New York route no. 10.
96. J. J. Talman, ed., *Loyalist Narratives from Upper Canada* (Champlain Society Publication no. XXVII, Toronto, 1946), pp. 56–61, "Journal of Adam Crysler."

CHAPTER SIX

1. George Heriot, *Analyses of New Voyages and Travels* (London, 1807), p. 74.
2. P.A.C., Haldimand Transcripts, B. 99, p. 9, Accounts of Taylor and Duffin, Feb. 2, 1779.
3. *Ibid.*, pp. 179-82, "Memorandum relative to the Trade in ye Upper Country," undated.
4. E. A. Benians, ed., *A Journal by Thomas Hughes for his amusement, & designed only for his perusal by the time he attains the age of 50 if he lives so long (1778-89)* (Cambridge University Press, 1947), p. 151.
5. Christian Schultz, *Travels on an inland voyage . . . 1807 & 1808 . . .* (2 vols., New York, 1810), I, p. 92.
6. Horatio Rogers, ed., *James Murray Hadden's Journal kept in Canada and upon Burgoyne's campaign* (Albany, 1884), p. 260fn.
7. Haldimand Transcripts, B. 96-1, p. 229, Bolton to Haldimand, Nov. 11, 1778.
8. Mrs. Anne Grant, *Memoirs of an American Lady: with sketches of the manners and scenery in America, as they existed previous to the revolution* (2 vols., London, 1808), II, p. 134.
9. *Ibid.*, pp. 120-38.
10. Haldimand Transcripts, B. 62, p. 259-60, Haldimand to Bolton, Oct. 1, 1778.
11. P.A.C., Colonial Office Records, M.G. 11, "Q" ser., 16-2, pp. 563-68, Haldimand to Lord Germain, Sept. 25, 1779.
12. Haldimand Transcripts, B. 62, pp. 259-60, Haldimand to Bolton, Oct. 7, 1778.
13. *Ibid.*, B. 96-1, p. 163, Haldimand to Bolton, April 8, 1779.
14. John Maude, *Visit to the Falls of Niagara in 1800* (London, 1826), p. 44.
15. O. Turner, *Pioneer History of the Holland Purchase of Western New York . . .* (Buffalo, 1849), p. 229.
16. Haldimand Transcripts, B. 96-1, pp. 248-50, Bolton to Haldimand, March 4, 1779.
17. *Ibid.*
18. *Ibid.*, B. 104, p. 28, Haldimand to Bolton, June 7, 1779.
19. Dates through the courtesy of Mr. Frederick Secord, Chicago, who is preparing a genealogy of the Secord-Goring families. These dates were procured from church records in New Rochelle and New York City and have been given preference over those mentioned in the reference given in note no. 21 with which they disagree.
20. *2nd Report Ontario Archives* (1904), p. 989, Evidence on claim of Solomon Secord.
21. Haldimand Transcripts, B. 105, p. 295A, "Return of Persons under the Description of Loyalists . . . Being Farmers Settled at This Post, Niagara 1st Dec[r] 1783."
22. P.A.C., William Merritt Papers, vol. 19, Goring Papers, Goring to Captain Robinson, Aug. 4, 1779.
23. Petition of Peter Secord, July 1, 1794, quoted in *Ontario Historical Society, Papers and Records*, vol. XXIV (1927), pp. 119-20.
24. Ontario Archives, Canniff Papers, Notes on the Goring Family, Goring to James Crespel, Sept. 23, 1779.
25. *Ibid.*, James Clark to Goring, June 10, 1779.
26. *Ibid.*, Alexander Cunningham to Goring, June 1, 1778.
27. *Ibid.*, Aug. 2, 1778.
28. *Ibid.*, Clunes to Goring, March 26, 1779.
29. William Merritt Papers, vol. 19, Goring Papers, Warren to Goring, Dec. 9, 1779.
30. *Ibid.*, Jan. 23, 1780.
31. Francis W. Halsey, *The Old New York Frontier* (New York, 1901), p. 283; Ernest Cruikshank, *The Story of Butler's Rangers* (Welland, 1893), p. 78.
32. William Merritt Papers, vol. 19, Goring Papers, Goring to Street, March 15, 1780.
33. *Ibid.*, Oct. 4, 1779.
34. Canniff Papers, Notes on the Goring Family, Hamilton to Goring, May 1, 1780.
35. Haldimand Transcripts, B. 109, p. 78.
36. D. W. Smith's *Map of Upper Canada* (London, 1800).
37. Haldimand Transcripts, B. 92-2, pp. 188-91; B. 104, p. 360.
38. *Ibid.*, B. 96-2, pp. 147-52, Haldimand to Bolton, July 13, 1780.
39. Toronto Public Library, MSS. Collection, Minutes of the Court of Common Pleas, District of Nassau, Oct. 23, 1792, *Street* v. *Pilkington*, testimony of Colonel Butler.
40. Haldimand Transcripts, B. 105, pp. 100-12.
41. *Ibid.*, B. 96-2, pp. 145-47, Haldimand to Bolton, July 7, 1780.
42. Canniff Papers, Fragment of a diary.
43. Petition of Peter Secord, July 1, 1794, pp. 119-20.
44. *19th Report Ontario Archives* (1931), Land Book B, p. 92.
45. Haldimand Transcripts, B. 105, pp. 233-34, Butler to Matthews, Dec. 7, 1780.
46. *Ibid.*
47. *Ibid.*

48. *Ibid.*, p. 217, Butler to Matthews, July 24, 1780.
49. *Ibid.*, p. 264, Butler to Matthews, Dec. 7, 1780.
50. *Ibid.*, pp. 259-60, Matthews to Butler, April 12, 1781.
51. *Ibid.*, B. 107, pp. 166-67, Haldimand to Johnson, Sept. 29, 1780.
52. *Ibid.*, pp. 224-25, Johnson to Haldimand, May 9, 1781.
53. *Ibid.*, B. 101, p. 72, Powell to Haldimand, May 20, 1781.
54. *Ibid.*, B. 105, p. 264, Walter Butler to Matthews, May 30, 1781.
55. *Ibid.*, B. 147, p. 35. Haldimand to Sir Henry Clinton, Sept. 29, 1781.
56. *Ibid.*, B. 105, pp. 300-3, Butler to Matthews, Dec. 1, 1781.
57. *Ibid.*
58. P.A.C., A.O. 1, bundle 2532, roll 666, p. 40.
59. R. Janet Powell, *Annals of the Forty*, no. 7 (Grimsby Historical Society, 1956), pp. 53-55.
60. Haldimand Transcripts, B. 105, p. 380, Return of Persons resident at Niagara Dec. 1, 1783.
61. *Ibid.*, B. 169, p. 1, A Survey of the Settlement at Niagara August 25, 1782.
62. Robert Rogers, *A Concise Account of North America . . .* (London, 1765), p. 174.
63. Patrick Campbell, *Travels in the Interior Inhabited Parts of North America in the Years 1791 and 1792* (Edinburgh, 1793), p. 180.
64. Upper Canada Land Petitions, 1797, T 2, no. 46. On March 27, 1797, Archibald Thomson deposed that land bounded by the north rim of the Whirlpool "was given to him . . . in the year 1782—by Gen¹ Powell, then Comd^t at Niagara, and he was marked in the Garrison Books by Major Sheen, as a Farmer."
65. *Ibid.*, B. 169, p. 1, A Survey of the Settlement at Niagara, August 25, 1782.
66. *Ibid.*, B. 103, pp. 484-85.
67. *Ibid.*, B. 169, p. 1, A Survey of the Settlement at Niagara, August 25, 1782.
68. Turner, *Pioneer History of the Holland Purchase*, p. 264.
69. *Ibid.*, p. 265.
70. Haldimand Transcripts, B. 102, pp. 99-100, Powell to Haldimand, June 27, 1782.
71. *Ibid.*, B. 169, p. 135, "An account of Surveying and Expences Done by Allan McDonell at Niagara for Government, April 24, 1783."
72. P.A.C., Brit Mus. Add. MSS., vol. 21, 829, ff 71-72, B. 169, p. 137.
73. Minutes of the Court of Common Pleas, Oct. 23, 1792, *Street* v. *Pilkington*, testimony of Elijah Phelps, witness.
74. McMicking Papers in possession of Miss Beatrice Dennis, Stamford, Ontario.
75. The *Royal George*, 26 guns, built at St. Johns, was stationed throughout the war on Lake Champlain not on Lake George (Ira Allen, *The Natural and Political History of the State of Vermont* (London, 1798), p. 170; Historical Section of the General Staff, ed., *A History of the Organization, Development and Service of the Military and Naval Forces of Canada from the Peace of Paris in 1763 to the Present Time*, vol. III (n.d.), p. 85).
76. McMicking Papers.
77. Haldimand Transcripts, B. 96-2, pp. 188-91.
78. *Ibid.*, B. 105, p. 321, Butler to Matthews, June 12, 1782.
79. *Ibid.*, pp. 328-30, Matthews to Butler, July 9, 1782.
80. *Ibid.*, p. 236, Butler to Matthews, Sept. 2, 1782.
81. *Ibid.*, B. 103, pp. 53-54, Maclean to Haldimand, March 29, 1783.
82. *Ibid.*, p. 445, De Peyster to Haldimand, July 15, 1784.
83. Commission of Daniel Servos in the Museum at Fort George, Niagara-on-the-Lake, Ontario.
84. Haldimand Transcripts, B. 103, p. 182, Maclean to Haldimand, May 18, 1783.
85. *Ibid.*, p. 131, Maclean to Haldimand, May 3, 1783.
86. *Ibid.*, B. 105, pp. 354-56, Butler to Matthews, March 31, 1783.
87. *Ibid.*, B. 103, pp. 492-93, Memorial of the Farmers at Niagara to Lt. Col. Butler, 1783.
88. *Ibid.*, B. 104, p. 421, Haldimand to Maclean, May 25, 1783.
89. *New-York Gazette and the weekly mercury*, June 2, 1783, *et seq.*
90. Monroe, *History of Delaware County*, p. 234.
91. New York Public Library, Rare Book Room, Josiah Priest, *The Captivity and Sufferings of Gen. Freegift Patchin of Blenheim, Schoharie County, among the Indians, under Brant, the noted chief, during the Border Warfare in the time of the American Revolution* (Albany, 1833), p. 30.
92. Ontario Archives, W. D. Reid's Data on the United Empire Loyalists under "Beacroft."
93. Haldimand Transcripts, B. 105, p. 408.

CHAPTER SEVEN

1. E. A. Benians, ed., *A Journal by Thomas Hughes for his amusement, & designed only for his perusal by the time he attains the age of 50 if he lives so long (1778–89)* (Cambridge University Press, 1947), p. 54.
2. *New-York Gazette and the weekly mercury*, Jan. 12, 1778.
3. Benians, ed., Hughes' *Journal*, p. 54.
4. *Ibid.*, p. 55.
5. P.A.C., M.G. 14, B. 11, 14, Port Roseway Associates, 1782–83, Original Minute Book.
6. P.A.C., Upper Canada Land Petitions 1793–1795, C 1, no. 96, March 25, 1793.
7. William M. McBean, *Biographical Register of St. Andrew's Society in the State of New York* (New York, 1922), pp. 69–70.
8. E. B. O'Callaghan, ed., *Calendar of Historical Manuscripts relating to the War of the Revolution, in the office of the Secretary of State, Albany, N.Y.* (2 vols., Albany, 1868), I, p. 315.
9. New York Historical Society, MSS. Division, Deposition of Normand Tolmie, March 21, 1766.
10. O'Callaghan, ed., *Calendar of Historical Manuscripts*, I, pp. 340–41.
11. *2nd Report Ontario Archives* (1904), p. 150, Evidence on claim of Alexander Robertson.
12. *Ibid.*, p. 139, Evidence on claim of Charles Bruff.
13. *New-York Gazette and the weekly mercury*, June 29, 1778.
14. *Ibid.*
15. *The Papers of Sir William Johnson* (10 vols., Albany, 1920–51), III, map facing p. 32.
16. *Ibid.*, VII, p. 359; IX, map facing p. 323.
17. P.R.O., Great Britain, AO 12/23.
18. Mrs. Martha J. Lamb and Mrs. Burton Harrison, *History of the City of New York: Its Origin, Rise and Progress* (3 vols., New York, 1880), II, p. 752.
19. R. Janet Powell, *Annals of the Forty*, no. 6 (Grimsby Historical Society, 1955), p. 6. This is the most authentic of all versions of the story according to John Coleman who published the results of his extensive research in "Robert Land and some Frontier Skirmishes," *Ontario History*, vol. XLVIII, no. 2 (1956), pp. 47–100.
20. Colonial Williamsburg (Williamsburg, Va.) and New York Public Library photostatic copies of British Headquarters (Carleton) Papers, May 23, 1779.
21. Benians, ed., Hughes' *Journal*, p. 101.
22. *New York Genealogical and Biographical Record*, vol. LXVIII (1937), cited in Coleman, "Robert Land," p. 60.
23. Hugh Hastings, ed., *Public Papers of George Clinton, First Governor of New York, 1777–1795* (8 vols., Albany, 1899–1904), no. 2603.
24. P.A.C., Haldimand Transcripts, B. 96-1, pp. 251–53, Bolton to Haldimand, March 5, 1779.
25. *Ibid.*, B. 100, p. 190, Butler to Bolton June 18, 1779.
26. Hastings, ed., *Clinton Papers*, no. 2656.
27. Haldimand Transcripts, B. 159, p. 351, Memorial of John and Alexander Macdonell, Feb. 21, 1780.
28. Hastings, ed., *Clinton Papers*, no. 2656.
29. *Ibid.*, no. 2555.
30. *Ibid.*, no. 2603, Allan Macdonell and Hugh Fraser to Clinton, Nov. 16, 1779.
31. Haldimand Transcripts, B. 175, p. 1, Powell to Van Schaik, Feb. 13, 1780.
32. *Ibid.*
33. *Ibid.*, p. 4, Van Schaik to Powell, Feb. 23, 1780.
34. Powell to Van Schaik, Sept. 22, 1780, quoted in William L. Stone, *Life of Joseph Brant–Thayendanegea including the Indian Wars of the American Revolution* (2 vols., Cooperstown, N.Y., 1845), II, p. 130.
35. Haldimand Transcripts, B. 159, p. 351, Memorial of John and Alexander Macdonell, Feb. 21, 1780.
36. *Ibid.*, B. 73, p. 54, John Macdonell to Captain Matthews, March 20, 1780.
37. *New-York Gazette and the weekly mercury*, Aug. 10, 1778.
38. Kenneth Holcomb Dunshee, *As You Pass By* (New York, 1952), p. 39.
39. *Ibid.*, p. 108.
40. *New-York Gazette and the weekly mercury*, Aug. 24, 1778.
41. *Ibid.*, March 2, 1779.
42. *Ibid.*, Feb. 19, 1783.
43. *Ibid.*, advertising in issues 1778 through 1783.
44. *Ibid.*
45. Thomas Jones, *History of New York during the Revolution* (2 vols., New York, 1879), I, p. 321.

46. Major-General Pattison to Lord Germain, Feb. 22, 1780, quoted in J. Almon, ed., *The Remembrancer, or Impartial Repository of Political Events for 1780* (vol. IX), p. 367.
47. *Ibid.*
48. *New-York Gazette and the weekly mercury*, July 3, 1780.
49. Upper Canada Land Petitions, 1797, C 3, no. 63A, May 1, 1797.
50. Jones, *History of New York*, I, p. 323.
51. *Ibid.*
52. Upper Canada Land Petitions 1797, C 3, no. 63A, May 1, 1797.
53. *New-York Gazette and the weekly mercury*, Sept. 27, 1779.
54. *Ibid.*, March 26, 1783.
55. *Ibid.*, May 8, 1780.
56. *Ibid.*, May 31. 1779.
57. *Royal Gazette*, No. 14, 1778.
58. *Ibid.*, Feb. 16, 1778.
59. *Ibid.*, June 15, 1778.
60. *Ibid.*, March 18, 1781.
61. *Ibid.*, May 2, 1778.
62. *New-York Gazette and the weekly mercury*, advertising in issues 1778 through 1783.
63. Oscar T. Barck, *New York City during the War for Independence with Special Reference to the Period of British Occupation* (Columbia University Press, 1931), p. 119.
64. Port Roseway Associates' Minute Book, p. 6.
65. *2nd Rept. Ont Arch.*, pp. 50–51, Evidence on the claim of Joseph Durfee.
66. *Ibid.*, p. 140, Evidence on the claim of Edward Bowlby.
67. Port Roseway Associates' Minute Book, p. 31.
68. *Ibid.*, pp. 59–64.
69. New York Public Library, MSS Division, American Loyalist Transcripts, vol. 17, pp. 19–20, Evidence on the claim of Hugh Fraser, March 25, 1786.
70. Port Roseway Associates' Minute Book, pp. 88–89.
71. British Headquarters (Carleton) Papers, no. 7272, M. Morgann to W. Elliott, March 1783 (no day given).
72. Port Roseway Associates' Minute Book, p. 94.
73. *Ibid.*, pp. 105–6.
74. British Headquarters (Carleton) Papers, no. 7192.
75. Port Roseway Associates' Minute Book, p. 93.
76. *New-York Gazette and the weekly mercury*, March 31, 1783.
77. Port Roseway Associates' Minute Book, p. 100.
78. British Headquarters (Carleton) Papers, no. 7400, Carleton to Thomas Townshend, April 12, 1783.
79. Esther Clark Wright, *The Loyalists of New Brunswick* (Fredericton, N.B., 1955), p. 299.
80. British Headquarters (Carleton) Papers, no. 9728.

CHAPTER EIGHT

1. *Report on Canadian Archives, 1884,* note C, pp. xxvii–lix, Report on Nova Scotia by Col. Robert Morse, R.E., 1784, p. xxxv.
2. W. O. Raymond, "The Founding of Shelburne," *New Brunswick Historical Society Collections*, no. 8 (St. John, N.B., 1909), p. 211.
3. *Ibid.*
4. P.A.N.S., White Collection of MSS., no. 210, James Courtney to Archibald Cunningham, July 1, 1783.
5. Raymond, "Founding of Shelburne," p. 219fn. The minister referred to was Reverend William Black, a Methodist.
6. Transcription of Simeon Perkins' Diary at Perkins House, Liverpool, Nova Scotia.
7. Colonial Williamsburg (Williamsburg, Va.) and New York Public Library, photostatic copies of British Headquarters (Carleton) Papers, no. 8526, Parr to Carleton, July 25, 1783.
8. Ward Chipman to Edward Winslow, Nov. 29, 1783, quoted in Esther Clark Wright, *The Loyalists of New Brunswick* (Fredericton, N.B., 1955), p. 67.
9. White Collection, no. 291.
10. *New-York Gazette and the weekly mercury*, Aug. 25, 1783.
11. Parr to Lord Sidney, May 12, 1784, quoted in Raymond, "Founding of Shelburne," p. 229.
12. *New-York Gazette and the weekly mercury*, Sept. 1, 1783.
13. J. Almon, *The Remembrancer, or Impartial Repository of Political Events for 1784*, pt. I, p. 375.

14. J. R. Campbell, *A History of the County of Yarmouth, Nova Scotia* (St. John, N.B., 1876), p. 87.
15. Shelburne Court House Records at Shelburne, Deed Book 1, pp. 45–48.
16. *Ibid.*, pp. 228–29.
17. P.A.N.S., Memorial of George Thomas and 14 others, April 5, 1784; Crown Grant of Lot 6, Mason's Division, to George Chisholm, April 24, 1784.
18. Nova Scotia, Department of Lands and Forests, Book 13, p. 66, Grant dated May 25, 1784, to Andrew Hogarth and others including Kenneth McKenzie, Charles Oliver Bruff, Joseph Pynchon, Hugh Fraser, Edward Bowlby, and other grantees of fifty-acre lots in Mason's Division.
19. Shelburne Court House Records, Deed Book 4, p. 113; New York Public Library, MSS. Division, Shelburne Tax Book, 1786–87.
20. Shelburne Historical Society MSS., Canon Morris, "Shelburne" read before the Nova Scotia Historical Society, undated.
21. P.A.C., Map Division, B 900-1702, [J. B. L. Franquelin], Carte de L'Acadie . . . 1702.
22. *Rept. Can. Arch., 1884*, Morse's Report, p. xxxvii.
23. *Report of the Public Archives of Nova Scotia, 1947*, App. C, "MS. History and description and state of the Southern and Western townships of Nova Scotia in 1795 by the Rev. James Munro, late of Antigonish."
24. *Rept. Can. Arch., 1884*, Morse's Report, p. xxvii.
25. Shelburne Court House Records, Deed Book 1, p. 228.
26. Raymond, "Founding of Shelburne," pp. 259, 268.
27. Robert Rogers, *A Concise Account of North America* (London, 1765), p. 19.
28. Perkins' Diary.
29. *The Present State of Nova Scotia: with a Brief Account of Canada and British Islands on the Coast of North America* (Edinburgh, 1787), quoted in G. S. Brown, *Yarmouth, N.S.* (Boston, 1888), p. 134.
30. P.A.N.S., Special Sessions of Shelburne, N.S., May 26, 1785.
31. P.A.N.S., Minutes of the Court of Quarter Sessions, Shelburne District, April 10, 1787.
32. *Rept. Can. Arch., 1884*, Morse's Report, p. xxvii.
33. *Ibid.*
34. *Rept. P.A.N.S., 1947*, Rev. Munro's MS.
35. Raymond, "Founding of Shelburne," p. 268.
36. New York Historical Society, Muster Roll of Captain John Spiers' Company of Loyalists mustered at Shelburne, July 1784.
37. P.A.N.S., Colonial Correspondence, Nova Scotia, vol. 16, p. 280, Memorial of Magistrates of Shelburne, Sept. 8, 1785.
38. *Shorter Oxford Dictionary* (3rd ed., London, 1947). This definition dates back to 1623.
39. *Rept. P.A.N.S., 1947*, Rev. Munro's MS.
40. Shelburne Court House Records, Deed Book 1, p. 541.
41. Raymond, "Founding of Shelburne," p. 269.
42. *The Present State of Nova Scotia*, in Brown, *Yarmouth*.
43. Shelburne Court House Records, Minutes of the Court of Quarter Sessions, Shelburne District, April 11, 15 and 22, 1785.
44. *Ibid.*, March 28, 1786.
45. *Ibid.*, Sept. 6, 1786.
46. Shelburne Tax Book, 1786–87.
47. Perkins' Diary, Dec. 4, 1788.
48. Shelburne Court House Records, Minutes of the Court of Quarter Sessions, Shelburne District, April 19, 1784.
49. *Rept. P.A.N.S., 1947*, Rev. Munro's MS.
50. *Ibid.*
51. *Ibid.*
52. *Rept. Can. Arch, 1884*, Morse's Report, p. xxviii.
53. White Collection, no. 300, Gideon White to Thomas Melish, Aug. 3, 1784.
54. Raymond, "Founding of Shelburne," p. 268.
55. *Ibid.*, p. 269.
56. *Ibid.*, pp. 262–63.
57. *Royal American Gazette*, Jan. 24, 1785.
58. Raymond, "Founding of Shelburne," Jan. 19, 1784.
59. Shelburne Court House Records, Special Sessions of Shelburne, N.S., July 14, 1785, tavern licence granted to Alexander Fraser; Assessment Roll, Town and County, Shelburne, 1787, Alex. Fraser, Tavern Keeper.
60. Shelburne Court House Records, Minutes of the Court of Quarter Sessions, Nov. 4, 1784.
61. Shelburne Tax Book, 1786–87
62. *Royal American Gazette*, Feb. 24, 1785.
63. P.A.N.S., Dorchester Collection, no. 169, Memorial of Mr. Hugh Fraser, Nov. 6, 1783.

64. Perkins' Diary.
65. P.A.C., M.G. 21, Brit. Mus. Add. MSS., 19071, fo. 220, Petition of the Loyalists of the Church of Scotland at Shelburne, Sept. 3, 1788.
66. Shelburne Court House Records, Special Sessions, Book A, p. 195.
67. P.R.O., Great Britain, AO 12/23.
68. *Ibid.*, AO 13/15.
69. *Ibid.*
70. *Ibid.*
71. P.A.C., Upper Canada Land Petitions, 1793-1795, C 1, no. 96, March 25, 1793.
72. Shelburne Tax Book, 1786-87.
73. *Royal American Gazette*, Jan. 24, 1785.
74. *Port Roseway Gazetteer and Shelburne Advertiser*, Aug. 11, 1785.
75. Shelburne Court House Records, Minutes of the Court of Quarter Sessions, Shelburne District, April 22, 1784.
76. P.A.C., Colonial Office Records, Nova Scotia, A 116, pp. 191-201, Petition of Merchants, Owners of Shipping, and Principal Inhabitants of the Town and Port of Shelburne in His Majesty's Province of Nova Scotia, June 16, 1791; Colonel Thomas Dundas quoted in *2nd Report Ontario Archives* (1904), p. 21; *Rept. P.A.N.S., 1947*, Rev. Munro's MS.
77. Shelburne Court House Records, Minutes of the Court of Quarter Sessions, July 3, 1790.
78. *Ibid.*
79. White Collection, nos. 552, 560.
80. *Rept. P.A.N.S., 1947*, Rev. Munro's MS.
81. *Ibid.*
82. J. Plimsoll Edwards, "Shelburne That Was and Is Not," *Dalhousie Review*, vol. II, no. 2 (July 1922), p. 325.
83. *Rept. P.A.N.S., 1947*, Rev. Munro's MS.
84. Petition of Merchants, June 16, 1791.
85. P.A.C., M.G. 14, B 11, 14, Port Roseway Associates 1782-83, Original Minute Book, pp. 58-64, Pynchon to Committee, Jan. 23, 1783.
86. *Rept. Can. Arch., 1884*, Morse's Report, p. xxxvii.
87. Port Roseway Associates' Minute Book, Pynchon to Committee, Jan 23, 1783.
88. Dorothy Dumbrille, *Up and Down the Glens* (Toronto, 1954), p. 7.
89. *2nd Rept. Ont. Arch.*, p. 1056, Evidence on claim of Philip Crislor [sic].
90. *Ibid.*, p. 1108, Evidence on claim of Jacob Stanburner [sic].
91. *Ibid.*
92. A. G. Morice, "A Canadian Pioneer: Spanish John," *Canadian Historical Review*, vol. X (1929), pp. 212-35.
93. P.A.N.S., Shelburne Records, 1766-1868, Burials (Anglican) by Rev. Dr. Walter.
94. Upper Canada Land Petitions, 1793-1795, C 1, no. 96, March 25, 1793.
95. Shelburne Court House Records, Deed Book 4, p. 52.
96. Document formerly in the possession of the late Mrs. Arthur Chisholm, Oakville, Ontario.
97. *Rept. Can. Arch., 1884*, Morse's Report, p. xxxvii.
98. White Collection, no. 500, June 30, 1789.

CHAPTER NINE

1. P.A.C., Haldimand Transcripts, B. 105, p. 408, Return of the Rise and Progress of a Settlement of Loyalists on the west side of the River Niagara, April 18, 1784.
2. E. A. Cruikshank, ed., *The Correspondence of Lieut-Governor John Graves Simcoe, with allied documents relating to his administration of the government of Upper Canada* (5 vols., Toronto, 1923-31), III, p. 191, "Letter from a gentleman to his friend . . .," Nov. 20, 1794.
3. George Heriot, *Analyses of New Voyages and Travels* (London, 1807), pp. 65-66.
4. Patrick Campbell, *Travels in the Interior Inhabited Parts of North America in the Years 1791 and 1792* (Edinburgh, 1793), p. 223; O. Turner, *Pioneer History of the Holland Purchase of Western New York* (Buffalo, 1849), p. 555.
5. Haldimand Transcripts, B. 105, p. 408, Return of Loyalists, April 18, 1784.
6. "Places Pointed Out for Erecting Mills," 1785, *Niagara Historical Society Publication*, no. 39 (n.d.), p. 84.
7. P.A.C., Upper Canada Land Petitions, 1797, T 2, no. 76, March 27, 1797.
8. *Ibid.*
9. Thomas Dundas to the Duke of Clarence, 1788, quoted in *2nd Report Ontario Archives* (1904), p. 23.
10. Ernest Green, "Twp. no. 2—Mount Dorchester—Stamford," *Ontario Historical Society, Papers and Records*, vol. XXV (1929), p. 260, Plan of Twp. no. 2, n.d.

11. *The Loyalist* (Niagara), March 14, 1829, obituary notice of Peter Thomson, Stamford.
12. Upper Canada Land Petitions, 1791–1796, B 1, no. 95, July 3, 1795.
13. United States Department of the Interior, Geographical Survey, *Niagara River and Vicinity, 1901* (reprinted 1923).
14. Upper Canada Land Petitions, 1791–1796, B 1, no. 78, Petition of John Burch, March 1793.
15. *Report on Canadian Archives, 1886*, p. ccxxvi. Journal of Capt. Enys, 28th Regiment, 1787.
16. Christian Schultz, *Travels on an Inland Voyage . . . 1807 & 1808* (2 vols., New York, 1810), I, p. 74.
17. Green, "Twp. no. 2—Mount Dorchester—Stamford," p. 319.
18. *Quebec Gazette*, June 29, 1786.
19. Cruikshank, ed., *Simcoe Correspondence*, I, p. 234, Richard Cartwright Jr., "Report on the Subject of Marriage . . .," Oct. 12, 1792.
20. P.R.O., Great Britain, AO 13/15.
21. *Ibid.*
22. Fletcher data through the courtesy of Mrs. Jessie H. Finch, Trumansburg, New York, a descendant of Alexander and compiler of a Fletcher genealogy. According to a tradition of Catherine's descendants which research has failed to verify or disprove one of her sisters was the wife of the Duke of Argyll and another married a MacNab, relative of Sir Allan MacNab of Dundurn Castle, Hamilton, Ontario. A third sister was Mrs. MacGlashan and a fourth Mrs. McQueen.
23. McMicking Papers, courtesy of Miss Beatrice Dennis, Stamford, Ontario.
24. Green, "Twp. no. 2—Mount Dorchester—Stamford," p. 260, Plan of Twp. no. 2.
25. Information received from Mrs. Calvin Roberts, Stamford, Ontario, a descendant.
26. Richard Thomson to his three brothers, Aug. 18, 1786, Thomson Papers, through the courtesy of Mrs. Calvin Roberts.
27. Turner, *Pioneer History of the Holland Purchase*, pp. 310–13.
28. Cruikshank, ed., *Simcoe Correspondence*, III, p. 191.
29. Turner, *Pioneer History of the Holland Purchase*, p. 490.
30. Cruikshank, ed., *Simcoe Correspondence*, III, p. 191.
31. McMicking Papers.
32. *Ibid.*
33. *Ibid.*
34. Haldimand Transcripts, B. 96-2, pp. 265–66, Petition of Merchants at Niagara, Aug 21, 1783.
35. P.R.O., AO 13/13.
36. *Ibid.*, AO 13/11, 13/16, 13/15.
37. *Ibid.*, AO 12/32.
38. *Ibid.*, AO 12/64.
39. *2nd Rept. Ont. Arch.* (1904), pp. 979–1010.
40. *Ibid.*, p. 223.
41. *Ibid.*, p. 21.
42. *Ibid.*
43. Alexander Flick, *Loyalism in New York* (New York, 1901), p. 167.
44. Augustus Jones' renumbering of lots in townships nos. 1 and 2 prevailed and the locations confirmed to the Scots by letters patent from the Crown are as follows:

Grantor	Grantee	Description	Date of patent
Township no. 2 (Mount Dorchester, Stamford)			
Crown	Thomas McMicking	Lots 1, 2	1798
„	Archibald Thomson	„ 19, 20	1802
„	James Park	„ 21, 40	1798
„	John Thomson	„ 58, 41	1802
„	John Chisholm	„ 75	1802
"Gore between Newark and Stamford" or "Gore of Stamford"			
Crown	Daniel Rose	Lot 1	1798
Township no. 1 (Newark, Niagara)			
Crown	Daniel Rose	„ 1	1798
„	John Chisholm	„ 2	1798

John Chisholm's land transactions, of which few records have been found, have proved difficult to resolve. Though he was granted and secured patent to lot no. 75 and the Broken Front along the gorge at the mouth of Muddy Run in township no. 2 there is ample proof that his place of residence for some years was his original location below the Mountain, lot no. 7, township no. 1, first called West Niagara, then Newark, and finally Niagara Township. (See Ontario Archives, Crown Lands Papers, Schedule of Loyalists *ca.* 1785–86; Schedule of Nassau no. 3, Twp. no. 1, p. 1.) This land extends from Dee Road, the northern border of the village of Queenston, to a line running back from the river somewhat north of the War Memorial on the Niagara Parkway. The gully cut by a stream is referred to in a contemporary document as "the deep Hollow at John Chisholm's." (Niagara-on-the-Lake Museum, Scrapbook of Letters relating to Niagara arranged by Mrs. H. Thompson, p. 5, "Memorandum respecting the Reserve at Niagara, June 11, 1787.) Chisholm owned lot no. 75 until he sold it to John Fralick on June 28, 1806. The additional lands granted as their families increased were in scattered locations throughout the province, but it was on their grants as shown above that the Scots lived out their lives (Registry offices for Lincoln and Welland counties).

45. Ontario Archives, Niagara Township Papers, lots nos. 42–45, Memorial of David Secord, June 21, 1794.
46. Toronto Public Library, MSS. Collection, Minutes of the Court of Common Pleas and General Quarter Sessions of the Peace, District of Nassau, 1789–93.
47. Upper Canada Land Petitions, 1797, T 2, no. 76, Arch^d Thompson's information, March 27, 1797.
48. *Ibid.*
49. W. H. Smith, *Canada: Past, Present and Future* (2 vols., Toronto, 1852), I, p. 205.
50. John Ross Robertson, ed., *The Diary of Mrs. John Graves Simcoe* (Toronto, 1911), p. 139.
51. McMicking Papers.
52. Ontario Archives, Canniff Papers, Notes on the Goring Family, Fragment of a Diary, June 17, 1789.
53. McMicking Papers.
54. Patrick Campbell, *Travels*, pp. 147–48.
55. P.A.C., Quebec Land Book, R.G. 1, L 1, vol. 18, Minutes of the Executive Council, Province of Quebec, Nov. 9, 1789.
56. Ontario Archives, United Empire Loyalist List.
57. *3rd Rept. Ont. Arch.* (1905), p. 299, Minutes of Land Board, District of Nassau.
58. Turner, *Pioneer History of the Holland Purchase*, p. 313.
59. Crown Lands Papers, District of Nassau Letter Book no. 5, pp. 35–38, Surveyor-General to Augustus Jones, Feb. 22, 1791.
60. Ontario Archives, Stamford Township Papers, lot no. 44, Certificate of Land Board, District of Nassau, April 12, 1792.
61. *Ibid.*
62. Thomson Papers, Richard Thomson to John Thomson, Oct. 23, 1793.
63. Petition of John Dun, in *Ontario Historical Society, Papers and Records*, vol. XXIV (1927), p. 57.
64. Knox College, Toronto, Photostat copy of Subscription List, Oct. 1, 1794, Stamford Presbyterian Church.
65. P.A.C., Q 278, pp. 133–35.
66. Ontario, Provincial Museum, *Thirty-fifth Annual Archaeological Report* (1924–25), pp. 81–83, Duke of Northumberland to Joseph Brant, Sept. 3, 1791.
67. Ernest Green, "The Niagara Portage Road," *Ontario Historical Society, Papers and Records*, vol. XXIII (1926), p. 260.
68. *13th Rept. Ont. Arch.* (1916), La Rochefoucault-Liancourt's Travels in Canada, 1795, p. 16.
69. Cruikshank, *Simcoe Correspondence*, III, p. 191.
70. P.A.C., Lord Selkirk's Diary, Nov. 20, 1803.
71. D. B. Read, *The Life and Times of Gen. John Graves Simcoe* (Toronto, 1890).
72. *Rivington's New-York Gazetteer*, Nov. 25, 1773.
73. Robertson, ed., *Mrs. Simcoe Diary*, p. 158.
74. *Ibid.*, p. 172.
75. *Ibid*, p. 307.
76. Minutes of the Court of Common Pleas, District of Nassau, Jan. 13, 1789.
77. *Ibid.*, Jan. 15, 1789.
78. Canniff Papers, Notes on the Goring Family, Fragment of a Diary, Sept. 7, 1789.
79. *Ibid.*, March 17–May 10, 1790.
80. *Niagara Historical Society Publication*, no. 36 (n.d.), pp. 61–62.
81. Thomson Papers, "James Thomson jr's Book, 1798."
82. P.A.C., William Merritt Papers, Goring Papers, "Statement of Fact of business done for the late Hon^{le} Robert Hamilton esq by Fra^s Goring," no date.
83. *Upper Canada Gazette*, Aug. 8, 1793.
84. Ernest Green, "Twp. No. 2," p. 268.

85. Cruikshank, ed., *Simcoe Correspondence*, I, p. 24, Return of Nassau Militia, May 2, 1791.
86. Ontario Archives, Journal of William Chewett, Deputy Provincial Surveyor, 1792–95, p. 20, July 10, 1792.
87. Ontario Archives, Thomas McMicking's Commission as ensign, Oct. 27, 1788.
88. Cruikshank, ed., *Simcoe Correspondence*, II, pp. 342–43.
89. *Upper Canada Gazette*, July 10, 1794, "Commissions signed by the Lieutenant of the County of Lincoln . . ., July 28, 1794."
90. Upper Canada Land Petitions, R 1, no. 57, July 8, 1795 (R.G. 1, L 3, vol. 423).
91. *Ibid.*, T 2, no. 12, Aug. 15, 1796.
92. Ontario, Department of Lands and Forests, Surveys Division, Plan no. 1037, "An accurate Plan of Township no. 8, and part of Township on the N:W: side of Lake Geneva, in the District of Nassau. . . . 25 October 1791. Augustus Jones." This is East Flamborough Township (this name was conferred by Governor Simcoe in 1793, thus replacing the original name of Geneva Township), and the lands granted to the Scots over a period of time were as follows: Archibald Thomson, lot 3, concession 4; lot 11, conc. 5; lot 12, conc. 6. James Park, lot 2, conc. 3; lot 12, conc. 4; north half of lot 13, conc. 5; lot 13, conc. 9. Daniel Rose, lot 1, south half of lot 4, and lot 11, all in conc. 4; lots 11 and 13, conc. 7. John Chisholm, lot 10, conc. 5; lot 11, conc. 6. Thomas McMicking's lands were located elsewhere.
93. *19th Rept. Ont. Arch.* (1931), Land Book B, p. 118, March 31, 1797.
94. Upper Canada Land Petitions, 1793–1795, C 1, no. 96, March 25, 1793.
95. P.A.C., Upper Canada Land Book A, 1792–96, p. 111.
96. Upper Canada Land Petitions, K 3, no. 15 (R.G. 1, L 3, vol. 269).
97. Cruikshank, ed., *Simcoe Correspondence*, IV, p. 106, Plan of "Lands purchased from the Indians," no date.
98. Indenture between Dr. Robert Kerr and Charles King, July 12, 1793, King Papers in possession of Mrs. Melba Long, Burlington, Ontario.
99. Ontario, Department of Lands and Forests, Surveys Division, "Surveyors' Letters—Augustus Jones," p. 103, "Names of the Rivers, and Creeks, as they are called by the Mississagues and the meaning thereof explained in English, beginning at Niagara, and extending along the shore, by Burlington Bay," undated.
100. *Ibid.*
101. E. A. Cruikshank and A. F. Hunter, eds., *The Correspondence of the Honourable Peter Russell with allied documents relating to his administration of the government of Upper Canada during the official term of Lieut. Governor J. G. Simcoe while on leave of absence* (3 vols., Toronto, 1936), III, pp. 301–3, Russell to Hugh Hood, Feb. 7, 1800.
102. Lord Selkirk's Diary, May 29, 1804.
103. *Ibid.*
104. Robertson, ed., *Mrs. Simcoe's Diary*, p. 298.
105. Lord Selkirk's Diary, May 29, 1804.
106. Patrick Campbell, *Travels*, pp. 182–83.
107. Chisholm Papers in possession of the author.
108. Cruikshank, *Simcoe Correspondence*, IV, p. 299, Hamilton to E. B. Littlehales, June 15, 1796.
109. "I have also mentioned to your Lordship my Idea that the temporary Barracks of the Troops (and their attendant Artificers) be built by the head of the Navigation of the Rivers, whilst the Troops shall be employed in opening the different Roads of Communication should be so erected as to be converted into public Houses to become the property of the Government to be let by Auction for the purpose of Revenue" (*Ibid.*, I, p. 20, Simcoe to Lord Grenville, Feb. 10, 1791.)
110. Robertson, ed., *Mrs. Simcoe's Diary*, p. 328.
111. Cruikshank, ed., *Simcoe Correspondence*, V, p. 328, E. B. Littlehales to Hamilton, July 10, 1796. Officers of the Crown being entitled to extra lands, Chisholm petitioned for and was granted an additional 800 acres as magistrate (Upper Canada Land Petitions, 1797, C 3, no. 62, May 1, 1797; order-in-council May 9, 1797). These lands were located as follows: Haldimand Township, Northumberland County, lot 30, concession 1; Whitchurch Township, York County (now North York), lots 34 and 35, conc. 2, 400 acres (now partly within the town of Newmarket), and lot 35, conc. 3, 200 acres; Elmsley Township, Leeds County, lot 1, conc. 1, 200 acres, and the east half of lot 1, conc. 2, 100 acres ((four miles south of Smith's Falls) (Registry offices for the respective counties).

A dispute arose in the spring of 1798 between George Chisholm, Charles King, and Reverend Robert Addison, Anglican missionary at Niagara, over the ownership of the Burlington Bay tract which was amicably settled by the parties concerned (Upper Canada Land Petitions, 1797–99, C 4, no. 86, April 20, 1798; Land Book C, April 20, 1798; *Ibid.*, D, May 29, 1798).

112. P.A.C., Upper Canada Sundries, William J. Kerr to Major Hillier, Dec. 10, 1827.

113. Quoted in R. Janet Powell, *Annals of the Forty*, no. 6 (Grimsby Historical Society, 1955), p. 59.
114. Will of John Chisholm, May 10, 1831, courtesy of Mrs. Violet Chisholm Kirby, Portland, Oregon.
115. Powell, *Annals of the Forty*, no. 6, p. 59.
116. Patrick Campbell, *Travels*, pp. 190–99.
117. *Historical Sketch of the Barton Lodge No. 6, G.R.C., A.F. and A.M.* (Hamilton, 1895), p. 184.
118. *Ibid.*
119. *Upper Canada Gazette*, March 1, 1797.
120. Cruikshank, ed., *Simcoe Correspondence*, IV, pp. 120–21, Littlehales to Oliver Jaffray, March 20, 1796.
121. Cruikshank and Hunter, eds., *Russell Correspondence*, I, p. 183, David Shank to James Green, June 3, 1797
122. *Ibid.*, p. 185, Joseph Brant to Peter Russell, May 8, 1797.
123. Cruikshank, ed., *Simcoe Correspondence*, IV, p. 106, Simcoe to John Butler, Oct. 20, 1795.
124. *Ibid.*, Butler to Littlehales, Nov. 2, 1795.
125. *Indian Treaties and Surrenders* (2 vols., Ottawa, 1891), I, p. 8. Chisholm and Nelles were appointed on Aug 11, 1797. Nelles' commission, signed by Peter Russell, is in the Colonel Robert Nelles Papers in possession of Mrs. Nelles Rutherford, Grimsby, Ontario.
126. Nells Papers, Memorandum, Aug. 21, 1797.
127. Toronto Public Library, Reference Division, D. W. Smith Collection of MSS., ser. B, vol. 9, p. 183, A Purchase of Further Lands from the Missisaguas for Joseph Brant, Aug. 3, 1797.
128. Nelles Papers, Brant to Nelles, March 9, 1800.
129. Francis Hall, *Travels in Canada and the United States in 1816 and 1817* (London, 1818), p. 212.
130. D. W. Smith, *A Short Topographical Description of His Majesty's Province of Upper Canada* (London, 1799), p. 29.
131. Cruikshank and Hunter, eds., *Russell Correspondence*, II, p. v.
132. *Ibid.*, p. 135, Brant to William Claus, April 5, 1798. Brant's dissatisfaction with the treatment of his people by the British government has been covered by Harvey Chalmers and Ethel Brant Montour in *Joseph Brant: Mohawk* (Michigan State University Press, 1955).
133. Cruikshank and Hunter, eds., *Russell Correspondence*, II, p. 21, Memoir of Wm. Dummer Powell, Nov. 20, 1797.
134. Order-in-council, Aug. 28, 1797.
135. Crown Lands Papers, General Correspondence of the Surveyor-General and Commissioner of Crown Lands, Jones to D. W. Smith, Jan 3, 1798.
136. *Ibid.*, Feb. 2, 1799.
137. Upper Canada Land Petitions, B 1804-8, no. 19, July 7, 1806.
138. Bates Papers in possession of Mr. W. A. Bates, Freelton, Ontario, Indenture between Augustus Bates and Thomas Thompson, "Doctor of Physick," April 2, 1795.
139. Roydon Woodward Vosburgh, ed., "Record of St. Peter's Episcopal Church in the Village of Hobart, Town of Stamford, Delaware County, N.Y., transcribed by the N.Y. Genealogical and Biographical Society, N.Y.C., 1921," Dec. 8, 1794.
140. Upper Canada Land Petitions, B 1804-8, no. 19, July 7, 1806.
141. William Bates to Augustus Bates, Sept. 14, 1799, quoted in J. H. Smith, *Historical Sketch of the County of Wentworth* (Hamilton, 1897), pp. 125–30. The original letter which was among the Bates Papers now in possession of Mr. W. A. Bates was borrowed by Mr. Smith who, being unacquainted with the names in Delaware County, New York, read the address as "Thorpsfield" instead of Harpersfield. As the letter was never returned his copy is unfortunately the only one extant. Augustus' wife, Elizabeth, was the daughter of Waldron Blauu, an addresser to Lord Howe and Sir William Howe. This prominent Loyalist of New York City, who suffered great losses through confiscation, was evacuated in 1783 and died five days after landing at St. John River, New Brunswick. Blauu's property in New York was later restored to his widow. (Lorenzo Sabine, *Biographical Sketches of the Loyalists of the American Revolution with an historical essay* (Boston, 1864); New York Public Library, MSS. Division, "'List of New York Loyalists against whom judgements have been rendered under the Confiscation Act of 1783.'")
142. J. H. Smith, *Historical Sketch of Wentworth*, pp. 125–30.

CHAPTER TEN

1. Fred Coyne Hamil, "Lord Selkirk in Upper Canada," *Ontario Historical Society, Papers and Records*, vol. XXXVII (1945), p. 39.
2. P.A.C., Macdonell Collection, vol. 12, p. 1.
3. P.A.C., Lord Selkirk's Diary, Nov. 16 and 17, 1803.
4. *Ibid.*, Nov 3, 1803.
5. Lord Selkirk to George Chisholm, Dec. 22, 1803, in possession of Lieut.-Col. F. H. Chisholm, Oakville, Ontario.
6. Macdonell Collection, Baldoon Settlement Correspondence, vol. 4, pp. 5-7, Account of Wm. Burn for Sundries for Lord Selkirk to Thomas Clark, Oct. 31, 1803–April 18, 1804.
7. O. Turner, *Pioneer History of the Holland Purchase of Western New York* (Buffalo, 1849), p. 311.
8. *13th Report Ontario Archives* (1916), La Rochefoucault-Liancourt's Travels in Canada, 1795, p. 15; Toronto Public Library, MSS. Collection, Charles Prentice's Journal, 1807.
9. *Sesquicentennial of Genesee County 1802–1952*, pp. 71-73.
10. Timothy Dwight, *Travels in New-England and New-York* (4 vols., London, 1823), IV, p. 46.
11. T. C., *A Ride to Niagara in 1809* (Rochester, 1915), p. 44.
12. Selkirk's Diary, Nov. 1, 1803.
13. T. C., *Ride to Niagara*, p. 44.
14. Turner, *Pioneer History of the Holland Purchase*, p. 412.
15. T. C., *Ride to Niagara*, p. 15.
16. Selkirk's Diary, Nov. 11, 1803.
17. John Maude, *Visit to the Falls of Niagara in 1800* (London, 1826), p. 119.
18. E. A. Cruikshank, ed., *The Correspondence of Lieut.-Governor John Graves Simcoe, with allied documents relating to his administration of the government of Upper Canada* (5 vols., Toronto, 1923-31), I, p. 213.
19. Selkirk's Diary, Nov. 10, 1803.
20. *Ibid.*, Nov. 7, 1803.
21. *Ibid.*, Nov. 10, 1803.
22. *Commercial and Agricultural Magazine* (London), Aug. 1799, pp. 42-43, "Account of Capt. Williamson's Establishment on Lake Ontario, in North America."
23. *Ibid.*
24. *Ibid.*
25. *Ibid.*
26. Selkirk's Diary, Nov. 13, 1803.
27. *Ibid.*
28. Turner, *Pioneer History of the Holland Purchase*, p. 303.
29. Maude, *Visit to the Falls of Niagara*, p. 41.
30. *Ibid.*, pp. 50-51.
31. *Ibid.*, p. 104.
32. *Ibid.*, pp. 47-48.
33. *A Guide in the Wilderness or the History of the First Settlement in the Western Counties of New York, with useful Instructions to Future Settlers. In a series of letters addressed by Judge Cooper, of Coopers-Town, to William Sampson, Barrister, of New York* (Dublin, 1810), pp. 17-18.
34. Dwight, *Travels*, p. 14.
35. De Witt Clinton, Journal, quoted in Ulysses P. Hedrick, *A History of Agriculture in the State of New York* (Albany, 1933), pp. 228-29.
36. Maude, *Visit to the Falls of Niagara*, p. 73.
37. J. H. Mather and H. L. Brockett, *Geographical History of New York* (Utica, 1848), p.202.
38. *Encyclopaedia Britannica*.
39. Mather and Brockett, *Geographical History*, p. 202.
40. *Encyclopaedia Britannica*.
41. Selkirk's Diary, May 14, 1804.
42. *Ibid.*
43. Charles Prentice's Journal, 1807.
44. Dwight, *Travels*, p. 27.
45. Selkirk's Diary, Nov. 6, 1803.
46. Macdonell Collection, Baldoon Settlement Correspondence, vol. 4, p. 1, "A list of the Inhabetents of Johnstown, Feby, 1804."
47. Mather and Brockett, *Geographical History*, p. 201.
48. Macdonell Collection, vol. 4, p. 1, "A list of the names of the inhabetans from Corriesbush, Feby 7, 1804."

NOTES

49. Dwight, *Travels*, p. 10.
50. *Ibid.*
51. John D. Monroe, *Chapters in the History of Delaware County, New York* (Delaware County Historical Association, 1949), p. 86.
52. David H. Burr, *An Atlas of the State of New York* (New York, 1829); *A New Universal Atlas comprising separate maps* ... (New York, undated), maps dated 1833-35.
53. New York Historical Society, Miscel. MSS., Tryon County, Affidavit of Walter Sabin, Feb. 8, 1786.
54. Bates Papers in possession of Mr. W. A. Bates, Freelton, Ontario, "Indenture between Augustus Bates and Thomas Thomson, Doctor of Physick of Kattskill Landing," April 20, 1795.
55. J. H. French, *Historical and Statistical Gazetteer of New York State* (Syracuse, 1860), p. 265fn.
56. Roydon Woodward Vosburgh, ed., "Record of St. Peter's Episcopal Church in the Village of Hobart, Town of Stamford, Delaware County, N.Y., transcribed by the N.Y. Genealogical and Biographical Society. N.Y.C., 1921," p. 3.
57. *History of Delaware County, New York, 1797-1880* (New York, 1880), p. 301.
58. Vosburgh, ed., "Record of St. Peter's Church."
59. *History of Delaware County, 1797-1880*, p. 292, "Map of the township of New Stamford ... agreeable to the law ... passed April 21, 1787. . . ."
60. David Murray, ed., *Centennial History of Delaware County, New York* (Delhi, N.Y., 1898), p. 521.
61. Dwight, *Travels*, p. 10.
62. Roydon Woodward Vosburgh, ed., "Records of the Presbyterian Congregation of Harpersfield, in the town of Harpersfield, Delaware County, N.Y., transcribed by the N.Y. Genealogical and Biographical Society (N.Y., 1921)," p. 2.
63. *History of Delaware County, 1797-1880*, pp. 225, 455.
64. John W. Barber and Henry Howe, *Historical Collections of the State of New York* (New York, 1844), p. 129fn.
65. *Ibid.*
66. William W. Campbell, *The Border Warfare of New York during the Revolution or, the Annals of Tryon County* (New York, 1849), pp. 383-85.
67. French, *Historical and Statistical Gazetteer*, p. 263.
68. Jay Gould, *History of Delaware County and Border Wars of New York* (Roxbury, N.Y., 1856), pp. 72-73.
69. *History of Delaware County, 1797-1880*, p. 241; Murray, ed., *Centennial History*, p. 223.
70. Murray, ed., *Centennial History*, p. 224.
71. French, *Historical and Statistical Gazetteer*, p. 263.
72. Montgomery County Clerk's Office, Liber 3, p. 45 *et seq.*, Descriptions of Roads in the towns of Harpersfield and Kortright, 1788-90.
73. *Ibid.*
74. Dwight, *Travels*, p. 12.
75. *Ibid.*, p. 14.
76. Gould, *History of Delaware County*, p. 143.
77. *History of Delaware County, 1797-1880*, p. 236. It is here stated that Wattles occupied the farm later owned by William Stoutenberg and the 1869 *Atlas* of the county shows W. Stoutenberg, the only one of that initial in the township, on lot 89, Kortright Patent.
78. Historical marker at site.
79. *Ibid.*
80. Macdonell Collection, Baldoon Settlement Correspondence, vol. 4, p. 1, "A list of the Inhabetents of Johnstown, Feby, 1804."
81. Selkirk's Diary, May 20-21, 1804.
82. *Ibid.*, May 24, 1804.
83. *Ibid.*, May 26-27, 1804.
84. *Ibid.*, May 27, 1804.
85. *Ibid.*, May 29, 1804.
86. *Ibid.*
87. *Ibid.*, July 8, 1804.
88. P.A.C., Transcripts of Selkirk Papers, vol. 58, p. 15422.
89. Macdonell Collection, Baldoon Settlement Correspondence, vol. 1, p. 18, Andrew Templeton to Alexander Macdonell, Sept. 16, 1804.
90. Selkirk Transcripts, vol. 53, p. 1423, Macdonell to Selkirk, Nov. 3, 1804.
91. Milo M. Quaife, ed., *John Askin Papers* (2 vols., Detroit, 1929), II, p. 446, Robert Hamilton to John Askin, Dec. 16, 1804.

CHAPTER ELEVEN

1. McMicking Papers in possession of Miss Beatrice Dennis, Stamford, Ontario.
2. Timothy Dwight, *Travels in New-England and New-York* (4 vols., London, 1823), I, pp. 72-73.
3. Thomson Papers, Articles of Agreement between William Sutherland and John Thomson, April 9, 1803, in possession of Mrs. Calvin Roberts, Stamford, Ontario.
4. Recollections of Mrs. William Breckon, great-granddaughter of Archibald Thomson and Daniel Rose, as told to the author in 1956.
5. John Hayes Jenkinson, "A Corwin Silverthorn Saga," MS. written for the United Empire Loyalists' Association.
6. *Ibid.*
7. Charles King to James and George King at Queenston Camp, in Captain Chisholm's company, Sept. 6, 1812, King Papers in possession of Mrs. Melba Long, Burlington, Ontario.
8. P.A.C., Upper Canada Land Petitions, 1817-22, C no. 53.
9. P.A.C., MSS., C. 1700, p. 109, Affidavit dated Niagara, April 1, 1819; *Ibid.*, C. 701, p. 130, Roll of Captain James Crooks' Flank Co. of Lincoln Militia, 1st Regiment.
10. Chisholm Family Bible; tombstone, Stamford Presbyterian Church.
11. Descendants of John Chisholm (Mrs. T. W. Kirby of Portland, Oregon, Cameron Hughson of Toronto, and Miss Helen Bishop of Owen Sound) verify the fact that this monument stood on his land though records at the Lincoln County Registry Office show no conveyance of land to the government. Indeed, the second monument's cornerstone had been laid three years before part of lot 2, originally granted to John Chisholm, and the adjoining section of lot 3, Niagara Township, was purchased by the government. Absolute proof would entail a survey of lot 2.
12. Ontario Archives, Samuel Street Papers, Letter of Francis Hall, Oct. 28, 1835.
13. *Ibid.*, Statement of David Thorburn, May 12, 1836.
14. McMicking Papers.
15. Data through the courtesy of Mrs. F. A. Blackburn, Toronto, descendant of James MacGlashan.
16. McMicking Papers.
17. Recollections of Mrs. William Breckon.
18. P.A.C., R.G. 19, War of 1812 losses claim no. 220.
19. *Ibid.*, no. 1000.
20. *Ibid.*, nos. 683, 225.
21. *Ibid.*, no. 1760.
22. John Buchanan, *Sketches of the History, Manners, and Customs of the North American Indians* (London, 1824), p. 32.
23. *Ibid.*, pp. 26-32.
24. *Western Mercury* (Hamilton), Aug. 30, 1832.
25. William L. Stone, *Life of Joseph Brant-Thayendanegea including the Indian Wars of the American Revolution* (2 vols., Cooperstown, N.Y., 1845), II, p. 537.
26. John Ross Robertson, *The History of Freemasonry in Canada* (2 vols., Toronto, 1900), I, p. 647.
27. *Historical Sketch of the Barton Lodge, No. 6, G.R.C., A.F., and A.M.* (Hamilton, 1895), pp. 104-5.
28. P.A.C., R.G. 19, War of 1812 losses claim no. 33.
29. George Laidler, "Historical Sketch of the King's Head Inn," MS. at Brant Museum, Burlington, Ontario.
30. P.A.C., Upper Canada Sundries, April 1, 1817.
31. P.A.C., R.G. 19, War of 1812 losses claim no. 616.
32. Welland County Registry Office, Memorial of the will of Archibald Thomson, registered Dec. 3, 1835.
33. *Niagara Historical Society Publication*, no. 10 (1903), p. 34.
34. Lincoln County Registry Office, Will of John Chisholm, no. 8304.
35. Upper Canada, *Journals of the House of Assembly*, 1834, Appendix, p. 221.
36. *Ibid.*
37. Ontario Archives, Nelson, Trafalgar, and Toronto Township Papers, Certificates of Settlement Duties.
38. Ontario, Department of Lands and Forests, Surveys Division, Surveys of Nelson, Trafalgar, and Toronto Townships, Samuel S. Wilmot, deputy surveyor, 1806.
39. P.A.C., Plans for the Burlington Bay Canal 1824—440.18, endorsed "Francis Hall, Engineer, Queenston 14th April 1824."
40. *U.E. Loyalist*, July 15, 1826, vol. 1, no. 7, quoted in John Ross Robertson, *Landmarks of Toronto* (Toronto, 1914), vol. VI, pp. 413-16.

41. *Western Mercury*, March 15, 1832.
42. *Hamilton Gazette* quoted in the *Montreal Gazette*, Feb. 27, 1836.
43. William Lyon Mackenzie's account quoted in Charles Lindsey, *The Life and Times of William Lyon Mackenzie* (2 vols., Toronto, 1862), I, pp. 109–12.
44. Lorne Pierce, *William Kirby* (Toronto, 1924), p. 69.
45. Smith and Chisholm Papers courtesy of the late Miss Helen Smith, Oakville, Ontario.
46. *Ibid.*
47. Robertson, *History of Freemasonry in Canada*, II, p. 468.
48. Inscription, very nearly illegible, on monument to the Rangers at the Butler Burying Ground, Niagara-on-the-Lake, Ontario.

GLOSSARY

Aunayza, *see* New Town.
Anaquaga, *see* Unadilla.

Banyar's Brook, now Wright's Brook, tributary of the West Branch of the Delaware River. Enters the Delaware at Bloomville, Delaware Co., N.Y.
Betty's Brook, tributary of the West Branch of the Delaware River. Enters the Delaware between Hobart and Bloomville, Delaware Co., N.Y.
Big Tree, *see* Chenussio.
Bloomville, *see* Four Corners.
Breakabean, German for rushes which grow at this place. Tributary of Schoharie Creek in Schoharie Co., N.Y.
Buffaloe Creek, a settlement where the creek of the same name enters the Niagara River. This name persisted until after the Holland Purchase, when in 1801–2 the settlement was surveyed into village lots on the north side of the creek, and renamed New Amsterdam. Modern Buffalo, Erie Co., N.Y.
Burlington Bay, *see* Little Lake.
Butlersbury, (1) home of Colonel John Butler in Tryon Co., Province of New York. Still standing north of Fonda, Montgomery Co., N.Y. (2) Same on west bank of the Niagara River. First name of settlement at river's mouth. When laid out as a town, named Lennox, then called West Niagara, Newark, Niagara, and finally Niagara-on-the-Lake, Lincoln Co., Ontario.

Canadarago (Canadaragae, Canaderagey, Candurago, Canaduraga, etc.) Lake, renamed Schuyler Lake after the Revolution. Modern Canadarago Lake, Otsego Co., N.Y.
Canadasaga (Canadasagoe, Canadasego. Kanadesaga, etc.), Old Castle, Seneca town $1\frac{1}{2}$ miles west of outlet of Seneca Lake. Destroyed 1779, not rebuilt. Modern Geneva, Ontario Co., N.Y.
Canajoharie Castle, *see* Upper Castle of the Mohawks.
Canaseraga, (1) Oneida village on Canaseraga Creek where it enters Oneida Lake, Onondaga Co., N.Y. (2) Indian village on Canaseraga Creek, a water of the Genesee River. Modern Dansville, Livingston Co., N.Y.
Cataraqui, called Fort Frontenac during the French régime in Canada. Modern Kingston, Frontenac Co., Ontario.
Catherine's Town, *see* French Catherine's Town.
Catskill, *see* Kaatskill.
Charlotte River, in Schoharie and Delaware cos., N.Y. Called Adaquightinge (Adoquetangy, etc.) by the Indians, it is now known as Charlotte Creek.
Chenussio (Chenesei, Tscheneshee, etc.), Great Seneca Castle at confluence of Canaseraga Creek with the Genesee River. Also called Big Tree after treaty oak and Little Beard's town after Indian chief. Destroyed 1779, not rebuilt. Site between modern Cuylerville and West Branch of the Genesee River in Livingston Co., N.Y.
Chippawa, *see* Upper Landing, west side Niagara River.
Cookoze (Cokeose), "owl's nest," corrupted into Cookhouse by white men. Modern Deposit, Broome Co., N.Y.
Cooperstown, *see* Croghan's.
Corry's Bush, southwest of Fort Hunter. Patent to William Corry and others of 1,500 acres situated northeast of New Turlach. About two-thirds of this grant now lies within the modern township of Charleston and the balance within the township of Root, Montgomery Co., N.Y. Includes the communities of Rural Grove, Lykers, Charleston, Four Corners which are reached by N.Y. route no. 162, an early road from Canajoharie to Schoharie.
Croghan's, modern Cooperstown, Otsego Co., N.Y.
Cushetunk (Cushietunk), meaning "low ground," was situated in Pennsylvania on the Delaware River opposite modern Cochecton, Sullivan Co., N.Y. Settled 1757 by families from Connecticut, the beginning of the Connecticut invasion of the Province of Pennsylvania.

GLOSSARY

Dansville, *see* Canaseraga (2)
Delaware River, called Kithane by Indians. The early name for the East Branch was the Popachton (Pepachton) or Popatunk (Papacunck) Branch, names which doubtless derived from those of Indian villages. The Mohawks Branch was the early name for the West Branch.
Deposit, *see* Cookoze.

Flockey, German for "swampy land," referring to an area situated within the limits of the present village of Fultonham, Schoharie Co., N.Y.
Forks of the Grand River, modern Paris, Brant Co., Ontario.
Four Corners, modern Bloomville, Delaware Co., N.Y.
Fort Defiance ("Deyfeyance") or Middle Fort, the stone house of Johannes Becker which stood in modern Middleburg, Schoharie Co., N.Y.
Fort Frontenac, *see* Cataraqui.
Fort Hunter, *see* Lower Castle of the Mohawks.
Fort Johnson, situated west of modern Amsterdam, Montgomery Co., N.Y.
Fort Schlosser, *see* Upper Landing, east side Niagara River.
Fort Schuyler (old), built 1758, modern Utica, Oneida Co., N.Y.
Fort Schuyler (new), *see* Fort Stanwix.
Fort Stanwix, renamed Fort Schuyler during the Revolution. Site of modern Rome, Oneida Co., N.Y.
Forty Mile Creek, enters Lake Ontario at Grimsby, Lincoln Co., Ontario.
French Catherine's Town, called Shechquego by Indians, situated four miles south of the head of Seneca Lake in Schuyler Co., N.Y.
Fultonham, *see* Flockey.

Geneva, *see* Canadasaga.
Geneva, Lake, *see* Burlington Bay.
German Flatts, Palatine settlement along the Mohawk River between modern Herkimer and Frankfort, Herkimer Co., N.Y.
Great Seneca Castle, *see* Chenussio.
Grimsby, *see* Forty Mile Creek.

Hobart, *see* Paine's Dale.

Kaatskill, Dutch for Wildcat Creek, one of many names which became Anglicized at the beginning of the nineteenth century and is now Catskill.
Kingston, *see* Cataraqui.
Kithane, *see* Delaware River.

Lambinicon, *see* Rambo Creek.
Landings, Niagara River, *see* Lower Landing; Upper Landing.
Lennox, *see* Butlersbury (2).
Lewiston, *see* Lower Landing, east side Niagara River.
Little Beard's town, *see* Chenussio.
Little Lake, the name for the head of Lake Ontario, called Wequatetong by Indians. Also called Lake Geneva until named Burlington Bay by Lieutenant-Governor Simcoe.
Little Lakes, *see* Youngsfield.
Lower Castle of the Mohawks, in 1711 became Fort Hunter, Schoharie Co., N.Y.
Lower Landing
 east side Niagara River, modern Lewiston, Niagara Co., N.Y.
 west side Niagara River, later Queens Town, now Queenston, Lincoln Co., Ontario.

Middleburg, *see* Fort Defiance.
Middle Fort, *see* Fort Defiance.
Minisink, settlement founded about 1690 by Dutch and Huguenots who reached it by the earliest known road running west from the Hudson River and said to have been built more than a century before by the Dutch. The settlement, covering an area of about ten miles, was situated west of modern Goshen and east of Port Jervis in Orange Co., N.Y.
Mohawks Branch, *see* Delaware River, West Branch.

New Amsterdam, *see* Buffaloe Creek.
New Stamford, now farm land in the valley of Town Brook east of Hobart, Delaware Co., N.Y.
New Town, called Aunayza (Oyenyange), a Seneca town on the Chemung River, destroyed 1779 and not rebuilt. Site is five miles south of Elmira, Chemung Co., N.Y.
Newark, *see* Butlersbury (2).
Niagara, Niagara-on-the-Lake, *see* Butlersbury (2).

Old England District, Tryon, Co., comprised a considerable part of modern Oneonta and Otego townships, Otsego Co., N.Y.
Old Seneca Castle, *see* Canadasaga.
Oneida Castle, retains that name today in Oneida Co., N.Y.
Onondaga Castle, called Salina by white settlers, now in the western section of Syracuse, Onondaga Co., N.Y.
Onondaga Lake, *see* Salt Lake.
Oquaga (Oghwage, Aughquaga, etc.), Indian town on the Susquehanna River, destroyed 1778, not rebuilt. Present site of Windsor, Broome Co., N.Y.
Ouleout (Aulyoulet) Creek, "a continuing voice," a tributary of the Susquehanna River, retains that name today.

Paine's Dale, modern Hobart, Delaware Co., N.Y.
Papacunck, also called Popatunk or Popachton (Pepachton), an Indian village whose site was submerged upon the building of the Downsville Dam, Delaware Co., N.Y.
Popachton, *see* Papacunck.
Popachton Branch, *see* Delaware River, Each Branch.
Port Roseway, *see* Shelburne.

Queenston, Queens Town, *see* Lower Landing, west side Niagara River.

Rambo Creek, called Lambinicon by Indians, in Burlington, Ontario.
Rome, *see* Fort Stanwix.

Salina, *see* Onondaga Castle.
Salt Lake, now Onondaga Lake, Onondaga Co., N.Y.
Shechquego, *see* French Catherine's Town.
Schoharie, translated from the Mohawk by Joseph Brant as "drift-wood," was so named for the accumulation which formed a natural bridge above Middle Fort, modern Middleburg, Schoharie Co., N.Y.
Schuyler Lake, *see* Canadarago Lake.
Shelburne, called Port Razoir by the French and later Port Roseway by the British until renamed 1783 by Governor Parr of Nova Scotia.
Springfield, colonial settlement at the head of Otsego Lake, now the area surrounding Springfield Center, Otsega Co., N.Y.
Stone Arabia, early Palatine settlement in the Mohawk Valley which retains that name in Montgomery Co., N.Y.
Syracuse, *see* Onondaga Castle.

Tioga (Teaoga), Seneca castle on the Susquehanna called Tioga Point by colonials until the removal in 1795 of the Senecas. Site is a short distance south of modern Athens, Bradford Co., N.Y.
Tioga Point, *see* Tioga.
Tonewanta (Tonwantee, etc.), Seneca for "swift running water," a tributary of the Niagara River; now Tonewanda Creek flowing through Genesee and Niagara cos., N.Y.
Tryon County, relatively the same area as modern Montgomery Co., N.Y.
Turlach (Turlagh, Torlock, Dorlach, etc.), after German patent of New Dorlach, 1730, pronounced New Turlach or New Dorloo. Comprised modern townships of Sharon, Seward, and a portion of Carlisle, Schoharie Co., N.Y.
Twenty Mile Creek, now part of the Welland Canal which enters Lake Ontario at Port Dalhousie, Lincoln Co., Ontario.

Unadilla (Tunadilla), called Anaquaga, Anaquaqua, or Onoghguagy by Indians, a town at the junction of the Unadilla and Susquehanna rivers. Destroyed 1778, not rebuilt.
Upper or Canajoharie Castle of the Mohawks, situated on the Mohawk River in the present township of Danube, Herkimer Co., N.Y. Not to be confused with the modern town of that name (Canajoharie) farther downriver.
Upper Landing
  east side Niagara River, called Little Niagara and Upper Landing before construction in 1760 of Fort Schlosser, now within the southeastern limits of modern Niagara Falls, Niagara Co., N.Y.
  west side Niagara River, modern Chippawa, Welland Co., Ontario.
Utica, *see* Fort Schuyler (old).
Utsayantha, Lake, Mohawk for "beautiful spring, cold and pure," headwater of the Delaware River in Stamford, Delaware Co., N.Y.

Vrooman's Nose, called Onistagrawa by Indians, is a promontory in the Schoharie Valley south of Middleburg, Schoharie Co., N.Y.

Vroomansland, a tract of 1,100 acres bordering Schoharie Creek, bought 1711 from Mohawk Indians by Adam Vrooman, a Dutchman from Schenectady. This area is now Fulton Township, Schoharie Co., N.Y., and a copy of the Mohawk land grant is exhibit no. 12 in the Old Stone Fort Museum at Schoharie.

Warren, *see* Youngsfield.
West Niagara, *see* Butlersbury (2).
Wildcat Creek, *see* Kaatskill.
Windsor, *see* Oquaga.
Wright's Brook, *see* Banyar's Brook.
Wyoming, Delaware Indian name for the fertile intervale of the Susquehanna River, 3-4 miles wide and 20 miles long, in Pennsylvania. By 1770 some 6,000 settlers had come from Connecticut to this area which is now north of Wilkes-Barre, Pennsylvania.

Youngsfield, the settlement of Frederick Adam Young (Jung) whose Palatine father Theobald had secured patent in 1752. This area around and northward of the Little Lakes which empty into Otsego Lake is that now surrounding Warren, Herkimer Co., N.Y.

INDEX

ADAMS, Samuel (1722–1803), 33
Albany (N.Y)
   Co.: xi, 9, 11; Committee of Safety, 40, 73
   town of: 5–7, 54, 73, 79
Alden, Ichabod, 52–53, 57
Alexander, Hugh: land of, 19, 28, 29, 171; mill of, 23, 69 156; during Revolution, 42, 45, 54
Alexander, Sir William (1567?–1640), 103, 122
Allan, Ebenezer ("Indian Allan") (1744–1813), 64fn., 149
Allcock, Henry (?–1808), 159
Allen, Ebenezer (1752–1813), 46
Allen, Ethan (1737–89), 33, 46
Allen, Ira (1751–1814), 46
Ancaster Twp. (Upper Canada), 91
Annan, Rev. R., 26
Annapolis (Nova Scotia): town of, 107, 112; Road, 113
Anne, Queen, 8, 18
Arnold, Benedict (1741–1801), 33, 44
"Ash Lawn" (Charlottesville, Va.), 28fn.
Askin, Catherine (1763–96), 81fn.
Askin, John (1739–1819), 81
Aspinwall, Hannah (Mrs. Lawrence Kortright), 5
Associations, signing of, 34–35, 38–39
Aunayza (New Town), 65, 202

BADEAU, Magdalena (Mrs. James Secord Sr.) (1739–?), 67
Baldoon, 160; see also Selkirk, Lord
Ballard, W. H., 52–53
Banyar, Goldsbrow (1724–1815), 5, 10, 13–14, 39; see also Banyar Patent
Banyar Patent, 39; location of, 5, 10–11, 154; settlement on, 13, 19, 171–73
Banyar's Brook (Wright's Brook), 26–29, 156, 202; settlement along, 19, 171–72; mill on, 23, 69, 156
Barck, Dr. Oscar T., 102
Barnhart, John, 64fn.
Barrington (Nova Scotia), 107
Bartholomew, Benjamin, 15
Bartholomew, James, 15
Bartholomew, John, 15
Bartholomew, Joseph, 15
Batholomew, Mary: see Harper, Mrs. Alexander
Bartholomew, Thomas, 15
Bartlett Hollow (Delaware Co., N.Y.), 158fn.
Barton Lodge, see Freemasonry
Barton Twp. (Wentworth Co., Ontario), 164fn.

Bartram, John (1701–77), 20
Bartram, William (1739–1823), 20fn.
Bartram's Garden, 20fn.
Batavia, town of (Genesee Co., N.Y.), 146, 147–48
Bates, Augustus (1765–1842), 143–44, 154, 197
Bates, Mrs. Augustus (Elizabeth Blauu) (1772–1848), 154, 197
Bates, Richard Waldron, 154
Bates, William (1758–1843), 143–44, 154, 159, 165
Bates, Mrs. William (Rebecca Murphy), 143
Bath (N.Y.), 148
Beacraft (Beacroft; Begraft), Benjamin, 70, 91
Beardsley, Bartholomew Crannel (1776–1855), 19fn.
Beardsley, John, 19fn.
Beardsley, Levi, 19, 25
Beasley, Joanna (1726–95), 140
Beasley, Richard (1761–1842), 140, 141, 143
Beaver Dams (Upper Canada), 163–64
Becker, Johannes, 43
"Bees," 18
Bender, Philip, 67, 87, 88, 129
Bergen Swamp (Genesee Co., N.Y.), 147
Betty's Brook, 15, 28, 72, 157, 173, 202
Big Springs, 149
Big Tree, 202; see also Chenussio
Big Tupper Lake, N.Y., 38fn.
Birch, Samuel, 112
Birchtown (Nova Scotia), 112
Black Creek (Welland Co., Upper Canada), 51fn.
"Black Pioneers," 105, 112
Black Rock (Erie Co., N.Y.), 146
Blauu, Elizabeth: see Bates, Mrs. Augustus
Blomidon, Cape (Nova Scotia), 113
Bloody Run, see Devil's Hole massacre
Bloomville (Delaware Co., N.Y.), 15 fn., 28, 202; see also Four Corners
Blowmedown, see Blomidon
Bluck, Stephen, 105, 112
Blue Mountains, 15
Bolton, Mason (?–1780), 50, 77–86 passim
"Boston tea party," 4, 32–33
"Bostonians," 70fn.
Boswell, James (1740–95), x, xi, 37
Bowlby, Edward, 103–4, 124
Bowman, Adam (1758–1842) 49, 50, 128, 137, 176
Bowman, Elizabeth (Mrs. Jacob), (1739–1800), 49–50, 128
Bowman, Jacob (1736–1815), 49, 50, 128, 176

Bowman Peter (1766-?), 49-50, 141
Bowman's Creek: Montgomery Co. N.Y., 50, 52; Stamford Twp., Ont., 128
Bradt, Arent (1684-1765), 13, 72, 171, 173
Braehead Hill Road (Kortright, N.Y.), 29
Brant, Catharine (Mrs. Joseph) (1759-1837), 68, 141, 164, 166
Brant, Elizabeth (Mrs. William Johnson Kerr), 138, 164
Brant, John (1794-1832), 164, 166
Brant, Joseph (Thayendanegea) (1742-1807), 34, 43, 61, 90, 130, 135, 142-43, 144, 159; guides surveyors, 12; biographical sketch of, 31-32; allies with British, 33-34; goes to Canada, 37; visits England, 37; evades capture, 40-41; leads Indians at Oriskany, 42, 44; commands company in Butler's Rangers, 48-49; seeks recruits and provisions, 50-51; attends war council at Tioga, 51; attacks frontier settlements, 52; aid from Tunnicliffs, 52-53; raids Mohawk Valley, 53; aid from Servos, 54-55; in Cherry Valley raid, 57-59; description of, 62; raids Wyoming, 62; raids Minisink, 64-65 wounded, 65; at battle of New Town, 65; marriage, 68; takes prisoners at Harpersfield, 69-70; "Indian letter," 70; raids Mohawk Valley, 71, 72; last raid, 75; encamps at Niagara, 83, 88; receives gift of pistols, 134; lives on Grand River, 140-41; as Freemason, 141; settles at Burlington Bay, 141-42; death and funeral, 164
Brant, Margaret, 12, 68
Brant, Mary (Molly), 31-32, 37, 44fn., 138
Brant, Susannah, 68
Brant's Block, 142, 166
Brant's Spring, 88
Brass, Davis, 43, 89
Breadalbane (Breadalbin) (Fulton Co., N.Y.), 145
Breakabean Creek (Schoharie Co., N.Y.), 42, 43, 153, 202
Brock, Sir Isaac (1769-1812), 162; monument to, 163, 167
Broon, Wullie: see Brown, William.
Brown, Alexander, 145, 159
Brown, John (1744-80), 46
Brown, William, 129, 134, 136, 137
Brown, Mrs. William: see McMicking, Janet
Bruff, Charles Oliver, 95, 103, 105
Bruff, James Earl, 95
Buck, Philip, 49, 50, 134, 166
Buffaloe Creek (New Amsterdam; Buffalo), 83, 147, 150fn., 202
Burch, John (1742-97), 53-54, 63, 128, 130, 134, 137
Burch, Mrs. John: see Ramsey, Martha
"Burch's Mills," 128
Burgoyne, John (1722-92), 42, 44-46, 82fn.
Burlington: Bay (Little Lake; Lake Geneva), 138-43 passim, 165-69 passim, 202, 203; Canal, 167; Heights, 165, 167
Burn, William (?-1804), 145, 146, 160
Butler, John (1725-96), 10, 31, 35, 38, 42, 61, 68, 175; biographical sketch, 36; sent to Niagara, 36-37; organizes Butler's Rangers, 45, 48; raids Wyoming, 50, 51; leads frontier raids, 63, 64; stands at New Town, 65-66; returns to Niagara, 66; raids Schoharie Valley, 71; assists in settlement at Niagara, 83, 85, 86, 89, 90-91; works for release of prisoners, 97; organizes militia, 137; purchases land from Missisaugas, 142; see also Butler's Rangers; Butlersbury
Butler, Mrs. John (Catherine Pollock) (1725-83), 36, 38, 58, 97, 98
Butler, Joseph (father of John), 31, 36
Butler, Walter N., (1752?-81) 36, 57-59, 60, 74, 75, 84, 86
Butler, William (Continental officer), 57
Butler's Purchase, 36
Butler's Rangers: organized, 45; purpose and function of, 48; Indian Department of, 48, 60-62 (see also Brant, Joseph); uniform of, 49; supplies for, 53-54; in Cherry Valley raid, 57-59; methods of warfare and survival, 60-62; barracks of, 67; in war parties, 68-71, 74-75; disbanding of, 127; see also Butler, John; names of individual Rangers
Butlersbury, 202; in N.Y., 31, 35, 36, 67, 75, 152; at Niagara, 133; see also Niagara (settlement)
Butternuts (the), 43, 53

CALDER, James, ix, 23, 123, 158, 171
Calder, William, ix, 69, 171
Caledonia (Livingston Co., N.Y.), 148-49
Cameron, John, 5, 7, 14, 123; holdings of, 21, 23, 171; during Revolution, 40, 42
Cameron, William, 123, 171
Campbell, James, 11
Campbell, Patrick: observations of, 60, 87, 132, 139, 140, 141
Campbell, Samuel, 12, 13, 33, 57, 97, 155-56
Campbell, Mrs. Samuel, 57, 58, 68, 96-98, 156
Campbell, William W., 98
Canadarago Lake, 19fn., 52, 202
Canadasaga (Old Seneca Castle), 57, 63, 65, 202
Canajoharie, settlement of, 12fn., 37, 63, 64, 71, 131, 152
Canajoharie Castle, see Upper Castle of the Mohawks
Canajoharie Creek, 7, 11, 12fn.
Canajoharie District (Tryon Co., N.Y.), 11, 33, 34, 74; see also Banyar Patent; Cherry Valley; Harpersfield; Kortright Patent
Canadaigua (Ontario Co., N.Y.), 151
Canaseraga: see Dansville
Canaseraga (near Oneida Lake, N.Y.), 37, 97, 202
Canawagorass, 65
Canawaugus, 61
Canisteo River, 65
Cannon, Hester, 5
Cannon, John, 5
Cape Sable Island (Nova Scotia), 106

INDEX

Carleton, Sir Guy (Lord Dorchester) (1724–1808): during Revolution, 46, 77, 103, 104, 111; as governor (after Revolution), 127, 131, 132, 135, 138, 166
Carleton Island, 65, 75, 81–83, 85
Carlisle (Schoharie Co., N.Y.), 34fn.
Carson, Alexander, 62, 171
Cartwright, Richard Sr., 6, 12, 54
Cartwright, Richard Jr. (1759–1815), 54, 63, 65, 83, 130, 140
Cataraqui, 202
Catherine's Town (Schuyler Co., N.Y.), 149, 202
Catskill, *see* Kaatskill
Catskill-Susquehanna Turnpike, 29, 153, 157, 158
Catskill Park (N.Y.), 15fn.
Cayuga, 147
Cayuga Indians, 7, 35fn., 61; *see also* Six Nations Indians
Cayuga Lake, 61, 150
Cedars (the), 37
Center Brook (Delaware Co., N.Y.), 23, 29
Champlain, Samuel de (1567–1635), 107, 111
Charlotte River, 5, 10, 23, 39, 202
Charlottenburgh Twp. (Upper Canada), 172–73
Chatham Twp. (Upper Canada), 145
Chauncey, Isaac (1772–1840), 165
Chemung River, 50, 58, 61, 63–65
Chenango River, 148, 151, 158
Chenussio (Great Seneca Castle), 61, 66, 202
Cherry Hill (Cooksville, Ontario), 162
Cherry Valley (Otsego Co., N.Y.), 23, 38; founding of, 10–12; during Revolution, 34, 52, 57–59; Presbyterian church in, 155–56
Chipman, Ward (1754–1824), 111
Chippawa: settlement of (Upper Landing), 128, 135, 147, 202; battle of, 164
Chippawa Creek, 87, 128, 131, 132, 134, 135, 137
Chisholm, Barbara (Mrs. George King) (1790–ca. 1817), 124, 162
Chisholm, Barbara: *see* Chisholm, Mrs. George Sr.
Chisholm, Christy (1795–?), 139
Chisholm, George Sr. (1752–1842)
  in Scotland, ix, x; emigrates, x
  in Province of N.Y., 21, 23; locates, 15, 17, 171; manufactures potash, 22; property seized, 40; joins British, 42; joins Burgoyne, 45; taken prisoner, 46; escapes to York Town, 93, 94; sets up as merchant, 94; in volunteer corps, 94, 100; acquaintances, 94–95; family life, 95–96; becomes Port Roseway Associate, 103, 105
  in Nova Scotia: locates in Shelburne, 109, 110; removes to Jordan Bay, 112–13, 114, 117; claim for losses, 120–21; family, 124; removes to Niagara, 124; his grants today, 124–25
  at Niagara, 129; on U.E. List, 133; signs address to Simcoe, 134; works at Fort Erie, 134, 138
  at Burlington Bay: purchases land and locates, 138–39; appointed magistrate, 139–40; as Freemason, 141, 164; as Crown commissioner for Indian purchase, 142; as bridge commissioner, 143; journey to Kortright, 144–58; in War of 1812, 162, 165; his last days, 167–69
Chisholm, Mrs. George Sr. (Barbara McKenzie) (1758–1824), 95–96, 135, 158, 169
Chisholm, George Jr. (1792–1872), 135, 162, 166, 169
Chisholm, George (son of John of Queenston) 1801–?), 141, 165
Chisholm, Hannah: *see* Smith, Mrs. Hiram
Chisholm, James (1786–?), 124
Chisholm, Jane (Mrs. Joseph Silverthorn) (1791–1879), 162, 166
Chisholm, Janet: *see* Chisholm, Mrs. John (Inverness)
Chisholm, Janet (daughter of George Sr.) (1779–?), 96
Chisholm, John (Inverness), x
Chisholm, Mrs. John (Inverness) (Janet MacGlashan), x, 163
Chisholm, John (of Queenston) (1746–1830)
  in Scotland, ix, x; emigrates, 20
  in Province of N.Y., 23; locates, 20, 171; joins British, 42; returns home, 45; joins Brant, 50, 51; in raids, 58, 62, 64; goes to Niagara, 66; property confiscated, 66
  at Niagara, 163; settles below Mountain, 89, 127; marriages, 128–29; claim for losses, 130; granted additional lands, 133; subscriber to Presbyterian church, 134; removes to Mountain, 137; family, 138; land on Grand River, 140–41; house of, 161, 162, 170; in War of 1812, 162; losses War of 1812, 164; death and will, 165
Chisholm, Mrs. John (of Queenston): *see* Fletcher, Catherine; Stuart, Christine
Chisholm, John Jr. (1794–1815), 163
Chisholm, John (son of George Sr.) (1784–1861), 124, 162, 166, 168
Chisholm, John Brant, 166
Chisholm, Mary Christina (Mrs. Ephraim Land) (1782–1865), 96, 124, 164–65
Chisholm, Nancy (1795–?), 139
Chisholm, William (son of John of Queenston) (1787–?), 129, 136
Chisholm, William "White Oak" (son of George Sr.) (1788–1842), 19fn., 124, 162, 166–67
Chrysler, Adam (*ca.* 1732–93), 23, 89, 153; during Revolution, 42–43, 45, 53, 67, 75
Chrysler, Philip, 45, 123
Clark, Thomas (1770–1837), 145, 146, 147, 159
Clarke, Hugh, 20, 40–41, 42, 47, 171
Claus, Daniel (1727–87), 9, 31–38 *passim*, 44–45
Claus, Mrs. Daniel (Ann Johnson), 31
Claus Manor (Mohawk Valley, N.Y.), 31
Clement, Janet, 54, 56
Clement, Joheph, 35
Clement, Lewis (?–1781), 35, 41, 134, 171
Clinton, George (1739–1812), 52, 53, 97, 111, 152
Clinton, Sir Henry (1738?–95), 86, 96
Clinton, James ((1736–1812), 47, 58, 63–64

Clothing, frontier: *see* Frontier practices
Clunes, John, 46, 82
Cochecton (Penn.), 55, 202
Cohocton River, 61, 65
Colden, Cadwallader (1688-1776), 5
Cole, Daniel, 64fn.
Cole, Joseph, 64fn.
Columbia College (N.Y. City), 96fn.
Conawagorass: *see* Canawagorass
Congress: *see* Continental Congress
Conspiracies, Commissioners for (detecting and defeating), 53, 54, 62, 95
Continental Congress, 33, 34, 39, 40, 44fn., 66, 90, 107
Cook, James (1728-79), 134
Cookoze (Cookhouse; Deposit), 61 154, 202
Cooksville (Toronto Twp., Ont.), 162
Cooper, James Sr., 36
Cooper, Mrs. James Sr.: *see* McMicking, Janet
Cooper, James Jr. (1772-?), 36, 73, 74, 129, 134
Cooper, James Fenimore (1789-1851), 13fn.
Cooper, Janet: *see* McMicking, Janet
Cooper, Thomas (1771-?), 36, 73, 74, 129, 134
Cooper, William (1754-1809), 13fn., 155; observations of, 17, 149, 150
Cooperstown ((Otsego Co., N.Y.), 13fn. 155, 202
Coote's Paradise ((Upper Canada), 140
Corn Planter, Chief, 71
Cornwall Twp. (Upper Canada), 171-74
Cornwallis, Lord Charles (1738-1805), 75, 130
Correspondence, committees of, 33, 34; *see also* Safety, committees of
Corry's Bush, 153, 202
Corwin, Esther (Mrs. John Silverthorn) (1764-1852), 162, 166
Courtney, Thomas, 103
Courtright (Lambton Co., Ont.), 160
Covenanters' Cemetery, 29
Cowley, St. Ledger, 72
Credit River (Upper Canada), 159
Croghan, George (?-1782), 13, 24, 63, 68
Croghan's, 202
Croghan's Lake: *see* Otsego Lake
Crops, frontier: *see* Frontier practices
Croy, Parish of (Inverness-shire, Scotland), ix-x, 169
Cruikshank, Robert, 65, 81
Crum, Benoni, 64fn.
Crum, William, 64fn.
Cummings, Ann (Mrs. Alexander Leah), ix, xi
Cummings, Thomas Sr., 54, 172
Cummings, Thomas Jr. (*ca.* 1758-1823), 54, 134, 160
Cushetunk (Penn.), 96, 202

DANFORTH, Asa, 151
Dansville (Livingston Co., N.Y.), 149-50, 203
Danube Twp. (Herkimer Co., N.Y.), 12fn.
Dartmouth College, 32fn.
Davenport (Delaware Co., N.Y.), 15fn.
Davis, Asahel (1774-1850), 165
Davis, Sarah, 166
Davis, William (1741-1834), 166

Davis, Mrs. William (Hannah Philipse), 166
DeCou's Mills, 164
Deer Island: *see* Carleton Island
Delaware (River), Head of the: early settlement at, 5, 10-16 *passim*, 17-26 *passim*; during Revolution, 30, 33-41 *passim*, 47-48, 59, 62, 63, 69-70, 72-73, 87; after Revolution, 91, 153-57; present-day, 26-28; *see also* Banyar Patent; Delaware River, West Branch; Kortright Patent; Harpersfield; New Stamford
Delaware Co. (N.Y.), 15fn., 145, 154
Delaware (Kithane) River, 7, 19
East (Popachton; Popatunk) Branch, 9, 10, 53, 203
West (Mohawks) Branch, 9-10, 11, 2 6-27, 203; *see also* Delaware, Head of the
Delaware Twp. ((Upper Canada), 149
Deposit (Broome Co., N.Y.), 154, 203
Depue, Charles, 143, 176
Depue, John, 50, 67, 86, 92 143 175
Depue, Mary (Mrs. John), 86
Devil's Hole massacre, 79-80, 83
Diblee, Rev. Ebenezer, 154
Dingwall, James, 19, 23, 123, 172
Dingwall, John, 19, 123, 172
Dole, James, 103, 104
Dolson, Elizabeth (Mrs. Isaac), 68, 80
Dolson, Isaac, 68, 80, 85, 87, 89, 91, 92, 187
Dolson, John Sr., 68, 80
Dolson, John Jr., 160
Dolson, Mathew, 160
Dorchester, Lord: *see* Carleton, Sir Guy
Dorchester, Mount: *see* Mount Dorchester
Douglas, Thomas: *see* Selkirk, Lord
Dover Twp. (Upper Canada), 145
Dun, Rev. John, 133
Dundas, Thomas, 120, 130-31
Dundas, village of (Upper Canada), 168
Dundas St. (Upper Canada), 162, 166
Dunlop, Rev. Samuel, 11, 33, 57, 97
Durfee, Joseph, 103
Durlach: *see* New Turlach
Dutch: along Hudson, 6; as frontier settlers, 7, 8, 11, 22, 30, 31, 67
Dwight, Timothy (1752-1817): observations of, 26, 150, 153, 155, 157, 158, 161
Dyott, William, 121

EAST FLAMBOROUGH: *see* Flamborough, East
Ellice, James, 97
Ellicott, Joseph (1760-1826), 147-48
Elliott, Walter, 70, 152
Ellsworth, Francis, 55, 87
Emery, Catharine (Mrs. Archibald Thomson Sr.) (?-1823), 129
Emery, Margaret (Mrs. James Thomson Sr.), 129
Empey, Adam, 64fn.
Erie Canal, 150fn., 153
Etobicoke Creek (Upper Canada), 159

FARMERS' MUSEUM (Cooperstown, N.Y.), 13fn.
Federal City (U.S.A.), 147
Fenimore House (Cooperstown, N.Y.), 13fn.

Fenn, Rev. Stephen, 155
Fergusonville (Delaware Co., N.Y.), 15fn.
Field, George (1721–85), 68, 86, 187
Field, Rebecca, 86
Filman's Point, Burlington Bay, 169
Fireman's Home (Hudson, N.Y.), 99fn.
Fisher, Frederick, 47
Five Nations Indians, 7; *see also* Six Nations Indians
Five Mile Meadow (Niagara), 84
Flamborough (Upper Canada): East, 138, 142, 159, 166, 169, 171, 196; West, 171
Fletcher, Alexander, 129
Fletcher, Archibald, 129
Fletcher, Mrs. Archibald (Flora MacNab), 129
Fletcher, Catherine (Mrs. John [of Queenston] Chisholm) (1761–1825), 129, 169
Flockey, battle of The, 42–43, 89, 153, 203
Fonda (Fulton Co., N.Y.), 36, 202
Forfeiture and Sequestration, Commission of, 39, 48, 53, 54, 66
Forsyth, George, 81
Fort Brewerton, 74
Fort Detroit, 76–82 *passim*, 136
Fort Defiance, 43, 47, 153, 203
Fort Erie, 57fn., 77, 83, 134–35, 138, 146, 159
Fort Frontenac, 31, 203
Fort Hunter, 8, 31, 32, 36, 152–53, 203
Fort Johnson, 75, 203
Fort Michilimackinac, 76–78, 92
Fort Niagara: as military headquarters, 48–49, 50, 54, 55, 59, 66, 67, 69, 71; Loyalists flee to, 66–68, 74; difficulties of provisioning, 75–79, 81, 82, 86; agricultural and settlement plan for, 78–84; *see also* Niagara (settlement); ceded to United States, 92, 133; post office at 135–36
Fort Ontario, 78
Fort Oswego, 66, 136, 151; as military post, 33, 42–44, 47, 74, 79: cultivation at, 78–79
Fort Pitt, 95
Fort Plain, 12fn.
Fort St. John's, 33, 35
Fort Schlosser, 77, 203; *see also* Niagara River, Upper Landing
Fort Schuyler: new, 47, 203 (*see also* Fort Stanwix); old, 203
Fort Stanwix, 38, 42–45, 203; Treaty, 9, 11, 13fn.
Forty Mile Creek ("the Forty") (south shore, Lake Ontario), 84, 142, 203
Four Corners (Delaware Co., N.Y.), 156, 157, 203; *see also* Bloomville
Four Mile Creek (Lincoln Co., Upper Canada), 83–84
Four Mile Pond (Lincoln Co., Upper Canada), 89
Foxes Creek (Schoharie Co., N.Y.), 153
Franklin (Delaware Co., N.Y.), 158fn.
Franklin, Benjamin, 13fn., 72
Franklin, William, 13fn.
Fraser, Alexander, 112
Fraser, Elizabeth (Mrs. Hugh), 97–98
Fraser, Hugh, 22, 23, 172; migrates, x; represents Highlanders in land negotiations, 5, 7, 13–14; during Revolution, 40, 41, 42, 45; at YorkTown, 73, 93, 96, 97, 104, 105; in Nova Scotia, 109, 110, 113, 120, 124
Fraser, Rev. Hugh, 119
Fraser, Simon, 19, 172
Fraser, William, 19, 172
Fraunces, Samuel, 102
Fraunces' Tavern, 101–2, 111
Freemasonry: in Scotland, x; at Johnstown, N.Y., 37; at Head of Lake Ontario (Barton Lodge), 141, 164–65
French Catherine's Town, 51, 203
Frey, Hendrick, 33, 37, 131
Frey, John (1740–1833), 33
Frey, Philip Rockell (?–1823), 138; during Revolution, 37, 52, 64, 175; as surveyor, 131, 133
"Frolics," 18
Frontier practices, 17–26; shelters and houses, 17, 18–19, 25–26; food, 17, 18, 20, 25; "frolics" or "bees," 18; clothing, 18, 25; land clearance, 19–21; crop cultivation and harvesting, 20, 22–23; potash, 21–22; maple sugar, 22; tools and implements, 22–23; milling, 23; farm animals, 23–24; spinning and weaving, 24–25; church-going, 26
Fulton Twp. (Schoharie Co., N.Y.), 43
Fultonham (Schoharie Co., N.Y.), 42, 153, 203

Gage, James (1774–1854), 166
Galinée, Father: quoted, 61
Gass, Isabella (Mrs. Thomas McMicking) (1767–1830), 129
Gass, William, 129
Gates, Horatio (*ca.* 1728–1806), 46
Gaylord, Levi, 157
Genesee fever, 150
Genesee Pike, 158; *see also* Seneca Turnpike
Genesee River, 7, 61, 66, 84, 147–49, 202; Falls, 149; Plain, 150
Geneva (Ontario Co., N.Y.), 148, 149, 159, 203
Geneva, Lake (Upper Canada): *see* Burlington Bay
Genishaau, 147
Germain, Lord George (1716–85), 52
German Flatts (Herkimer Co., N.Y.), 31, 33, 49, 203; raided by Brant, 53, 69
Germans: *see* Palatines, German
Glengarry (Upper Canada), 123
Goldie, John (1793–1814), 142fn.
Gore District, 166–67
Gore Militia, 167, 168
Goring, Francis (1755–1842), 46, 63, 64, 65, 77, 80–85 *passim*, 136–37
Gould, Jay (1836–92), 155fn., 156
Grand River (Upper Canada), 140–41, 164, 203
Grant, Alexander, 156
Grant, Mrs. Anne (1755–1838), 18, 78–79
Grant, George, 154
Great Hardenburgh Patent, 10, 53
Great Meadow (Niagara), 84, 85

Great Seneca Castle, 203; *see also* Chenussio
Green, Diana, 165
Green, Ernest, 135
Green Mountain Boys, 33, 46
Guy Park (Mohawk Valley, N.Y.), 31

HAGAR, Jacob, 75
Haldimand, Sir Frederick (1718-91), 140; during Revolution, 34, 57, 70, 71, 98; ideas re Niagara settlement, 79, 80, 83-91 *passim*
Hall, Francis, 142fn., 163, 167
Halton Co. (Upper Canada), 166-67
Hamilton (Wentworth Co., Upper Canada), 164fn., 167
Hamilton, Robert (1750-1809), 64, 130, 136, 138; as trader, 83, 134, 135, 137; and Lord Selkirk, 87fn., 145, 159, 160
Hammond, Sir Andrew Snape (1738-1828), 103, 104, 105, 115
Hardenburgh, Johannes, 53
Hardenburgh Patent, 10, 53
Hare, Henry (?-1779), 64
Hare, Peter (1748-1834), 64
Harper, Alexander, 10, 15, 154, 155; during Revolution, 41, 48, 69-70, 152
Harper, Mrs. Alexander (Mary Bartholomew) (1773-?), 15, 69-70
Harper, James (1731-60), 10
Harper, John Sr., 10
Harper, John Jr. (1734-1811), 10, 12, 13, 23, 29; during Revolution, 38-41, 43, 47-48; after Revolution, 155, 157
Harper, Joseph, 10, 155
Harper, Miriam (Mrs. John Jr.), 13
Harper, William (1729-?), 10, 12, 13, 155; during Revolution, 39, 40, 47, 58
Harper and Bros., 155fn.
Harper Patent, 10-13: *see also* Harpersfield
Harpersfield: early settlement at, 12-16 *passim*, 17-26 *passim*, 171-74; during Revolution, 30, 34-35, 38-41, 45, 50, 69-70; after Revolution, 153-57; present day, 26-29
Harpur: *see* Harper
Hatt, Richard (?-1820), 159
Hayden Lake (Nova Scotia), 110
Hebert, Louis, 111
Hendrick, King (Mohawk chief) (*ca.* 1680-1755), 18, 31
Hendry, James (1745-80), 69fn.
Hendry, Thomas, 69fn.
Herkimer, Nicholas (1728-77), 33, 34, 41, 44
"High Dutch": *see* Palatines, German
Highland Volunteer Militia (York Town), 94, 100
Highlanders: *see* Scottish Highlanders
Hill, Aaron (Little Aaron), 31, 48, 57, 63, 136
Hill, David (Little David; Little Mohawk Chief), 31, 48, 63, 140
Hobart (Delaware Co., N.Y.), 15fn., 203: *see also* Paine's Dale
Holland Land Company, 146
Holland Purchase (N.Y.), 147-48
Hoosick (Rensselaer Co., N.Y.), 97
Howe, William (1729-1814), 42

Hudson (Columbia Co., N.Y.), 99fn.
Hudson River, 5-7, 42, 45-46
Huff, Hendrick, 39-40, 41, 64fn., 70, 140
Huff, John, 64fn., 140
Huffson, Henry: *see* Huff, Hendrick
Hughes, Thomas (1759?-90): observations of, 77, 93, 94, 96
Hunter, Robert (?-1734), 8

"INDIAN ALLAN": *see* Allan, Ebenezer
Indian Charity School, 12, 32
Indian Department: of Butler's Ranger: *see* Butler's Rangers; in Province of N.Y., 9, 32, 36, 66, 67, 86
Indian Prayer Book, 32, 88
Indians: *see* Missisauga Indians; Six Nations Indians
Inverness (Livingstone Co., N.Y.), 149
Inverness-shire (Scotland), emigrants from, ix-xi, 171-73
Ireland, emigrants from, 13
Iroquois Indians: *see* Six Nations Indians

JACOB, Capt.: *see* Lewis, Capt. Jacob
Jefferson, Thomas (1743-1826), 28
Jesuit missionaries, 18, 150, 151
Johnson, Ann (Nancy) (Mrs. Daniel Claus), 31
Johnson, Elizabeth (Mrs. Robert Kerr) (1762-94), 138
Johnson, Guy (1740-88), 9, 31, 32; during Revolution, 33, 35, 36, 52, 66, 68, 83-84, 86
Johnson, Mrs. Guy (Mary[Polly]), 31
Johnson, Isabella (Mrs. Murdoch McKenzie), 124fn.
Johnson, Sir John (1732-1830), 31; during Revolution, 37-38, 42, 43, 50, 70-72, 97; after Revolution, 123; *see also* King's Royal Regiment of New York
Johnson, Lady Mary (wife of Sir John) (Mary Watts), 31, 38
Johnson, Mary (Polly) (Mrs. Guy Johnson), 31
Johnson, Rudolph, 64fn.
Johnson, Dr. Samuel (1709-84), x-xi
Johnson, Sir William (1715-74), 8, 18, 23, 36, 66; as landholder, xi, 9, 10, 13, 14, 95; relations with Indians, 8-9, 31-32, 79, 90; family, 31, 138
Johnson, William "Jr." (half breed), 31, 48, 57, 58
Johnson Hall (Johnstown, Fulton Co., N.Y.), 7, 37, 38, 71, 138, 152
Johnson's Bush, 14, 31, 36, 71, 152
Johnson's Greens: *see* King's Royal Regiment of New York
Johnstown (Fulton Co., N.Y.), 7, 11, 14, 31, 46fn., 152; gaol at, 37, 55, 152; court house at, 11, 152,; Episcopal church at, 152
Jones, Augustus (1763-1836), 139, 141; as surveyor, 131, 138, 142, 143, 160, 194
Jones, Thomas (1731-92), 100
Jordan Bay (Nova Scotia): lots on, 110, 114; description of area, 113-14, 117-18; decline of area, 121, 122, 124; area today, 124-25

Jordan River (Nova Scotia), 110, 114, 117, 122; Falls, 114

KAATSKILL, 6, 7, 203
Kaatskill Mountains, 7, 15-16, 28, 29
Kerr, Dr. Robert Kerr (1755-1824), 138, 141, 164
Kerr, Mrs. Robert: see Johnson, Elizabeth
Kerr, William Johnson (1813-45), 164, 167-68
Kerr, Mrs. William Johnson (Elizabeth Brant), 164
Kinderhook, 95
King, Charles Sr. (1765-1832), 138-39, 162-63, 168, 169
King, George, 162-63
King, Mrs. George: see Chisholm, Barbara
King, James, 162
King's College (N.Y.), 96
King's Head Inn (Burlington Beach, Upper Canada), 141, 143, 159, 165
King's Royal Regiment of New York (Johnson's Greens; Royal Yorkers), 38, 42-45, 64fn., 123, 129, 138, 171-74
Kingston (Upper Canada), 66, 140, 203
Kithane, 9, 203; see also Delaware River
Klock, Johannes, 52, 152
Knox, Henry (1750-1806), 111
Kortreght, Louwrens: see Kortright, Lawrence
Kortright
   Center, 29, 156-57
   Patent: location of, 5, 10-11, 154; early settlement, 13-16 passim, 17-26 passim, 171-74; during Revolution, 35, 38-40, 45, 50, 62; after Revolution, 91, 154, 155, 156-57; present-day, 26-29
   Twp., 10, 91, 154; see also Kortright Patent
Kortright, Cornelius Jansen, 5
Kortright, Elizabeth (Eliza) (Mrs. James Monroe) (?-ca. 1830), 28fn.
Kortright, Lawrence (1728-94), 39, 105; as landholder, 5, 10, 13-14, 20, 91; see also Kortright Patent
Kortright, Mrs. Lawrence (Hannah Aspinwall), 5

LACROSSE, 132
Lake George, 18, 89
Lake Erie, 76; settlement along, 92, 127, 145, 160
Lake Ontario, 76, 77, 84, 92, 127; Head of, 84; settlement at, 138-44, 165, 166-67
Lake Rodney (Nova Scotia), 117
Lake Salubria, 158fn.
Lake St. Clair, 145
Lambinicon (Rambo Creek), 142, 203
Lancaster Twp. (Upper Canada), 172
Land, Abel (?-1848), 96, 166
Land, Ephraim (1774-1841), 96, 164
Land, Mrs Ephraim: see Chisholm, Mary Christina
Land, John, 96
Land, Robert (1739-1818), 55, 96, 141, 164fn.
Land, Mrs. Robert (Phoebe Scott) (1733-1826), 96, 105, 164fn.
Leal, Alexander (1740-1813), ix, xi, 29, 59, 91, 156-57

Leal, Mrs. Alexander (Ann Cummings), ix, xi
Leckie, Alexander, 95, 102, 120
Lennox (Upper Canada), 133, 203; see also Niagara (settlement)
Lennox, Charles, 4th Duke of Richmond (1764-1819), 133
Lewis, Jacob, 48, 57, 58, 136
Lewis, Morgan, 150fn.
Lewiston (Niagara Co., N.Y.), 146, 150fn., 203; see also Niagara River, Lower Landing
Lincoln Militia, 1st Regiment of, 163
Lincoln and Norfolk, county of (Upper Canada), 51fn., 135
Lindesay, James, 11
Lindesay's Bush, 11
"Line of Property," 9
Little Aaron: see Hill, Aaron
Little Bear Creek (Baldoon, Upper Canada), 159
Little Beard's town, 203; see also Chenussio
Little David: see Hill, David
Little Falls (Mohawk River), 33, 65
Little Lake (Upper Canada), see Burlington Bay
Little Lakes (Otsego Co., N.Y.), 47, 203
Little Mohawk Chief: see Hill, David
Little Niagara, 77; see also Niagara River, Upper Landing
Liverpool (Nova Scotia), 107, 109
Livingston, John, 20, 23, 40, 42, 172
Livingston, Neil, 20, 172
Lockeport (Nova Scotia), 107
Log houses: see Frontier practices
London Associates, 148-49
Long (Capt.), 56
Lower Canada: founding of, 134
Lower Castle of the Mohawks, 8, 31, 203; see also Fort Hunter
Lower Landing: see Niagara River
Loyal Confederate Valley, 88
Lucy, Miss, 149
Lundy's Lane, battle of, 164
Lutes, Samson, 85
Lutes, Samuel, 63, 92

McALISTER, Terence, 35, 41, 42, 172
McAlister, Mrs. Terence, 47
McAslin (McCausland?), Dougal, 19, 29, 172
McAuley, Thomas, 157
McCauley, Rev. William, 156
McClellan, William, 58
MacDonald, John: see Macdonell, John (of Scottos)
Macdonell, Alexander (of Aberchalder), ix; represents Highlanders in land negotiations, 5, 7, 13-14; holdings of, 14, 23, 29, 172
Macdonell, Alexander (sheriff of Home District, Upper Canada), 145, 146, 159, 168
Macdonell, Allan (of Collachie), ix, 7, 14, 123; during Revolution, 37, 40; at York Town, 96, 97
Macdonell, Mrs. Allan (of Collachie), 97-98
Macdonell, Allan (surveyor), 88-89, 133

Macdonell, Catherine (Mrs. John [of Scottos]), x, 47, 98
Macdonell, John (of Leek), ix
Macdonell, John (of Scottos) (Spanish John) (1728-1810): migrates, x; holdings of, 14, 23, 29, 172; during Revolution, 39, 40, 42-44, 98, 153; after Revolution, 123, 137
Macdonell, Mrs. John (of Scottos): see Macdonell, Catherine.
Macdonell, Mary, 98
Macdonell, Miles (1769-1828), 123, 159
Macdonell, Roderick (Rory), 14, 23, 29, 40, 123, 172
Macdonell, Sheriff: see Macdonell, Alexander
Macdonell, Spanish John: see Macdonell, John (of Scottos)
Macdonell, William Johnson, 123
McGillivrae, Daniel, 29, 59, 91
MacGlashan, James, 163
MacGlashan, Janet (Mrs. John [Inverness] Chisholm), x, 163
McGlashen, John, 163
MacGrath, James, 163
MacGregor, Mille, 149
McIntosh, Angus, 62
McKay, Catherine (Mrs. John), 114
McKay, John, 23, 121, 123, 172; during Revolution, 42, 45, 73; in Nova Scotia, 110, 113, 114, 124
McKay, Neil, 26, 121, 123, 172; during Revolution, 42, 45, 47, 73, 93; in Nova Scotia, 110, 124
McKee, Ann, 72
McKenzie, Barbara: see Chisholm, Mrs. George Sr.
McKenzie, Duncan, 23, 173
McKenzie, Kenneth, 112
McKenzie, Mary (Mrs. William), (1730-?), ix, xi
McKenzie, Murdoch, 105, 109, 110, 120, 124fn.
McKenzie, Mrs. Murdoch (Isabella Johnson), 124fn.
McKenzie, William (1729-ca. 1787): migrates, ix, xi; at Scotch Settlement, 95, 158; at York Town, 95, 100, 103, 105, 158; in Nova Scotia, 109, 110, 113, 114, 117, 120, 121
McKenzie, Mrs. William: see McKenzie, Mary
Mackenzie, William Lyon (1795-1861), 168
Maclean, Allan, 88
McLean's Island (Nova Scotia), 114
McLeod, Donald, 40
McMicking, Janet Mulwain (1717-9?), 36, 72-73, 89, 134
McMicking, Janet (Mrs. James Cooper; later Mrs. William Brown) (1739-1809), 36, 73, 74, 129
McMicking, John (1753-?), ix, xi, 36, 72-73, 74, 173
McMicking, Sarah (1754-75), 36
McMicking, Thomas (1750-1830)
 in Scotland, ix; emigrates, xi, 36
 in Province of N.Y., 23, 31: locates, 19, 36, 173; joins British, 42; returns home, 45;
 in Patriot service, 48, 54; arrested, 62; supplies British, 63, 69; as prisoner of Senecas, 72-74
 at Niagara; ransomed, 74; settles, 87-88, 91, 92, 127, 130, 132; marriage, 129; claim for losses, 130; granted additional lands, 133; subscriber to and trustee of Presbyterian church, 133-34; signs address to Simcoe, 134; as township warden, 137; receives military commission, 137; house of, 161, 169; losses War of 1812, 164; death, 165
McMicking, Mrs. Thomas: see Gass, Isabella
McMullin, Angus, 48
McMullin, Hugh, 40, 173
MacNab, Sir Allan, 169fn.
MacNab, Flora (Mrs. Archibald Fletcher), 129
Maitland, Sir Peregrine, 167
Mann, George, 43, 153
Maple sugar, making of, 12, 22
Marbletown (Ulster Co., N.Y.), 56
"Mark of Honour," 132-33
Marston, Benjamin, 107, 108, 120; observations of, 107-19 passim
Marston's Division (Shelburne, Nova Scotia), 110
Mason, Charles, 110
Mason, Rev. Dr. John M., 96
Masonry: see Freemasonry
Mason's Division (Shelburne, Nova Scotia), 110, 112-13
Maude, John, 80, 149, 151
Mayfield Twp. (Fulton Co., N.Y.), 151
"Meanasinks": see Minisink
Meredith Twp. (Delaware Co., N.Y.), 157
Middle Fort, 203
Middleburg (Schoharie Co., N.Y.), 153, 203
Milbrook (Nine Partners), 86
Military Tract (N.Y.), 151-52
Militia
 in Province of New York, 34-35, 50, 55, 74-75; see also Highland Volunteer
 in Upper Canada, 137, 162; see also Gore; Lincoln; York
Miller, Nicholas, 64fn.
Mills, Alexander, 15, 91, 156, 173
Minisink, 55, 149, 203; Brant's raid on, 64-65
Missisauga Indians, 139, 140; and land negotiations, 80-81, 83-84, 86, 142
Mohawk-Susquehanna Trail, 10-11
Mohawk Chapel: see Queen Anne's Royal Chapel of the Mohawks
Mohawk Indians: country of, 7-8, 10; relations with white men, 11, 18, 31-32, 34; village on Grand River (Upper Canada), 164; see also Brant, Joseph; Six Nations Indians
Mohawk River Valley, 51; settlement in, 7-9, 11, 20, 30-31 (see also names of individual settlements); during Revolution, 42, 69, 70-71
Mohawks Branch: see Delaware River, West Branch
Molly, Miss: see Brant, Mary
Monroe, James (1758-1831), 28fn.

Monroe, Mrs. James: *see* Kortright, Elizabeth
Monroe, John D.: observations of, 39, 55fn., 70–71
Montgomery, Richard, 152
Montgomery, Samuel, 134, 165
Montgomery Co. (N.Y.), 145, 152, 154
"Monticello" (Charlottesville, Va.), 28fn.
Montour, Catherine, 51
Montour, Esther, 51
Moore, Jane, 68
Moore, John, 33, 35, 57
Moore, Mrs. John, 57, 58, 68, 96–98
Morden, Ralph (?–1778), 96
More, Alexander, 19
More, John, 19, 155
Moresville (Delaware Co., N.Y.), 155
Morse, Robert (1743–1818), 122
Mount Defiance: *see* Sugar Loaf Hill
Mount Dorchester (the Mountain; Niagara Escarpment), 84; area settled, 85, 86–90, 91–92; settlement expands, 127–30, 131–38, 161–62; in War of 1812, 163–64; township of, *see* Stamford Twp.
Mount Independence, 46
Mount Johnson (Mohawk Valley, N.Y.), 31
"Mount Vernon," 111
Mountain (the): at Burlington Bay, 139; at Niagara, *see* Mount Dorchester
Muirhead, Dr. James (*ca.* 1742–*ca.* 1811), 141
Munro, Rev. James, 117, 122
Murphy, Rebecca (Mrs. William Bates), 143
Murphy, Timothy (1751–1818), 55fn.
Murray, John, 73, 173

NASSAU, District of (Upper Canada), 131, 133, 136
Navy Island (Niagara River), 168
Negroes: as slaves, 35, 87–88, 121, 141, 165; taken prisoner, 57–58, 73; "Black Pioneers," 105, 112
Nelles, Hendrick William (1735–91), 50, 67–68, 69–70, 141
Nelles, Priscilla (Mrs. Hendrick William), 68
Nelles, Robert, 68, 134, 140, 142
Nelles, William (1769–1850), 67
Nelson Twp. (Upper Canada), 166
New Amsterdam (Buffaloe Creek; Buffalo) (Erie Co., N.Y.), 147, 203
New Rochelle (N.Y.), 67
"New Scotland": *see* Nova Scotia
New Scottos (Glengarry Twp., Upper Canada), 123
New Stamford (Delaware Co., N.Y.): early settlement at, 17, 19, 171–72; during Revolution, 35; after Revolution, 143, 153, 155
New Sweden, 18
New Town (Aunayza), 65–66, 203
New Turlach, 34, 45, 47, 74, 123
New York, Province of: immigration to, ix–xi; spread of colonization in 7–15, 171–74; frontier practices in, *see* Frontier practices; during Revolution, 30–75 *passim*; *see also* names of individual settlements in; York Town

New York City: *see* York Town
New York Highlanders: *see* Highland Volunteer Militia
New York State: in 1804, 146–59; present-day, 26–29
Newark (Upper Canada): town of, 143, 202; *see also* Niagara (settlement); Twp., 135, 161
Newberry, Sgt., 64
Niagara
  Fort: *see* Fort Niagara
  settlement on west bank of Niagara River (Butlersbury; Lennox; West Niagara; Newark; Niagara-on-the-Lake), 203; plan for, 79–81, 83–84; topography of, 84; first settlers, 85, 86–88; first survey, 88–89; mills built, 89–90; dissatisfaction at, 91; progress of, 91–92, 127–29; second survey, 131; newcomers to, 132–33; district town chosen, 133; portage road through, *see* Niagara River; court sessions at, 136; education at, 136; government at, 137; militia at, 137; houses at, 161–62, 170; during War of 1812, 163–64; outposts of, *see* Burlington Bay
Niagara-on-the-Lake (Ontario), 202; *see also* Niagara (settlement)
Niagara River, 76, 84, 92, 146
  Gorge of, 76, 87, 128, 137; rattlesnakes in, 129–30
  Great Falls of, 76, 84; portage around, *see* portage road
  Lower Landing: east side, 77, 85, 88, 203; *see also* Lewiston; west side, 85, 87, 127, 134, 135, 203; *see also* Queens Town
  portage road along: east side, 77, 79–80; west side, 87, 133, 134–35, 169–70
  settlement along: *see* Fort Niagara; Niagara (settlement)
  Upper Landing: east side (Little Niagara; Fort Schlosser), 77, 80, 204; west side, 87, 134, 135, 204; *see also* Chippawa
  Whirlpool of, 79, 87, 127–28, 159
Niagara Twp. (Upper Canada), 173
Nine Partners (Milbrook) (N.Y.), 86
Nixon, Janet (Mrs. John Thomson), 128
North West Company, 123
North West Settlement, 123
Northumberland, Duke of, 37, 134, 141
Nova Scotia, 107–26, 166; *see also* Jordan Bay; Port Roseway; Shelburne

OAKVILLE (Ontario), 19fn., 167
Odell's Lake (Delaware Co., N.Y.), 72
Ogdensburg (N.Y.), 150fn.
Ogsada, 35
Ohio Road (Nova Scotia), 114, 125
Old England District (Tryon Co., N.Y.), 11, 38, 50, 95, 158, 204
Old Iroquois Trail, 51
Old Seneca Castle: *see* Canadasaga
Old Stone Fort Museum (Schoharie, N.Y.), 153fn.
Oneida Castle, 204

Oneida Indians, 7, 37, 61; *see also* Six Nations Indians
Oneonta (Otsego Co., N.Y.), 12
Onondaga Castle, 204
Onondaga Hollow, 151
Onondaga Indians, 7, 35fn., 61, 69; *see also* Six Nations Indians
Onondaga (Salt) Lake, 37, 151, 204
Oquaga, 8, 11, 40, 64, 56-57, 204
O'Reilly, James, 133
Oriskany, battle of, 44
Osnabruck Twp. (Upper Canada), 173-74
Oswego: *see* Fort Oswego
Otego Patent, 5
Otsego Co. (N.Y.), 23fn., 154-55
Otsego Lake, 12, 13, 23, 47, 52, 63-64, 74
Ouleout Creek (Delaware Co., N.Y.), 95, 157-58, 204

PAINE, Ezra, 154
Paine, John, 154
Paine, Joshua, 154
Paine's Dale (Hobart), 143, 154, 155, 204; mills at, 143, 154, 157
Palatine Bridge, 152
Palatine District (Tryon Co., N.Y.), 11, 32, 40
Palatine Hill, 131
Palatines, German: as frontier settlers, 7, 8, 11, 18-19, 22, 30, 31, 67
Papacunck (Popatunk; Popachton), 53-55, 64fn., 67, 128, 204
Paris, Isaac, 33
Park, Hagar, 129, 132
Park, John, 42, 73, 132, 173
Park, James (*ca.* 1751-*ca.* 1796)
 in Scotland, ix; emigrates, xi
 in Province of N.Y.: locates, 15, 173; joins British, 42; returns home, 45; joins Brant, 50, 51; in raids, 58, 62; goes to Niagara, 66; property confiscated, 66
 at Niagara, 132; settles, 127; marriage, 129; claim for losses, 130; granted additional lands, 133; on jury, 136; death, 137; family, 138
Parkman, Francis: descriptions by, 7, 15, 18, 60
Parr, John (1729-91), 104, 107, 111, 115
Patchin, Freegift (1759-1831), 70, 155
Pattison, James (1723-1805), 94, 100
Pearl-ash: *see* Potash
Pelham Manor (N.Y.), 103
Pell, Joshua, 103
Pells' Road (Nova Scotia), 113
Pemberton, Jeremy, 130
"Pennsylvania Dutch": *see* Palatines, German
Perkins, Simeon: observations of, 109, 114, 117, 119
Peters, Caroline, 31
Phelps, Elijah Sr. (1724-?), 86
Phelps, Mrs. Elijah Sr. (Jemima Wilcox), 86
Phelps, Elijah Jr. (1750-1843), 86-87, 89, 91
Philipse, Hannah (Mrs. William Davis), 166
Pimmebetonggonk, 139
Pollard, Edward, 81
Pollock, Catherine: *see* Butler, Mrs. John
Popachton (Popatunk): *see* Papacunck

Popachton (Popatunk) Branch: *see* Delaware River, East Branch
Portage road: *see* Niagara River
Port L'Hebert (Nova Scotia), 110, 114, 124
Port Razoir: *see* Port Roseway
Port Roseway (Nova Scotia), 103-6, 107, 204; Loyalists arrive at, 107-8, 110; settlement begins at, 108-11; name changed to Shelburne, 111; *see also* Port Roseway Associates; Shelburne
Port Roseway Associates (Associated Loyalists): organized, 103; send delegates to Nova Scotia, 104; make departure preparations, 104-5; embark, 106; arrive in Nova Scotia, 107-8, 110; lots assigned to, 108-9, 110; erect shelters, 109; dig wells, 109; *see also* names of individual Associates
Port Royal (Nova Scotia), 107
Port Talbot (Upper Canada), 159
Potash, making of, 21-22
Powell, Henry Watson (1733-1814), 46, 85, 87
Powell, John, 68
Prentice, Charles, 151
Priest, Josiah, 70
Purchase Line (Upper Canada), 139, 166
Pynchon, Joseph, 103-4, 122

QUEEN ANNE, 8, 18
Queen Anne's Royal Chapel of the Mohawks, 8, 32, 152
Queen Esther (Montour), 51
Queen Esther's town, 51
Queen's Rangers, 48, 49, 134, 135, 143
Queens Town (Queenston) (Upper Canada), 135, 145, 146, 159, 167, 204
Queenston: *see* Queens Town
Queenston Heights (Upper Canada), 163

RAGGED ISLANDS (Nova Scotia), 107
Rambo Creek (Lambinicon) (Nelson Twp., Upper Canada), 142, 204
Ramsey, David, 11
Ramsey, George, 39-40
Ramsey, James, 58
Ramsey, Martha (Mrs. John Burch) (1746-1823), 63fn., 128
Rebellion of 1837 (Upper Canada), 167-68
Regiments
 British: 42 Highlanders (Black Watch), x; 8th or King's, 37, 77, 131, 140; 3rd, 65; 9th of Foot, 77; Royal Engineers, 82, 86, 88; 71st Highland, 119; 29th, 128-29
 provincial, 64fn., 129, 138, 171-74; Royal Emigrants, 65; *see also* King's Royal Regiment of New York; Queen's Rangers
Richelieu River, 42, 89
Richfield, 19fn.
Richmond, Duke of: *see* Lennox, Charles
Rivière des Jardins, 113
Riviere aux Raisins (St. Andrew's), 123
Rivington, James, 4
Robertson, Alexander, 95, 103, 105
Robinson, Beverley (1723-92), 19fn., 96, 104
Robinson, Samuel, 80, 81, 82
Rochester (Monroe Co., N.Y.), 149fn., 150fn.

INDEX

Rogers, Robert (1731–95): observations of, 87, 114
Rogers' Rangers, 48, 49, 52fn.
Rome (Oneida Co., N.Y.), 204
Romney, George (1734–1802), 37
Roosevelt, John, 4
Rose, Daniel (1757–ca. 1827)
  in Scotland, ix, emigrates, xi
  in Province of N.Y., 23; locates, 15, 17, 19, 173; manufactures potash, 22; joins British, 42; returns home, 45; joins Brant, 50, 51; in raids, 58, 62; goes to Niagara, 66; property confiscated, 66
  at Niagara: settles, 87, 88, 127; claim for losses, 130; granted additional lands, 133; subscriber to Presbyterian church, 134; receives militia commission, 136; family, 138; losses War of 1812, 164; death, 165
Rose, Mrs. Daniel: see Rose, Jane
Rose, Eunice (Mrs. Hugh [son of Daniel]), 164
Rose, Hugh (1737–1824): migrates, ix, xi; land of, 19, 28, 144; mill of, 23, 69, 154; during Revolution, 62; after Revolution, 154, 156
Rose, Hugh (son of Daniel (1778–1847), 87, 156, 164, 166
Rose, James, ix, xi, 15, 173
Rose, Jane (Mrs. Daniel), 42, 87, 164
Rose, John, 87
Rose, Margaret, 163
Rose, William: migrates, ix, xi; holdings of, 15, 17, 21, 23, 28, 144; during Revolution, 42
Rose's Brook, 15, 19, 23, 154
Roseville (Delaware Co., N.Y.), 154
Roseway River (Nova Scotia), 109, 114; lots on, 110, 112, 113; area today, 125–26
Ross, George, 116
Ross, Robert, 116
Rosse, Donald: see Rose, Daniel
Ross-Thomson House (Shelburne, Nova Scotia), 116
Royal Yorkers: see King's Royal Regiment of New York
Roxbury Twp. (Delaware Co., N.Y.), 155

SAFETY, committees of, 33, 34, 35, 38, 39–40, 47, 73
St. Andrew's (Upper Canada), 123
St. Clair River, 160
St. John River (New Brunswick), 91
St. Johnsville (Montgomery Co., N.Y.), 152
St. Lawrence River: difficulties of transportation in, 76–78
St. Leger, Barry, 42, 44–45
St. Louis River, 76
Salina (Onondaga Co., N.Y.), 151, 204
Salt, manufacture of, 151
Salt (Onondaga) Lake, 37, 151, 204
Salt Point, 151
Saratoga, District of, 178
Sawyer, Isaac, 72
Schenectady (Schenectady Co., N.Y.), 37, 75, 97, 131, 135

Schoharie, settlement of, 13, 22, 36; during Revolution, 50, 52, 55, 56, 57, 59, 75
Schoharie Co. (N.Y.), 43fn.
Schoharie Kill (Creek), 7, 8, 10, 11, 13, 56, 69, 204; Upper Fort on, 69, 75; Lower Fort on, 153; Middle Fort on, 153
Schultz, Christian: description by, 77
Schuyler, Peter, 31
Schuyler, Philip (1733–1804), 38, 40, 74
Schuyler Lake, 53, 204
Scotch Settlement (Ouleout Creek, Delaware Co., N.Y.), 95, 158
Scotch-Irish, as frontier settlers, 8, 11–13, 19, 30, 31
Scothouse: see Scottos
Scott, Phoebe: see Land, Mrs. Robert
Scottish Highlanders: as emigrants, ix–xi, 4, 5, 7, 13, 14–15, 171–74; as frontier settlers, 17–26, 30–32; see also names of individual Highlanders
Scottos: Isle of Skye, x; New, 123; John of: see Macdonell, John
Scotus: see Scottos
Secord, Abigail (Mrs. Peter) (1743–?), 80
Secord, David (1759–1844), 80, 85fn., 176
Secord, James Sr. (1732–84): during Revolution, 49, 50, 67, 97, 175; settles at Niagara, 80, 85, 88, 89
Secord, Mrs. James Sr. (Magdalena Badeau), 67
Secord, John (ca. 1750–1830), 67, 176
Secord, Peter (1721–1818): during Revolution, 67, 176; settles at Niagara, 80, 85, 89, 92, 134
Secord, Mrs. Peter: see Secord, Abigail
Secord, Solomon (1755–99), 80, 176
Secord, Stephen (1757–?), 80, 176
Seeley, Lodovic (ca. 1757–?), 64fn.
Selkirk, Lord (Thomas Douglas) (1771–1820), 87fn., 123, 148, 149, 153, 158–59: settlement in Upper Canada, 145–46, 153, 159–60
Seneca Indians: country of, 7, 35fn., 147; during Revolution, 58–59, 72–74, 177; in Devil's Hole massacre, 79–80, 83; see also Six Nations Indians
Seneca Lake, 7, 58, 61, 148, 202
Seneca Turnpike, 147; see also Genesee Pike
Sequestration: see Forfeiture and Sequestration, Commission of
Servos, Christopher (ca. 1670–1778), 90; holdings of, 14–15, 22, 23, 29, 173; during Revolution, 54–56
Servos, Clara (Mrs. Christopher), 55
Servos, Daniel, 39, 55, 67, 90, 134, 173
Servos, Jacob, 67
Servos, John, 55, 173
Servos, Magdalene (ca. 1773–1854), 55
Seth's Henry (Seth Hendrick), 72
Seward (Schoharie Co., N.Y.), 34fn.
Shandaken, 15
Sharon (Schoharie Co., N.Y.), 34fn.
Shearer, Thomas, 19, 123, 173
Shechquego, 204
Shehawken, 55

Shelburne (Nova Scotia), 204; founding of, *see* Port Roseway; named, 111; rise of, 111–13, 115–18; sawmills, 114–15; fisheries, 115–16; shipbuilding, 116; transportation, 116–17; shops and taverns, 118; merchants, tradesmen, and advertising, 119; religion at, 119–20; decline of, 121–22
Ships: *Brindle Cow*, 5; *Caroline*, 168; *Cherry Bounce*, 112; *General Brock*, 167; *Jackie*, 36; *Ontario*, 85; *Peace and Plenty*, xi; *Pearl*, xi, 4–5; *Prince William Henry*, 114; *Sophie*, 111
Short Hills (Upper Canada), 163
Showers, Hannah (Mrs. Michael), 85
Showers, Michael, 49, 50, 85, 86
Sicard, Ambroise, 67
Silverthorn, John (1764–1846), 162, 166
Silverthorn, Mrs. John: *see* Corwin, Esther
Silverthorn, Joseph (1785–1879), 162, 166
Silverthorn, Mrs. Joseph: *see* Chisholm, Jane
Silverthorn, Rebecca (Mrs. William "White Oak" Chisholm) (1795–1865), 166
Simcoe, John Graves (1752–1806), 48; as governor of Upper Canada, 134–43 *passim*, 148
Simcoe, Mrs. John Graves (1766–1850), 139–40
Six Nations (Iroquois) Indians
 confederacy, 7–8, 66
 homeland of, 7–8, 9, 51; devastated, 63–66; ceded to United States, 90, 92; settled by white men, 147–52
 practices of, 18, 20, 22, 23, 25, 58, 60–62, 129–30, 132
 as British allies during Revolution, 33–59 *passim*, 64–66, 69–72, 74–75, 90; *see also* Brant, Joseph
 at Niagara: take refuge, 66, 78, 83, 88; land of, 79–80
 at Grand River, 140–41
 in War of 1812, 164; in 1837 Rebellion, 168
 see also Cayugas; Mohawks; Oneidas; Senecas; Tuscaroras
Sixteen Mile Creek (north side, Lake Ontario), 159
Smith, Charles, 55–56
Smith, Deborah: observations of, 112
Smith, Hiram (1803–76), 168
Smith, Mrs. Hiram (Hannah Chisholm) (1809–60), 168
Smith, Richard (1735–1803), 5–7, 12–13
Smith, William, 70
Smith, Judge William, 3–4
Smith's Tavern (Barton Twp., Upper Canada), 141
Sodus Bay (Lake Ontario), 148
South Worcester (Otsego Co., N.Y.), 23, 55fn.
Springfield, 50, 52, 63, 204
Stamford Twp.
 Delaware Co. (N.Y.), 15fn., 153–54, 159
 Upper Canada: Presbyterian church in, 127, 133–34, 163, 165; named, 135; settlers in, 171, 173–74; portage road through, *see* Niagara River
Stark, John (1728–1822), 52, 53, 56

Stedman, John (1731–1808), 79–80, 83, 135
Steenbrander: *see* Stoneburner
Stevens, James (?–1780), 69fn.
Stewart, Peter, 145, 152, 159
Stone, William L.: comments of, 40, 71–72
Stone Arabia, 33, 68, 204
Stoneburner, Jacob, 19, 43, 47, 123, 144, 174
Stoneburner, Jacob Jr., 123, 174
Stoneburner, John, 123, 174
Stoneburner, Joseph, 123, 174
Stoneburner, Leonard, 123, 174
Strasburgh Patent, 10
Street, John (?–1790), 82, 146
Street, Samuel (1750–1815), 82–83, 147
Stuart, Christine (Mrs. John [of Queenston] Chisholm) (?–1788), 129
Stuart, Dr. James, 154; migrates, x; holdings of, 19, 21, 23, 144, 174; during Revolution, 41, 42, 129; after Revolution, 123, 129
Stuart, Rev. John, 32
Sugar Loaf Hill, 45–46
Sullivan, John (1740–95), 61, 63–66
Summit Lake (Delaware Co., N.Y.), 11
Susquehannah Turnpike: *see* Catskill-Susquehanna Turnpike
Sutherland, William, 161, 162
Swart, Peter, 40, 43
Switzer Hill (Fonda, Fulton Co., N.Y.), 36, 152
Sydney (Cape Breton, Nova Scotia), 172
Syracuse (Onondaga Co., N.Y.), 204

TAGEHUENTO: *see* Johnson, Capt. William "Jr."
Terry, Partial (?–1809), 51–52, 176
Thayendanegea: *see* Brant, Joseph
Thomas, George, 113
Thom(p)son, Archibald Sr. (1749–1821)
 in Scotland, ix, emigrates, xi
 in Province of N.Y., 23; locates, 15, 174; joins British, 42; returns home, 45; in Patriot militia, 48; joins Brant, 50, 51; taken prisoner and escapes, 56; in raids, 58, 62; goes to Niagara, 66; property confiscated, 66
 at Niagara, 131; in war party, 69–70; settles, 87, 127–28, 189; marriage, 129; claim for losses, 130; granted additional lands, 133; subscriber to and trustee of Presbyterian church, 133–34; on jury, 136; as township warden, 137; family, 138; land on Grand River, 140; winters Selkirk's sheep, 159; house of, 161–62, 169; losses War of 1812, 164; death, 165
Thom(p)son, Mrs. Archibald: *see* Emery, Catharine
Thom(p)son, Archibald Jr., 165
Thom(p)son, Benjamin (1796–1885), 164, 165, 166
Thom(p)son, James Sr. (1752–1832), 128, 129, 131–32, 136, 137
Thom(p)son, Mrs. James Sr. (Margaret Emery), 129
Thom(p)son, James Jr. (1786–1850), 136
Thom(p)son, James (son of Archibald), 165, 166

Thom(p)son, John (1758-1814), 128, 131-32, 134, 161
Thom(p)son, Mrs. John (Janet Nixon)), 128
Thom(p)son, John (son of Archibald), 164
Thom(p)son, Peter (1749-1828), 128, 131-32, 134, 137
Thom(p)son, Richard, 129, 133
Thom(p)son, Richard (son of Archibald), 165
Tice, Gilbert (?-1791), 33, 36-38, 44, 53, 74-75, 128
Tice, Mrs. Gilbert (Christian Van Slyke), 37, 128
Tinling, William, 88
Tioga Castle: see Queen Esther's town
Tioga Point, 51, 52, 61, 63, 64, 71, 72, 73, 204
Tonewanta Creek, 147, 204,
Tolmie, Normand, 94-95, 100
Toronto Twp. (Upper Canada), 162, 166
Town Brook, 26, 72, 143, 153-55; settlement along, 19, 171-72, 174
Trafalgar Twp. (Upper Canada), 166
Tribes (Tripes) Hill (Mohawk Valley), 35, 41
Tryon, William (1725-88), 11, 34, 94, 100
Tryon Co. (N.Y.), 11, 152, 204; during Revolution, 33, 39, 42, 47 : see also Canajoharie District; Old English District; Palatine District
Tunnicliff, John, 19fn., 52, 56, 73
Tunnicliff, William, 52-53, 56
Turlach: see New Turlach
Tuscarora Indians, 7, 61 : see also Six Nations Indians
Twelve Mile Creek (north shore, Lake Ontario), 90, 159
Twenty Mile Creek (south shore, Lake Ontario), 84, 164, 204
Twenty Mile Pond, 84
Twiss, William, 45, 82, 85
Tyler, Comfort, 151

U.E. List, 132-33
Unadilla, 41, 49-51, 53-54, 56-57, 95, 204
Unadilla River, 71
Upper Canada, Province of, 51fn., 88, 151; formation of, 127, 134; first governor of: see Simcoe, John Graves; settlements in, see Baldoon; Burlington Bay; Mount Dorchester; Niagara (settlement)
Upper (Canajoharie) Castle of the Mohawks, 12, 18, 31-32, 44fn., 88, 204
Upper posts : see Forts Detroit; Michilimackinac; Niagara
Upper Landing: see Niagara River
Utica (Oneida Co., N.Y.), 204
Utsayantha: Mount, 75; Lake, 9-10, 153, 204

Van Slyke, Christian (Mrs. Gilbert Tice), 128
Vigilance Committee, 34
Vrooman, Peter (1736-?), 35, 43, 70
Vrooman's Nose, 153, 205
Vroomansland, 23, 43, 205

War of 1812, 162-65
Warren: see Youngsfield
Warren, John, 82

Warren, Sir Peter (1703-52), 8, 36
Warren's (Corners) (Niagara Co., N.Y.), 146
Warren's Bush, 8, 31, 36, 74-75
Warwick, Earl of, 37
Washington, George (1732-99), 111, 156
Wattles, Nathaniel, 158
Wattles, Sluman (1753-1837), 157-58
Wattles' Ferry, 153, 158
Watts, John, 34
Watts, Mary (Polly) (Lady Mary Johnson), 31, 38
Welland River (Upper Canada): see Chippawa Creek
"Wellington Square" (home of Joseph Brant), 142, 164
Wellington Square, village of (Upper Canada), 166, 168
Wells, Jane, 97
Wequatetong, 139 : see also Burlington Bay
West Canada Creek (Herkimer Co., N.Y.), 75
West Niagara, 205 : see also Niagara (settlement)
Westbrook, Anthony, 64fn.
Westbrook, Elizabeth, 91
Wheelock, Eleazor (1711-79), 12, 32, 34
Whirlpool, see Niagara River
Whiskey Hollow, 72
White, Gideon, 118
"White Oak Chisholm" : see Chisholm, William
Whitestown (Oneida Co., N.Y.), 147, 149
Wilcox, Jemima (Mrs. Elijah Phelps Sr.), 86
Wildcat-Creek, 205
Willett, Marinus, 75
William of Canajoharie: see Johnson, Capt. William "Jr."
William Henry, Prince (William IV) (1765-1837): visits Shelburne, 121, 124
Williamson, Charles (1757-1808), 148-49, 158fn.
Wills, William, 40
Wilsey, Abel, 136
Wilson, James, 112
Windsor (Broome Co., N.Y.), 205
Wirt, David, 43
Wright, Daniel, 112-13
Wright's Brook, see Banyar's Brook
Wright's Road (Nova Scotia), 112-13, 125
Wyoming valley (of the Susquehanna), 205; some settlers join British, 45, 67, 68, 86; raids on, 50, 51-52, 58, 62; Continentals at, 63, 64

Yale College, 26, 32fn., 46fn., 150, 155, 157fn.
Yates, Christopher P., 33
York, town of (Province of Upper Canada), 143, 145, 159
York Co. (Upper Canada), 166
York Town
  in 1773, 3-4
  during Revolution, 39, 55, 67; as haven for Loyalists, 41, 93-98; hardships at, 93-94, 98-100, 102; entertainments at, 101-2; merchandise available at, 102; evacuation started, 102-6, completed, 111

York Island (Province of N.Y.), 3, 37, 93–94; *see also* York Town
York Militia (Upper Canada), 2nd Regiment of, 162
Young, Adam, 47, 50, 140
Young, Daniel, 140, 176
Young, Frederick (1726–?), 140
Young, John, 47, 140, 175
Young's Island (Grand River, Upper Canada), 141
Youngsfield, 47, 140, 205

www.ingramcontent.com/pod-product-compliance
Lightning Source LLC
Chambersburg PA
CBHW051351070526
44584CB00025B/3714